Regulation of Extractive Industries

This book intends to inform the key participants in extractive projects – namely, the communities, the host governments and the investors – about good practice for effective community engagement, based on analysis of international standards and expectations, lessons from selected case-studies and innovations in public participation.

The extent of extractive industries varies widely around the Arctic as do governmental and social attitudes towards resource development. Whilst most Arctic communities are united in seeking investment to fund education, healthcare, housing, transport and other essential services, as well as wanting to benefit from improved employment and business opportunities, they have different views as to the role that extractive industries should play in this. Within each community, there are multiple perspectives and the goal of public participation is to draw out these perspectives and seek consensus. Part I of the book analyses the international standards that have emerged in recent years regarding public participation, in particular, in respect of indigenous peoples. Part II presents six case studies that aim to identify both good and bad practices and to reflect upon the distinct conditions, needs, expectations, strategies and results for each community examined. Part III explores the importance of meaningful participation from a corporate perspective and identifies some common themes that require consideration if Arctic voices are to shape extractive industries in Arctic communities.

In drawing together international law and standards, case studies and examples of good practice, this anthology is a timely and invaluable resource for academics, legal advisors and those working in resource development and public policy.

Rachael Lorna Johnstone is adjunct professor of law at Ilisimatusarfik (University of Greenland) and professor of law at the University of Akureyri, Iceland.

Anne Merrild Hansen is professor of social science and director of the PhD school at Ilisimatusarfik and professor in planning and impact assessment in the Arctic at Aalborg University, Denmark.

Between 2016 and 2018, Rachael and Anne directed the Arctic Oil and Gas Research Centre at Ilisimatusarfik.

Routledge Research in Polar Law

Emerging Legal Orders in the Arctic
The Role of Non-Arctic Actors
Edited by Akiho Shibata, Leilei Zou, Nikolas Sellheim & Marzia Scopelliti

For a full list of titles in this series, visit https://www.routledge.com/law/series/RRPL

Regulation of Extractive Industries

Community Engagement in the Arctic

Edited by
Rachael Lorna Johnstone and
Anne Merrild Hansen

LONDON AND NEW YORK

First published 2020
by Routledge
2 Park Square, Milton Park, Abingdon, Oxon OX14 4RN

and by Routledge
605 Third Avenue, New York, NY 10017

Routledge is an imprint of the Taylor & Francis Group, an informa business

First issued in paperback 2021

© 2020 selection and editorial matter, Rachael Lorna Johnstone and Anne Merrild Hansen; individual chapters, the contributors

The right of Rachael Lorna Johnstone and Anne Merrild Hansen to be identified as the authors of the editorial material, and of the authors for their individual chapters, has been asserted in accordance with sections 77 and 78 of the Copyright, Designs and Patents Act 1988.

All rights reserved. No part of this book may be reprinted or reproduced or utilised in any form or by any electronic, mechanical, or other means, now known or hereafter invented, including photocopying and recording, or in any information storage or retrieval system, without permission in writing from the publishers.

Trademark notice: Product or corporate names may be trademarks or registered trademarks, and are used only for identification and explanation without intent to infringe.

Publisher's Note
The publisher has gone to great lengths to ensure the quality of this reprint but points out that some imperfections in the original copies may be apparent.

British Library Cataloguing-in-Publication Data
A catalogue record for this book is available from the British Library

Library of Congress Cataloging-in-Publication Data
A catalog record has been requested for this book

ISBN 13: 978-0-367-18179-6 (hbk)
ISBN 13: 978-1-03-223822-7 (pbk)
ISBN 13: 978-0-429-05993-3 (ebk)

DOI: 10.4324/9780429059933

Typeset in Galliard
by Taylor & Francis Books

Contents

List of illustrations vii
List of contributors ix
Abbreviations and acronyms xiii

1 Introduction 1
  RACHAEL LORNA JOHNSTONE AND ANNE MERRILD HANSEN

PART I
Participation in principle 9

2 Indigenous rights and resource development in the Arctic: An overview of international standards and principles for consultation, participation and consent 11
  EMMA WILSON

3 What is required for free, prior and informed consent and where does it apply? 47
  RACHAEL LORNA JOHNSTONE

4 Meaningful stakeholder engagement as an aspect of risk-based due diligence between the economy, politics and law: The constitutive role of the business and human rights regime 78
  KARIN BUHMANN

PART II
Participation in practice 99

5 Youth as a resource in extractive industry decision-making processes: A case study using social media and visual methods to engage young Greenlanders 101
  ANNA-SOFIE SKJERVEDAL

6 Comparative expectations of resource development in selected
  Greenland communities 125
  RACHAEL LORNA JOHNSTONE AND ANNE MERRILD HANSEN

7 "Our consent was taken for granted": A relational justice perspective
  on the participation of Komi people in oil development in northern
  Russia 156
  JULIA LOGINOVA AND EMMA WILSON

8 Local views on oil development in a village on the North Slope of
  Alaska 185
  ANNE MERRILD HANSEN AND PANIGRUAQ IPALOOK

9 Land claims agreements in Canada and the promise of enhanced
  participation 200
  NIGEL BANKES

10 Participation in a small archipelago: The Shetland negotiations 225
  JAMES MITCHELL

PART III
Participation improved 243

11 The relationship between host government contracts for oil and gas
  activities and public participation 245
  EDUARDO GUEDES PEREIRA AND MARIANTHI PAPPA

12 Achieving excellence in public participation and consultation 265
  PENNY NORTON

13 Arctic voices: Strategies for community engagement 286
  ANNE MERRILD HANSEN AND RACHAEL LORNA JOHNSTONE

  Index 298

Illustrations

Figures

5.1 "The most important things in my life are my son (him with the branches in the stroller) and my freedom. The freedom to do what I want: study, draw, or go make discoveries with my son." 111

5.2 "In 10 years I will be a nurse, live in Nuuk and have a family of my own. Up till then I will have had an internship in Tanzania and Vietnam, worked as a nurse at Doctors Without Borders and in a war zone. The picture symbolises the road forward at the only 'highway' in Greenland: The ice by Uummannaq." 112

5.3 "My family, my friends and the experiences I gather are most important in my life. This picture also shows my passion for physical activities, both indoors and outdoors." 113

5.4 "The most important thing for me is my work, travelling, new challenges, new experiences, proving to myself that I can do even better, nature and my family." 113

5.5 "In my home I have two shelves with things that remind me of my origin, my home. Greenland has changed through the years I have lived abroad, so I am not sure what to expect when I return. I hope I will be able to feel at home. I am consistently fighting against these objects becoming 'tourist artefacts' in my own home, trying to keep the traditions they represent alive through me." 115

5.6 "I have a wish and expectation that I one day will return to my home town with my boyfriend and our daughter. In the mean-time my daughter learns about Greenland through Greenlandic books." 115

5.7 "This is a picture of a block of flats, 'Blok P,' which was torn down in 2012. The flag on the building symbolises change and expectations attached to the implementation of self-rule in Greenland. One of my fears for the future is that the economic situation, and the problem with housing, does not improve, and that the social inequalities become even bigger so that even more people decide to emigrate. Many, especially young people, lack a proper home, which can make it hard for them to focus on studies and their future. Having a roof over their head is a vital prerequisite for young people to grow as humans, learn and prepare for their future." 117

6.1 Greenland geology and selected mineral occurrences 132
7.1 Map of the Komi Republic (top right) and settlements in Izhma and Usinsk districts mentioned in the study 161
12.1 The circular approach to strategy development 271

Tables

6.1 Summary of fieldwork, 2017–2019 134
6.2 Perceptions of opportunities, risks, decision-making process and influence of extractive industries in four regions of Greenland 148
8.1 Overview of themes and questions raised in debates about oil and gas in Nuiqsut 192
12.1 A strategic approach to public consultation 268
12.2 Ten principles of good public participation 284

Contributors

Nigel Bankes is Professor of Law and holder of the Chair of Natural Resources Law at the University of Calgary. He was Adjunct Professor of Law with the KG Jebsen Centre for the Law of the Sea, at UiT (the University of Tromsø), the Arctic University of Norway from 2012 to August 2019. His main fields of research are property law; natural resources and energy law; oil and gas law; and international environmental law. In 2010 the University of Akureyri, Iceland conferred an honorary doctoral degree on Nigel in recognition of his contributions to the development of Arctic law in the areas of natural resources law, international environment law and the rights of indigenous peoples. In 2019, he was awarded a Killam Annual Professorship for excellence in research, mentorship and teaching. Nigel has a law degree from Cambridge University and an LLM from the University of British Columbia. He posts on developments in Canadian oil and gas and energy law at ABlawg: http://ablawg.ca

Karin Buhmann is Professor in the Department of Management, Society and Communication at Copenhagen Business School. Her dedicated charge is the field of Business and Human Rights. Her teaching and research interests are in the areas of business responsibilities for human rights; corporate social responsibility; sustainability; public-private regulation; and the interaction between public law and policy and private sector (self-)regulation. She has published widely on these and related areas. She leads the University of the Arctic's Thematic Network on Arctic Sustainable Resources and Social Responsibility. Karin was educated in law and East Asian Studies at the University of Copenhagen and has a master's degree in International Law from the Raoul Wallenberg Institute of Human Rights and Humanitarian Law at the University of Lund, Sweden. Her Ph.D. in law from Aarhus University was awarded for a thesis providing a cross-cultural analysis of the implementation of international human rights law. Her advanced post-doc dissertation at Roskilde University earned her the title Dr.scient.adm. based on an extensive analysis of the evolution of the business and human rights regime poised between law, business ethics and management, and communicative strategies.

Anne Merrild Hansen is Professor at the Danish Centre for Environmental Assessment and head of the cross faculty platform, AAU Arctic, at Aalborg University.

She is also the head of the Ph.D. school at Ilisimatusarfik (University of Greenland). Anne has been engaged in many international research projects. She is a Fulbright Arctic Alumni and has participated in various projects including the Arctic Council project *Adaptation Actions for a Changing Arctic* and the *Arctic Challenge* project on social implications of oil activities in Norway, Alaska and Greenland. Anne's research focuses on the social impacts and benefits related to resource development in Arctic communities. She also studies impact assessment processes with a particular focus on participation procedures and inclusion of Indigenous knowledge and local knowledge in the assessments. Anne published more than thirty scientific articles on these topics and several chapters in scientific books. She holds a master's degree in engineering and a Ph.D. in Strategic Environmental Assessment from Aalborg University.

Panigruaq Ipalook was educated as an Oral Historian. He has recently coordinated a large survey across the North Slope as a team leader in the North Slope Borough's Oral History Program. He travelled to all the villages in the region, collecting household data on language and interviewing elders. Being born and raised in Nuiqsut, a village heavily influenced by oil development, Panigruaq has been involved in public meetings, and engaged in various debates on management of oil projects and oil related funds for the past ten years.

Rachael Lorna Johnstone is Professor of Law at the University of Akureyri, Iceland and Adjunct Professor of Law at Ilisimatusarfik (University of Greenland). Rachael specialises in Polar law: the governance of the Arctic and the Antarctic under international and domestic law. She has published widely on the rights of indigenous people; international human rights law; governance of extractive industries in the Arctic; international environmental law; due diligence; state responsibility; and Arctic strategies. Major publications include *Arctic Governance in a Changing World* (Rowman and Littlefield, 2019) with co-author Mary Durfee and *Offshore Oil and Gas Development in the Arctic under International Law: Risk and Responsibility* (Brill, 2015). Professor Johnstone holds an S.J.D. from the University of Toronto (2004), an M.A. in Polar Law from the University of Akureyri (2014), an LL.M. in Legal Theory from the European Academy of Legal Theory (2000) and an LL.B.(Hons) from the University of Glasgow (1999).

Julia Loginova works as a Postdoctoral Research Fellow at the University of Queensland, Australia. Julia was born and raised in the Republic of Komi in northern Russia where extensive resource extraction industries are operating. Since 2010, she has assisted regional and rural development projects in Indigenous communities in the Circumpolar North linked to the University of the Arctic. Julia holds a Ph.D. from the University of Melbourne. Her thesis uncovers the development of oil extraction projects by exposing the justice challenges related to climate change and recognition of indigenous perspectives. Julia also has an undergraduate degree in Circumpolar Studies from Finnmark University College (University of Tromsø) and is an Arctic-FROST early career research fellow.

James Mitchell is Professor of Public Policy at the University of Edinburgh. He has held the Chair in Public Policy since 2013, prior to which he held the Chair in Politics at the University of Strathclyde (2000–2013) and the Chair in Public Policy at the University of Sheffield (1998–2000). His research interests are primarily in sub-state politics, public policy and government and political behaviour. In his work, James emphasises: multi-level governance and the territorial dimensions of public policy; regionalism and nationalism; and political behaviour with reference to sub-state levels of government. James has an undergraduate degree from Aberdeen University and a doctorate from Nuffield College, University of Oxford.

Penny Norton is a public consultation and community relations consultant with twenty years' expertise in the planning, development and regeneration sector in the UK. Penny runs the consultancy PNPR Limited and, as the founder of *ConsultOnline*, has made pioneering use of web-based communications and social media in consultation. Penny is the author of *Public Consultation and Community Involvement in Planning: A Twenty-first Century Guide* (Routledge, 2018) and edited *Communicating Construction: Insight, Experience and Best Practice*, and *Promoting Property: Insight, Experience and Best Practice* (both Routledge, 2020). Penny has written extensively for property publications and regularly provides policy advice and training on consultation and community relations. She is an Associate of The Consultation Institute, an active member of the Town and Country Planning Association and a Fellow of the Chartered Institute of Public Relations.

Marianthi Pappa is Assistant Professor in Law at the University of Nottingham. She specialises in international law of the sea; energy and investment law; and space law. Her research covers multiple topics, including contemporary issues in extractive industries; the place of private actors in the international plane; and the interplay between different areas of law. Marianthi also delivers training workshops to governmental and business organisations on issues of boundary disputes and energy law. Marianthi studied law at the Aristotle University of Thessaloniki, before practising law in Greece and Cyprus, consulting individuals and multinational corporations operating in the fields of finance and energy. She earned an LL.M. in Oil & Gas Law and a Ph.D. in International Law of the Sea, both from the University of Aberdeen, and is an associate fellow in the Higher Education Academy of the UK.

Eduardo G. Pereira is professor of natural resources and energy law as a full-time scholar at the Siberian Federal University, and part-time, adjunct and/or visiting scholar in a number of leading academic institutions around the world. Eduardo has been active in the oil and gas industry for over ten years and is an international expert on joint operating agreements. He has practical experience of oil and gas governance in over forty jurisdictions covering America, Europe, Africa and Asia. Eduardo is also a managing editor for the *African Journal on Energy, Natural Resources and Environmental Law* and an associate editor of

OGEL. He is the author and editor of several leading oil and gas textbooks. Eduardo concluded his doctoral thesis on oil and gas joint ventures at the University of Aberdeen and conducted postdoctoral research at the Oxford Institute for Energy Studies (University of Oxford) and at the Scandinavian Institute of Maritime Law (University of Oslo). Further information about his profile and publications can be found at: www.eduardogpereira.com

Anna-Sofie Skjervedal has roots in Greenland and specialises in current public participation practices in relation to extractive industry development in Greenland. Anna-Sofie currently works as a special consultant at Sermersooq Municipality in Nuuk, where she advises on and leads public participation initiatives. She is responsible for ensuring that the municipality meets the objectives as set forth in their public participation strategy. She is also an active member of the Global Research and Engagement Network for Socially Responsible Transitions (GREEN-SORT) focusing on best practice for meaningful stakeholder involvement within the renewable energy and mining sector in the Nordic Arctic and Canada. She has contributed to the *Arctic Challenge* project (2014–2017) and the *To the Benefit of Greenland* report of the Committee for Greenlandic Mineral Resources to the Benefit of Society (2014). Anna-Sofie holds a Ph.D. from Ilisimatusarfik (University of Greenland) and Aalborg University in which she focused on meaningful youth engagement through visual means and social media (*Towards Meaningful Youth Engagement: Breaking the Frame of the Current Public Participation Practice in Greenland*, 2018).

Emma Wilson is an independent researcher and consultant, director of ECW Energy Ltd., and Associate of the Scott Polar Research Institute, Cambridge University, and the Consultation Institute, UK. She has over twenty years' experience of researching and consulting on issues related to oil, gas, mining and renewable energy, Indigenous rights, community relations and corporate responsibility. This includes social impact assessment and social audit of industrial projects; company–community relations; and anthropological and sociological field research methodologies. She speaks fluent Russian and has worked in Russia, Uzbekistan, Turkmenistan, Kazakhstan, Azerbaijan, Ukraine, Norway, Greenland, Nigeria, Ghana, South Africa and Qatar. Emma holds a Ph.D. from Cambridge University (2002) on the topic of local community engagement and participation in oil and gas development on Sakhalin Island in the Russian Far East. She has since published regularly in academic journals and other research publications. From 2007 to 2015, she worked at the International Institute for Environment and Development (IIED), where she was a Principal Researcher and Energy Team Leader.

Abbreviations and acronyms

Aarhus Convention	Convention on Access to Information, Public Participation in Decision-Making and Access to Justice in Environmental Matters, 1998
APF	Asia Pacific Forum
CBD	Convention on Biological Diversity, 1992
CCH	Chisana Caribou Herd
CERD	Convention on the Elimination of All Forms of Racial Discrimination, 1965
CHLOE	Conceptual Hexagonal Land Use Overlay Engine
CSR	Corporate social responsibility
DO	Designated office
EIA	Environmental impact assessment
Espoo Convention	Convention on Environmental Impact Assessment in a Transboundary Context, 1991
FPIC	Free, prior and informed consent
IA	Impact assessment
IBA	Impact benefit agreement
ICCPR	International Covenant on Civil and Political Rights, 1966
ICESCR	International Covenant on Economic, Social and Cultural Rights, 1966
ICMM	International Council on Mining and Metals
ICP	Informed consultation and participation
IFC	International Finance Corporation
ILO	International Labour Organisation
ILO C169	Indigenous and Tribal Peoples Convention, 1989
INGO	International Non-Governmental Organisation
IPIECA	The Global Oil and Gas Industry Association for Advancing Environmental and Social Performance
Kiev Protocol	Protocol on Strategic Environmental Assessment to the Convention on Environmental Impact Assessment in a Transboundary Context, 2003
LILCA	Labrador Inuit Land Claims Agreement, 2005
MVRMA	Mackenzie Valley Resources Management Act, 1998

NCP	National contact point
NFA	Nunavut Land Claims Agreement, 1993
NSIP	Nationally significant infrastructure project
OECD	Organization for Economic Cooperation and Development
OHCHR	Office of the United Nations High Commissioner for Human Rights
PEST	Political, economic, social and technological
QIA	Qikiqtani Inuit Association
RLUPC	Regional land use planning commission
SIA	Social impact assessment
SLO	Social licence to operate
SWOT	Strengths, weaknesses, opportunities, threats
Tłı̨chǫ Agreement	Tłı̨chǫ Land Claims and Self Government Agreement, 2003
UN	United Nations
UN Framework	UN Protect, Respect and Remedy: A Framework for Business and Human Rights, 2008
UNDRIP	United Nations Declaration on the Rights of Indigenous Peoples, 2007
UNGPs	UN Guiding Principles on Business and Human Rights, 2011
WRFN	White River First Nation
YESAA	Yukon Environmental and Socio-Economic Assessment Act, 2003

1 Introduction

Rachael Lorna Johnstone and Anne Merrild Hansen

The Arctic has, over the past decade, been the subject of increasing international attention, in light of climate change, geopolitical security, resource expectations and shipping. But the Arctic is also home to approximately 4 million people, over 10 per cent of whom are indigenous, including Saami, Inuit, Nenets and Aleuts.[1]

The first Arctic peoples came to the area thousands of years ago and their descendants continue to live there today.[2] They have adapted to the challenges posed by the region's severe climate and extreme environment. Eight states now claim sovereignty above the Arctic Circle: Canada, the Kingdom of Denmark (in respect of Greenland), Finland, Iceland, Norway, Russia, Sweden and the USA (in respect of Alaska). They vary enormously in population, population density, territorial size, economy and style of government.[3] Non-Arctic states are also demanding an increasing say in Arctic governance.[4]

The extent of extractive industries varies widely around the Arctic according to known resource deposits, climate, physical accessibility, economic history, commercial interest, technology and political will. Governmental and social attitudes to extractives vary, depending on whether they are seen as strategic resources (e.g., Greenland and Russia), economic resources (e.g., Canada), or public goods (Norway).[5] All persons potentially affected by resource development projects enjoy rights to participation in the decision-making processes by virtue of domestic laws in all the Arctic States as well as under the Aarhus Convention in the Nordic countries (excluding Greenland).[6] Indigenous peoples live in all the

1 Mary Durfee and Rachael Lorna Johnstone, *Arctic Governance in a Changing World* (Lanham, MD: Rowman and Littlefield, 2019), 52–55.
2 Ibid., 33–38.
3 Ibid., 55–67.
4 Ibid., 68–79.
5 Cécile Pelaudeix, "Governance of Offshore Hydrocarbon Activities in the Arctic and Energy Policies: A Comparative Approach between Norway, Canada and Greenland/Denmark," and Roman Sidortsov, "The Russian Offshore Oil And Gas Regime: When Tight Control Means Less Order," in *Governance of Arctic Offshore Oil and Gas* (Abingdon: Routledge, 2017).
6 "Convention on Access to Information, Public Participation in Decision-Making and Access to Justice in Environmental Matters 1998," *International Legal Materials* 38 (1999): 517.

Arctic States except Iceland, which complicates the participation requirements further, in particular through the requirement to implement the principle of free, prior and informed consent (FPIC).

The desire of Arctic peoples and their elected governments for improved socio-economic conditions is at least as much of a driver of extractive industries as the climatic changes and technological developments that are making Arctic natural resources more accessible. Whilst most Arctic communities are united in seeking investment to fund education, healthcare, housing, transport, and other essential services, and whilst most could benefit from improved job opportunities and in turn demographic stability, citizens have different views as to the role that extractive industries should play. Extractive ventures, even at very early stages, introduce change and uncertainty to communities.[7] Disasters in other parts of the world, or historic experiences locally of projects that caused widespread contamination or were never cleaned up, effectively trigger fears that the same might happen in their homes. As Hansen, et al., explain, "while companies can move on to other projects when reserves are exhausted or if mistakes are made, a community generally only has one chance at development of extractives, and therefore it is of utmost importance to get it right the first time."[8]

Within each community, there are multiple perspectives. The purpose of the public participation process is to draw out those perspectives and – ideally – seek a path that all community members can accept. Rapid evolution of international law and standards on human rights, environmental protection and the rights of indigenous peoples is making it increasingly rare for governments and corporations to deal directly with one another, ignoring the people whose lands and lives will be most affected by industrial development.

Demands for high-quality, informed and influential public participation in large-scale extractive industries in the Arctic are growing, especially since the principle of FPIC for activities affecting indigenous land and resources was endorsed in the UN Declaration on the Rights of Indigenous Peoples 2007 (UNDRIP).[9] Questions remain regarding what FPIC entails, how it applies when the indigenous population is a majority in their jurisdiction, whether FPIC is a binding principle

See also, Ellen Margrethe Basse, "Juridisk responsum om den gældende grønlandske lovgivning vurderet i lyset af Århuskonventione" (2014), June 21, 2014, https://naalakkersuisut.gl//~/media/Nanoq/Files/Attached%20Files/Miljoe/Gr%C3%B8nlandsrapport%20%C3%85rhuskonventionen%20dk.pdf (on the implications for Greenland of joining the Aarhus Convention).

7 Emma Wilson, Anne Merrild Hansen, and Elana Wilson Rowe, "Imagining the Future: Local Perceptions of Arctic Extractive Projects That Didn't Happen," in *Arcticness and Change: Power and Voice from the North*, ed. I. Kelman (London: University College London Press, 2017), 130–149.
8 Anne Merrild Hansen, Frank Vanclay, Peter Croal, and Anna-Sofie Hurup Skjervedal, "Managing the Social Impacts of the Rapidly-Expanding Extractive Industries in Greenland," *The Extractive Industries and Society* 3, no. 1 (2016): 25–33, 25, https://doi.org/10.1016/j.exis.2015.11.013
9 UN General Assembly, Declaration on the Rights of Indigenous Peoples, UNGA Res 61/295, September 13, 2007 (UNDRIP).

of law, in what circumstances and to what extent it is relevant to non-indigenous populations, and how it is implemented in practice. The right to and experiences of participation of non-indigenous individuals and groups is of increasing importance; for example under the Aarhus Convention. James Mitchell's case study of Shetland, and Penny Norton's examination of the UK consultation framework provide insights into good practice and benchmarks against which to assess FPIC and the notion of consent more broadly. From these chapters we can also explore the differences, if any, that the presence of indigenous peoples makes to the decision-making and management systems for large-scale resource projects.

In addition to reflecting on both indigenous and non-indigenous contexts, the contributions to this volume examine situations where indigeneity is contested – including in Greenland and in respect of the Komi people of northern Russia who are not recognised as an indigenous people nor protected as such within the Russian legal system. This is an underdeveloped issue in the existing literature – how far is self-identification as indigenous relevant? What if a government does not recognise a people as indigenous and denies them protection under that framework? What if the community does not have a united view of its own indigeneity? This anthology delivers important and original insights on these questions, offering governments, developers, indigenous and other local communities, international organisations and civil society organisations knowledge and opportunities for reflection that can be used to improve processes for the better protection of land and resource rights.

This book adds to the rich body of case studies and analysis that already exists on extractive industries and public engagement; for example, in such collections as *The Will to Drill; Public Brainpower, Northern Sustainabilities; Natural Resource Extraction and Indigenous Livelihoods,* and *Sharing the Costs and Benefits of Energy and Resource Activity: Legal Change and Impact on Communities*.[10] There is also an increasing amount of journal special issues as well as some excellent "grey literature."[11] *The Will to Drill* concludes with a call for further research targeted at improving planning and decision-making processes to include more effectively local stakeholders; and to improve administrative capacity within communities when dealing with extractive industries. It is our aim in this anthology to pursue those goals. We do this by drawing from more general work on public participation and

---

10 Brigt Dale, Ingrid Bay-Larsen, and Berit Skorstad, *The Will to Drill: Mining in Arctic Communites* (Cham, Switzerland: Springer, 2018); *Public Brainpower: Civil Society and Natural Resource Management*, ed. Indra Øverland (Basingstoke: Palgrave Macmillan, 2018); *Northern Sustainabilities*, eds Gail Fondahl and Gary Wilson (Prince George: University of British Colombia, 2017); *Natural Resource Extraction and Indigenous Livelihoods: Development Challenges in an Era of Globalisation*, eds Emma Gilberthorpe and Gavin Hilson (Farmham UK and Burlington VT: Ashgate Publishing, 2014); *Sharing the Costs and Benefits of Energy and Resource Activity: Legal Change and Impact on Communities*, ed. Lila Barrera-Hernández et al. (Oxford: Oxford University Press, 2016).

11 See, e.g., Emma Wilson et al., *Meaningful Stakeholder Engagement in the Extractive Industries* (London: International Institute for Environment and Development, 2016).

decision-making and especially in the contribution of Penny Norton, who has written widely on public consultation strategies from the planner's perspective.[12]

A 2018 study demonstrated the connection between meaningful participatory processes and public support for projects in Northern Canada and Northern Sweden.[13] The researchers found that support for mining projects correlated with their confidence in the decision-makers and the location of decision-making.[14] Those who believed that local actors had influence over the projects were more supportive while those who believed that local or indigenous actors should have more influence were less supportive.[15]

While history has shown that it is certainly possible to operate highly profitably in the absence of any genuine dialogue with local communities where democracy is lacking, it is rather more difficult in democratic countries with an effective fourth estate, a lively non-governmental sector, and increasing expectations of corporate social responsibility. No-one in the Arctic – from the corporate sector, to the government representatives, to the hundreds of citizens with whom our contributors engaged in the course of their research for this book – expressed support for a "resource-curse" economy combining highly profitable (for some) extractive projects with high levels of oppression. That no one took such an extreme position is unsurprising, but there was a wide consensus that extractive industries could not come at the cost of social cohesion or personal well-being and that top-down decision-making in some abstract "national interest" is not acceptable. However, community support for and community benefit from extractive projects is only possible where there is good, ongoing communication between all parties. Conversely, poor communication and low local social acceptance can also be very costly for developers.

This book intends to inform the key participants in extractive projects – namely, the communities, the host governments and the investors – about good practice for effective community engagement. This is based on analysis of international standards and expectations, lessons from the selected case studies, and innovations in public participation. Aside from the practical implications of the volume, as all academic works intend it also contributes to the theoretical debate.

The contributions in the present volume are based on recent research led and conducted by the authors. The overall theme and the selection of chapters is primarily based on presentations given by the contributors at a public seminar in Nuuk, held in October 2017, followed by a half-day closed workshop where the main concepts were further explored. Seven of the twelve contributors

---

12 See, e.g., Penny Norton and Martin Hughes, *Public Consultation and Community Involvement in Planning: A Twenty-first Century Guide* (Abingdon: Routledge, 2017); and "Penny Norton," PNPR, https://www.pnprlimited.co.uk/penny-norton
13 Sverker C. Jagers, Simon Matti, Greg Poelzer, and Stan Yu, "The Impact of Local Participation on Community Support for Natural Resource Management: The Case of Mining in Northern Canada and Northern Sweden," *Arctic Review on Law and Politics* 9 (2018): 124–47, https://doi.org/10.23865/arctic.v9.730
14 Ibid., 140.
15 Ibid., 141.

participated in the seminar and workshop, which offered an opportunity to discuss and share research and experiences relating to international standards and principles combined with local experience and expectations in a range of community contexts. The presentations and public seminar discussion can be viewed on the website of the Arctic Oil and Gas Research Centre.[16] Reflecting on the success of the conference and workshop as well as its gaps, we then sought out a number of other experts to contribute to the anthology.

Following this introduction are three complementary parts, which examine in turn international standards, selected case studies, and proposals for reform. The methodological approaches vary between the chapters but most of the contributors work in interdisciplinary spheres. Between them, they have formal educations in engineering, law, social science, anthropology, human geography, economics and history.

Part I, "Participation in Principle," considers the international standards that have emerged in recent years regarding public participation, especially in respect of indigenous peoples. This part examines a mix of binding treaties, "soft law" (voluntary or guiding) standards and the UNDRIP which straddles both hard and soft law, containing elements of both. These instruments are usually at a fairly high degree of abstraction and need to be sufficiently flexible to take account of widely different circumstances. The three chapters in this Part each provide insights into the current international standards and their application to public participation in the Arctic. Wilson provides an overview of the pertinent international legal and ethical frameworks, including international hard and soft law standards applicable to governments, as well as some of the key international standards and principles applicable to the private sector. Johnstone considers the requirements of the principle of FPIC and its applicability in Greenland within the Self-Government regime. She provides a detailed examination of the status of FPIC in international law and a critique of what it requires in practice, especially since the endorsement of the UNDRIP in 2007. Buhmann follows with an assessment of international guidance standards and their relevance to good governance of extractive industries. She asks: to what extent can international standards be implemented effectively at the local level and what does effective implementation depend on? Part I hence sets out the general frameworks against which one can assess participation in practice.

Part II, "Participation in Practice," presents six case studies with the aim of identifying lessons for improving community engagement in Arctic extractive industries. Each of these is quite distinct, examining different aspects of the participatory processes, to facilitate an assessment of what works in the particular context investigated. How is participation conducted? In what ways is the experience different for indigenous and non-indigenous populations, for older and younger generations? What

---

16 Anne Merrild Hansen and Rachael Lorna Johnstone, "Videos," Arctic Oil & Gas Research Centre, https://uk.uni.gl/research/arctic-oil-gas-research-centre.aspx. A decision was taken not to record the workshop, in order to facilitate the most candid discussion.

has worked well and what has worked less well? How do specific circumstances affect the utility of different strategies and have any bespoke solutions been tested? Skjervedal reports on the challenges of involving young people in public participation and examines tools to boost their engagement. How can youth be involved in an effective and meaningful way? Staying in Greenland, Johnstone and Hansen present the views of different communities in Greenland on resource development, including both those living close to sites of interest and those hundreds of kilometres away. They consider the gap between people's expectations of the consultation process and their experiences. Loginova and Wilson present insights from Russia's Komi Republic, illustrating the efforts of the indigenous Komi people (who are not recognised as such according to Russian law) to participate effectively in decision-making related to oil projects in the region. The Komi case study provides a different perspective on indigeneity and critical reflections on the relevance of official recognition of indigeneity to participation, in theory and practice. Hansen and Ipalook then present insights on Inuit reflections on engagement in oil development on the North Slope of Alaska. After decades of oil extraction and a broad acceptance of the industry, proposals for new developments appear to be creating divisions in small communities. How can this be addressed? Nigel Bankes discusses the provisions of Inuit land claims agreements in Canada that ostensibly guarantee co-management in respect of resource governance. By reviewing case law, Bankes shows how the promises of the land claims agreements for meaningful participation and leadership are not being upheld and explores what would be required to close the gap. Mitchell concludes the case studies with a historic review of the Shetland oil negotiations which have not, up until now, been the object of academic analysis. Lessons can still be learned from this episode in how small and relatively isolated communities can protect their cultural heritage and economic traditions in the face of an oil or mineral discovery when decision-making seems to take place in far distant cities.

Part III, "Participation Improved," contains three contributions that look to the potential to improve public participation and community engagement in Arctic communities. Pereira and Pappa discuss the responsibilities of host governments, the choices they have to make to find the appropriate balance between the requirements of investors and of citizens, in particular, in high-risk environments. This chapter considers the choices and trade-offs that have to be made to secure investment in "high-risk" or "frontier" resource areas, and provides the necessary context to understand how requirements for public participation fit into the broader framework of resource governance. Why should governments and investors prioritise effective community engagement in a challenging and high-risk venture? Norton follows with an examination of innovations in public participation in the context of the UK planning process and assesses their effectiveness. She considers the difficulties of ensuring participation that is meaningful for all parties and different strategies to bring in a representative selection of views into the decision-making process. Norton's chapter reminds the corporate decision-makers of why quality participation is valuable for them and encourages them to seek out means to maximise its effectiveness, rather than viewing it as a bureaucratic hurdle to be surmounted.

Hansen and Johnstone conclude the volume with a critical review of the previous chapters and identification of the key issues that require attention if participation is to be more effective for all parties in the Arctic extractive context. They consider the contributions in light of seven main themes: upholding human rights and the rights of indigenous peoples; identifying the public to be involved; non-traditional means of dialogue; quality information and necessary time to digest it; power relations; the importance of ongoing communication and (ideally) consent; and the complexity and diversity of views within and between different stakeholder groups. There is no one-size-fits-all participation strategy for the Arctic, but the contributions to this anthology aim to assist decision-makers in selecting the strategy that fits best for each project.

Bibliography

Barrera-Hernández, Lila, Barry Barton, Lee Godden, Alistair Lucas, and Anita Rønne (eds). *Sharing the Costs and Benefits of Energy and Resource Activity: Legal Change and Impact on Communities*. Oxford: Oxford University Press, 2016.

Basse, Ellen Margrethe. "Juridisk responsum om den gældende grønlandske lovgivning vurderet i lyset af Århuskonventionen" (2014) https://naalakkersuisut.gl//~/media/Nanoq/Files/Attached%20Files/Miljoe/Gr%C3%B8nlandsrapport%20%C3%85rhuskonventionen%20dk.pdf

"Convention on Access to Information, Public Participation in Decision-Making and Access to Justice in Environmental Matters 1998" (Aarhus Convention). *International Legal Materials* 38, no. 517 (1999).

Dale, Brigt, Ingrid Bay-Larsen, and Berit Skorstad. *The Will to Drill: Mining in Arctic Communites*. Cham, Switzerland: Springer, 2018.

Durfee, Mary and Rachael Lorna Johnstone. *Arctic Governance in a Changing World*. Lanham MD: Rowman and Littlefield, 2019.

Fondahl, Gail and Gary Wilson. *Northern Sustainabilities*. Prince George: University of British Colombia, 2017.

Gilberthorpe, Emma and Gavin Hilson. *Natural Resource Extraction and Indigenous Livelihoods: Development Challenges in an Era of Globalisation*. Farnham UK and Burlington VT: Ashgate Publishing, 2014.

Hansen, Anne Merrild and Rachael Lorna Johnstone. "Videos."*Arctic Oil & Gas Research Centre*. Accessed August 16, 2019. https://uk.uni.gl/research/arctic-oil-gas-research-centre.aspx

Hansen, Anne Merrild, Frank Vanclay, Peter Croal, and Anna-Sofie Hurup Skjervedal. "Managing the Social Impacts of the Rapidly-Expanding Extractive Industries in Greenland." *The Extractive Industries and Society* 3, no. 1 (2016): 25–33. https://doi.org/10.1016/j.exis.2015.11.013

Jagers, Sverker C., Simon Matti, Greg Poelzer, and Stan Yu. "The Impact of Local Participation on Community Support for Natural Resource Management: The Case of Mining in Northern Canada and Northern Sweden." *Arctic Review on Law and Politics* 9 (2018): 124–147. https://doi.org/10.23865/arctic.v9.730

Norton, Penny and Martin Hughes. *Public Consultation and Community Involvement in Planning: A Twenty-first Century Guide*. Abingdon: Routledge, 2017.

Øverland, Indra (ed.) *Public Brainpower: Civil Society and Natural Resource Management.* Cham, Switzerland: Palgrave Macmillan, 2018.

Pelaudeix, Cécile. "Governance of Offshore Hydrocarbon Activities in the Arctic and Energy Policies: a Comparative Approach between Norway, Canada and Greenland/Denmark." In *Governance of Arctic Offshore Oil and Gas*, edited by Cécile Pelaudeix and Ellen Margrethe Basse, 108–126. Abingdon: Routledge, 2017.

"Penny Norton." PNPR. Accessed August 16, 2019. https://www.pnprlimited.co.uk/penny-norton

Sidortsov, Roman. "The Russian Offshore Oil and Gas Regime: When Tight Control Means Less Order." In *Governance of Arctic Offshore Oil and Gas*, edited by Cécile Pelaudeix and Ellen Margrethe Basse, 127–147. Abingdon: Routledge, 2017.

UN General Assembly. Declaration on the Rights of Indigenous Peoples, UNGA Res 61/295. September 13, 2007.

Wilson, Emma, Sarah Best, Emma Blackmore, and Saule Ospanova. *Meaningful Stakeholder Engagement in the Extractive Industries.* London: International Institute for Environment and Development, 2016.

Wilson, Emma, Anne Merrild Hansen, and Elana Wilson Rowe. "Imagining the Future: Local Perceptions of Arctic Extractive Projects That Didn't Happen." In *Arcticness and Change: Power and Voice from the North*, edited by I. Kelman, 130–149. London: UCL Press, 2017.

Part I
Participation in principle

2 Indigenous rights and resource development in the Arctic
An overview of international standards and principles for consultation, participation and consent

Emma Wilson

1 Introduction[1]

International standards and principles for the protection of the environment, human rights and indigenous rights have been evolving over recent decades, increasingly through international, multi-stakeholder dialogue. Yet the social and cultural issues related to resource development continue to be an area of contention and frequently poor performance by resource industries, particularly with regard to indigenous rights and community consultation, participation and consent. Often this is due to a lack of adequate understanding of the underlying social and cultural issues and the mechanisms of meaningful community engagement and free, prior and informed consent (FPIC). It also relates to the lack of involvement of affected communities in early-stage impact assessments and strategic decision-making, and in determining the nature of the engagement itself.

This chapter provides an overview of some of the key international standards and principles that are relevant to indigenous peoples and resource development, focusing in particular on the concepts of engagement, participation, consultation and consent – aspects that are directly related to indigenous peoples' right to self-determination. Drawing on evidence of good practice and lessons learned, it highlights some of the critical challenges in the application of international standards in Arctic (and sub-Arctic) community contexts. It refers not only to indigenous rights instruments, but also to those that apply to public engagement more widely and can be used by indigenous groups to gain a more meaningful voice in decision-making around natural resource development on their lands.

Section 2 provides some background and context to the chapter. Section 3 provides an overview of selected standards and instruments related to indigenous

---

1 Research for this chapter was supported by the Norwegian Ministry of Foreign Affairs as part of the project *Indigenous Peoples and Resource Extraction in the Arctic: Evaluating Ethical Guidelines*, led by the Árran Lule Sami Centre, Ájluokta/Drag, Norway. See the related paper: Emma Wilson, *Evaluating International Ethical Standards and Instruments for Indigenous Rights and the Extractive Industries* (Ájluokta/Drag, Norway: Árran Lule Sami Centre, 2016), https://tinyurl.com/IndigenousStandards

rights and public engagement in the context of resource development. Section 4 focuses in on the question "Who is indigenous?" and the implications of this for the application of standards. Section 5 looks in more depth at key terms employed in standards and instruments, including engagement, due diligence, consultation, participation, consent, and access to remedy and justice, with particular consideration of the relative responsibilities of governments and business. Section 6 offers some concluding thoughts, reflecting on the relevance for Greenland.[2]

2 Background and context

With growing pressures on their lands and resources, indigenous groups are increasingly asserting their rights under international hard and soft law.[3] Governments and the private sector are realising that by applying international standards (over and above national law where necessary) they can avoid and reduce conflicts, which can otherwise be costly.[4] A greater shared understanding of international standards and principles, and the ways in which they are applied, can help to promote mutual understanding and constructive engagement among stakeholders.

To date, threats to indigenous lands, waters and resources have frequently come from the expansion of the extractive industries, including mining, forestry and petroleum development. In the Arctic, as elsewhere, concerns about the damaging effects of extractive industries are now extending to industrial activity related to "green transitions," as indigenous and local communities encounter encroachment from wind farms or the extraction of rare earth minerals to supply green technologies, while hydropower projects continue to engender high levels of concern.[5] Communities may also experience the cumulative effects of multiple interventions, for instance wind turbines, mining infrastructure, roads and tourism development, and it may be difficult for affected people to ascertain the full picture of who needs to be held to account and how to do so.[6] Multiple different interventions may

---

2 See also, Emma Wilson, *Energy and Minerals in Greenland: Governance, Corporate Responsibility and Social Resilience* (London: International Institute for Environment and Development, 2015).
3 "Hard law" is a binding source of law (e.g. the human rights treaties), while the term "soft law" is used for voluntary or guiding standards (see Section 3); see also Johnstone, this volume.
4 Rebecca Adamson and Nick Pelosi, *Indigenous Rights Risk Report* (Vancouver: First Peoples Worldwide, 2014); Rachel Davis and Daniel Franks, *Costs of Company-Community Conflict in the Extractive Sector* (Cambridge MA: Harvard Kennedy School, 2014).
5 Rebecca Lawrence, "Internal Colonisation and Indigenous Resource Sovereignty: Wind Power Developments on Traditional Saami Land," *Environment and Planning D: Society and Space* 32, no. 6 (2014): 1036; Raman Sujatha, "Fossilizing Renewable Energies," *Science as Culture* 22, no. 2 (2013): 172; Mark Nuttall, "Zero-Tolerance, Uranium and Greenland's Mining Future," *The Polar Journal* 3, no. 2 (2013): 368–383.
6 Vigdis Nygaard, "Do Indigenous Interests Have a Say in Planning of New Mining Projects? Experiences from Finnmark, Norway," *The Extractive Industries and Society* 3, no. 1 (2016): 17; Lawrence, "Internal Colonisation."

have multiple protagonists, and may therefore follow multiple different environmental and social standards, reporting to different monitoring bodies.

Over recent years, debates around indigenous rights and resource development have focused heavily on the principle of free, prior and informed consent (FPIC).[7] FPIC is a mechanism by which indigenous peoples can exercise their right to self-determination and other universal human rights, including the right to property, culture and non-discrimination.[8] The principle of FPIC is enshrined in international hard and soft law, notably the International Labour Organisation's 1989 Convention No. 169 on Indigenous and Tribal Peoples (ILO C169) and the 2007 United Nations Declaration on the Rights of Indigenous Peoples (UNDRIP).[9] The inclusion of FPIC specifically in relation to resource development in UNDRIP was a significant development in international law (see Section 3).[10]

There is no universally accepted definition of FPIC, but a much-used definition was provided in a legal commentary submitted in 2005 to the UN Working Group on Indigenous Populations:

- Indigenous peoples are not coerced, pressured or intimidated in their choices of development;
- Their consent is sought and freely given prior to the authorisation and start of development activities;
- Indigenous peoples have full information about the scope and impacts of the proposed development activities on their lands, resources and well-being;
- Their choice to give or withhold consent over developments affecting them is respected and upheld.[11]

---

7 Amy K. Lehr and Gare A. Smith, *Implementing a Corporate Free, Prior, and Informed Consent Policy: Benefits and Challenges* (Boston: Foley Hoag LLP, 2010); Cathal Doyle and Jill Cariño, *Making Free, Prior and Informed Consent a Reality: Indigenous Peoples and the Extractive Sector* (London: Indigenous Peoples Links/PIPLinks; Middlesex University School of Law; The Ecumenical Council for Corporate Responsibility, 2013); Emily Greenspan, *Free, Prior and Informed Consent in Africa: An Emerging Standard for Extractive Industry Projects* (Washington DC: Oxfam America, 2014); Ginger Gibson Macdonald and Gaby Zezulka, *Understanding Successful Approaches to Free, Prior and Informed Consent in Canada. Part 1* (Ottawa: Boreal Leadership Council, 2015); Emma Wilson, *What Is Free, Prior and Informed Consent?* (Ájluokta/Drag, Norway: Árran Lule Sami Centre, 2016).
8 Matthias Åhrén, *Indigenous Peoples' Status in the International Legal System* (Oxford: Oxford University Press, 2016), 119.
9 Indigenous and Tribal Peoples Convention 1989, ILO Convention 169, 1989; UN General Assembly, Declaration on the Rights of Indigenous Peoples, UNGA Res 61/295, September 13, 2007 (UNDRIP).
10 See also Johnstone, this volume.
11 Antoanella-Iulia Motoc and the Tebtebba Foundation, *Standard-Setting: Legal Commentary on the Concept of Free, Prior and Informed Consent*, submitted to the UN Commission on Human Rights, Sub-Commission on the Promotion and Protection of Human Rights, Working Group on Indigenous Populations, UN Doc. E/CN.4/Sub.2/AC.4/2005/WP.1, 15, para. 57.

The UN Expert Mechanism on the Rights of Indigenous Peoples has emphasised the close links between FPIC and indigenous peoples' right to determine the outcomes of decision-making, stating:

> The duty of the State to obtain indigenous peoples' free, prior and informed consent entitles indigenous peoples to effectively determine the outcome of decision-making that affects them, not merely a right to be involved in such processes.[12]

This entitlement to "determine the outcome of decision-making that affects them" has been under-explored in debates around indigenous rights and natural resource development (see Section 5.1).

The debate around FPIC has perhaps overshadowed the evolution of other concepts within international standards and principles, such as meaningful stakeholder consultation and engagement, and public participation in decision-making, which have been just as significant – both for indigenous and local populations. Considerable volumes of guidance have been prepared on how to carry out stakeholder engagement in an industrial context.[13] The 2011 UN Guiding Principles on Business and Human Rights (UNGPs)[14] have greatly influenced debates on stakeholder engagement, in particular the notion of "meaningful" consultation and engagement with communities and other stakeholders.[15]

International instruments are evolving all the time and have influenced one another. For instance, the adoption of UNDRIP also resulted in the UN human rights treaty bodies placing increased emphasis on FPIC and has triggered the inclusion and strengthening of FPIC clauses in private sector standards and guidance,[16] while the OECD Guidelines for Multinational Enterprises incorporated the UNGPs in their 2011 update (see Section 5.2).

---

12 Asia Pacific Forum of National Human Rights Institutions and the Office of the United Nations High Commissioner for Human Rights, *The United Nations Declaration on the Rights of Indigenous Peoples: A Manual for National Human Rights Institutions* (Geneva: APF and OHCHR, 2013), 20.

13 For example: IFC, *Stakeholder Engagement: A Good Practice Handbook for Companies Doing Business in Emerging Markets* (Washington DC: International Finance Corporation, 2007); Kirk Herbertson, Athena R. Ballesteros, Robert Goodland and Isabel Munilla, *Breaking Ground: Engaging Communities in Extractive and Infrastructure Projects* (Washington DC: World Resources Institute, 2009); ICMM, *Community Development Toolkit* (London: International Council on Mining and Metals, 2016); "Community Engagement and Indigenous Peoples," IPIECA, www.ipieca.org/our-work/social/indigenous-peoples/.

14 John Ruggie, *Guiding Principles on Business and Human Rights: Implementing the United Nations "Protect, Respect and Remedy" Framework*, UN Doc. A/HRC/17/31, March 21, 2011 (UNGPs).

15 OECD, *Due Diligence Guidance for Meaningful Stakeholder Engagement in the Extractive Sector* (Geneva: OECD, 2016); Emma Wilson, Sarah Best, Emma Blackmore, and Saule Ospanova, *Meaningful Community Engagement in the Extractive Industries* (London: International Institute for Environment and Development, 2016).

16 Doyle and Cariño, *Making FPIC a Reality*; Wilson, *What Is Free, Prior and Informed Consent (FPIC)?*; see Johnstone, this volume.

Due diligence is a key area where consultation and engagement are critical. Due diligence seeks to identify risks to an investment or contractual relationship and to develop strategies and plans to mitigate and manage those risks.[17] Environmental and social due diligence seek to mitigate and manage risks to the environment and local society, as these also represent risks to the success of a project and the security of an investment. At the project level, due diligence comprises an ongoing set of assessment and monitoring activities, starting early and continuing over the life of the project. These activities tend to be funded by the project proponent, as required by national legislation and/or the requirements of project finance. The assessment of impacts on health, human rights and culture may be integrated into a larger comprehensive assessment or carried out as discrete impact assessments.[18] Related monitoring and oversight measures may include third party monitoring, such as environmental and social audits carried out on behalf of project lenders, or participatory monitoring by civil society representatives. Communities are calling for greater local control over the impact assessment process, including choice of consultants, priority setting, participation in data gathering and analysis, and influence over subsequent decision-making and outcomes.[19]

Individual states encounter specific challenges in meeting their commitments, especially when it comes to balancing indigenous rights with industrial development imperatives.[20] In practice, international hard-law instruments – legally binding international treaties – may have only a limited scope of application (for instance there may be a limited number of state parties). Soft-law instruments, such as UN Declarations, may be deemed universal in their application, while not being legally binding, but they may be influential in other ways, such as in the drafting of binding standards or national legislation, or the way that they are used by civil society groups in campaigns and disputes.

A key challenge for interpretation is the level at which requirements ought to be applied, for instance in what level of decision-making local communities have the

17 See Buhmann, this volume.
18 See, Martin Birley, *Health Impact Assessment: Principles and Practice* (Abingdon: Routledge, 2012) (for more on health impact assessment); see Désirée Abrahams and Yann Wyss, *Guide to Human Rights Impact Assessment and Management* (Washington DC: International Finance Corporation, UN Global Compact and the International Business Leaders Forum, 2010) (for more on human rights impact assessment). See also Convention on Biological Diversity, *Akwé:Kon Voluntary Guidelines for the Conduct of Cultural, Environmental and Social Impact Assessment Regarding Developments Proposed to Take Place on, or which are Likely to Impact on, Sacred Sites and on Lands and Waters Traditionally Occupied or Used by Indigenous and Local Communities* (Montreal: Secretariat of the Convention on Biological Diversity, 2004) (on socio-cultural assessment).
19 Ciaran O'Faircheallaigh, "Effectiveness in Social Impact Assessment: Aboriginal Peoples and Resource Development in Australia," *Impact Assessment and Project Appraisal* 27, no. 2 (2009): 95–110; Hansen et al., "Managing the Social Impacts of the Rapidly-Expanding Extractive Industries in Greenland," *The Extractive Industries and Society* 3 (2016): 25–33; Martin Papillon and Thierry Rodon, "Proponent–Indigenous Agreements and the Implementation of the Right to Free, Prior and Informed Consent in Canada," *Environmental Impact Assessment Review* 62 (2017): 216.
20 See Part II of this volume.

right to be involved. For instance, Greenland's leaders have tended to see the granting of self-government by Denmark as the equivalent of granting Greenlanders the rights inherent in UNDRIP.[21] However, this position has been challenged by opposition politicians, notably when a presumed moratorium on uranium mining was repealed in 2013 by the Greenland Parliament by a majority of a single vote.[22] By contrast, in Norway, a successful effort to block the reopening of a gold mine in a Sami community was made possible by decentralised democratic decision-making mechanisms, rather than the application of Norway's commitments under ILO C169 and UNDRIP.[23] Meanwhile, Russia has not signed up to ILO C169 or officially endorsed UNDRIP, but the liquefied natural gas (LNG) project Yamal LNG in Western Siberia implemented a process of securing the FPIC of local indigenous communities in order to comply with the requirements of the project lenders.[24]

The public and the media often focus more on the responsibility of business to engage and consult with communities, rather than on the responsibility of governments to do the same. This may be due to the fact that companies are often a more obvious target in relation to a specific project in a specific location. It might also be because states tend to expect corporations to run public consultation exercises (and to pay for them), and so governments delegate their own legal responsibility. Yet by doing so, they are putting off the consultation to a time when many of the critical strategic decisions have already been made, and may be failing to meet their obligations under international law. These state obligations are stipulated clearly in several international instruments (see Section 5.1). The importance of early strategic engagement and consultation prior to the allocation of land and exploration licences is increasingly well understood by researchers and advocacy groups, and is becoming a critical area of concern for the private sector and international financial institutions.[25] Without this, companies may be invited to invest considerable amounts of money in exploration activities, only to discover that the community is opposed to the project, and may be able to halt it.[26]

The UNGPs help to clarify the relative human rights responsibilities of governments and business through the "Protect, Respect and Remedy" framework.

21 See Johnstone, this volume.
22 Mark Nuttall, "Imagining and Governing the Greenlandic Resource Frontier," *The Polar Journal* 2, no. 1 (2012): 113.
23 Nygaard, *Indigenous Interests*; Tone Magnussen and Brigt Dale, "The Municipal No to Mining: The Case Concerning the Reopening of the Biedjovaggi Gold Mine in Guovdageainnu Municipality, Norway," in *The Will to Drill: Mining in Arctic Communities*, eds Brigt Dale, Ingrid Bay-Larsen and Berit Skorstad (Geneva, Switzerland: Springer International Publishing, 2018), 175.
24 Wilson, *Evaluating International Ethical Standards*.
25 Shift and the Institute for Human Rights and Business, *Oil and Gas Sector Guide on Implementing the UN Guiding Principles on Business and Human Rights* (Brussels: European Commission, 2011); IFC, *ILO Convention 169 and the Private Sector* (Washington DC: IFC, 2007).
26 Magnussen and Dale, "The Municipal No."

These comprise: the government responsibility to protect human rights; the corporate responsibility to respect human rights; and effective access to remedies in cases of human rights abuses.[27] The UNGPs were welcomed as the global recognition of business responsibilities in relation to human rights. They have also been welcomed (especially by business) for the way that they balance consideration of the responsibilities of business and government, and help to build understanding of the interplay between the two (see Section 5).

For the private sector, the standards set by international financial institutions – such as the International Finance Corporation (IFC) for project finance – are highly influential but are only mandatory for those companies that are receiving finance from the financial institutions in question (see Section 3). Companies may also sign up to voluntary corporate responsibility initiatives, such as the UN Global Compact or the Voluntary Principles on Security and Human Rights, while industry associations have also developed their own good practice standards and guidance (see Section 3). In practice, in many cases, a company that is a member of one or more industry associations or voluntary initiatives may partner with a company that has not made the same commitments (e.g. a state-owned company). In such cases, the policies and practices of the joint venture need to be agreed between the partners.

Even after establishing which standards might apply to a project, there is frequently a lack of agreement on how they are applied in practice. Accepted understandings are often developed for particular contexts through the analysis of legal case history,[28] or the function of monitoring bodies, complaints mechanisms and ombudsmen.[29] These experiences are important in understanding, for example, how an obligation to obtain FPIC according to international law plays out in a particular location with its own set of national and subnational legal and regulatory requirements, and local cultural norms and practices.

---

27 John Ruggie, *Protect, Respect and Remedy: a Framework for Business and Human Rights. Report of the Special Representative on Human Rights, Transnational Corporations and Other Business Enterprises*, UN Doc. A/HRC/8/5, April 7, 2008; see also Buhmann, this volume.

28 Amy K. Lehr, *Indigenous Peoples' Rights and the Role of Free, Prior and Informed Consent* (New York: UN Global Compact, 2014); Leena Heinämäki, "The Rapidly Evolving International Status of Indigenous Peoples: The Example of the Sami People in Finland," in *Indigenous Rights in Scandinavia*, eds Christina Allard and Susann F. Skogvang (Farnham, UK and Burlington VT: Ashgate Publishing, 2015); Mattias Åhrén, *Indigenous Peoples' Status*.

29 Martijn Scheltema, "Assessing the Effectiveness of Remedy Outcomes of Non-judicial Grievance Mechanisms," *The Dovenschmidt Quarterly* 4 (2013): 190; Emma Wilson and Emma Blackmore, eds, *Dispute or Dialogue? Community Perspectives on Company-Led Grievance Mechanisms* (London: International Institute for Environment and Development, 2013); Shift and Mazars, *UN Guiding Principles Reporting Framework* (Cambridge MA: Shift and Mazars, 2017); "ACCESS," ACCESS Facility, accessed June 25, 2019, www.accessfacility.org/

3 Overview of selected international standards and principles

This section offers a brief overview of selected international standards and principles relevant to indigenous rights, resource extraction, meaningful consultation and engagement, and public participation, including participation in strategic-level natural resource planning.[30] Individual indigenous people enjoy the same human rights as any other individuals, but also enjoy additional – collective – indigenous rights.[31] The cornerstone of indigenous rights is the right to self-determination, along with the rights to land, property and the means of subsistence.

The Universal Declaration of Human Rights (UDHR) (1948) is a declaration of the UN General Assembly. Although formally a non-binding international soft-law instrument, it provided the foundation for a number of legally binding human rights treaties, and many argue that it has attained customary law status.[32] Article 17 recognises the right to individual and collective ownership of land and states that "no one shall arbitrarily be deprived of his property." The UDHR was developed into two complementary binding treaties: the International Covenant on Economic, Social and Cultural Rights (ICESCR) and the International Covenant on Civil and Political Rights (ICCPR).[33] They were adopted by the UN General Assembly in 1966 and came into force in 1976. Article 1 of both covenants contains the following:

1. All peoples have the right of self-determination. By virtue of that right they freely determine their political status and freely pursue their economic, social and cultural development.
2. All peoples may, for their own ends, freely dispose of their natural wealth and resources without prejudice to any obligations arising out of international economic co-operation, based upon the principle of mutual benefit, and international law. In no case may a people be deprived of its own means of subsistence.

The right to self-determination and other human rights were reinforced by participating governments through the Vienna Declaration, adopted by the World

---

30 See Wilson, *Evaluating International Standards* (for a more detailed evaluation of these instruments).
31 See Johnstone, this volume.
32 UN General Assembly, *Universal Declaration of Human Rights*, UNGA Res A/RES/217(III), December 10, 1948. See also, Richard Lillich, "The Growing Importance of Customary International Human Rights Law," *Georgia Journal of International and Comparative Law* 25, no. 1 (1995): 1; Jochen von Bernstorff, "The Changing Fortunes of the Universal Declaration of Human Rights: Genesis and Symbolic Dimensions of the Turn to Rights in International Law" *The European Journal of International Law*, 19, no. 5 (2008): 903; John Gerard Ruggie, "Business and Human Rights: the Evolving International Agenda," *American Journal of International Law*, 101, no. 4 (2007): 819–840.
33 International Covenant on Civil and Political Rights 1966 (ICCPR); International Covenant on Economic, Social and Cultural Rights 1966 (ICESCR).

Conference on Human Rights in 1993.[34] In addition, the Declaration urged states "to ensure the full and free participation of indigenous people in all aspects of society, in particular in matters of concern to them."[35]

Indigenous peoples' rights to meaningful participation, consultation and engagement derive from their rights to self-determination, property and the means of subsistence, as well as the right to non-discrimination. The two key indigenous rights instruments most referred to in the context of extractive industry development are the aforementioned ILO C169 and UNDRIP.

In 1989, ILO C169 replaced the outdated 1957 ILO Convention 107 on Indigenous Peoples. It is legally binding on the 23 countries that have ratified the Convention. This includes Norway (1990) and the Kingdom of Denmark (1996) but none of the other Arctic states. UNDRIP was adopted in 2007 by the UN General Assembly (following 25 years of deliberation between UN member states and indigenous groups). It was initially adopted by a majority of 144 states (including Denmark, Finland, Iceland, Norway and Sweden), with four votes against (Canada, the United States, New Zealand and Australia) and 11 abstentions, while over 30 countries did not turn up for the vote.[36] Today the four states which voted against the Declaration have now endorsed it, although most of the abstaining states (including the Russian Federation) and the absent states have yet to do so.

As a General Assembly Resolution, rather than a treaty, UNDRIP is not legally binding on its own terms. However, some of its provisions are binding because they reflect customary international law, while others may become binding over time to the extent that customary international law evolves in the same direction.[37] Moreover, UNDRIP has been widely used by indigenous groups in articulating and defending their rights, and by indigenous and other experts in the drafting of national legislation, including in Russia.[38] Full implementation of UNDRIP at the national level has been challenging in practice for some countries, particularly with regard to the matter of FPIC.[39]

34 "UN World Conference on Human Rights, Vienna Declaration and Programme of Action," *International Legal Materials* 32 (1993): 1661.
35 Ibid., para. B1.31; see also Buhmann, this volume.
36 The eleven countries that abstained from voting on UNDRIP in 2007 were Azerbaijan, Bangladesh, Bhutan, Burundi, Colombia, Georgia, Kenya, Nigeria, the Russian Federation, Samoa and Ukraine. Ukraine endorsed UNDRIP in May 2014 following the annexation of Crimea by Russia. Of the 144 nations that voted for UNDRIP, 101 do not have officially recognised indigenous populations, while all of those who voted against, all the abstaining nations and most of those who were absent do have indigenous populations. See: "United Nations Declaration on the Rights of Indigenous Peoples," United Nations, accessed 25 June 2019, https://www.un.org/development/desa/indigenouspeoples/declaration-on-the-rights-of-indigenous-peoples.html
37 Customary international law is based on state practice and is a form of hard law. See Statute of the International Court of Justice 1945, article 38(1)(d).
38 Natalia I Novikova, *Okhotniki i neftyaniki: issledovaniya v yuridicheskoy antropologii* [Hunters and Oil Workers: Research in Legal Anthropology] (Moscow: Nauka. 2014).
39 Wilson, *Evaluating International Ethical Standards*.

Other binding treaties, principles, action plans and declarations have influenced public participation and consultation, and can be used by indigenous communities. Notably, a suite of instruments resulted from the 1992 UN Conference on Environment and Development (UNCED), including the Rio Declaration on Environment and Development (1992), which was adopted by over 170 countries, including all the Arctic states.[40] The Convention on Biological Diversity (CBD) (1992), a key output of UNCED, has been ratified by 198 parties, including all the Arctic states, apart from the United States, which has signed but not ratified the Convention.[41] Agenda 21 was adopted at UNCED by over 178 governments, including all the Arctic states, as a non-binding action plan for the UN, other multilateral organisations and individual governments to promote sustainable development at local, national and global levels.[42] Among other things, it recommends strengthening national dispute-resolution arrangements for settling land and resource-management conflicts.

Principle 10 of the Rio Declaration requires governments to facilitate public awareness and participation in environmental decision-making by making information widely available. It gave rise to the UN Economic Commission for Europe (UNECE)'s Convention on Access to Information, Public Participation in Decision-making and Access to Justice in Environmental Matters (1998) (the Aarhus Convention).[43] The UNECE covers all of Europe, the USA and Canada, the Caucasus and Central Asia but in 2011 the Aarhus Convention was opened up for accession by states outside of the UNECE.[44] There are currently 47 parties to the Aarhus Convention, including – among Arctic states – Denmark (but not Greenland), Finland, Iceland, Norway and Sweden.

UNECE also promulgated the Convention on Environmental Impact Assessment in a Transboundary Context (the Espoo Convention) in 1991 and its Protocol on Strategic Environmental Assessment (SEA) in 2003 (the Kiev Protocol).[45] As with the Aarhus Convention, they are open to all states, not only UNECE members. The Espoo Convention currently has 45 state parties (including Canada, the entire Kingdom of Denmark, Finland, Norway and Sweden), while the Kiev Protocol has 33, including Denmark and Greenland, Finland, Norway and Sweden.[46]

---

40 "Rio Declaration on Environment and Development 1992," *International Legal Materials* 31 (1992): 876.
41 Convention on Biological Diversity 1992 (CBD).
42 United Nations Conference on Environment and Development, *Agenda 21, Rio Declaration, Forest Principles*. New York: United Nations, 1992.
43 Convention on Access to Information, Public Participation in Decision-Making and Access to Justice in Environmental Matters 1998 (Aarhus Convention); see also Buhmann, this volume.
44 "Landmark Meeting of Aarhus Convention Welcomes Global Accession," UNECE, accessed July 2, 2019, https://www.unece.org/press/pr2011/11env_p32e.html
45 Convention on Environmental Impact Assessment in a Transboundary Context 1991 (Espoo Convention); Protocol on Strategic Environmental Assessment to the Convention on Environmental Impact Assessment in a Transboundary Context (Kiev Protocol).
46 United Nations Treaty Collection, Chapter XXVII.4, Convention on Environmental Impact Assessment in a Transboundary Context, status as at July 23, 2019, https://treaties.un.org/Pages/ViewDetails.aspx?src=TREATY&mtdsg_no=XXVII-4&chapter=27&

A highly influential instrument in the sphere of human rights is the 2011 UN Guiding Principles on Business and Human Rights (UNGPs).[47] The principles evolved out of a long UN process, in which John Ruggie played a key role as Special Representative to the UN Secretary General on Business and Human Rights. The UNGPs were unanimously endorsed in 2011 by the UN Human Rights Council (made up of 47 UN member states).[48] Indigenous rights are not a core element of the UNGPs. However, the commentary to Article 12 (which relates to the human rights referred to by the Principles) indicates that indigenous rights instruments may also need to be taken into account by business enterprises. The UNGPs have also been analysed and interpreted for their relevance to indigenous rights, notably in a 2013 UN-endorsed report by James Anaya, the then-UN Special Rapporteur on the Rights of Indigenous Peoples (see below).[49] Targeted sectoral guidance on applying UNDRIP has also been developed for the oil and gas industry, in which indigenous rights are identified as a leading human rights issue.[50]

In 2011, the Organization for Economic Co-operation and Development (OECD) Guidelines for Multinational Enterprises were updated, following a multi-stakeholder process, including a new section on human rights, reflecting the influence of the UNGPs. The OECD Guidelines were launched in 1976, and are recommendations addressed by signatory governments to multinational enterprises operating within or out of adhering countries, covering environmental protection, employment and labour rights, corruption and taxation, in addition to the new human rights section. All 36 OECD countries (including Canada, Denmark, Finland, Iceland, Norway, Sweden and the United States) and 12 non-OECD countries (*not* including Russia) have subscribed to the Declaration. In 2016, the OECD issued due diligence guidance on meaningful stakeholder engagement for the extractive sector, which includes an annex relating to meaningful engagement with indigenous peoples.[51]

A key area where industry standards are being developed – and are still evolving – is in the sphere of so-called voluntary standards. In this context, the term "voluntary" is sometimes misleading. For instance, a company might

---

clang=_en; and UN Treaty Collection, Chapter XXVII.4.b, Protocol on Strategic Environmental Assessment to the Convention on Environmental Impact Assessment in a Transboundary Context, status as at July 23, 2019, https://treaties.un.org/Pages/ViewDetails.aspx?src=TREATY&mtdsg_no=XXVII-4-b&chapter=27&clang=_en

47 UNGPs.
48 The UN Human Rights Council is an inter-governmental body comprising 47 member states elected for three-year terms by members of the UN General Assembly. See, UN Human Rights Council, "List of Past Members of the Human Rights Council," accessed July 23, 2019, https://www.ohchr.org/EN/HRBodies/HRC/Pages/PastMembers.aspx (for the membership in 2011)
49 James Anaya, *Report of the Special Rapporteur on the Rights of Indigenous Peoples, James Anaya: Extractive Industries and Indigenous Peoples*, 2013. UN Human Rights Council, UN Doc. A/HRC/24/41.
50 Shift and IHRB, *Oil and Gas*.
51 OECD, *Due Diligence*.

voluntarily seek finance from a financial institution, but in doing so commit itself to following a set of binding standards and principles, which have associated penalties if the company fails to follow the standards (see below). In some cases, such as the ISO 14001 standard (see below), contracting companies may be unable to take supply chain jobs if they are not certified to the standard. At the same time, companies using their own finance or state funding that does not have the same strict regulations, are not obliged to follow these environmental and social standards; they are limited only by the national legislation of the countries in which they operate and any standards that apply from their home jurisdictions.

Project finance is the long-term financing of infrastructure and industrial projects, involving both equity investors and project lenders. International financial institutions, such as the International Finance Corporation (IFC),[52] the private sector lending arm of the World Bank Group, have developed comprehensive sets of environmental and social performance standards which issue obligations on their clients receiving the loans. Institutional investors have their own sets of standards, notably the Principles for Responsible Investment,[53] while the export credit agencies of OECD member states are covered by the OECD Common Approaches for Officially Supported Export Credits and Environmental and Social Due Diligence.[54]

In this chapter, the focus is primarily on the text of the IFC Performance Standards for Environmental and Social Sustainability,[55] as they are seen as a benchmark for good industry practice and have been influential on the development of other standards. Other international financial institutions have been developing and updating their own standards (broadly similar, sometimes more or less progressive than the IFC standards); these include the World Bank itself, and regional development banks such as the European Bank for Reconstruction and Development (EBRD), which has financed some projects in Russia.[56] The 97 Equator Principles Financial Institutions have also committed to follow the IFC standards as part of their wider due diligence framework.[57]

Voluntary corporate responsibility initiatives also include the UN Global Compact, the Voluntary Principles on Security and Human Rights, and the Global

---

52 "IFC Performance Standards on Environmental and Social Sustainability – Effective January 1, 2012," International Finance Corporation, accessed June 27, 2019, https://www.ifc.org/wps/wcm/connect/topics_ext_content/ifc_external_corporate_site/sustainability-at-ifc/publications/publications_handbook_pps
53 "Principles for Responsible Investment," PRI, accessed June 27, 2019, https://www.unpri.org/
54 "Environmental and Social Due Diligence," OECD, accessed June 27, 2017, www.oecd.org/trade/topics/export-credits/environmental-and-social-due-dilligence/
55 International Finance Corporation, "IFC Performance Standards."
56 See, e.g., "Sakhalin II (Phase 1) Oil Project," European Bank for Reconstruction and Development, accessed July 28, 2019, https://www.ebrd.com/work-with-us/projects/psd/sakhalin-ii-phase-1-oil-project.html
57 "The Equator Principles," Equator Principles, accessed June 27, 2017, https://equator-principles.com/about/

Reporting Initiative.[58] Such initiatives require companies to report against a set of principles to which they commit when they sign up to the initiative.[59] Industry associations have also developed their own good practice standards. For instance, the 27 companies that are members of the International Council on Mining and Metals (ICMM) are obliged to commit to a set of ten principles and eight position statements, and transparent reporting.[60] By contrast, the oil and gas industry association for advancing environmental and social issues, known as IPIECA, does not impose binding commitments on its 35 corporate members, focusing instead on building knowledge networks and developing good practice guidance within its member-based working groups.[61]

The first enterprises to start work on an extractive industry project are generally involved in some form of exploration work, such as seismic testing or exploratory drilling. Frequently, these are smaller junior companies, with less money and fewer staff resources to expend on in-depth stakeholder engagement efforts, and they are less likely to be members of industry associations and global corporate responsibility initiatives. Often their aim is ultimately to sell the project to a larger company once the reserve potential has been confirmed. Such companies may have fewer incentives to engage in meaningful community engagement in the earliest stages of project development, and yet this is a critical time for community engagement, as recognised by the IFC among others.[62]

Official commentaries and guidance documents play an important role in the interpretation of international standards. Of particular relevance here is the above-mentioned 2013 commentary by the former UN Special Rapporteur on the Rights of Indigenous Peoples, James Anaya, relating to the UNGPs and how they relate to indigenous rights and the extractive industries.[63] Anaya's "preferred model" of development, *if resource extraction is to go ahead*, is for indigenous peoples to have greater control over the developments, through involvement in strategic-level decision-making, benefit-sharing, and implementation of industrial projects. Anaya also emphasises indigenous peoples' right to decline to pursue industrial development, and refers to the principle of FPIC as the "general rule" for extractive projects taking place within indigenous peoples' territories.

---

58 "Who We Are," United Nations Global Compact, accessed 28 July 2019, https://www.unglobalcompact.org/; "Voluntary Principles on Security and Human Rights," Voluntary Principles on Security and Human Rights, accessed July 28, 2019, www.voluntaryprinciples.org/; "GRI Standards," Global Reporting Initiative, accessed July 28, 2019, https://www.globalreporting.org/
59 See Wilson, *Evaluating International Ethical Standards* (for more on these and other initiatives).
60 "International Council on Mining and Metals," ICMM, accessed June 27, 2019, https://www.icmm.com/
61 "The Global Oil and Gas Industry Association for Advancing Environmental and Social Issues," IPIECA, accessed June 27, 2019, www.ipieca.org.
62 IFC, *A Strategic Approach to Early Stakeholder Engagement: A Good Practice Handbook for Junior Companies in the Extractive Industries* (Washington DC: IFC, 2014).
63 Anaya, *Report of the Special Rapporteur*.

4 Who is indigenous?

A key challenge frequently highlighted by companies and financial institutions is how to identify the indigenous people who may be affected by a particular project or development. In some cases, such as in Greenland, not all members of a population may necessarily self-identify as "indigenous";[64] in other cases, such as the Komi people of Russia's Komi Republic, a people may self-identify as indigenous, but may not officially be recognised as indigenous by the national government.[65]

In many cases, the need to identify whether or not a community or group is indigenous is an unwanted distraction from the goal of ensuring that isolated, vulnerable and/or land- and resource-dependent people are adequately protected from the potential impacts of industrial development. However, the questions of self-determination and the protection of traditionally-used land and resources also need to be considered (separately from resource-dependency, marginalisation and vulnerability).[66] The need for definitions has generated some worthwhile debate and has led to the development of useful clarifications and guidance, some of which are discussed in this section.

Indigenous peoples themselves have long argued against formal definitions of "indigenous," preferring to self-identify.[67] The UN has various working definitions, a widely cited one being from a 1986 study by the then-UN Special Rapporteur on the Prevention of Discrimination and the Protection of Minorities, José Martínez Cobo:

> Indigenous communities, peoples and nations are those which, having a historical continuity with pre-invasion and pre-colonial societies that developed on their territories, consider themselves distinct from other sectors of the societies now prevailing on those territories, or parts of them. They form at present non-dominant sectors of society and are determined to preserve, develop and transmit to future generations their ancestral territories, and their ethnic identity, as the basis of their continued existence as peoples, in accordance with their own cultural patterns, social institutions and legal system.[68]

The same study defines an indigenous person as "one who belongs to these indigenous populations through self-identification as indigenous (group consciousness) and is recognised and accepted by these populations as one of its members (acceptance by the group)."[69]

---

64 See Johnstone, this volume.
65 See Loginova and Wilson, this volume.
66 See Johnstone, this volume.
67 Asia Pacific Forum and OHCHR, *The United Nations Declaration*.
68 José Martínez Cobo, UN Special Rapporteur, *Study of the Problem of Discrimination against Indigenous Populations* (Report) (New York: United Nations. 1986), UN Doc. E/CN.4/Sub.2/1986/7 Add. 4, para 379.
69 Ibid., paras 381–382.

Article 1 of ILO C169 states that the Convention applies to:

> peoples in independent countries who are regarded as indigenous on account of their descent from the populations which inhabited the country, or a geographical region to which the country belongs, at the time of conquest or colonisation or the establishment of present state boundaries and who, irrespective of their legal status, retain some or all of their own social, economic, cultural and political institutions.

ILO C169 applies also to "tribal peoples," who may not be descended from peoples who lived in a place prior to colonisation or the establishment of current state boundaries, but "whose social, cultural and economic conditions distinguish them from other sections of the national community, and whose status is regulated wholly or partially by their own customs or traditions or by special laws or regulations" (Article 1). Article 2 of the Convention states: "Self-identification as indigenous or tribal shall be regarded as a fundamental criterion for determining the groups to which the provisions of this Convention apply."

UNDRIP does not seek to define "indigenous," recognising that "indigenous peoples have the right to determine their own identity or membership in accordance with their customs and traditions" (Article 3). Åhrén observes that UNDRIP was instrumental in confirming indigenous peoples' status as "peoples" under international law:

> One must now reasonably conclude that the term "peoples" can no longer be understood to exclusively refer to aggregate populations of states. Rather, also populations with certain distinct cultural and ethnic characteristics within a state can also be peoples for international legal purposes, at least in an indigenous peoples' context. In other words, in states with indigenous populations there can be more than one people in a state, and the territory of a people can also stretch across state borders.[70]

The OECD Due Diligence Guidance for Meaningful Stakeholder Engagement in the Extractive Sector (Annex B) follows ILO C169 with its definition of indigenous (not tribal) peoples, adding: "Enterprises should consider the unique characteristics of indigenous peoples and identify the collective rights claimed by indigenous peoples, as well as the human rights of indigenous individuals who are potentially impacted by activities."[71] The guidance also states:

> [C]ertain characteristics of indigenous peoples will require special consideration including: their governance institutions, practices and any associated right to self-determination; their relationship with land; their spiritual and cultural heritage; historical discrimination they have suffered; their unique and at times

---

70 Åhrén, *Indigenous Peoples' Status*.
71 OECD, *Due Diligence*, 78.

vulnerable position in society; their recognition under international law, as well as at times special legal status under national legislation and policy. Extractive activities that affect indigenous peoples should be aware of these unique considerations.[72]

The IFC Performance Standard 7 on Indigenous Peoples (clauses 4–6) states that while there is no universally accepted definition of indigenous peoples, the Performance Standard uses the term:

> in a generic sense to refer to a distinct social and cultural group possessing the following characteristics in varying degrees:
>
> - self-identification as members of a distinct indigenous cultural group and recognition of this identity by others;
> - collective attachment to geographically distinct habitats or ancestral territories in the project area and to the natural resources in these habitats and territories;
> - customary cultural, economic, social, or political institutions that are separate from those of the mainstream society or culture; or
> - a distinct language or dialect, often different from the official language or languages of the country or region in which they reside.

Performance Standard 7 goes further to state:

> This Performance Standard applies to communities or groups of Indigenous Peoples who maintain a collective attachment, i.e. whose identity as a community or group is linked to distinct habitats or ancestral territories and the natural resources therein. It may also apply to communities or groups that have lost collective attachment to distinct habitats or ancestral territories in the project area, occurring within the concerned group members' lifetime, because of forced severance, conflict, government resettlement programs, dispossession of their lands, natural disasters, or incorporation of such areas into an urban area.

As part of a due diligence process, clients of the IFC are required to demonstrate whether or not Performance Standard 7 is to be triggered, along with the requirement to implement a process of FPIC (see Section 5.2). To do this, an assessment is carried out (by appropriate third party experts) to determine whether or not affected communities are indigenous. However, it is also worth noting that the IFC's requirement to carry out "informed consultation and participation" (ICP), which requires in-depth engagement with the local community leading to the client "incorporating into their decision-making process the views of the Affected Communities on matters that affect them directly," applies to all people

---

72 OECD, *Due Diligence*, 75.

who are likely to suffer "significant adverse impacts," whether or not they are defined as being "indigenous" (see Section 5.2).

More guidance is needed for practitioners to understand how to tackle this question sensitively. "Vulnerability" and "marginalisation" are possible entry points and are frequently used by industry standards and guidance (see Section 5.2). However, the vulnerability and marginalisation of indigenous communities is an additional consideration to the right to self-determination and the need to protect traditionally used land and resources, and the implications of these in a project context. Therefore, these considerations need to be addressed at the same time but separately.

The Forest Stewardship Council (FSC) sought to address the challenge of identifying indigenous communities in the context of its forest certification standards. The 2012 revision of the standard extends the application of FPIC not only to indigenous peoples, but also "local communities" and "traditional peoples."[73] Self-identification is a key criterion in the definition of "indigenous peoples," which aligns with the definitions described above; the other categories are for people who do not self-identify as being indigenous. The FSC definition of "local communities" is:

> Communities of any size that are in or adjacent to the Management Unit [the unit of managed forest subject to certification], and also those that are close enough to have a significant impact on the economy or the environmental values of the Management Unit or to have their economies, rights or environments significantly affected by the management activities or the biophysical aspects of the Management Unit.[74]

The FSC definition of "traditional peoples" is:

> Social groups or peoples who do not self-identify as indigenous and who affirm rights to their lands, forests and other resources based on long established custom or traditional occupation and use.[75]

The FSC also emphasises the importance of recognising not only people's legal rights to land and resources, but also their customary rights. It also states that "indigenous peoples who are uncontacted or who live in voluntary isolation" are "extremely vulnerable and any contact with them must be avoided."[76]

In December 2018, the UN General Assembly adopted the UN Declaration on the Rights of Peasants and Other People Working in Rural Areas. This declaration protects those who practice traditional land-, water- and resource-dependent livelihoods, including fisherfolk, hunters, gatherers, nomads, pastoralists, agricultural

---

73 Forest Stewardship Council, *FSC Guidelines for the Implementation of the Right to Free, Prior and Informed Consent (FPIC)* (Bonn: Forest Stewardship Council, 2012).
74 Ibid., 21.
75 Ibid., 22.
76 Ibid., 22.

workers and others, whether or not they are indigenous or officially recognised as such.[77] The Declaration aims to protect workers' rights and improve their living conditions, strengthen food sovereignty, tackle climate change and promote biodiversity conservation.[78] The declaration includes requirements for states to undertake good-faith consultation and co-operation, and free, meaningful and informed participation of peasants and other rural workers in decision-making processes relating to matters that affect them directly. However, no Arctic states have supported it (the US and Sweden voted against it, while the others abstained).[79]

5 Key principles and responsibilities

This section explores the texts of selected international standards and instruments, focusing in particular on indigenous peoples' rights to consultation, participation and consent in the context of extractive industry activity. It considers the balance of responsibilities of government and business, and follows the structure of the "Protect, Respect and Remedy" framework.[80]

5.1. The responsibilities of government

In the UNGPs (and elsewhere), government responsibility is largely framed as providing the appropriate legal framework; clarifying certain areas of law and policy, such as land rights; establishing appropriate regulations for companies to follow; and ensuring oversight and enforcement. However, governments also have their own responsibilities to engage in public consultation and engagement at the earliest stages of resource development, including during the drafting of national energy or mineral strategies or the allocation of land and waters for mineral or petroleum exploration.

The Aarhus Convention requires governments to seek public participation in decision-making during the preparation of plans, programmes and policies that relate to the environment (Article 7); and in developing executive regulations and legally-binding instruments that relate to the environment (Article 8). Article 6(4) states: "Each Party shall provide for early public participation, when all options are open and effective public participation can take place." The Kiev Protocol acknowledges the Aarhus Convention, and Article 8(1) states: "Each Party shall ensure early, timely and

---

77 UN General Assembly, *Declaration on the Rights of Peasants and Other People Working in Rural Areas*, UNGA Resolution 73/165, December 17, 2018 (Peasants' Declaration).
78 Ibid.
79 See Johnstone, this volume.
80 See also, Emma Wilson and Kirill Istomin, "Beads and Trinkets? Stakeholder Perspectives on Benefit Sharing and Corporate Responsibility in a Russian Oil Province," *Europe-Asia Studies* (2019), doi: 10.1080/09668136.2019.1641585; and Emma Wilson, "What Is Benefit Sharing? Respecting Indigenous Rights and Addressing Inequities in Arctic Resource Projects," *Resources* 8, no. 2 (2019), https://doi.org/10.3390/resources8020074 (on other related issues, such as negotiation and benefit sharing).

effective opportunities for public participation, when all options are open, in the strategic environmental assessment of plans and programmes."

The Convention on Biological Diversity (CBD) requires states to make environmental impact assessments mandatory for projects likely to have "significant adverse effects on biological diversity" and "where appropriate, allow for public participation in such procedures" (Article 14(1)(a)).[81] In 2004, the Secretariat of the CBD published the Akwe:Kon Guidelines, which comprise detailed (non-binding, but highly respected) guidance on conducting environmental and socio-cultural impact assessments for projects that are due to take place on sacred and traditionally used lands.[82]

The government responsibility to enable the participation of indigenous people in decision-making related to resource management that may affect them is established in Agenda 21, where paragraph 26.3 states:

> In full partnership with indigenous people and their communities, Governments and, where appropriate, intergovernmental organizations should aim at fulfilling the following objectives: ... (b) Establishment, where appropriate, of arrangements to strengthen the active participation of indigenous people and their communities in the national formulation of policies, laws and programmes relating to resource management and other development processes that may affect them, and their initiation of proposals for such policies and programmes.

ILO C169 and UNDRIP confirm indigenous peoples' right to consultation and participation in the early stages of strategic planning. For instance, Article 7(1) of ILO C169 states:

> The peoples concerned shall have the right to decide their own priorities for the process of development as it affects their lives, beliefs, institutions and spiritual well-being and the lands they occupy or otherwise use, and to exercise control, to the extent possible, over their own economic, social and cultural development. In addition, they shall participate in the formulation, implementation and evaluation of plans and programmes for national and regional development which may affect them directly.

Article 6(1)(a) of ILO C169 underscores the right to be consulted on legislative and administrative measures, which may include those that relate to resource development:

---

81 Although the United States is not a party to the CBD, it was already a pioneer in the development of EIA legislation through the National Environmental Policy Act 1969, 42 US Code §§ 4321–27 (2000).
82 Convention on Biological Diversity, *Akwé: Kon Voluntary Guidelines*.

> In applying the provisions of this Convention, governments shall: ... consult the peoples concerned, through appropriate procedures and in particular through their representative institutions, whenever consideration is being given to legislative or administrative measures which may affect them directly.

Article 15(2) further confirms that indigenous peoples have the right to be consulted prior to resource exploration or exploitation:

> [G]overnments shall establish or maintain procedures through which they shall consult these peoples, with a view to ascertaining whether and to what degree their interests would be prejudiced, before undertaking or permitting any programmes for the exploration or exploitation of such resources pertaining to their lands.

Article 6(2) of ILO C169 underscores the need for consultation to be conducted in good faith, with the aim of reaching agreement or consent:

> The consultations carried out in application of this Convention shall be undertaken, in good faith and in a form appropriate to the circumstances, with the objective of achieving agreement or consent to the proposed measures.

This should not, however, be interpreted as a veto right. The Handbook for ILO Tripartite Constituents on understanding ILO C169 emphasises that Article 6(2) "does not provide Indigenous peoples with a veto right, as obtaining the agreement or consent is the purpose of engaging in the consultation process, and is not an independent requirement."[83] A 2010 General Observation by the Committee of Experts on the Application of Conventions and Recommendations (CEACR) outlines the process by which the final wording of ILO C169 was agreed. The note explains that Article 15(2) (on resource development), had originally contained the phrase "seek the consent" but this "was not acceptable to a sufficiently large proportion of the membership" and was therefore altered to "they shall consult these peoples."[84]

The CEACR Observation notes: "It is only in Article 16, concerning removal, relocation and the right of return to their traditional lands that a very precise formulation of consent exists." Article 16(2) states:

> Where the relocation of these peoples is considered necessary as an exceptional measure, such relocation shall take place only with their free and

---

83 ILO, *Understanding the Indigenous and Tribal Peoples* Convention, *1989 (No.169): Handbook for ILO Tripartite Constituents* (Geneva: ILO, 2013).
84 ILO, *General Observation (Committee of Experts on the Application of Conventions and Recommendations) – Indigenous and Tribal Peoples* Convention, *1989 (No.169) –* Adopted 2010, published 100th ILC session (2011) (Geneva: ILO, 2011) 5.

informed consent. Where their consent cannot be obtained, such relocation shall take place only following appropriate procedures established by national laws and regulations, including public inquiries where appropriate, which provide the opportunity for effective representation of the peoples concerned.

Thus to a great extent, the term "consent" is used in ILO C169 as a way of establishing that consultation needs to be carried out in good faith and with the aim of reaching agreement. Even where a clear statement is made regarding relocation, the requirement for consent is followed by a description of the process to follow if consent cannot be obtained.

Nonetheless, the requirement for good faith consultation with the aim of reaching agreement or consent is a strong formulation of the requirement to consult. It is also worth noting that according to Article 7(3) of ILO C169 governments are obliged to ensure that impact assessment studies are carried out in co-operation with the affected indigenous peoples:[85]

> Governments shall ensure that, whenever appropriate, studies are carried out, in co-operation with the peoples concerned, to assess the social, spiritual, cultural and environmental impact on them of planned development activities. The results of these studies shall be considered as fundamental criteria for the implementation of these activities.

The direct involvement of indigenous representatives in negotiating the text of UNDRIP – and in defending the draft text against subsequent changes – resulted in more explicit clarification of rights and principles, including stronger wording around consultation and consent, and a clear requirement for FPIC in relation to resource development.[86]

Article 32(2) of UNDRIP states: "Indigenous peoples have the right to determine and develop priorities and strategies for the development or use of their lands or territories and other resources." According to Article 19, FPIC is required in the development of legislative and administrative measures that may affect indigenous peoples. On resettlement, Article 10 of UNDRIP states: "No relocation shall take place without the free, prior and informed consent of the indigenous peoples concerned and after agreement on just and fair compensation and, where possible, with the option of return." Similarly, no storage or disposal of hazardous materials shall take place without FPIC (Article 29).

Critically for the resource development context, Article 32(2) explicitly requires FPIC prior to the approval of any project affecting indigenous peoples' lands, territories or resources:

---

85 Emma Wilson, *What Is Social Impact Assessment?* (Ájluokta/Drag, Norway: Árran Lule Sami Centre, 2017).
86 Claire Charters and Rodolfo Stavenhagen, *Making the Declaration Work: The United Nations Declaration on the Rights of Indigenous Peoples* (Copenhagen: International Working Group for Indigenous Affairs, 2009).

States shall consult and co-operate in good faith with the indigenous peoples concerned through their own representative institutions to obtain their free and informed consent prior to the approval of any project affecting their lands or territories and other resources, particularly in connection with the development, utilization or exploitation of mineral, water, or other resources.

5.2 The responsibilities of business

It is important to consider the responsibilities of government and business in relation to one another and not in isolation. Frequently, the ability of businesses to carry out their own responsibilities effectively is dependent on whether governments have met their own obligations prior to the involvement of individual companies in exploration or extraction activities.

The UNGPs do not make explicit reference to government responsibilities to engage or consult with local communities prior to the involvement of business in individual projects, referring only to the responsibility of business to carry out meaningful consultation as part of their due diligence processes (see below). However, European Commission guidance for the oil and gas sector on the implementation of the UNGPs draws attention to the human rights risks for oil and gas companies if governments have not carried out legally-mandated early community consultation, or have done so inadequately.[87] The guidance recommends that "companies keep track of government-led consultations with stakeholders on issues related to their projects," adding that "where there are questions about this consultation process or unresolved stakeholder issues, it is in the company's interests to find out about them and, as far as possible, to address them."[88]

Similarly, a Guidance Note on ILO C169 produced by the IFC for its private sector clients highlights the potential risks to companies if a (signatory) government fails to meet its obligations to consult with affected indigenous people: "For example, if a State fails to comply with obligations on prior consultation on a project, a private company may find that the licenses that have been granted are subject to legal challenge."[89] To minimise risks, the IFC urges its clients to look into whether "appropriate consultation takes place prior to the granting of exploration and exploitation licenses" and to consider what they might do to promote consultation and the government role in it.[90]

The requirement for companies themselves to engage with indigenous and local communities at the earliest opportunity is also written into certain standards and is considered good practice within resource sectors. The OECD Guidelines (General policies, A14) state that enterprises should:

---

87 Shift and the Institute for Human Rights and Business, *Oil and Gas Sector Guide*, 36.
88 Ibid., 36.
89 IFC, *ILO Convention 169*, 3.
90 Ibid., 6.

Engage with relevant stakeholders to provide meaningful opportunities for their views to be taken into account in relation to planning and decision making for projects or other activities that could significantly impact local communities.

The reference to "planning" clearly indicates an early stage for enterprises to start engagement. The related OECD Due Diligence Guidance for Meaningful Stakeholder Engagement in the Extractive Sector defines "meaningful stakeholder engagement" as "ongoing engagement with stakeholders that is two-way, conducted in good faith and responsive."[91] Enterprises should also "[c]arry out human rights due diligence as appropriate to their size, the nature and context of operations, and the severity of the risks of adverse human rights impacts" (Chapter IV(5)). The same Due Diligence Guidance recognises the Akwe:Kon Guidelines as best practice for impact assessment and due diligence relating to indigenous peoples.[92]

The UNGPs require companies to have in place a human-rights due-diligence process and act upon the findings; the due-diligence process should be ongoing throughout the life of the project, extend to an enterprise's business relationships, and be able to respond to changing circumstances (Principles 15, 17 and 19). Principle 18b states that human rights due diligence should:

Involve meaningful consultation with potentially affected groups and other relevant stakeholders as appropriate to the size of the business enterprise and the nature and context of the operation.

The commentary to Principle 18b emphasises that "business enterprises should pay special attention to any particular human rights impacts on individuals from groups or populations that may be at heightened risk of vulnerability or marginalization."

The UNGPs themselves do not define "meaningful consultation," even within their Reporting Framework.[93] However, the EC-commissioned Oil and Gas Sector Guide provides detailed guidance on how to engage and consult meaningfully with communities and stakeholders, including indigenous peoples, who are included within an overall category of "vulnerable and marginalised groups."[94] The guide makes reference to IFC Performance Standard 7 for guidance on engagement with indigenous peoples.

IFC's Performance Standard 7 relates specifically to indigenous peoples, but Performance Standard 1 provides important guidance on public consultation and participation more generally. Performance Standard 1(5) requires the client ("in co-ordination with other responsible government agencies and third parties as appropriate") to carry out an Environmental and Social Assessment, incorporating

---

91 OECD, *Due Diligence*, 9.
92 Ibid., Annex B.
93 Shift and Mazars, *UN Guiding Principles*.
94 Shift and the Institute for Human Rights and Business, *Oil and Gas Sector Guide*.

stakeholder engagement, and to establish and maintain an Environmental and Social Management System for the life of the project. These are expected to cover issues related to indigenous people, who are identified in screening and scoping exercises at the start of the due diligence process.[95]

The IFC distinguishes between regular "consultation" (required for all affected communities) and a more in-depth process of "Informed Consultation and Participation (ICP)" for those likely to experience significant adverse impacts. Performance Standard 1(30) states that (regular) consultation "provides the Affected Communities with opportunities to express their views on project risks, impacts and mitigation measures, and allows the client to consider and respond to them." Effective consultation should be a "two-way" process and should:

- Begin early in the process of identification of environmental and social risks and impacts and continue on an ongoing basis as risks and impacts arise;
- Be based on prior disclosure/dissemination of relevant, transparent, objective, meaningful and easily accessible information, in culturally appropriate local language(s) and format, understandable to Affected Communities;
- Focus inclusive engagement on those directly affected as opposed to those not directly affected;
- Be free of external manipulation, interference, coercion, or intimidation;
- Enable meaningful participation, where applicable; and
- Be documented.

If, following scoping and screening, a project is deemed likely to have significant adverse impacts on affected communities, a process of ICP is triggered (Performance Standard 1(31)):

> ICP involves a more in-depth exchange of views and information, and an organised and iterative consultation, leading to the client's incorporating into their decision-making process the views of the Affected Communities on matters that affect them directly, such as the proposed mitigation measures, the sharing of development benefits and opportunities, and implementation issues. The consultation process should (i) capture both men's and women's views, if necessary through separate forums or engagements, and (ii) reflect men's and women's different concerns and priorities about impacts, mitigation mechanisms, and benefits, where appropriate. The client will document the process, in particular the measures to avoid or minimize risks to and adverse impacts on the Affected Communities, and will inform those affected about how their concerns have been considered.

---

95 Companies using finance from the IFC or other international financial institutions, and their contractors, are frequently required to become certified to the International Standards Organisation (ISO) 14001 standard on environmental management systems, which includes a requirement for stakeholder engagement.

A key difference between (regular) consultation and ICP relates to the obligation on the part of the developer to incorporate the views of the consultees into their decision-making process, and informing them how their concerns have been considered. It is worth emphasising that the recommended procedures for an ICP process apply whether or not a community is identified as being indigenous.

For projects with potential adverse effects on indigenous people, Performance Standard 7 requires IFC clients to implement an Indigenous Peoples' Development Plan, including consideration of impacts and a benefit-sharing programme. It requires the client to engage affected indigenous communities in a process of ICP, and in defined circumstances to obtain their FPIC.

The requirement for FPIC is based on IFC's recognition of the particular vulnerability of indigenous peoples to project impacts (Performance Standard 7(11)):

> Affected Communities of Indigenous Peoples may be particularly vulnerable to the loss of, alienation from or exploitation of their land and access to natural and cultural resources. In recognition of this vulnerability, in addition to the General Requirements of this Performance Standard, the client will obtain the FPIC of the Affected Communities of Indigenous Peoples in the circumstances described in paragraphs 13–17 of this Performance Standard. FPIC applies to project design, implementation, and expected outcomes related to impacts affecting the communities of Indigenous Peoples.

Paragraphs 13–17 relate to: locating a project on, or commercially using natural resources on traditionally used lands (13, 14); relocation from communally held lands and natural resources subject to traditional ownership or under customary use (15); and in the case of significant project impacts on critical cultural heritage (16, 17).

According to Performance Standard 7(12):

> FPIC builds on and expands the process of ICP described in Performance Standard 1 and will be established through good faith negotiation between the client and the Affected Communities of Indigenous Peoples. The client will document: (i) the mutually accepted process between the client and Affected Communities of Indigenous Peoples, and (ii) evidence of agreement between the parties as the outcome of the negotiations. FPIC does not necessarily require unanimity and may be achieved even when individuals or groups within the community explicitly disagree.

The UNGPs and the OECD Guidelines do not contain language on FPIC. However, the related sectoral guidance documents do provide guidance on FPIC.[96] It is perhaps worth highlighting the following discussion in the OECD Due Diligence Guidance, which draws attention to the risks associated with consent not being granted:

---

96 OECD, *Due Diligence*; Shift and the Institute for Human Rights and Business, *Oil and Gas Sector Guide*.

In cases where their consent is not forthcoming or where indigenous peoples refuse to engage, material risks to the enterprise and adverse impacts to indigenous peoples may be generated. In situations where proceeding with projects will cause adverse impacts to indigenous peoples an enterprise should take the necessary steps to cease or prevent such impacts. If through its due diligence processes an enterprise concludes that consent is required to proceed with an activity, and the agreed process has not arrived at consent, activities should not proceed unless FPIC is subsequently forthcoming.

Not all industry guidance is as definitive about whether or not industrial activities should go ahead if consent is not granted.[97] However, the risks of pushing ahead without community consent are increasingly well understood.[98]

A key challenge in relation to FPIC, or indeed any community engagement, relates to the extent to which a community can agree internally on their future development options, and who represents the interests of the community in engagement and negotiations with industry proponents. Internal community consensus may be difficult to achieve as some members of the community may support a proposed development, while others firmly oppose it. Business guidance tends to emphasise the need to agree approaches, methods and goals in advance with the community. Some guidance contains specific reference to community protocols – community charters of rules, procedures and responsibilities, in which communities set out their legal and customary rights to land and resources, and their position in relation to any proposed development on their territories.[99] Community protocols enable communities to build consensus in advance of external negotiations, and to clarify their priorities, expectations and favoured engagement procedures in advance. As such, they have the potential to provide clarity and reduce risk in resource development activities.

5.3 Access to remedy and justice

International standards and principles also contain obligations on governments to ensure judicial and non-judicial access to remedy, and on companies and project developers to establish their own complaints procedures or grievance mechanisms, by which local communities can raise their concerns about a project and have them addressed in a fair and timely manner.[100] At the heart of these requirements lies the need for ongoing meaningful engagement.

97 Wilson, *Evaluating International Ethical Standards*.
98 Shift and the Institute for Human Rights and Business, *Oil and Gas Sector Guide*; Herbertson et al., *Breaking Ground*.
99 Krystyna Swiderska, ed., *Biodiversity and Culture: Exploring Community Protocols, Rights and Consent: Participatory Learning and Action* (London: International Institute for Environment and Development, 2012), 65; Gibson Macdonald and Zezulka, *Understanding Successful Approaches*.
100 Wilson and Blackmore, *Dispute or Dialogue?*; Caroline Rees, *Piloting Principles for Effective Company–Stakeholder Grievance Mechanisms: A Report of Lessons Learned* (Cambridge MA: CSR Initiative, Harvard Kennedy School, 2011).

The third pillar of the UNGPs is "access to remedy". According to Principles 25–28, states must ensure that the people affected by any abuse of human rights by business can access an effective remedy through the court system or other legitimate non-judicial process. Business enterprises themselves are expected to have processes in place to remediate negative human rights impacts that they cause or contribute to (Principle 15), and they should establish or participate in effective grievance mechanisms for any individuals or communities negatively affected by their operations (Principle 29). Principle 31 provides effectiveness criteria for non-judicial grievance mechanisms. The UNGPs have also stimulated the wider development of procedures and approaches for resolving project-level grievances, and for measuring their effectiveness.[101]

The third pillar of the Aarhus Convention is "access to justice." Article 9(3) states that each Party should ensure that "members of the public have access to administrative or judicial procedures to challenge acts and omissions by private persons and public authorities which contravene provisions of its national law relating to the environment."

The provisions of ILO C169 include the right for indigenous people to receive fair compensation for any damages or losses caused by natural resource developments and/or relocation (Articles 15(2) and 16(5)). Article 18 states: "Adequate penalties shall be established by law for unauthorised intrusion upon, or use of, the lands of the peoples concerned, and governments shall take measures to prevent such offences."

UNDRIP obliges states to provide redress for damage to indigenous peoples' lands, territories and resources, through restitution and compensation (Articles 11 (2), 28 and 32(3)). Article 40 states:

> Indigenous peoples have the right to have access to and prompt decision through just and fair procedures for the resolution of conflicts and disputes with States or other parties, as well as to effective remedies for all infringements of their individual and collective rights. Such a decision shall give due consideration to the customs, traditions, rules and legal systems of the indigenous peoples concerned and international human rights.

IFC Performance Standard 1 "supports the use of an effective grievance mechanism that can facilitate early indication of, and prompt remediation for those that believe that they have been harmed by a client's actions." Clause 35 provides more detail on the required grievance mechanism, which applies to all affected communities:

> The grievance mechanism should be scaled to the risks and adverse impacts of the project and have Affected Communities as its primary user. It should seek to resolve concerns promptly, using an understandable and transparent consultative process that is culturally appropriate and readily accessible, and at no

---

101 Rees, *Piloting Principles*; Scheltema, *Assessing the Effectiveness*.

cost and without retribution to the party that originated the issue or concern. The mechanism should not impede access to judicial or administrative remedies. The client will inform the Affected Communities about the mechanism in the course of the stakeholder engagement process.

IFC Performance Standard 7 does not mention a grievance mechanism, as it is assumed that Performance Standard 1 also applies to indigenous communities (given that the latter includes the criterion that such mechanisms be "culturally appropriate"). Performance Standard 7(9) does however address remediation. Thus, where adverse impacts on Indigenous people are unavoidable:

> [T]he client will minimize, restore, and/or compensate for these impacts in a culturally appropriate manner commensurate with the nature and scale of such impacts and the vulnerability of Affected Communities of Indigenous Peoples. The client's proposed actions will be developed with the ICP of the Affected Communities of Indigenous Peoples and contained in a time-bound plan, such as an Indigenous Peoples Plan, or a broader community development plan with separate components for indigenous peoples.

Most international instruments also have their own accountability mechanisms. For instance, each party to the CBD sets up National Focal Points which facilitate implementation of the Convention and report to the Conference of Parties. The Aarhus Convention Compliance Committee addresses complaints relating to the Aarhus Convention. Governments make regular reports on their implementation of ILO C169 and every five years the ILO reports to the UN. UNDRIP is not a treaty and has no enforcement or monitoring system of its own, but complaints can be addressed by National Human Rights Institutions.[102] Countries adhering to the OECD Guidelines establish National Contact Points (NCPs), which investigate complaints relating to business activities in that country, or overseas activities by companies based in that country.[103] These NCPs can also address complaints relating to the UNGPs. Clients of the IFC or other international financial institutions are regularly audited by the lenders' environmental and social auditors. The lenders can withhold the next tranche of finance if there is a serious breach. Project-affected communities can also turn to the Compliance Advisor Ombudsman, which is the independent recourse mechanism for the World Bank Group.

6 Conclusions

Individual indigenous people have the same human rights as any other individuals, but also have additional – collective – indigenous rights. The cornerstone of indigenous rights is the right to self-determination, along with the rights to land, property and the means of subsistence. Indigenous peoples' entitlement to

---

102 Asia Pacific Forum and OHCHR, *The United Nations Declaration*.
103 See Buhmann, this volume.

determine the outcome of decision-making that affects them has been under-explored – and under-delivered – in the context of resource development to date. While FPIC has tended to be at the centre of debates around indigenous rights and resource development, indigenous rights to consultation and participation are also significant in this regard.

A key challenge highlighted by businesses and investors is establishing who is indigenous in a specific context. This should not detract from the goal of ensuring that isolated, vulnerable and/or land- and resource-dependent people are adequately protected from the potential impacts of industrial development. Self-determination and the protection of traditionally used land and resources are issues to be considered separately, alongside vulnerability and resource-dependency. For Greenland, there are issues around whether or not Greenlanders want to be considered indigenous, and the extent to which the Inuit Self-Government is entitled to make resource development decisions on behalf of the wider population.[104] While not yet approved by any Arctic state, the UN Peasants Declaration, alongside the work of organisations such as the Forest Stewardship Council, highlight the importance of enabling the meaningful participation of local land- and resource users in decision-making that affects them, whether or not they are identified as being indigenous, and whether or not the government of the wider territory is itself indigenous.

Under international law, states are ultimately responsible for setting and ensuring compliance with indigenous and human rights norms within their jurisdictions. In addition, international instruments confirm the responsibility of governments to ensure that indigenous people participate in strategic-level decision-making relating to natural resource management that may affect them, and that adequate consultation takes place prior to the allocation of exploration licences. Indigenous peoples have the right not only to influence, but to *determine* priorities and strategies, and to participate in the formulation of development plans and programmes, before the allocation of licences and lands to industrial developers. A key priority for Greenlanders is thus to develop a nuanced understanding of what level of decision-making and at what stage in a project life-cycle or in the development of a resource sector project-affected communities have the right to determine the outcomes of decision-making.

Governments and companies both have important roles to play in due diligence and sharing information with the public relating to project risks. Official guidance for business urges companies to be aware of the reputational and investment-related risks of operating in situations where governments have failed to carry out early consultation or have done so inadequately. As part of their project due diligence, companies are urged to consider whether or not government consultation has taken place, and make efforts to involve government in their own early consultation processes.

International standards emphasise the importance of carrying out impact assessments in collaboration with affected indigenous communities, and the need to assess

[104] See Johnstone, this volume.

social, spiritual, cultural and environmental impacts. An impact assessment is not a one-off process, but forms the basis of management plans and a management system, with the results being treated as fundamental criteria for project implementation. Meaningful consultation is an essential element of due diligence. It is important in Greenland to ensure that local communities are able to collaborate fully in the assessment of social, spiritual, cultural and environmental impacts of projects likely to affect their lands, resources and traditional livelihood practices.[105]

Governments and companies have ongoing responsibilities for public engagement, but in practice once a project is underway, operating companies take on the primary responsibility for public consultation and engagement. At this stage the role of government agencies might become more focused on oversight and access to justice or remedy. Governments also have an ongoing responsibility to ensure the public has access to relevant information and that companies have clear guidance on the type of engagement that they are expected to undertake with communities, including whether or not there is a requirement for an impact and benefit agreement (which is required in some but not all cases of resource development activity in Greenland).[106]

Companies need to continue meaningful consultation and engagement with affected communities throughout the life of a project. Following the IFC performance standards, in-depth consultation and engagement are required for all local communities if they are likely to be significantly affected by project activities, whether or not they are indigenous. In such cases, developers are obliged to incorporate the views of the consultees into their decision-making process, and inform them how their concerns have been considered. Indigenous communities have the additional right to a process of FPIC in certain circumstances.

FPIC is a mechanism by which indigenous peoples can (collectively) assert their rights to self-determination, property and non-discrimination, and to "determine" the outcomes of decision-making relating to resource development policy and projects. FPIC is primarily a government responsibility and it needs to take place prior to the involvement of individual businesses in resource development projects. However, FPIC is not a one-off activity. Standards for the private sector increasingly require companies to follow processes of FPIC for particular activities and when project plans change, and it is increasingly viewed as an important risk-mitigation strategy.

Key elements of an FPIC process are found in standards and guidance aimed at the private sector, and will often require collaboration with government bodies. These activities include: prior agreement between the community and project proponent of the process to be followed and the objectives to be achieved; identification of land and resource rights and traditional resource use; documentation of the negotiation process, including agreed impact mitigation and avoidance measures; and evidence of any agreement made between the parties. While different standards and instruments have different advice regarding what to do if

---

105 See Johnstone and Hansen, this volume.
106 See Johnstone and Hansen, this volume.

consent is withheld, it is increasingly accepted that it is not appropriate to move ahead with a project in such cases, especially in light of the high risks of taking such a step, and even where governments may be in favour of overriding the result of an FPIC process.

International standards and guidance recommend that project proponents and communities agree processes, procedures and values in advance of engagement, consultation and consent processes. While not explicitly required by international instruments, so-called community protocols – charters of rules, procedures and responsibilities developed by the community – are a potentially effective way for communities to establish and articulate their expectations and demands in advance of engaging with external developers. This is a particularly interesting area for local Greenlandic communities and resource users to explore in light of future potential developments on their lands.

International instruments often have their own accountability mechanisms and may also contain obligations on governments to ensure judicial and non-judicial access to remedy and on companies to establish project-level grievance mechanisms. At the heart of these requirements lies the need for ongoing information disclosure and meaningful community engagement.

Each individual project context will be different, including the ethnic mix of local communities, levels of resource dependency, and the nature of cultural practices and decision-making structures. Further factors include the status of indigenous rights, according to government commitments under international conventions and declarations, and national legislation; the policy commitments made by the companies and financial institutions involved in the project; and the levels of interest on the part of national and global civil society organisations, including levels of social media exposure. A greater – shared – understanding of the range of international standards and instruments, and the key principles inherent in them, will help to build mutual trust and ensure that if a project goes ahead, it does so with the support of indigenous and local communities, and with full respect for their rights.

References

Abrahams, Désirée and Yann Wyss. *Guide to Human Rights Impact Assessment and Management.* Washington DC: International Finance Corporation, UN Global Compact and the International Business Leaders Forum, 2010. www.globalgovernancewatch.org/docLib/20140206_hriam-guide-092011.pdf

ACCESS Facility. "ACCESS." Accessed June 25, 2019. www.accessfacility.org/

Adamson, Rebecca and Pelosi, Nick. *Indigenous Rights Risk Report.* Vancouver: First Peoples Worldwide, 2014. www.nationalunitygovernment.org/pdf/2014/Indigenous-Rights-Risk-Report-Nov-2014.pdf

Åhrén, Matthias. *Indigenous Peoples' Status in the International Legal System.* Oxford: Oxford University Press, 2016.

Anaya, James. *Report of the Special Rapporteur on the Rights of Indigenous Peoples, James Anaya: Extractive Industries and Indigenous Peoples, 2013.* UN Human Rights Council. UN Doc. A/HRC/24/41.

Asia Pacific Forum and OHCHR. *The United Nations Declaration on the Rights of Indigenous Peoples: A Manual for National Human Rights Institutions.* Sydney and Geneva: Asia Pacific Forum of National Human Rights Institutions/Office of the United Nations High Commissioner for Human Rights, 2013. www.ohchr.org/Documents/Issues/IPeoples/UNDRIPManualForNHRIs.pdf

Birley, Martin. *Health Impact Assessment: Principles and Practice.* Abingdon: Routledge, 2012.

Charters, Claire and Rodolfo Stavenhagen. *Making the Declaration Work: The United Nations Declaration on the Rights of Indigenous Peoples.* Copenhagen: International Working Group for Indigenous Affairs, 2009.

Convention on Access to Information, Public Participation in Decision-Making and Access to Justice in Environmental Matters 1998. Adopted June 25, 1998, entered into force October 30, 2001. United Nations Treaty Series 2161, 447 (Aarhus Convention).

Convention on Biological Diversity 1992. United Nations Treaty Series1760, 79.

Convention on Biological Diversity. *Akwé:Kon Voluntary Guidelines for the Conduct of Cultural, Environmental and Social Impact Assessment Regarding Developments Proposed to Take Place On, or Which Are Likely to Impact On, Sacred Sites and on Lands and Waters Traditionally Occupied or Used by Indigenous and Local Communities.* Montreal: Secretariat of the Convention on Biological Diversity, 2004.

"Convention on Environmental Impact Assessment in a Transboundary Context 1991." *International Legal Materials* 30: 800 (Espoo Convention).

Davis, Rachel and Daniel Franks. *Costs of Company–Community Conflict in the Extractive Sector.* Corporate Social Responsibility Initiative, Report no. 66. Cambridge MA: Harvard Kennedy School, 2014. https://www.hks.harvard.edu/m-rcbg/CSRI/research/Costs%20of%20Conflict_Davis%20%20Franks.pdf

Doyle, Cathal and Jill Cariño. *Making Free, Prior and Informed Consent a Reality: Indigenous Peoples and the Extractive Sector.* London: Indigenous Peoples Links/PIPLinks; Middlesex University School of Law; The Ecumenical Council for Corporate Responsibility, 2013. www.ecojesuit.com/wp-content/uploads/2014/09/Making-FPIC-a-Reality-Report.pdf

Equator Principles. "The Equator Principles." Accessed June 27, 2017. https://equator-principles.com/about/.

European Bank for Reconstruction and Development. "Sakhalin II (Phase 1) Oil Project." Accessed July 28, 2019. https://www.ebrd.com/work-with-us/projects/psd/sakhalin-ii-phase-1-oil-project.html.

Forest Stewardship Council. *FSC Guidelines for the Implementation of the Right to Free, Prior and Informed Consent (FPIC).* Bonn: Forest Stewardship Council, 2012.

Gibson Macdonald, Ginger and Gaby Zezulka. *Understanding Successful Approaches to Free, Prior and Informed Consent in Canada. Part 1.* Ottawa: Boreal Leadership Council, Canada, 2015. http://borealcouncil.ca/reports/understanding-successful-approaches-to-free-prior-and-informed-consent-in-canada/

Global Reporting Initiative. "GRI Standards." Accessed July 28, 2019. https://www.globalreporting.org/

Greenspan, Emily. *Free, Prior and Informed Consent in Africa: An Emerging Standard for Extractive Industry Projects.* Oxfam America Research Backgrounder series. Washington DC: Oxfam America, 2014. https://www.oxfamamerica.org/publications/fpic-in-africa/

Hansen, Anne Merrild, Frank Vanclay, Peter Croal, and Anna-Sofie Hurup Skjervedal. "Managing the Social Impacts of the Rapidly-Expanding Extractive Industries in Greenland." *The Extractive Industries and Society* 3, no. 1 (2016): 25–33. https://doi.org/10.1016/j.exis.2015.11.013

Heinämäki, Leena. "The Rapidly Evolving International Status of Indigenous Peoples: the Example of the Sami People in Finland." In *Indigenous Rights in Scandinavia*, edited by C. Allard and S.F. Skogvang, 189–206. Farnham UK and Burlington VT: Ashgate Publishing, 2015.

Herbertson, Kirk, Athena R. Ballesteros, Robert Goodland and Isabel Munilla. *Breaking Ground: Engaging Communities in Extractive and Infrastructure Projects*. Washington DC: World Resources Institute, 2009.

ICMM. "International Council on Mining and Metals." Accessed June 27, 2019. https://www.icmm.com/

ICMM. *Community Development Toolkit*. London: International Council on Mining and Metals, 2016. www.icmm.com/en-gb/publications/community-development-toolkit

IFC. *ILO Convention 169 and the Private Sector*. Washington DC: IFC, 2007.

IFC. *Stakeholder Engagement: A Good Practice Handbook for Companies Doing Business in Emerging Markets*. Washington DC: International Finance Corporation, 2007.

IFC. *A Strategic Approach to Early Stakeholder Engagement: A Good Practice Handbook for Junior Companies in the Extractive Industries*. Washington DC: International Finance Corporation, 2014. https://commdev.org/userfiles/FINAL_IFC_131208_ESSE%20Handbook_web%201013.pdf

IFC. "IFC Performance Standards on Environmental and Social Sustainability – Effective January 1, 2012." Accessed June 27, 2019. https://www.ifc.org/wps/wcm/connect/topics_ext_content/ifc_external_corporate_site/sustainability-at-ifc/publications/publications_handbook_pps

ILO Convention 169 (1989). "Indigenous and Tribal Peoples Convention. Adopted 27 June 1989, entered into force 5 September 1991." *International Legal Materials* 28, 1382.

ILO. *General Observation (Committee of Experts on the Application of Conventions and Recommendations) – Indigenous and Tribal Peoples Convention, 1989 (No.169)*. Adopted 2010, published 100th ILC session (2011) Geneva: ILO, 2011.

ILO. *Understanding the Indigenous and Tribal Peoples Convention, 1989 (No.169): Handbook for ILO Tripartite Constituents*. Geneva: ILO, 2013.

International Covenant on Civil and Political Rights 1966. United Nations Treaty Series 999, 171.

International Covenant on Economic, Social and Cultural Rights 1966. United Nations Treaty Series 993, 3.

IPIECA. "Community Engagement and Indigenous Peoples." Accessed July 201, 2019. www.ipieca.org/our-work/social/indigenous-peoples/

IPIECA. "The Global Oil and Gas Industry Association for Advancing Environmental and Social Issues." Accessed June 27, 2019. www.ipieca.org/

Lawrence, Rebecca. "Internal Colonisation and Indigenous Resource Sovereignty: Wind Power Developments on Traditional Saami Land." *Environment and Planning D: Society and Space* 32, no. 6 (2014): 1036–1053. https://doi.org/10.1068/d9012

Lehr, Amy K. and Gare A. Smith. *Implementing a Corporate Free, Prior, and Informed Consent Policy: Benefits and Challenges*. Boston: Foley Hoag LLP, 2010. www.foleyhoag.com/publications/ebooks-and-white-papers/2010/may/implementing-a-corporate-free-prior-and-informed-consent-policy

Lehr, Amy. *Indigenous Peoples' Rights and the Role of Free, Prior and Informed Consent*. New York: UN Global Compact, 2014. www.foleyhoag.com/publications/alerts-and-updates/2014/april/united-nation-global-compact-indigenous-peoples

Lillich, Richard. "The Growing Importance of Customary International Human Rights Law." *Georgia Journal of International and Comparative Law* 25, no. 1 (1995): 1–30.

Magnussen, Tone and Brigt Dale. "The Municipal No to Mining. the Case Concerning the Reopening of the Biedjovaggi Gold Mine in Guovdageainnu Municipality, Norway." In *The Will to Drill: Mining in Arctic Communities*, edited by Brigt Dale, Ingrid Bay-Larsen and Berit Skorstad, 175–195. Geneva, Switzerland: Springer International, 2018.

Martínez Cobo, Jóse R., UN Special Rapporteur. *Study of the Problem of Discrimination against Indigenous Populations*. Report. New York: United Nations, 1986. UN Doc. E/CN.4/Sub.2/1986/7 Add. 4.

Motoc, Antoanella-Iulia and the Tebtebba Foundation. *Standard-Setting: Legal Commentary on the Concept of Free, Prior and Informed Consent. Submitted to the UN Commission on Human Rights, Sub-Commission on the Promotion and Protection of Human Rights, Working Group on Indigenous Populations*. July 14, 2005. UN Doc. E/CN.4/Sub.2/AC.4/2005/WP.1.

National Environmental Policy Act 1969, 42 US Code §§ 4321–27(2000) (United States).

Novikova, Natalia I. *Okhotniki i neftyaniki: issledovaniya v yuridicheskoy antropologii* [Hunters and Oil Workers: Research in Legal Anthropology]. Moscow: Nauka, 2014.

Nuttall, Mark. "Imagining and Governing the Greenlandic Resource Frontier." *The Polar Journal* 2, no. 1 (2012): 113–124.

Nuttall, Mark. "Zero-Tolerance, Uranium and Greenland's Mining Future." *The Polar Journal* 3, no. 2 (2013): 368–383.

Nygaard, Vigdis. "Do Indigenous Interests Have a Say in Planning of New Mining Projects? Experiences from Finnmark, Norway." *The Extractive Industries and Society* 3, no. 1 (2016): 17–24.

O'Faircheallaigh, Ciaran. "Effectiveness in Social Impact Assessment: Aboriginal Peoples and Resource Development in Australia." *Impact Assessment and Project Appraisal* 27, no. 2 (2009): 95–110.

OECD. "Environmental and Social Due Diligence." Accessed June 27, 2017. www.oecd.org/trade/topics/export-credits/environmental-and-social-due-dilligence/

OECD. *Due Diligence Guidance for Meaningful Stakeholder Engagement in the Extractive Sector*. Geneva: OECD, 2016. https://mneguidelines.oecd.org/stakeholder-engagement-extractive-industries.htm

Papillon, Martin and Theirry Rodon. "Proponent-Indigenous Agreements and the Implementation of the Right to Free, Prior and Informed Consent in Canada." *Environmental Impact Assessment Review* 62 (2017): 216–224.

PRI. "Principles for Responsible Investment." Accessed June 27, 2019. https://www.unpri.org/

Protocol on Strategic Environmental Assessment to the Convention on Environmental Impact Assessment in a Transboundary Context, 2003. UN Doc. ECE/MP.EIA/2003/2 [Kiev Protocol].

Rees, Caroline. *Piloting Principles for Effective Company-Stakeholder Grievance Mechanisms: A Report of Lessons Learned*. Cambridge MA: CSR Initiative, Harvard Kennedy School, 2011. www.hks.harvard.edu/m-rcbg/CSRI/publications/report_46_GM_pilots.pdf

"Rio Declaration on Environment and Development 1992." *International Legal Materials* 31 (1992): 876.

Ruggie, John. "Business and Human Rights: the Evolving International Agenda." *American Journal of International Law* 101, no. 4 (2007): 819–840.

Ruggie, John. *Guiding Principles on Business and Human Rights: Implementing the United Nations "Protect, Respect and Remedy" Framework*. Geneva and New York: United Nations, 2011 (UNGPs). UN Doc. A/HRC/17/31. March 21.

Ruggie, John. *Protect, Respect and Remedy: A Framework for Business and Human Rights. Report of the Special Representative on Human Rights, Transnational Corporations and Other Business Enterprises.* UN Doc. A/HRC/8/5. April 7, 2008.
Scheltema, Martijn. "Assessing the Effectiveness of Remedy Outcomes of Non-Judicial Grievance Mechanisms." *The Dovenschmidt Quarterly* 4 (2013): 190–197.
Shift and Mazars. *UN Guiding Principles Reporting Framework.* Harvard University, Cambridge MA: Shift and Mazars, 2017. https://www.shiftproject.org/resources/publications/un-guiding-principles-reporting-framework/
Shift and the Institute for Human Rights and Business. *Oil and Gas Sector Guide on Implementing the UN Guiding Principles on Business and Human Rights.* Brussels: European Commission, 2011. https://www.ihrb.org/pdf/eu-sector-guidance/EC-Guides/O&G/EC-Guide_O&G.pdf
Sujatha, Raman. "Fossilizing Renewable Energies." *Science as Culture* 22, no. 2 (2013): 172–180.
Swiderska, Krystyna (ed.) *Biodiversity and Culture: Exploring Community Protocols, Rights and Consent.* Participatory Learning and Action, vol. 65. London: International Institute for Environment and Development, 2012. http://pubs.iied.org/14618IIED.html
UN Conference on Environment and Development. *Agenda 21, Rio Declaration, Forest Principles.* New York: United Nations, 1992.
UN General Assembly. Declaration on the Rights of Indigenous Peoples, UNGA Res 61/295. September 13, 2007 (UNDRIP).
UN General Assembly. Declaration on the Rights of Peasants and Other People Working in Rural Areas, UNGA Res 73/165. December 17, 2018.
UN General Assembly. Universal Declaration of Human Rights, UNGA Res A/RES/217 (III). December 10, 1948.
UN Global Compact. "Who We Are." Accessed July 28, 2019. https://www.unglobalcompact.org/
UN Human Rights Council. "List of Past Members of the Human Rights Council." Accessed July 23, 2019. https://www.ohchr.org/EN/HRBodies/HRC/Pages/PastMembers.aspx
UN Treaty Collection. "Chapter XXVII.4, Convention on Environmental Impact Assessment in a Transboundary Context, status as at July 23, 2019." https://treaties.un.org/Pages/ViewDetails.aspx?src=TREATY&mtdsg_no=XXVII-4&chapter=27&clang=_en
UN Treaty Collection. "Chapter XXVII.4.b, Protocol on Strategic Environmental Assessment to the Convention on Environmental Impact Assessment in a Transboundary Context, status as at July 23, 2019." https://treaties.un.org/Pages/ViewDetails.aspx?src=TREATY&mtdsg_no=XXVII-4-b&chapter=27&clang=_en
UN World Conference on Human Rights. "Vienna Declaration and Programme of Action." *International Legal Materials* 32, 1661 (1993).
UNECE. "Landmark Meeting of Aarhus Convention Welcomes Global Accession." Accessed July 2, 2019. https://www.unece.org/press/pr2011/11env_p32e.html
Von Bernstorff, Jochen. "The Changing Fortunes of the Universal Declaration of Human Rights: Genesis and Symbolic Dimensions of the Turn to Rights in International Law." *European Journal of International Law* 19, no. 5 (2008): 903–924.
Wilson, Emma. *Energy and Minerals in Greenland: Governance, Corporate Responsibility and Social Resilience.* London: International Institute for Environment and Development, 2015.
Wilson, Emma. *Evaluating International Ethical Standards and Instruments for Indigenous Rights and the Extractive Industries.* Ájluokta/Drag, Norway: Árran Lule Sami Centre, 2016. https://tinyurl.com/IndigenousStandards

Wilson, Emma. *What Is Free, Prior and Informed Consent (FPIC)?* Ájluokta/Drag, Norway: Árran Lule Sami Centre, 2016.

Wilson, Emma. *What Is Social Impact Assessment?* Ájluokta/Drag, Norway: Árran Lule Sami Centre, 2017.

Wilson, Emma. "What is Benefit-Sharing? Respecting Indigenous Rights and Addressing Inequities in Arctic Resource Projects." *Resources* 8, no. 2 (2019): 74. doi:10.3390/resources8020074

Wilson, Emma and Emma Blackmore. *Dispute or Dialogue? Community Perspectives on Company-Led Grievance Mechanisms.* London: International Institute for Environment and Development, 2013. http://pubs.iied.org/16529IIED.html

Wilson, Emma and Kirill Istomin. "Beads and Trinkets? Stakeholder Perspectives on Benefit Sharing and Corporate Responsibility in a Russian Oil Province." *Europe-Asia Studies* (2019). doi:10.1080/09668136.2019.1641585

Wilson, Emma, Sarah Best, Emma Blackmore and Saule Ospanova. *Meaningful Community Engagement in the Extractive Industries.* London: International Institute for Environment and Development, 2016. http://pubs.iied.org/16047IIED/

3 What is required for free, prior and informed consent and where does it apply?

Rachael Lorna Johnstone

Introduction

This chapter explores in depth the concept of free, prior and informed consent (FPIC) and its applicability in Greenland. FPIC was promised in respect of extractive industries for indigenous peoples in the UN Declaration on the Rights of Indigenous Peoples in 2007 (UNDRIP).[1] However, since then, both the Danish and Greenlandic governments have taken the view that the 2009 Self-Government Act constitutes full implementation of UNDRIP because decisions are taken by the Self-Government in Nuuk on most matters, including on extractive industries. Therefore, difficult questions arise as to whether the Greenlanders continue to enjoy rights as an indigenous people, against whom they would hold such rights and whether FPIC is one of those rights.

After explaining the legal and theoretical bases for FPIC, the chapter interrogates the "indigeneity" of Greenlanders based on legal history, the current constitutional framework and the potentially distinct status of the minorities in North and East Greenland. It then draws on the work of the UN expert committees that monitor selected international human rights treaties to analyse the legal status and content of FPIC, demonstrating increasing recognition of the principle as a legally binding duty on States that permit extractive industries on indigenous territories before engaging in an extended discussion of the potential to implement FPIC in Greenland.

Free, Prior and Informed Consent (FPIC)

The evolution of the principle of free, prior and informed consent (FPIC) was discussed at length in the previous chapter. Its inclusion in the 2007 UN Declaration on the Rights of Indigenous Peoples (UNDRIP) in respect of resource development marks a significant development in international law. As a General Assembly Resolution, UNDRIP is not intrinsically binding. However, as noted in the preceding chapter by Emma Wilson, UNDRIP is closely connected

---

1 UN General Assembly, Declaration on the Rights of Indigenous Peoples, UNGA Res 61/295, September 13, 2007 (UNDRIP).

to customary international law, both by virtue of codifying some pre-existing norms of international law and by encouraging the necessary state practice and *opinio iuris* that will lead other norms to obtain (binding) customary status over time.[2] Irrespective of its legal status, there is strong political commitment to UNDRIP, in particular, from the Danish government.

The only international treaty dedicated to the rights of indigenous peoples is ILO Convention 169 on the rights of indigenous and tribal peoples from 1989 (ILO C169).[3] The Kingdom of Denmark, including Greenland, has been a party to this convention since 1996.[4] ILO C169 defines indigenous "land" as "the total environment of the areas which the peoples concerned occupy or otherwise use" thus clearly including maritime spaces where there has been longstanding indigenous use.[5] Article 15 requires States to consult with indigenous and tribal people "with a view to ascertaining whether and to what degree their interests would be prejudiced" before facilitating extractive projects on indigenous territory. States should also ensure that indigenous peoples "wherever possible participate in the benefits of such activities, and receive fair compensation for any damages." It further requires that "measures shall be taken in appropriate cases to safeguard the right of the peoples concerned to use lands not exclusively occupied by them, but to which they have traditionally had access for their subsistence and traditional activities."[6] Indigenous peoples should, according to the convention, "decide their own priorities for the process of development as it affects their lives, beliefs, institutions and spiritual well-being and the lands they occupy or otherwise use."[7] However, ILO C169 does *not* require the consent of indigenous peoples whose territory is exploited unless the interference reaches such a level that they are forced from their lands.[8]

UNDRIP, by contrast, states that:

1   Indigenous peoples have the right to determine and develop priorities and strategies for the development or use of their lands or territories and other resources.
2   States shall consult and cooperate in good faith with the indigenous peoples concerned through their own representative institutions in order to obtain their free and informed consent prior to the approval of any project affecting their lands or territories and other resources, particularly in connection with the development, utilization or exploitation of mineral, water or other resources.

---

2   Customary international law is based on state practice (what states do) and *opinio iuris* (how states describe their actions and those of other states). It is a binding source of law, i.e. it is hard law, not soft law. See Statute of the International Court of Justice 1945, article 38(1)(b).
3   Indigenous and Tribal Peoples Convention 1989, ILO C169, 1989.
4   See ILO, "Normlex: Ratifications of C169" for the current status of signatures and ratifications.
5   ILO C169, article 13(2).
6   Ibid., article 14(1).
7   Ibid., article 7(1) (emphasis added).
8   Ibid., article 16. Under ILO C169, a people can even be relocated without consent where such consent "cannot" be obtained, ibid., article 16(2).

3   States shall provide effective mechanisms for just and fair redress for any such activities, and appropriate measures shall be taken to mitigate adverse environmental, economic, social, cultural or spiritual impact.[9]

The provisions on FPIC are notoriously ambiguous. Must a state *obtain* the consent of indigenous peoples before engaging in or permitting resource exploitation or is it sufficient that they take extensive measures in good faith to *seek* consent? In short, does the indigenous people concerned have a "veto" on extractive industries on their territory?[10] This ambiguity is not a drafting failure but rather the result of compromises between the indigenous and state representatives negotiating the text.

The application of FPIC *as a right* pivots on *indigeneity*. It is not a right that is available to all communities. Non-indigenous groups do not have a right to FPIC, not even under a "soft" law instrument such as a UN Declaration. Other groups do have certain rights to public participation under general human rights treaties (such as the International Covenant on Civil and Political Rights[11]), regional instruments (such as the European Convention on Human Rights, the American Convention on Human Rights, the African Charter and the UNECE Aarhus Convention[12]) and the (non-binding) General Assembly's 2018 Peasants Declaration.[13] However, none of these introduce requirements for *consent* and not all are applicable in Greenland.

This is because indigenous rights are not of the same nature as human rights. Human rights are possessed simply by virtue of being human, on the basis of human dignity. But indigenous rights are based on the collective right to exist *as a people* and are based upon indigenous sovereignty – the occupation of the indigenous people on the territory concerned before colonisation by the population now dominant.[14] Indigenous rights are a necessary response to colonialism. Many indigenous rights, including the right to FPIC, can only be enjoyed in community and do not make sense on an individual basis. It is not the right of each and every indigenous person to grant – or deny – consent to extractives on their communities traditional lands, but a right of the community *as a whole*.

---

9   UNDRIP, article 32; compare ILO C169, articles 7 and 15.
10 Mauro Barelli, "Development projects and indigenous peoples' land: Defining the scope of free, prior and informed consent," in *Handbook of Indigenous Peoples' Rights*, eds Corrine Lennox and Damien Short (Abingdon: Routledge, 2016).
11 International Covenant on Civil and Political Rights 1966 (ICCPR).
12 Convention for the Protection of Human Rights and Fundamental Freedoms 1950 (ECHR); American Convention on Human Rights 1969 (ACHR); African Charter on Human and Peoples' Rights 1981 (African Charter); Convention on Access to Information, Public Participation in Decision-Making and Access to Justice in Environmental Matters 1998 (Aarhus Convention).
13 UN General Assembly, Declaration on the Rights of Peasants and Other People Working in Rural Areas, UNGA Resolution 73/165, December 17, 2018 (Peasants Declaration).
14 See Paul Patton, "Philosophical Justifications for Indigenous Rights," in *Handbook of Indigenous Peoples' Rights*.

Sometimes, indigenous rights are justified on the basis of historic oppression – and often that oppression is ongoing. However, indigenous rights are not remedial rights; they are not "temporary special measures" as we have for other disadvantaged minorities.[15] Indigenous rights continue even when a community has overcome historic marginalisation and is treated as an equal party.

FPIC is a response to colonialism but its function is not to provide a remedy for the wrongful taking of land and resources. Rather, its function is to protect a people, a *nation*, from uses of territories that are essential to its survival *qua people*. In *Saramaka*, the Inter-American Court held that:

> Members of tribal and indigenous communities have the right to own the natural resources they have traditionally used within their territory for the same reasons that they have a right to own the land they have traditionally used and occupied for centuries. Without them, the very physical and cultural survival of such peoples is at stake. Hence the need to protect the land and resources they have traditionally used to prevent their extinction as a people. That is, the aim and purpose of the special measures required on behalf of the members of indigenous and tribal communities is to guarantee that they may continue living their traditional way of life, and that their distinct cultural identity, social structure, economic system, customs, beliefs and traditions are respected, guaranteed and protected by States.[16]

FPIC is nothing less than a provision against cultural genocide.

A (brief) legal history of Greenland

The settlement of Greenland began over 4,000 years ago beginning with the immigration of the Saqqaq people. Further waves, representing distinct cultures (Independence I and II, Early and Late Dorset) arrived from the North (what is now Canada) but apparently disappeared, before the Thule people, ancestors of today's Inuit population, built coastal settlements around the island (from 1300 onwards). Norsemen, arriving from Iceland, established two main settlements in Greenland in the late tenth century, known, somewhat misleadingly, as the Western and Eastern settlements, but these died out some time in the fifteenth century.

Danish-Norwegian missionary, Hans Egede, set out in 1721 to find the Norse settlements and educate the inhabitants into the ways of the Reformation but on arrival, he found no surviving Norsemen. Instead, he found the Inuit communities. Egede rejected the evidence of a well-functioning legal order and began his mission to impose Scandinavian norms, prohibit dispute-settlement practices and convert the

---

15 E.g., Convention on the Elimination of Racial Discrimination 1965 (CERD).
16 *Saramaka People v. Suriname*, Preliminary Objections, Merits, Reparation and Costs, 2007, Inter-American Court of Human Rights, Petition 12338, para. 121.

Inuit to Lutheranism – a project with lasting impact as today the overwhelming majority of Greenlanders are Christian, of whom nearly all are Lutheran.[17]

The Scandinavians settled and – under European norms of international law – established sovereignty over what they considered a *terra nullius*: a land formerly devoid of law.

The indigenous people of Greenland were not considered capable of forming a state recognisable to their European occupiers.[18] Nevertheless, they were a *people*, possibly even three peoples. They were not familiar with the notion of "sovereignty" but they knew the land and sea on which they depended for their livings and they knew they were a part of it. In any practical sense of the term, they enjoyed sovereignty over their territory and resources until the arrival of Egede's expedition.

Danish colonisation changed all that. Self-serving European norms dictated that territories – and their resources – fell under the control of the colonial state – and these norms could be upheld by force if necessary. Denmark established control through the Royal Greenland Trading Department.[19] It not only enforced a trade monopoly (with restriction on the products available to Inuit and different prices for Danes and Inuit) but was also responsible for administration in Greenland until 1908.[20] The trade monopoly was not lifted until 1950.[21]

Gustav Holm led the first European expedition to East Greenland from 1883 to 1885. His team, including a number of indigenous guides from South Greenland, "discovered" eleven settlements, previously unknown to the Europeans (though the West Greenlanders were aware that there were settlements in the region). The traditions and language of the people they met were distinct from those of other Greenlanders – and remain distinct to this day.[22] One Marine officer noted that the East Greenlanders enjoyed better conditions in many respects, in particular as

17 Søren Rud, *Colonialism in Greenland: Tradition, Governance and Legacy* (Cham, Switzerland: Palgrave Macmillan, 2017), 17–21; "Table: Christian Population as Percentages of Total Population by Country," Pew Research Center, *Religion and Public Life*, December 19, 2011, www.pewforum.org/2011/12/19/table-christian-population-as-percentages-of-total-population-by-country/
18 See, Steven Newcomb, "Domination in Relation to indigenous ('Dominated') Peoples in International Law," and Marcelle Burns, "The 'Natural' Law of Nations: Society and the Exclusion of First Nations as Subjects of International Law," in *Indigenous Peoples as Subjects of International Law: We Were Here First*, ed. Irene Watson (Abingdon: Routledge, 2018) (for indigenous critiques of the European application of the concept of sovereignty to justify colonial expansion and domination, challenging positivist law accounts and natural law accounts respectively).
19 *Legal Status of Eastern Greenland (Denmark v. Norway)*, 1933, P.C.I.J. (ser. A/B) No. 53 (Apr. 5), para 30.
20 Aage V. Strøm Tejsen, "The History of the Royal Greeland Trade Department," *Polar Record* 18, 116 (1977): 451–474, 456 and 460.
21 Ibid., 454; meanwhile, the trade monopoly in the Faroe Islands was lifted in 1856, ibid., 459.
22 For a full report of the expedition, including clear distinctions between the cultural practices of the East Greenlanders and other Greenlanders, see Gustav Holm, et al., *The Ammassalik Eskimo: Contributions to the Ethnology of the East Greenland Natives*,

regards clothing, than those in the West who had been colonised for a century. This was attributed to the West Greenlanders trading their resources with the settlers for imports.[23]

American explorer Robert Edwin Peary had led a number of ventures to the far northwest of Greenland, the Avanersuaq or Thule area, but there was no American occupation as such.[24] A Danish trading station was established in 1920.[25] In 1916, the US gave up any claim to Greenland as part of an agreement to purchase the Danish West Indies (now the US Virgin Islands) from Denmark and recognised Danish sovereignty over the north.[26] The people of the Avanersuaq region (known as the Inughuit) are also distinct in language and customs from those of the West Greenland majority.[27]

A Norwegian challenge to Danish sovereignty over the whole island was defeated by Denmark – peacefully – through a legal challenge before the Permanent Court of International Justice in 1933. The Court considered the respective Danish and Norwegian claims but did not consider whether the centuries-long presence of the Inuit could constitute occupation in the legal sense. In the judgment, the "Eskimos" (sic) are referred to as an "aboriginal population" that could not constitute a state for the purposes of establishing sovereignty, even if they had, as suspected, had a hand in the destruction of the Norse settlements.[28] Their welfare is considered, especially as Denmark argues that its sovereignty is crucial for their protection, but their views as to which monarch they prefer, let alone whether they would prefer no monarch at all, are never explored.[29]

Thus, at the time of the formation of the United Nations, the whole of Greenland was considered a Danish colony. Denmark listed the whole of Greenland under Part XI as a "non-self-governing territory." However, under the Charter, sovereignty of colonial powers is limited: non-self-governing peoples also have certain rights. The interests of the indigenous inhabitants are "paramount" in the administration of the colony; and the colonial power should work to ensure "their political, economic, social and educational advancement, their just treatment, and their protection against abuses [and] to develop self-government."[30]

Shortly after World War II, the decolonisation movement around the World emerged and grew rapidly. Although there was no significant independence

William Thalbitzer, ed., Parts I and II (English translation) (Copenhagen: Bianco Luno, 1914).
23 Rud, 15–16 and 22.
24 Kenn Harper, *Minik: The New York Eskimo* (Hanover NH: Steer Forth Press, 2017).
25 Rud, *Colonialism in Greenland*, 24.
26 Astrid Nonbo Andersen, "The Reparations Movement in the United States Virgin Islands," *The Journal of African American History* 103, 1–2 (Winter/Spring 2018): 104–132.
27 See, Terto Ngiviu, "The Inughuit of Northwest Greenland: An Unacknowledged Indigenous People," *Yearbook of Polar Law* 6 (2016): 142–161.
28 *Legal Status of Eastern Greenland*, para. 101.
29 Ibid., e.g., paras 226, 363 and 389.
30 Charter of the United Nations 1945, article 73.

movement in Greenland at this time, its potential was clear, especially after India and Pakistan became independent in 1948. Denmark – influenced by its defence agreement with the United States that permits to this day the latter to maintain a military base on Greenland territory – was under pressure to secure its control over the territory and pre-empt any challenges that might disrupt this arrangement. Denmark proposed to integrate Greenland as a county of Denmark as part of wide-ranging constitutional reform.

The process of purported consultation with the Grønlands Landsråd has been extensively discussed elsewhere.[31] Unlike the population in Denmark, the Greenlanders were not invited to vote on the final constitutional text – precisely because they were still a colony! Just five days before the new constitution came into force – granting protections for the Greenlanders equivalent to the Danes – the Inughuit population was forcibly relocated to make way for the expansion of the US Thule base at Pituffik in the far north of Greenland's west coast.[32] The 1953 constitution granted Danes and Greenlanders equal status as citizens and Greenland has ever since elected two seats to the Danish Parliament (Folketing). Following representations from the Danish government, the UN General Assembly voted to remove Greenland from the list of non-self-governing territories on November 22, 1954.[33]

Denmark's accession to the EEC in 1973 would prove decisive for Greenlanders seeking to reclaim their sovereignty. In the national referendum, while 63 per cent voted in favour of membership in Denmark, in Greenland, only 30 per cent of votes cast were in favour.[34] Entry to the EEC against the wishes of the Greenlanders, in particular, their inclusion in the Common Fisheries Policy while the Faroe Islands remained outside because of their Home Rule agreement, sparked the campaign for increased self-government in Greenland.

The Home Rule Act of 1979 allowed the Greenland government to repatriate various fields of competence, including rights usually associated with sovereignty such as taxation, fisheries, hunting, agriculture and commerce.[35] Denmark now

---

31 Gudmundur Alfredsson, "Greenland and the Law of Political Decolonization," *German Yearbook of International Law* 25 (1982): 290; Mininnguaq Kleist, "En etisk-politisk analyse af dokumenterne angående Grønlands indlemmelse I Danmark," in *Kilder til Færøernes og Grønlands historie*, eds Hallbera West and Maria Amalia Heinesen (Thorshavn: Føroya Fróðskaparfelag, 2004).
32 See also, e.g., Erik Beukel, Frede P. Jensen, and Jens Elo Rytter, *Phasing Out the Colonial Status of Greenland, 1945–1954: A Historical Study* (Copenhagen: Museum Tusculanum Press, University of Copenhagen, 2010), 68.
33 UN General Assembly, Cessation of the Transmission of Information under Article 73 e of the Charter in Respect of Greenland, UNGA Res 849 (IX), November 22, 1954. "Non-self governing territories" is the term used in the UN Charter to describe colonies.
34 Cindy Vestergaard, "The European Union, Its Overseas Territories and Non-Proliferation: The Case of Arctic Yellowcake," EU Non-Proliferation Consortium, *Non-Proliferatoin Papers* no. 25 (January 2013): 4; "Referendums on the European Union," House of Commons Briefing Paper 7570, April 22, 2016.
35 Greenland Home Rule Act, Act No. 577 of November 29, 1978.

recognised the Greenlanders as a "distinct community" within its Realm – a society of people (særligt folkesamfund).[36] With their new status, the Greenland Home Rule government immediately set about the process to leave the EEC, a process that was completed in 1985 through a bespoke treaty.[37] Greenland became – and remains – an overseas country of the EU.

Under the Home Rule Act, sovereignty was increasingly shared as Greenland controlled more of its own affairs, but the Greenlanders still did not enjoy rights over their mineral resources. This had been promised to colonial peoples by a General Assembly Resolution of 1960.[38] However, following integration as a county, Denmark no longer recognised the Greenlanders as a colonial people.

Denmark ratified ILO C169 in 1996, according to which it recognised the Greenland Inuit as an indigenous people and promised to respect and fulfil the rights in the Convention, including resource rights. However, Denmark included a declaration with its ratification, stating that:

> There is only one indigenous people in Denmark in the sense of Convention 169, viz. the original population of Greenland, the Inuit.[39]

This statement is limiting in two respects. While it recognises the rights of the Greenlanders as indigenous, it reinforces the distinction between indigenous and colonial peoples and denies the Greenlanders the more extensive rights – including to complete independence – that colonial peoples by this point enjoy under customary international law.[40] ILO C169 itself contains the caveat that:

> The use of the term peoples in this Convention shall not be construed as having any implications as regards the rights which may attach to the term under international law.[41]

---

36 Ibid., ss1(1), see also Ngiviu, "The Inughuit of Northwest Greenland," 155.
37 Treaty amending, with regard to Greenland, the Treaties establishing the European Communities 1985; see also, Council Decision 2014/137/EU of 14 March 2014 on relations between the European Union on the one hand, and Greenland and the Kingdom of Denmark on the other, OJ L. 76/1, 2014.
38 UN General Assembly, Declaration on the Granting of Independence to Colonial Countries and Peoples, UNGA Res 1514 (XV), December 14, 1960.
39 Report of the Committee Set Up to Examine the Representation Alleging Non-Observance by Denmark of the Indigenous and Tribal Peoples Convention, 1989 (No. 169), made under article 24 of the ILO Constitution by the National Confederation of Trade Unions of Greenland (Sulinermik Inuussutissarsiuteqartut Kattuffiat–SIK) (*SIK v. Denmark*), GB.277/18/3; GB.280/18/5, para 20.
40 UN General Assembly Resolution Defining the Three Options for Self-Determination, UNGA Res 1541 (XV) December 15, 1960; UN General Assembly Declaration on Principles of International Law Concerning Friendly Relations and Co-operation among States in Accordance with the Charter of the United Nations, UNGA Res 2625(XXV), October 24, 1970.
41 ILO C169, article 1(3).

This provision was included to make it clear that indigenous peoples were not to have the same legal rights as colonial peoples, in particular, the right to full independence as a sovereign state.

Furthermore, the Danish declaration on signing ILO C169 entrenches the Danish position that Greenland contains only *one* indigenous people, rejecting the status of the two minorities, in North and East Greenland respectively, as distinct indigenous peoples (see below).

Nevertheless, ratification of ILO C169 was the first time that the Kingdom of Denmark recognised any mineral resource management rights of the Greenlanders under international law, limited as these are.

The view that the Greenlanders might indeed be a colonial people grew around the turn of the century and thereafter, both in Greenland and Denmark. From 1999–2002, a Greenland Home Rule appointed commission explored the options for Greenland and concluded that the Greenlanders are a [colonial] "people" under international law. In 2004, a joint commission (with eight members each from the Greenland and Danish parliaments) began to work on proposals to enable Greenland to take over more of her own affairs. The latter commission's starting point was that the Greenlanders enjoy the right to self-determination and their conclusion was that the Greenlanders are indeed a colonial people.[42] This work would form the basis for the Self Government Act of 2009, which begins by:

> Recognising that the people of Greenland is a people pursuant to international law with the right of self-determination, the Act is based on a wish to foster equality and mutual respect in the partnership between Denmark and Greenland.[43]

Meanwhile, UNDRIP was approved by the UN General Assembly in 2007 with strong Danish and Inuit support.[44] The rights of indigenous peoples are weaker than those of colonial peoples – pointedly excluding the right to independence. Denmark's position was and remains ambiguous but Denmark is an ardent supporter of UNDRIP, for example, pressing the Canadian government in 2009 which had initially voted against the Declaration, to endorse and implement it.[45]

---

42 The Greenland–Danish Self-Government Commission's report on self-government in Greenland: Executive summary, April 2008, 4, https://naalakkersuisut.gl// ~/media/Nanoq/Files/Attached%20Files/Engelske-tekster/Summary%20of%20the% 20paper.pdf
43 Act on Greenland Self-Government, Act no. 473 of June 12, 2009.
44 Statement by H.E. Ambassador Carsten Staur, 11th Session of the UN Permanent Forum on Indigenous Issues, Statement by Denmark and Greenland on agenda item 9, New York, May 17, 2012. See also Irene Watson and Sharon Venne, "Talking Up Indigenous Peoples' Original Intent in a Space Dominated by State Interventions," in *Indigenous Rights in the Age of the UN Declaration*, ed. Elvira Pulitano (Cambridge: Cambridge University Press) (on the drafting history and the UN process).
45 United Nations Human Rights Council Working Group on Universal Periodic Review 2009, *Canada*. UN Doc. A/HRC/11/17, paras 24, 48 and 76.

The Greenlanders and indigenous rights

Denmark views Greenland self-government as the answer to the promises of UNDRIP, notwithstanding the uncertainty about UNDRIP's legal status.[46]

Kuupik Kleist, the Premier of Greenland in 2009 when the Self-Government Act was passed, stated that:

> [T]his new development in Greenland and in the relationship between Denmark and Greenland should be seen as a *de facto* implementation of the Declaration and, in this regard, hopefully an inspiration to others.[47]

What is the basis for this position? The use of *de facto* is important: the electorate, Parliament and Government of Greenland are not "indigenous" bodies. The right to vote in Greenland is based on *Danish* citizenship and residence in Greenland for six months or more.[48] (There is no such thing as Greenlandic citizenship in law.) Around 88 per cent of the electorate self-identify as Inuit, but this is not the basis for their rights to vote or stand for election. Nevertheless, the self-government and parliament are *de facto* composed entirely of persons who self-identify as Inuit and it is very likely that Inuit will remain the overwhelming majority of elected representatives for the foreseeable future. Consequently, *de facto*, Greenlanders, principally Greenlanders who self-identify as Inuit, control their own affairs, including natural resource governance. In fact, jurisdiction over mineral resource activities and regulation of the offshore working environment were the first two powers that Greenland repatriated after the coming into force of the Self-Government Act.[49]

Although there is no officially accepted definition of indigeneity, most working definitions require that the indigenous community be politically non-dominant in their society. They need not be a numerical minority but they should "form at present non-dominant sectors of society" and "consider themselves distinct from other sectors of the societies now prevailing on those territories."[50] The former UN special rapporteur on the rights of indigenous peoples, James Anaya, considers

---

46 Statement by H.E. Ambassador Carsten Staur; DANIDA: International Development and Cooperation, *Review Report: Strategy for Danish Support to Indigenous Peoples, 2001–2010* (Ministry of Foreign Affairs of Denmark, 2011) 8.
47 Greenland (Delegation of Denmark), "Statement by Mr. Kuupik Kliest, Premier of Greenland," Delivered to the Expert Mechanism on the Rights of Indigenous Peoples, 2nd Sess., Geneva, 11 August 2009, 2.
48 Mininnguaq Kleist, "Greenland's Self-Government," in *Polar Law Textbook*, ed. Natalia Loukacheva (Copenhagen: Nordic Council of Ministers, 2011), 181.
49 "Fields of Responsibility assumed by the Greenland Home Rule Government (I and II) and Greenland Self-Government (III) respectively," accessed February 7, 2019, www.stm.dk/multimedia/GR_oversigt_sagsomr_270110_UK.pdf
50 José R. Martínez Cobo, UN Special Rapporteur, *Study of the Problem of Discrimination Against Indigenous Populations*, 1987, UN Doc. E/CN.4/Sub.2/1986/7 Add. 4, para. 379.

that the term "indigenous" "refers broadly to the living descendants of pre-invasion habitants of lands now dominated by others."[51]

When it comes to decision-making regarding extractive industries, it can no longer be said that the Danes "prevail on those territories" or that the Inuit are "dominated by others." Elected (Inuit) Greenlanders make the decisions.

A further criterion of indigeneity that complicates matters in Greenland is self-identification: the community must *want* to continue to be viewed as an indigenous people.[52] Many Greenlanders are increasingly questioning their status as indigenous. This stems in the main from the view that Greenlanders are no longer marginalised politically, socially or economically because of the Self-Government Act. However, for some, it is also a response to a belief that the indigenous label has negative connotations, that it describes somehow "backward" peoples and has no relevance for a modern nation like Greenland. While recognising the importance of indigenous rights for vulnerable indigenous minorities in other countries, they do not think they need them anymore in Greenland. This view is problematic, indicating the success of the colonial endeavour to convert the Greenlanders into good Scandinavians, but it is more complicated than might first appear because the same people who might reject the indigenous label would be proud to self-identify as "Inuit."[53]

The Greenland government's view is that the government and the parliament are *the* representative institutions of the Greenlanders. The civil service in Greenland does not mainstream indigenous rights in its working methods: in fact, it barely considers them at all. Their view is that indigenous rights do not apply in Greenland because the (indigenous) Greenlanders are not underrepresented. The government voice is purportedly the voice of all Greenlanders.[54] Further, they assume that Inuit values are necessarily integrated into decision-making simply because the decision-makers are themselves Inuit.[55]

In short, the Greenland government's position is that the legal status of UNDRIP is a moot point: binding or not, it is not opposable *against the Greenland government*.

There are, of course, alternative views. Greenlanders are still a minority within the Realm – constituting barely 1 per cent of the total population – and they remain subject to the Danish Constitution and the Danish Supreme Court. In this wider context they are clearly "non-dominant" and the Danish majority undoubtedly "prevails." Although the Greenland Self-Government enjoys very broad powers to govern mineral resources, even these sometimes come into tension with Danish competence regarding security – such as in the Kuannersuit

---

51 Anaya, S. James, *Indigenous Peoples in International Law*, 2nd edn (Oxford: Oxford University Press, 2004) 3.
52 Martínez Cobo, *Study of the Problem of Discrimination*.
53 Apprentice, personal communication, Nuuk, March 30, 2019.
54 Anne Merrild Hansen et al., "Managing the Social Impacts of the Rapidly-Expanding Extractive Industries in Greenland," *The Extractive Industries and Society* 3 (2016): 25–33, 31.
55 Ibid.

(Kvanefjeld) mining project for rare earth elements and uranium.[56] Others take the view that "indigeneity" is based on culture, tradition, ways of life and value systems, and emphasise the need for indigenous rights to ensure their survival.[57] This would be the view of the Inuit Circumpolar Council's Greenland chapter. Indigenous traditional activities need not be frozen in time, using pre-colonial tools, in order to be recognised as cultural rights. In other words, modern tools and techniques and Scandinavian living standards are not a bar to indigenous rights.[58]

Does the Self-Government Act eliminate the need for FPIC at community level?

If the Greenlanders cease to be indigenous *or* cease to be a colonial people because they have obtained a sufficient degree of autonomy, is FPIC irrelevant? It is counterintuitive that Greenlandic citizens, on obtaining self-government, now enjoy fewer protections against the decision-makers than they had when the Kingdom of Denmark held the reins.

In States that have never been colonised, there is no particular right to FPIC. The simple, representative-democracy model of decision-making is regarded as sufficient for decision-making regarding extractives as for other social and economic issues. The provisions of human rights law apply at an individual level – private property may not be taken without due process and compensation; activities cannot infringe the home or individuals' privacy – but "the people" do not enjoy collective rights to inclusive decision-making. The Aarhus Convention provides rights of consultation and remedies for activities with an environmental impact – but Greenland is not a party to that treaty and the very fact that there *is* such a treaty and that so many States are *not* party to it suggests that these provisions are not customary law. Thus the current situation is that the Greenland government applies neither the participatory rights of indigenous peoples, nor the participatory rights afforded to citizens elsewhere in the Realm.

As considered at the beginning of this chapter, indigenous rights recognise the existence of indigenous peoples as distinct peoples with sovereignty rights necessary to ensure their continued existence *qua* peoples. But is this still necessary in a decolonised country? There is no "outsider" threatening the survival or cultural integrity of the group. There are only some members of the group – duly and democratically elected – making decisions about which their electorate has mixed views. One recent study of attitudes amongst government officials found that they did not consider FPIC relevant in Greenland because the Inuit are not a minority

---

56 See, Cindy Vestergaard and Gry Thomasen, *Governing Uranium in the Danish Realm*, DIIS Report 2015: 17 (Danish Institute of International Studies, 2015).
57 Apprentice, personal communication, Nuuk, March 30, 2019.
58 See, e.g., *Länsman, Ilmari et al. v. Finland*, Human Rights Committee, 1994; *Mahuika et al. v. New Zealand*, Human Rights Committee, 2000.

and since the government was composed of Inuit, they considered "Inuit values" to be sufficiently integrated in decision-making.[59]

The question is thus not about the legal status of FPIC under international law but rather about whether the Greenlanders (still) have the status to enjoy it. The right to FPIC (if indeed it *is* a right) is not a general right of all communities, but only a right of indigenous ones. So if Greenlanders are not indigenous, they do not possess this right.

Under the Mineral Resources Act and its various implementing regulations, indigenous rights are not integrated into the process. The rules on social impact assessments do not refer to indigenous rights at all (instead referring only to "traditional and local knowledge") and hence it is no surprise that the companies undertaking social impact assessments rarely refer to indigenous rights.[60]

The "consent" part of FPIC in Greenland is the consent of the government as the legitimately elected representatives of the people.[61] Consent is manifested, indirectly, through the democratic process. This is no different from any other Western representative democracy but differs fundamentally from the consensus-based decision-making that is more common in indigenous societies.[62] Within the legal framework for mineral resource development, the Greenlanders have no distinct indigenous rights against their own government. Greenlanders have fewer rights against those making decisions on extractive industries than they had when they were governed by Denmark.

The Greenland government's position has not gone unchallenged. Sara Olsvig, former leader of the opposition *Inuit Ataqatigiit* (IA) party and erstwhile representative of the Greenland Parliament at Inuit Circumpolar Council Greenland (ICC Greenland), rejects the position of Kleist (also of the IA party) and others. She agrees that the Self-Government Act implements *some* provisions of the UNDRIP, in particular, those on self-government, but she does not agree that it introduces them all, certainly not those on FPIC.[63] Now that the Greenland Parliament has the power to legislate for extractive industries and to require FPIC, the government claims that it is no longer needed because they are they only organ whose consent is required.[64] The position of ICC Greenland is that

---

59 Hansen et al., "Managing the Social Impacts," 31.
60 Jeppe Strandsbjerg, "Making Sense of Contemporary Greenland: Indigeneity, Resources and Sovereignty," in *Polar Geopolitics: Knowledges, Resources and Legal Regimes*, eds Richard C. Powell and Klaus Dodds (Cheltenham: Edward Elgar, 2014) 270–271; Government of Greenland, *Social Impact Assessment (SIA) Guidelines on the Process and Preparation of the SIA Report for Mineral Projects*, Version 2 (Nuuk: Ministry of Industry, Labour and Trade, 2016) 24–25.
61 Act on Mineral Resources and Mineral Resource Activities of December 7, 2009, Parliament of Greenland, articles 2–4.
62 See, e.g., Irene Watson, *Aboriginal Peoples, Colonialism and International Law: Raw Law* (Abingdon: Routledge, 2015), 17 (explaining that consensus-based decision-making discovers not necessarily the most popular option but rather the option that all participants are able to accept).
63 Sara Olsvig, personal communication, November 7, 2018.
64 Ibid.

indigenous rights remain very much applicable and that FPIC is required for projects such as that at Kuannersuit.[65] The Reconciliation Commission that was established to gather evidence, open discussion and promote healing also concluded that FPIC be obtained whenever "major social changes" are planned.[66]

Beyond indigeneity, in *Saramaka*, the Inter-American Court of Human Rights protected non-indigenous "tribal" peoples who live a traditional lifestyle, requiring FPIC where developments threaten their very way of life.[67] This was an exceptional case, as the Saramaka people were the direct descendants of slaves, but the crucial factor was that they continued to maintain their distinct traditions and rely on subsistence activities. Support for improved participation (though not FPIC) in Greenland from at least those communities that rely on traditional subsistence activities for their livelihoods might be found in the General Assembly Declaration on the Rights of Peasants and Other People Working in Rural Areas from December 2018.[68] The declaration extends rights to meaningful participation to all persons who rely on the land for their living at a small scale, as well as a share of the benefits.[69] However, none of the Arctic states supported the declaration.[70]

The (indigenous?) minorities of East and North Greenland

As alluded to in the brief section on Greenland's legal history, Eastern and North Greenland were integrated into the Danish Realm much later than West Greenland and the colonisation of these regions was led both by Danes and by other Greenlanders. Some people in these areas feel themselves as much colonised by the West Greenlanders as they were by the Danes.[71] The East Greenlanders and North Greenlanders (Inughuit) self-identify as Inuit but enjoy and seek to retain distinct languages and cultural identities. There are around 3,000 speakers of *Tunumiit oraasiat* (the language of the East Greenlanders) and around 1,000 speakers of *Inuktun* (the language of the North Greenlanders), compared with around 50,000 of speakers of Kalaallisut, the official language of Greenland.[72]

---

65 Mia Olsen Siegstad and Mads Fægteborg, *"Ajorpoq" – vi Får Ingen Svar! Bedre Borgerinddragelse Om Kuannersuit* (Inuit Circumpolar Council, Greenland, 2015), http://naalakkersuisut.gl/~/media/Nanoq/Files/Attached%20Files/Formandens%20Departement/Puljemidler/Ajorpoq%20Kuannersuit.pdf
66 Greenland Reconciliation Commission, *Vi Forstår Fortiden; Vi Tager Ansvar for Nutiden; Vi Arbejder for en Bedre Fremtid.* Final Report, December 2017, 46, Recommendation no. 7.
67 *Saramaka v. Suriname.*
68 UN General Assembly, Peasants Declaration.
69 Ibid., especially article 5.
70 "Voting Record," United Nations Bibliographic Information System, accessed March 12, 2019, http://unbisnet.un.org:8080/ipac20/ipac.jsp?profile=voting&menu=search. The US and Sweden voted against; the other Arctic states, including the Kingdom of Denmark, abstained.
71 Member of Greenland Parliament, personal communication, Nuuk, October 25, 2017.
72 Mauro Mazzi, *Aurora borealis: Diritto polare e comparazione giuridica* (Bologna: Filo diritto editore, 2014) 300.

Although formally classed as "dialects" of Greenlandic, these three tongues are not mutually comprehensible. They have distinct traditions of clothing, hunting and spirituality.[73] The Greenland government does not recognise the distinctiveness of the groups, a position that originated in Denmark but is now followed by Greenland.[74] However, under international law, the existence of an indigenous people is a question of fact and States cannot deprive indigenous peoples of their rights under international law by failing to recognise them. The Greenland/Danish position has been repeatedly challenged both within Greenland and by the UN human rights treaty bodies that emphasise the importance of self-identification and express concern in particular with regard to the Inughuit position.[75]

As linguistic and even possibly ethnic minorities, the Inughuit and the East Greenlanders enjoy certain rights under article 27 of the ICCPR (see below). However, if they are in fact an indigenous people *within Greenland*, then the Self-Government must uphold the same rights for them that the (West) Greenlanders demanded against the Kingdom of Denmark. A failure to recognise these distinct communities risks a repetition of the assimilationist practices that have scarred Inuit communities throughout the Arctic under European colonisation. As indigenous peoples, East and North Greenlanders have a right to continue to exist in some respects distinct from the dominant Greenland population – and that includes a right to FPIC opposable against the Greenland government.

FPIC under international treaty law

Notwithstanding the opacity of the UNDRIP provisions on FPIC, not to mention uncertainty regarding their legal status, some of the UN human rights treaty bodies have been engaging with the principle in their engagement with States under the human rights treaties. This system has the advantage of being based on binding treaties entered into by States, including the Kingdom of Denmark, including Greenland. This is not the same as asking if UNDRIP is customary international law – or even if FPIC is customary international law. Instead, it is asking about what standards States have to meet *vis á vis* extractive industries *under treaties they have already agreed to uphold as a matter of law*.

Relying on human rights treaties (and their committees) to promote indigenous rights is a pragmatic and influential approach because of the basis in binding treaty instruments and the high regard of the independent experts from all over the world who serve on the committees. When they write collectively, they might

---

73 On the North Greenlanders, see, Ngiviu, "The Inughuit of Northwest Greenland."
74 Ibid., 149; see also Statement by H.E. Ambasador Carsten Staur.
75 Committee on Economic, Social and Cultural Rights, Concluding Observations on the fifth periodic report of Denmark, 2013, para 21; Concluding observations of the Committee on the Elimination of Racial Discrimination: Denmark, 2002, para. 18; Concluding observations of the Committee on the Elimination of Racial Discrimination: Denmark, 2010, para. 17; Human Rights Committee, Concluding Observations on the Sixth Periodic Report of Denmark, 2008, para. 13.

even be considered to have the status of "publicists" – which gives their statements authority as a source of international law.[76]

Even before the text of UNDRIP was finalised and adopted by the General Assembly, the committees that monitor the treaties were pressing States on indigenous rights, including in respect of extractive industries. Later, at the first World Conference on Indigenous Peoples, States from all over the world invited the treaty bodies "to consider UNDRIP in accordance with their respective mandates" and encouraged States to integrate it into their state reports.[77]

The most important human rights treaties for indigenous peoples are as follows:

- The Convention on the Elimination of All Forms of Racial Discrimination 1965 (supervised by the Committee on the Elimination of Racial Discrimination);
- The International Covenant on Civil and Political Rights 1966 (supervised by the Human Rights Committee);
- The International Covenant on Economic, Social and Cultural Rights[78] (supervised by the Committee on Economic, Social and Cultural Rights); and
- The Convention on the Elimination of All Forms of Discrimination Against Women[79] (supervised by the Committee on the Elimination of Discrimination Against Women).

Other committees, including the Committee on the Rights of the Child, the Committee Against Torture, and the Committee on the Rights of Persons with Disabilities, also consider indigenous rights but tend not to address issues around indigenous participation in decision-making in extractive industries.

None of the treaties discusses FPIC as such, nor in the older treaties are indigenous peoples mentioned as a distinct category of rights-bearers. Nevertheless, there are some provisions that the expert committees have interpreted to protect indigenous peoples – e.g.:

International Covenant on Civil and Political Rights (ICCPR) and International Covenant on Economic, Social and Cultural Rights (ICESCR)
Article 1(1): All peoples have the right of self-determination. By virtue of that right they freely determine their political status and freely pursue their economic, social and cultural development.

---

76 Publicists are esteemed scholars of international law whose doctrinal treaties can be regarded as a material but not a formal source of law. This means they do not *create* law (unlike treaties or customary law) but that their expert writings are regarded as an authoritative *description and interpretation* of the law. See Statute of the International Court of Justice 1945, article 38(1)(d).
77 Outcome document of the high-level plenary meeting of the General Assembly known as the World Conference on Indigenous Peoples, September 25, 2014, para. 29.
78 International Covenant on Economic, Social and Cultural Rights 1966 (ICESCR).
79 Convention on the Elimination of All Forms of Discrimination Against Women 1979.

(2) All peoples may, for their own ends, freely dispose of their natural wealth and resources without prejudice to any obligations arising out of international economic co-operation, based upon the principle of mutual benefit, and international law. In no case may a people be deprived of its own means of subsistence.

International Covenant on Civil and Political Rights (ICCPR)

Article 27: In those States in which ethnic, religious or linguistic minorities exist, persons belonging to such minorities shall not be denied the right, in community with the other members of their group, to enjoy their own culture, to profess and practise their own religion, or to use their own language.

International Covenant on Economic, Social and Cultural Rights (ICESCR)

Article 15(1): The States Parties to the present Covenant recognize the right of everyone: (a) To take part in cultural life... etc.

Convention on the Elimination of All Forms of Racial Discrimination

Article 2(1): States Parties condemn racial discrimination and undertake to pursue by all appropriate means and without delay a policy of eliminating racial discrimination in all its forms and promoting understanding among all races...

The committees review the compliance of States through the state report process: the state sends a report of its efforts and its challenges to implement the treaties and the expert committees give them feedback including recommendations for action. There are also a number of important Views (committee opinions based on complaints from affected persons) based on article 27 of the ICCPR – especially from Canada, Sápmi and Peru. The committees also make general comments or general recommendations that are addressed to all state parties. A number of these are pertinent to indigenous issues of resource governance.

Human rights treaties and FPIC

The Special Rapporteur on the rights of indigenous peoples, Victoria Tauli-Corpuz, reported in 2015 that:

> Human rights treaty bodies have consistently affirmed the principle of free, prior and informed consent of indigenous peoples in matters relating to their rights and interests and specifically in relation to their ancestral lands and conservation.[80]

But what exactly do they say about FPIC?

Certainly, an original interpretation of the treaties would not endorse an "FPIC as veto" approach – given that the treaties are up to 50 years old and at their time,

---

80 Victoria Tauli-Corpuz, *Report of the Special Rapporteur of the Human Rights Council on the Rights of Indigenous Peoples (Conservation and Indigenous Peoples' Rights)*, A/71/229, July 29, 2016, para. 23.

indigenous rights were barely scratching the surface of UN human rights system. However, treaties must be interpreted dynamically and contextually – taking into account more recent developments on similar issues or in related areas of international law – including the emergence of FPIC under customary law and under UNDRIP.[81]

The Committee on the Elimination of Racial Discrimination has been addressing indigenous peoples for over two decades, including with an important General Recommendation back in 1997 where it addressed "informed consent" as regards all decisions affecting indigenous peoples and especially recognised rights to lands, territories and resources.

> The Committee calls in particular upon States parties to: ... Ensure that members of indigenous peoples have equal rights in respect of effective participation in public life and that no decisions directly relating to their rights and interests are taken without their informed consent.
>
> The Committee especially calls upon States parties to recognize and protect the rights of indigenous peoples to own, develop, control and use their communal lands, territories and resources and, where they have been deprived of their lands and territories traditionally owned or otherwise inhabited or used without their free and informed consent, to take steps to return those lands and territories.[82]

From 2007, when UNDRIP was adopted, the Committee asked States to use it "as a guide to interpret obligations under the Convention relating to indigenous peoples."[83] This was addressed, amongst others, to the United States – even before the US had endorsed the declaration. In the same report, they call on the State "to consult and cooperate in good faith" with indigenous peoples as regards extractive industries, but they do not address FPIC as such.[84]

In 2009, the Committee on the Elimination of Racial Discrimination made a very important statement regarding indigenous rights which clarifies their distinction from "non-discrimination" standards. The committee pointed out that indigenous rights are *not* temporary special measures, i.e. this is not about affirmative action to allow indigenous peoples to catch up or to rectify past discrimination.[85] Rather, indigenous rights, including rights to land traditionally occupied, are *permanent* rights based on their rights to exist *as peoples*.

---

81 Vienna Convention on the Law of Treaties 1969, articles 31–32. UNDRIP is not strictly speaking a source of "law" but to the extent that it reflects customary international law, it must be taken into account.
82 Committee on the Elimination of Racial Discrimination, General Recommendation XXIII on the Rights of Indigenous Peoples, 1997, para 5.
83 Committee on the Elimination of Racial Discrimination, Concluding Comments on the State Report of United States of America, 2008, para. 29.
84 Ibid., para. 29.
85 Committee on the Elimination of Racial Discrimination, General Recommendation XXXII on the Meaning and Scope of Special Measures in the International Convention on the Elimination of Racial Discrimination, 2009, para. 15.

The Committee has recently addressed FPIC explicitly in a number of state report processes, including in Norway, expressing concern that the Finnmark Act is inadequate. It tends to approach FPIC as a good faith process rather than as an outcome.[86]

Although the Human Rights Committee eschews communications from aggrieved individuals under article 1 (the right to self-determination), it applies article 27 on the rights of persons belonging to minority groups to enjoy their culture to defend indigenous peoples' rights on an effectively *collective* basis.[87] The *Poma Poma* case is the most important so far in this respect. In that case, regarding an indigenous Peruvian llama farmer, the committee recognised that:

> raising llamas is an essential element of the culture of the Aymara community, since it is a form of subsistence and an ancestral tradition handed down from parent to child.[88]

Where industrial activities "substantially compromise or interfere with the culturally significant economic activities of an indigenous community," development can only lawfully take place with the "free, prior and informed consent" of the community, following full participation in the decision-making process and even then, only if interference is proportionate "so as not to endanger the very survival of the community and its members."[89]

In dialogue with Sweden and Namibia as part of the state report and review process, the Human Rights Committee has indicated that consultation *aimed* at FPIC – i.e. a good faith consultation process – is adequate and that it is sufficient to "give primary consideration" to the opinions of the indigenous peoples concerned.[90] The degree of impact on the people concerned is likely to be a key factor.

The Committee on Economic, Social and Cultural Rights was already pressing States "to consult and seek consent" in 2005 – before UNDRIP was agreed.[91] It has been more willing than the Human Rights Committee to address the right of self-determination under article 1 in its dialogue with States over their reports, for example, in respect of the Saami.[92] However, the committee has not yet considered any petitions in respect of indigenous peoples.

---

86 Committee on the Elimination of Racial Discrimination, Concluding Comments on the State Report of Norway, 2015, para 29(b).
87 *Ominayak and the Lubicon Lake Band v. Canada*, Human Rights Committee, 1990.
88 *Poma Poma v. Peru*, Human Rights Committee, 2009, para. 7.3.
89 Ibid., para. 7.6.
90 Human Rights Committee, Concluding Observations on the Second Report of Namibia, 2016, para. 44; see also Human Rights Committee, Concluding Observations on the Sixth Report of Sweden, 2016, para. 39.
91 Concluding Observations of the Committee on Economic, Social and Cultural Rights on the Fourth Periodic Report of Colombia, 2001, para. 33.
92 E.g. Committee on Economic, Social and Cultural Rights, Concluding Observations on the Sixth Periodic Report of Finland, 2014, para. 9.

In 2011, the Committee issued a General Comment on the right to take part in cultural life (article 15) in which they addressed the rights of indigenous peoples explicitly. It concluded with the broad provision that:

> States parties should respect the principle of free, prior and informed consent of indigenous peoples in all matters covered by their specific rights.[93]

Messages on the substantive content of FPIC are a little mixed, however, in the state report process, in some cases indicating that FPIC is a process but in others promoting the view that consent must be obtained.[94]

The Committee on the Elimination of Discrimination Against Women has identified problems with extractive industries impinging on the rights of indigenous women. In its general inquiry into missing and murdered aboriginal women in Canada, a topic that is not *obviously* connected to extractives, the Committee deliberately referenced the right to FPIC.[95] However, while concerned about the full participation of indigenous women in decision-making processes, it seems to be sticking to a cautious "FPIC as process" approach – asking States, for example, to "systematically consult and seek free, prior and informed consent" without indicating the legal consequences should consent not be forthcoming.[96]

The two committees with the most obvious mandate over indigenous land and resource rights are the Human Rights Committee and the Committee on Economic, Social and Cultural Rights – by virtue of common article 1 on the right to self-determination. However, they are just as likely to apply the right to culture – sometimes in *preference* to politically-charged arguments about self-determination – to protect indigenous peoples. The Committee on the Elimination of Racial Discrimination has also been proactive on protecting indigenous peoples. Pointedly, it emphasises that indigenous rights are *not* temporary special measures. The Committees the Elimination of Discrimination Against Women is also applying FPIC to indigenous women's land and resource rights.

---

93 Committee on Economic, Social and Cultural Rights, General Comment No. 21, Right of Everyone to Take Part in Cultural Life (art. 15, para. 1(a), of the International Covenant on Economic, Social and Cultural Rights), 2009, para. 37.
94 See Committee on Economic, Social and Cultural Rights, Concluding Observations on the Sixth Periodic Report of Finland, 2014, para. 9; Concluding Observations on the Sixth Periodic Report of Sweden, 2016, para. 14; and Concluding Observations on the Sixth Periodic Report of Canada, 2016, para. 14 (indicating FPIC as process). But see, Concluding Observations on the Combined Second to Fourth Reports of Guyana, 2015, paras 14–15; and Concluding Observations on the Combined Fifth and Sixth Reports of the Philippines, 2016, paras 13–14 (indicating FPIC as outcome).
95 Committee on the Elimination of Discrimination Against Women, Report of the Inquiry Concerning Canada, 2015, para. 265.
96 See, e.g., Committee on the Elimination of Discrimination Against Women, Concluding Observations on the Combined Eighth and Ninth Periodic Reports of Ecuador, 2015, para. 39.

Discussion: (how) can Greenland perform free, prior and informed consent?

Having been leaders in the fight for the rights of indigenous peoples over the past decades, Greenlanders are now in a position to implement them. The Self-Government Act allows the government of Greenland – a *de facto* Inuit government – a wide discretion in managing extractive industries. It requires only political will to legislate for FPIC and thoughtful reforms to make it happen.

The status of the Greenlanders as indigenous or not is less important than a willingness on the part of the authorities to ensure that their people do not enjoy fewer rights under self-government than the very same political leaders demanded of Denmark. The question of "can" is very simply answered in the affirmative; the harder question is "how?"

The distinction between process and outcome is of limited importance. Under the current regulatory framework, Greenland is not even conducting a genuine process of *seeking* FPIC of local communities in extractive projects, let alone ensuring that consent is granted before going ahead.

As we will see in Chapter 6, there is a great deal of dissatisfaction with the decision-making processes in Greenland. We have suggested elsewhere fairly simple reforms that could improve the process:

> Proposal 1: That initiatives are taken by actors such as authorities, research institutions, educational institutions and the media, to inform and engage the public about extractive projects before or during early exploration.
>
> Proposal 2: That during the consultation phases in impact assessment processes, people are given the opportunity to meet with or hear from people from other communities where exploration and/or production of minerals or hydrocarbons have taken place.
>
> Proposal 3: That companies and authorities consider how to accept and consider confidential information and to facilitate anonymous submission of views.
>
> Proposal 4: That companies and authorities consider how to hold smaller, targeted meetings to ensure both a safe space and to encourage people to speak up.
>
> Proposal 5: That initiatives are taken to evaluate former extractive projects in Greenland and consider what lessons can be applied for future management.[97]

These proposals are focussed on effective participation and not explicitly on FPIC. They do not pivot on the indigeneity of the participants. However, they each contribute to an improvement in FPIC. The first proposal speaks both to the conditions of "prior" and "informed." In our fieldwork, we discovered a very

---

[97] Anne Merrild Hansen and Rachael Lorna Johnstone, "Improving Public Participation in Greenland Extractive Industries," in *Current Developments in Arctic Law: Vol. V*, eds Kamrul Hossain and Anna Petrétei (Rovaniemi: Arctic Law Thematic Network, 2018).

high degree of dissatisfaction with information provided, considering it too little, too late, and of the wrong sort.[98] People wanted to know more about the extractive potential of their region even before industry demonstrated an interest and certainly as soon as geologists began scanning their mountains.[99] Further, they wanted to have information from a wide range of sources, including sources they perceived as neutral, such as academic institutions. It is only with adequate information in advance that people can genuinely participate in the formal consultation process.[100]

However, in some cases, even the formal consultation is lacking. Under Greenlandic law, no social impact assessment is undertaken prior to the granting of an exploration licence for onshore mining activities. GME began exploratory drilling on the Kuannersuit mountain in 2005.[101] By the end of 2018, neither the social impact assessment nor the environmental impact assessment had been published. The requirement for prior *information*, let alone *consent*, is clearly not being upheld. The legislation should be revised to require studies of environmental *and social* impacts at much earlier stages, especially where traditional practices, including hunting, may be affected.

The second proposal also refers to the criterion of "informed." As well as "professional" information, communities can also be informed by their peers in other communities that have experienced extractive projects – and even by communities where large-scale projects have been proposed but never come to fruition. In fact, given the low proportion of projects that ever make it from the prospecting to the extraction and processing stages, this might be even more important in giving people a genuinely informed perspective on the projects proposed. These grassroots communities are the real experts on the social impacts of extractive projects.

The third and fourth proposals are relevant to the "informed" aspect of decision-making – this time ensuring that the decision-makers themselves are genuinely informed of all relevant circumstances and hear from all interest groups. It also reflects on the standard of "free." In much of the literature, the emphasis on "informed" is about informing the public in general and indigenous peoples in particular about the details of proposed projects and the anticipated social and environmental impacts. However, truly informed decision-making requires a multi-directional transfer of knowledge. Without diminishing in any way the importance of project developers transmitting important information to

---

98 Anne Merrild Hansen and Rachael Lorna Johnstone, "In the Shadow of the Mountain: Assessing Early Impacts on Community Development from Two Mining Prospects in South Greenland," *The Extractive Industries and Society* 6, 2 (2019): 480–488. doi: 10.1016/j.exis.2019.01.012
99 Ibid., 484; Entrepreneur, personal communication, Tasiilaq, August 21, 2017.
100 Ibid., 484.
101 Government of Greenland, *Report to Inatsisartut, the Parliament of Greenland, Concerning Mineral Resources Activities in Greenland* (Nuuk: Bureau of Minerals and Petroleum, June 2012).

communities in appropriate formats, it is equally important that they actively seek out and integrate the information they receive from the community.

In small communities, social pressures can make it difficult for people to stand up in large public meetings to express their views.[102] They fear bullying and exclusion if they are seen to support a position that is not shared by the more influential members of the community. Special efforts also need to be made to include hard-to-reach individuals who do not usually take part in traditional public meetings.

The fifth proposal also contributes to the criterion of "informed," in this case both for communities and for decision-makers. There have not been sufficient reviews of prior projects, including those that have never reached the extractive stage.[103]

Unsurprisingly, these five proposals having been aimed primarily at public participation do not exhaust FPIC. They allude to the need for decision-makers also to be informed, but it is necessary to expand on this. Reports of consultation processes, both from our own fieldwork and from other studies, describe sessions of "lectures" by project proponents with very limited opportunities to ask questions.[104]

Returning to the importance of multidirectional knowledge transfer, no party is properly "informed" by the traditional "death by PowerPoint" presentation at a public meeting. Mark Nuttall's study of the consultation meetings for the Isukasia iron ore mining project in the Nuuk fjord provides some examples of how *not* to do it.[105] In this case, four three-hour public meetings were held at the University of Greenland in Nuuk within two calendar months. The developers, London Mining, organised the meetings although a local consultancy firm was hired to chair the meetings.[106] At the meetings, representatives of London Mining and consultants hired by London Mining "summarized several thousand pages of technical reports in a dizzying array of short, colourful PowerPoint presentations."[107] There were difficulties of translation between English, Danish and Greenland, especially as regards complex technical terms. No presenters were opposed to the projects. Only at the end of the meeting (after hours of lectures) were attendees invited to ask questions. However, the questions were not answered but only recorded for (possibly) an answer at the next meeting, some two weeks later.[108]

---

102 Hansen and Johnstone, "Improving Public Participation," 32; Astrid Nonbo Andersen, "Restorative Justice and the Greenlandic Reconciliation Process," *Yearbook of Polar Law* 11 (2019).
103 Hansen and Johnstone, "Improving Public Participation," 32–33.
104 Hansen and Johnstone, "In the Shadow of the Mountain," 485; Mark Nuttall, "The Isukasia Iron Ore Mine Controversy: Extractive Industries and Public Consultation in Greenland," *Nordia Geographical Publications* 41, 5, 23–34.
105 Nuttall, ibid.
106 Ibid., 28.
107 Ibid.
108 Ibid., 29.

This failure to listen had significant consequences for the project design as well as the public attitudes towards it. The environmental impact assessment had been conducted by Danish consultants who made a short trip to the area and concluded that no one lived there and that it was an area of low biodiversity.[109] However, although nobody lived permanently in the area, it is easily reached in summer by boat and is used extensively in the summer for hunting and berry-picking. The local people had a very different story to tell about the richness of the area and its importance to their subsistence activities.[110]

Unfortunately, the failure to hold a genuine dialogue with the people who used the area meant that their expertise regarding the area was not considered. Further, the reliance on these external reports and the ignorance of local use undermined confidence in the whole consultation process and trust in the developers. Such devaluation of the Greenlanders' experience is incongruent with ILO C169's requirement to respect indigenous territory, rights to continue to use lands to which they "traditionally had access for their subsistence and traditional activities" and to decide their own priorities for development of "the lands they occupy or otherwise use."[111]

Aside from the limitations of the public meeting format of consultation – which reaches only a narrow group from local communities and does not give adequate time for people to digest complex technical information – the Isukasia mining information meetings also failed to be effective because they did not communicate the information that was most relevant to the people concerned. It is not enough for a company to provide the information that it thinks is most important or the information that is easy for it to obtain. It must also listen carefully to questions and have available experts who can answer different types of questions. Geologists cannot answer questions about impacts of the project on hunting, job opportunities, or the needs of an immigrant workforce, etc. It is unlikely that a developer can anticipate every question that will arise; but it can anticipate broadly the range of topics and ensure that its panels do not include only natural scientists and public relations personnel. It is likely that it will be necessary to include people familiar with the history of the area and others who understand its social importance, including in some cases spiritual values.

As well as seeking out hard-to-reach groups as mentioned above (proposal 4), genuine information sharing needs considering and integrating knowledge when it is presented in formats with which the developers are unfamiliar, including storytelling and other oral forms of communication.

In order both to engage in a meaningful dialogue with the public and to integrate submissions in a multitude of forms, it is likely that indigenous experts will be needed to interpret and translate between different epistemologies.

Multi-decade extractive projects naturally evolve during their lifetimes, in response to environmental and market changes as well as geological and social

---

109 Ibid.
110 Ibid.
111 ILO C169, articles 7 and 14(1); see also articles 13 and 15.

surprises. Communities need to be involved on a continuous basis. Back in 1995, Judge Weeramantry of the International Court of Justice coined the term, the "continuous environmental impact assessment":

> I wish in this opinion to clarify further the scope and extent of the environmental impact principle in the sense that environmental impact assessment means not merely an assessment prior to the commencement of the project, but a continuing assessment and evaluation as long as the project is in operation. This follows from the fact that EIA is a dynamic principle and is not confined to a pre-project evaluation of possible environmental consequences. As long as a project of some magnitude is in operation, EIA must continue, for every such project can have unexpected consequences; and considerations of prudence would point to the need for continuous monitoring.[112]

In light of the developments in human rights law and the rights of indigenous peoples, today analogous considerations apply to social impact assessments. Communities must be informed at an early stage of project development and should equally have an opportunity to supply their own information to the developers and government. However, this two-way exchange of information must be ongoing through the life of the project and beyond, as long as the project is having an influence on the local community.

Given that at any given time only *some* of the parties elected are in government, it is hard to accept the view of the Greenland government that its decisions reflect *the* voice of the Greenland people. Even accepting that the people of Greenland can delegate their decision-making through the electoral process, the government includes at any given time only some of the parties chosen by the people. Thus it is hard to agree that the consent of the government is the consent of all Greenlanders. Furthermore, even if one accepts the possibility to delegate consent in this manner, the degree to which those decisions are truly "free" is also debatable, given the party disciplinary system and the will to maintain fragile coalitions. Finally, given the deficiencies in the participatory processes, the government cannot be said to be granting truly informed consent – it does not have the full information on which to reach a decision.

The above suggestions will all improve the process of *seeking* consent from communities in Greenland. However, if the test is to be stricter, and the Greenland authorities will *obtain* consent before licensing projects, how can such consent be measured? It has already been argued that the government itself cannot grant or withhold genuine consent on behalf of all Greenlanders in the sense of FPIC. Who does have the power to consent and how can that consent be demonstrated? On highly contested issues that have national implications, such as permitting the extraction and export of uranium, a Greenland-wide, single-issue

---

112 *Case Concerning the Gabčíkovo-Nagymaros Project (Hungary v. Slovakia) (Separate Opinion of Weeramantry), ICJ Reports* 1997, 88, paras 111–112 (citing also *Trail Smelter Arbitration (United States v. Canada)* 1941, RIAA 3, 1905 in support).

referendum is probably the only way to assess the general public view. "Winner-takes-all" referenda are inevitably divisive and do not fit well with traditional indigenous forms of decision-making, which tend to be consensus-based.[113] Given Greenland's relatively strong incorporation of Nordic electoral processes, a referendum on this issue may be the only way to settle the matter at the level of principle. However, for such a referendum to be meaningful, it requires a lengthy, informed, accessible and inclusive debate.

The cost-benefit analysis of each project on its own merits and the terms of licensing agreements to protect the rights and interests of local communities can come later. This needs to be more focussed on those most directly affected. As regards the Kuannersuit project, emphasis should be placed on those living in the locality – in the Kujalleq region of South Greenland. The municipality needs to engage in effective consultations that are distinct from those of the national government to provide the space for a clear local voice (or, more likely, "voices"). In projects that have limited social and environmental impacts beyond the area, there must be strong engagement of local communities. While the Kujalleq region is small by Greenland standards and its municipal government can take the lead, this can hardly be effective for projects in the two very large regions: Avannaata and Sermersooq, each of which exceeds half a million square kilometres. Residents of the East Coast settlements would have reason to be aggrieved if the nearly 17,700 inhabitants of Nuuk (of a total of 21,200 for the entire municipality) could effectively determine the futures of communities in Tasiilaq (680 km away) or Ittoqqortoormiit (1436 km away). In such cases, localised participation processes and, if necessary, evaluation of public attitudes, are essential.

Finally, if consent is to be truly free, then it cannot be necessary for communities to justify the granting or withholding of consent. Such consent does not have to meet Western standards of "rationality" – in other words, an indigenous community's decision does not have to make sense to anyone else. It will no doubt help a community politically to give reasons, but it is not necessary to do so. The freedom to grant consent includes the freedom to withhold it for any reason whatsoever or even no apparent reason at all. It is not reviewable.

Conclusions

This chapter has showed the place and potential for FPIC in Greenland. It began by explaining the general legal and theoretical bases for FPIC and indigenous rights broadly. It examined and analysed the history of Greenland as well as the current government's position regarding indigenous rights. It found that the rejection of indigenous rights in Greenland is not convincing, in particular, in respect of the minorities (possibly distinct indigenous groups) of East and North Greenland. It then examined in more detail the treaty basis for FPIC in international law before proposing some innovations that could enable Greenland to implement it on the ground.

---

113 Watson, *Aboriginal Peoples*, 17.

References

Act on Greenland Self-Government, Act no. 473 of June 12, 2009. Parliament of the Kingdom of Denmark.

Act on Mineral Resources and Mineral Resource Activities of December 7, 2009. Parliament of Greenland.

"African Charter on Human and Peoples' Rights 1981." *International Legal Materials* 21, 58 (1982).

Alfredsson, Gudmundur. "Greenland and the Law of Political Decolonization." *German Yearbook of International Law* 25 (1982): 290–308.

American Convention on Human Rights 1969. OAS Treaty Series No. 36; United Nations Treaty Series 1144, 123.

Anaya, James S. *Indigenous Peoples in International Law*, 2nd edn. Oxford: Oxford University Press, 2004.

Barelli, Mauro. "Development Projects and Indigenous Peoples' Land: Defining the Scope of Free, Prior and Informed Consent." In *Handbook of Indigenous Peoples' Rights*, edited by Corrine Lennox and Damien Short, 69–82. Abingdon: Routledge, 2016.

Beukel, Erik, Frede P. Jensen, and Jens Elo Rytter. *Phasing Out the Colonial Status of Greenland, 1945–1954: A Historical Study.* Copenhagen: Museum Tusculanum Press, University of Copenhagen, 2010.

Burns, Marcelle. "The 'Natural' Law of Nations: Society and the Exclusion of First Nations as Subjects of International Law." In *Indigenous Peoples as Subjects of International Law: We Were Here First*, edited by Irene Watson, 38–53. Abingdon: Routledge, 2018.

Case Concerning the Gabčíkovo-Nagymaros Project (Hungary v. Slovakia) Separate Opinion of Weeramantry. ICJ Reports 1997, 88.

Charter of the United Nations 1945. Adopted June 26, 1945, entered into force October 24, 1945. United Nations Treaty Series 1, XVI.

Convention on Access to Information, Public Participation in Decision-Making and Access to Justice in Environmental Matters 1998. Adopted June 25, 1998, entered into force October 30, 2001. United Nations Treaty Series 2161, 447 (Aarhus Convention).

Convention for the Protection of Human Rights and Fundamental Freedoms 1950. European Treaty Series 005.

Convention on the Elimination of All Forms of Discrimination Against Women 1979. United Nations Treaty Series 1249, 13.

Convention on the Elimination of Racial Discrimination 1965. United Nations Treaty Series 660, 195.

Council Decision 2014/137/EU of March 14, 2014 on relations between the European Union on the one hand, and Greenland and the Kingdom of Denmark on the other, OJ L. 76/1, 2014.

DANIDA. *Strategy for Danish Support to Indigenous Peoples. 2001–2010.* Report. Copenhagen: Ministry of Foreign Affairs of Denmark, 2011.

Expert Mechanism on the Rights of Indigenous Peoples, 2nd Sess., Geneva, 11 August 2009.

"Fields of Responsibility assumed by the Greenland Home Rule Government (I and II) and Greenland Self-Government (III) respectively." Accessed February 7, 2019. www.stm.dk/multimedia/GR_oversigt_sagsomr_270110_UK.pdf

Government of Greenland. *Social Impact Assessment (SIA) Guidelines on the Process and Preparation of the SIA Report for Mineral Projects, Version 2.* Nuuk: Ministry of Industry, Labour and Trade, 2016.

Government of Greenland. *Report to Inatsisartut, the Parliament of Greenland, Concerning Mineral Resources Activities in Greenland*. Nuuk: Greenland Bureau of Minerals and Petroleum, June 2012.

Greenland (Delegation of Denmark). "Statement by Mr. Kuupik Kliest, Premier of Greenland", Delivered to the Expert Mechanism on the Rights of Indigenous Peoples, 2nd Sess., Geneva, August 11, 2009.

Greenland Home Rule Act, Act No. 577, November 29, 1978. Parliament of the Kingdom of Denmark.

Greenland Reconciliation Commission. *Vi Forstår Fortiden; Vi Tager Ansvar for Nutiden; Vi Arbejder for en Bedre Fremtid*. Final Report, December 2017. https://saammaatta.gl//~/media/Forsoningskommission/Diverse/Endelig%20bet%C3%A6nking%20DK.pdf

"Greenland-Danish Self-Government Commission's Report on Self-Government in Greenland: Executive Summary," April 2008. https://naalakkersuisut.gl//~/media/Nanoq/Files/Attached%20Files/Engelske-tekster/Summary%20of%20the%20paper.pdf

Hansen, Anne Merrild and Rachael Lorna Johnstone. "Improving Public Participation in Greenland Extractive Industries." In *Current Developments in Arctic Law: Vol. V*, edited by Kamrul Hossain and Anna Petrétei, 29–33. Rovaniemi: Arctic Law Thematic Network, 2018.

Hansen, Anne Merrild and Rachael Lorna Johnstone. "In the Shadow of the Mountain: Assessing Early Impacts on Community Development from Two Mining Prospects in South Greenland." *The Extractive Industries and Society* 6, 2 (2019): 480–488. doi:10.1016/j.exis.2019.01.012

Hansen, Anne Merrild, Frank Vanclay, Peter Croal, and Anna-Sofie Hurup Skjervedal. "Managing the Social Impacts of the Rapidly-Expanding Extractive Industries in Greenland." *The Extractive Industries and Society* 3, 1 (2016): 25–33. https://doi.org/10.1016/j.exis.2015.11.013

Harper, Kenn. *Minik: The New York Eskimo*. Hanover NH: Steer Forth Press, 2017.

Holm, Gustav, Thalbitzer, William, and Amdrup, Georg Carl. *The Ammassalik Eskimo: Contributions to the Ethnology of the East Greenland Natives* (English translation). Copenhagen: Bianco Luno, 1914.

ILO Convention 169 (1989). "Indigenous and Tribal Peoples Convention. Adopted 27 June 1989, entered into force 5 September 1991." *International Legal Materials* 28, 1382.

ILO. "Normlex: Ratifications of C169." Accessed September 26, 2019. https://www.ilo.org/dyn/normlex/en/f?p=1000:11300:0::NO:11300:P11300_INSTRUMENT_ID:312314

International Covenant on Civil and Political Rights 1966. United Nations Treaty Series 999, 171.

International Covenant on Economic, Social and Cultural Rights 1966. United Nations Treaty Series 993, 3.

Kleist, Kuupik. Statement delivered to the Expert Mechanism on the Rights of Indigenous Peoples, 2nd Session, Geneva, 11 August 2009, 2.

Kleist, Mininnguaq. "En etisk-politisk analyse af dokumenterne angående Grønlands indlemmelse I Danmark." In *Kilder til Færøernes og Grønlands historie*, edited by Hallbera West and Maria Amalia Heinesen, 129–183. Thorshavn: Føroya Fróðskaparfelag, 2004.

Kleist, Mininnguaq. "Greenland's Self-Government." In *Polar Law Textbook*, edited by Natalia Loukacheva, 171–198. Copenhagen: Nordic Council of Ministers, 2011.

Länsman, Ilmari et al. v. Finland, Human Rights Committee, Communication no. 511/1992, November 8, 1994. UN Doc. CCPR/C/52/D/511/1992.

Legal Status of Eastern Greenland (Denmark v. Norway), 1933 P.C.I.J. (ser. A/B) No. 53 (Apr. 5).

Mahuika et al.*v*. New Zealand, Human Rights Committee Communication no. 547/1993, November 15, 2000. UN Doc. CCPR/C/70/D/547/1933.

Martínez Cobo, Jóse R., UN Special Rapporteur. *Study of the Problem of Discrimination against Indigenous Populations*. Report. New York: United Nations, 1986. UN Doc. E/CN.4/Sub.2/1986/7 Add. 4.

Mazzi, Mauro. *Aurora borealis: Diritto polare e comparazione giuridica*. Bologna: Filo Diritto Editore, 2014.

Newcomb, Steven. "Domination in Relation to Indigenous ('Dominated') Peoples in International Law." In *Indigenous Peoples as Subjects of International Law: We Were Here First*, edited by Irene Watson, 18–37. Abingdon: Routledge, 2018.

Ngiviu, Terto. "The Inughuit of Northwest Greenland: An Unacknowledged Indigenous People." *Yearbook of Polar Law* 6 (2014): 142–161.

Nonbo Andersen, Astrid. "The Reparations Movement in the United States Virgin Islands." *The Journal of African American History* 103, 1–2 (2018): 104–132. doi:10.1086/696335

Nonbo Andersen, Astrid. "Restorative Justice and the Greenlandic Reconciliation Process." *Yearbook of Polar Law* 11 (2019).

Nuttall, Mark. "The Isukasia Iron Ore Mine Controversy: Extractive Industries and Public Consultation in Greenland." *Nordia Geographical Publications* 41, 5 (2012): 23–34.

Ominayak and the Lubicon Lake Band v. Canada, Human Rights Committee, Communication no. 167/1984. May 10, 1990. UN Doc. CCPR/C/38/D/167/1984.

Patton, Paul. "Philosophical Justifications for Indigenous Rights." In *Handbook of Indigenous Peoples' Rights*, edited by Corrine Lennox and Damien Short, 13–23. Abingdon: Routledge, 2016.

Pew Research Center. "Religion and Public Life, Table: 'Christian Population as Percentages of Total Population by Country.'" December 19, 2011. www.pewforum.org/2011/12/19/table-christian-population-as-percentages-of-total-population-by-country/

Poma Poma v. Peru, Human Rights Committee, Communication No. 1457/2006. March 27, 2009. UN Doc. CCPR/C/95/D/1457/2006.

"Referendums on the European Union." House of Commons Briefing Paper 7570, April 22, 2016.

Report of the Committee Set Up to Examine the Representation Alleging Non-Observance by Denmark of the Indigenous and Tribal Peoples Convention, 1989 (No. 169), Made Under Article 24 of the ILO Constitution by the National Confederation of Trade Unions of Greenland (Sulinermik Inuussutissarsiuteqartut Kattuffiat–SIK) (*SIK v. Denmark*), GB.277/18/3; GB.280/18/5.

Rud, Søren. *Colonialism in Greenland: Tradition, Governance and Legacy*. Cham, Switzerland: Palgrave Macmillan, 2017.

Saramaka People v. Suriname, Case of the, Preliminary Objections, Merits, Reparation and Costs. Petition 12338, Inter-American Court of Human Rights Series C No 172, November 28, 2007.

Siegstad, Mia Olsen and Mads Fægteborg. *"Ajorpoq" – vi Får Ingen Svar! Bedre Borgerinddragelse Om Kuannersuit*. Inuit Circumpolar Council, Greenland, December 2015. http://naalakkersuisut.gl/~/media/Nanoq/Files/Attached%20Files/Formandens%20Departement/Puljemidler/Ajorpoq%20Kuannersuit.pdf

Statute of the International Court of Justice 1945. Adopted June 26, 1945, entered into force October 24, 1945. *Bevans* 3, 1179; *Stat.* 59, 1031; Treaty Series 993.

Staur, Carsten. Statement by H.E. Ambassador Carsten Staur, 11th Session of the UN Permanent Forum on Indigenous Issues, Statement by Denmark and Greenland on agenda item 9, New York, May 17, 2012.

Strandsbjerg, Jeppe. "Making Sense of Contemporary Greenland: Indigeneity, Resources and Sovereignty." In *Polar Geopolitics: Knowledges, Resources and Legal Regimes*, edited by Richard C. Powell and Klaus Dodds, 259–276. Cheltenham: Edward Elgar, 2014.

Strøm Tejsen, Aago V. "The History of the Royal Greenland Trade Department." *Polar Record* 18, 116 (1977): 451–474.

Tauli-Corpuz, Victoria, UN Special Rapporteur on the Rights of Indigenous Peoples. *Report of the Special Rapporteur of the Human Rights Council on the rights of indigenous peoples: conservation and Indigenous Peoples' rights*. UN Doc. A/71/229. July 29, 2016.

Trail Smelter Arbitration (*United States v. Canada*) 1941, RIAA 3, 1905.

Treaty amending, with regard to Greenland, the Treaties establishing the European Communities, OJ No I. 29/1, 1985.

UN Bibliographic Information System. "Voting Records." Accessed March 12, 2019. http://unbisnet.un.org:8080/ipac20/ipac.jsp?profile=voting&menu=search

UN Committee on Economic, Social and Cultural Rights. Concluding Observations on the Combined Second to Fourth Reports of Guyana. UN Doc. E/C.12/GUY/CO/2–4. October 28, 2015.

UN Committee on Economic, Social and Cultural Rights. Concluding Observations on the Combined Fifth and Sixth Reports of the Philippines. UN Doc. E/C.12/PHL/CO/5–6. October 26, 2016.

UN Committee on Economic, Social and Cultural Rights. Concluding Observations on the Fifth Periodic Report of Denmark. UN Doc. E/C.12/DNK/CO/. June 6, 2013.

UN Committee on Economic, Social and Cultural Rights. Concluding Observations on the Fourth Periodic Report of Colombia. UN Doc. E/C.12/1/Add.74. December 6, 2001.

UN Committee on Economic, Social and Cultural Rights. Concluding Observations on the Sixth Periodic Report of Canada. UN Doc. E/C.12/CAN/CO/6. March 23, 2016.

UN Committee on Economic, Social and Cultural Rights. Concluding Observations on the Sixth Periodic Report of Finland. UN Doc. E/C.12/FIN/CO/6. November 28, 2014.

UN Committee on Economic, Social and Cultural Rights. Concluding Observations on the Sixth Periodic Report of Sweden. UN Doc. E/C.12/SWE/CO/6. July 14, 2016.

UN Committee on Economic, Social and Cultural Rights. General Comment No. 21, Right of Everyone to Take Part tn Cultural Life (art. 15, para. 1 (a), of the International Covenant on Economic, Social and Cultural Rights). UN Doc. E/C.12/GC/21. December 21, 2009.

UN Committee on the Elimination of Discrimination Against Women. Concluding Observations on the Combined Eighth and Ninth Periodic Reports of Ecuador. UN Doc. CEDAW/C/ECU/CO/8–9. March 11, 2015.

UN Committee on the Elimination of Discrimination Against Women. Report of the Inquiry Concerning Canada. UN Doc. CEDAW/C/OP.8/CAN/1. March 30, 2015.

UN Committee on the Elimination of Racial Discrimination. Concluding Comments of the Committee on the Elimination of Racial Discrimination: Denmark. UN Doc. CERD/C/60/CO/5. May 21, 2002.

UN Committee on the Elimination of Racial Discrimination. Concluding Comments of the Committee on the Elimination of Racial Discrimination: Denmark. UN Doc. CERD/C/DNK/CO/18–19. September 20, 2010.

UN Committee on the Elimination of Racial Discrimination. Concluding Comments on the State Report of Norway. UN Doc. CERD/C/NOR/CO/21–22. September 25, 2015.

UN Committee on the Elimination of Racial Discrimination. Concluding Comments on the State Report of United States of America. UN Doc. CERD/C/USA/CO/6. May 8, 2008.

UN Committee on the Elimination of Racial Discrimination. General Recommendation XXIII on the Rights of Indigenous Peoples. UN Doc. A/52/18, annex V. September 26, 1997.

UN Committee on the Elimination of Racial Discrimination. General Recommendation XXXII on the Meaning and Scope of Special Measures in the International Convention on the Elimination of Racial Discrimination. UN Doc. CERD/C/GC/32. September 24, 2009.

UN General Assembly. Cessation of the Transmission of Information under Article 73 e of the Charter in Respect of Greenland. UNGA Res 849 (IX). November 22, 1954.

UN General Assembly. Declaration on Principles of International Law Concerning Friendly Relations and Co-operation among States in Accordance with the Charter of the United Nations. UNGA Res 2625(XXV). October 24, 1970.

UN General Assembly. Declaration on the Granting of Independence to Colonial Countries and Peoples. UNGA Res 1514 (XV). December 14, 1960.

UN General Assembly. Declaration on the Rights of Indigenous Peoples. UNGA Res 61/295. September 13, 2007 (UNDRIP).

UN General Assembly. Declaration on the Rights of Peasants and Other People Working in Rural Areas. UNGA Res 73/165. December 17, 2018.

UN General Assembly. Resolution Defining the Three Options for Self-Determination. UNGA Res 1541 (XV). December 15, 1960.

UN Human Rights Committee. Concluding Observations on the Second Report of Namibia. UN Doc. CCPR/C/NAM/CO/2. April 22, 2016.

UN Human Rights Committee. Concluding Observations on the Sixth Periodic Report of Denmark. UN Doc. CCPR/C/DNK/CO/5. December 16, 2008.

UN Human Rights Committee. Concluding Observations on the Sixth Report of Sweden. UN Doc. CCPR/C/SWE/CO/7. April 28, 2016.

UN Human Rights Council Working Group on Universal Periodic Review. Canada. UN Doc. A/HRC/11/17. May 25, 2009.

UN World Conference on Indigenous Peoples. Outcome Document of the High-Level Plenary Meeting of the General Assembly Known As the World Conference on Indigenous Peoples. UN Doc. A/RES/69/2. September 25, 2014.

Vestergaard, Cindy and Gry Thomasen. *Governing Uranium in the Danish Realm*. Danish Institute for International Studies, Research Report 2015: 17. January 18, 2016. https://www.diis.dk/en/research/governing-uranium-in-the-realm

Vestergaard, Cindy. "The European Union, Its Overseas Territories, and Non-Proliferation: The Case of Arctic Yellowcake." SIPRI, Paper no. 25. January 2013. https://www.sipri.org/publications/2013/eu-non-proliferation-papers/european-union-its-overseas-territories-and-non-proliferation-case-arctic-yellowcake

Vienna Convention on the Law of Treaties 1969. Adopted May 25, 1969, entered into force January 27, 1980. United Nations Treaty Series 1155, UNTS 331.

Watson, Irene and Sharon Venne. "Talking up Indigenous Peoples' Original Intent in a Space Dominated by State Interventions." In *Indigenous Rights in the Age of the UN Declaration*, edited by Elvira Pulitano, 87–107. Cambridge: Cambridge University Press, 2012.

Watson, Irene. *Aboriginal Peoples, Colonialism and International Law: Raw Law*. Abingdon: Routledge, 2016.

4 Meaningful stakeholder engagement as an aspect of risk-based due diligence between the economy, politics and law

The constitutive role of the business and human rights regime

Karin Buhmann[1]

1 Introduction

In recent years the concept and regulatory implications of corporate social responsibility (CSR) have changed from being mainly an issue of private self-regulation to becoming increasingly institutionalised, with normative guidance based on specific norms of conduct grounded in international law. Such processes of institutionalisation of norms issued by public regulators are responses to policy concerns and testify to an increasing political will at various levels of governance to issue normative directives addressing transnational business operations beyond the territorial reach of nation states' jurisdictions. The endorsement in 2011 by the United Nations (UN) Human Rights Council of the UN Guiding Principles on Business and Human Rights[2] (UNGPs) and the Council's unanimous "welcoming" in 2008 of the predecessor of the UNGPs, the UN Protect, Respect and Remedy Framework[3] ("UN Framework") underscore that

---

1 This chapter draws on research made possible through several grants held by the author: grant (2015) from the Danish Agency for Science and Higher Education (DAFSHE) with the University of the Arctic (UArctic) for establishing the interdisciplinary Thematic Network on Arctic Sustainability and Social Responsibility; NOS-HS grant (2017) for the project "Best practice for Impact Assessment of infrastructure projects in the Nordic Arctic: Popular participation and Local Needs, Concerns and Benefits; DAFSHE grant (2017) for the project "Natural Resources, Risk-Based Due Diligence, Stakeholder Engagement and Public Participation in Decision-making: Building Comparative Arctic-Global South Sustainability Research"; and grant No. 0602–08420B from the Danish Research Council for Independent Research (Social Sciences) project "The Legal Character of CSR (Corporate Social Responsibility): Reflections between CSR and Public International Law, and Implications for Corporate Regulation."
2 John Ruggie, *Guiding Principles on Business and Human Rights: Implementing the United Nations "Protect, Respect and Remedy" Framework*, UN Doc. A/HRC/17/31, March 21, 2011 (UNGPs).
3 John Ruggie, *Protect, Respect and Remedy: a Framework for Business and Human Rights. Report of the Special Representative on Human Rights, Transnational Corporations and Other Business Enterprises*, UN Doc. A/HRC/8/5, April 7, 2008 (UN Framework).

tendency. Both are based on three pillars: the State Duty to Protect, the Corporate Responsibility to Respect, and Access to Remedy for violations. Between them, the UNGPs and the UN Framework clarify that in addition to the obligation of states to protect human rights against abuse caused by companies, companies of all types and sizes have a responsibility to respect human rights. That responsibility requires companies to comply with applicable national law and to self-regulate to fill governance gaps between national law and international law where the former is deficient, either in the letter of the law or in implementation. Both state and non-state actors must also ensure that victims have access to remedies. Business organisations should conduct human rights due diligence to identify, prevent and remedy adverse human rights impact, while states should provide guidance for businesses in that respect. With an emphasis on the risk caused by the company to society (rather than risk to the company), this approach has come to be adopted by several other international, regional and national governance frameworks for business conduct[4] and is now often referred to as "risk-based due diligence," as further explained below.

In constructing the corporate responsibility to respect, the 2008 UN Framework referred explicitly to the concept of the social licence to operate. The text applied the social licence to operate as an argument for responsible business conduct, connecting to social expectations and policy and bridging to public regulation.[5] The connection highlighted the economic implications for a company or sector that flow from society's views of its actions and impact, and the fact that social actors often resort to non-judicial sanctions that can have significant implications for a company, for example due to reduced orders or investment. The social licence to operate argument formed part of a larger argumentation strategy to create political support for the UN Framework and UNGPs, which has had a bearing on how public regulators seek to regulate business conduct beyond human rights to broader CSR policy concerns. The UNGPs have influenced other international instruments related to sustainability governance, in particular, OECD's Guidelines for Multinational Enterprises (MNEs) as well as French, Dutch, British and Australian law on due diligence in general or for particular problems, and Chinese guidance for minerals supply chains and investment in the mining sector. Risk-based due diligence as set out by the UNGPs and OECD's Guidelines stresses the value of stakeholder engagement as a means to identify proactively and manage adverse impacts. Guidance developed by the OECD in regard to the extractive sector also emphasises stakeholder engagement as a modality to enhance the positive impacts that may be generated by business activity.[6] For example, OECD's Guidelines

---

4 See Karin Buhmann, "Business and Human Rights: Understanding the UN Guiding Principles from the Perspective of Transnational Business Governance Interactions," *Transnational Legal Theory* 6, 1 (2015): 399–434, https://doi.org/10.1080/20414005.2015.1073516 (for details).
5 UN Framework, para. 54.
6 OECD, *Due Diligence Guidance for Responsible Business Conduct* (Paris: OECD, 2018) https://www.oecd.org/investment/due-diligence-guidance-for-responsible-business-conduct.htm

include provisions on actions that companies should take to contribute to employment of locally-based labour and to capacity building.

The UN Framework and UNGPs apply globally. OECD's Guidelines apply to companies that operate in or out of adhering states. Given that the majority of the world's MNEs are registered in OECD states, the Guidelines are therefore of relevance to such companies for their operation. By implication, they are also of relevance to many companies operating in the extractives sector in the Arctic, because the company's home or host state adheres to the Guidelines.

This contribution discusses the role that the risk-based due diligence approach to human rights plays as normative guidance for companies in regard to participation, having particular regard to the access of affected stakeholders to decision-making relating to the communities in which they live, and drawing out some implications for companies in the extractives sector. Section 2 introduces the Business and Human Rights regime as a response to political concerns with societal impacts of economic activities. Section 3 explains the objective of risk-based due diligence, while section 4 elaborates on meaningful stakeholder consultation as an aspect of this due diligence approach. Section 5 introduces some guidance related to due diligence and participation, based on statements ("jurisprudence") of OECD National Contact Points (NCPs), which are the remedial institutions for OECD's Guidelines and de facto also for the UNGPs. Finally, Section 6 concludes and draws up implications for companies involved in extractives activities in the Arctic.

2 Business and human rights: an emergent legal regime responding to political concerns with societal impacts of economic activities

During the 1990s several incidents relating to natural resource extraction (e.g. adverse social and environmental impacts resulting from oil extraction in the Niger Delta) and production processes in value chains (e.g. for apparel) contributed to political and civil society concern with the potential of business to cause societal harm. At the time, this was mainly phrased as issues of CSR or corporate responsibilities to adopt a triple bottom line entailing "people, planet, and profits." Many of the impacts on local communities and workers essentially constituted human rights infringements. In addition to infringements on rights to land, culture, rights at work and an adequate standard of living, the right to participation in processes of decision-making relating to projects impacting lands and communities was also at stake.

Following in the steps of various private and civil society-based initiatives to help firms identify and manage their adverse impacts, the UN initiated steps towards clarifying the social responsibilities of companies and developing guidance. A process undertaken between 2005 and 2011 resulted in the evolution of a theory-based set of recommendations that can be described as an emergent autonomous regime within the greater international law regime. Set apart from the conventional state-centrist regime of international human rights law, the Business & Human Rights (sometimes abbreviated BHR) regime formally recognises that business organisations as well as states have responsibilities in regard to standards of conduct developed under international law. So far this has occurred on a soft law (i.e. non-binding or guiding) basis at the international level (in contrast to the legally binding – hard law – nature of Conventions), but statutory requirements introduced by various countries are turning the emergent regime into binding national law (hard law). The adoption of the UN Framework and subsequently of the UNGPs represent a major shift in the idea of what types of actors carry responsibilities for human rights. The shift brought about the emergence of a new legal regime, which recognises businesses as having explicit responsibilities under international law, despite their status as so-called for-profit non-state actors. Even if those responsibilities are currently framed in policy and soft law documents, they refer explicitly to international legal standards in international human rights and labour instruments, which were originally developed and adopted as obligations for states. The recognition of businesses as bearers of international responsibilities, even on a soft law (guiding) basis, is a major change in the way that bearers of international obligations are perceived. However, as the instruments set out human rights standards of conduct for states, turning this into business conduct often requires a sort of "translation" into the operational business context.[7]

An international regime may be defined as a set of implicit or explicit principles, norms, rules, and decision-making procedures around which actor expectations converge.[8] Norms refer to standards of conduct in terms of rights and obligations, whereas rules and procedures are instructions for action and practices of making and realising collective choices.[9] In international relations studies, regimes are forms of cooperation that exist despite the restrictions that they place on involved actors.[10] In the past, treaty-related normative developments such as the prevention of nuclear proliferation have been defined as emergent autonomous regimes.[11] Convergence on a regime is attractive despite such restrictions because it offers order in place of anarchy.[12] The evolution of the conventional state-centrist human rights regime, which evolved based on ethics, political philosophy and national law and which became codified in international law during the twentieth century, is a case in point. This human rights regime limits each state's power vis-à-vis individuals within its jurisdiction, but on balance, the international human rights regime contributes to global order by reducing abuse of power that threatens peace and co-existence.

---

7 See also, Monash University, *Human Rights Translated 2.0: a Business Reference Guide* (Geneva: OHCHR, 2017), https://www.ohchr.org/documents/publications/HRT_2_0_EN.pdf
8 Stephen D. Krasner, "Structural Causes and Regime Consequences: Regimes as Intervening Variables," *International Organization* 36, 2 (1982): 185–205, 206, https://doi.org/10.1017/s0020818300018920
9 Ibid.
10 Nina Seppala, "Business and the International Human Rights Regime: A Comparison of UN Initiatives," *Journal of Business Ethics* 87, S2 (2009): 401–417, https://doi.org/10.1007/s10551-009-0297-4
11 Andreas Hasenclever, Peter Mayer, and Volker Rittberger, *Theories of International Regimes* (Cambridge: Cambridge University Press, 1997), 9 (referring to the Treaty on the Non-Proliferation of Nuclear Weapons).
12 Seppala, "Business and the International Human Rights Regime."

Like studies of international law and international relations in general, regime theory takes a state-centric point of departure. It may be expanded to issue-specific cooperation involving non-state actors where the extension to such actors is generated by the difference between the existing lack of order and the order offered by the regime.[13] The normative convergence that evolved with the broad support from non-state actors, states and international organisations for the UN Framework and UNGPs respectively represents an example of such an emergent regime. The emergent Business & Human Rights regime breaks off from conventional state-centrist human rights by explicitly recognising pro-profit non-state actors as bearers of specifically defined responsibilities.

Through its support for the UN Framework and UNGPs, the UN Human Rights Council has provided normative directives for both states and businesses to prevent, manage and remedy adverse impacts on human rights caused by businesses. The UN Framework, which the Human Rights Council adopted in 2008, sets out the theory-basis and defines the basic elements of the state duty to protect against human rights abuse caused by third parties, the corporate responsibility to respect human rights, and access for victims to remedy. At only 30 pages, the relative brevity of the UN Framework for treating a complex topic was due to formal UN requirements. Similar to some other key UN human rights texts, such as the Universal Declaration on Human Rights (UDHR), the brevity invites elaboration. Adopted in 2011, the UNGPs were developed to spell out the general normative directives of the UN Framework into operational steps. Responding to a request from the Human Rights Council for an operationalisation of the UN Framework, the UNGPs explain how states and businesses should act in order to honour their legal obligations and, in the case of businesses, also social expectations with regard to adverse human rights impacts caused by businesses. Like the UN Framework, the UNGPs are limited to a 30-page document. In the case of both, a series of much more extensive sub-reports and other UN documents add additional information. A series of guidance texts on due diligence issued by the OECD add further details.

With several of the UNGPs relating to management processes, the UN Framework argues the need for business enterprises to understand human rights and undertake activities to manage their harmful impacts partly with reference to the social licence to operate.[14] Operationalising the UN Framework, the UNGPs thereby also implicitly build on this. Originating in the extractives field as an issue of considerable practical relevance to business operations that came to be theorised in management literature,[15] the idea of the social licence to operate has spread to

---

13 Ibid.
14 UN Framework, paras 54–55.
15 Jason Prno and D. Scott Slocombe, "Exploring the Origins of 'Social License to Operate' in the Mining Sector: Perspectives from Governance and Sustainability Theories," *Resources Policy* 37, 3 (2012): 346–357, https://doi.org/10.1016/j.resourpol.2012.04.002; John R. Owen and Deanna Kemp, "Social Licence and Mining: a Critical Perspective," *Resources Policy* 38, 1 (2012): 29–35; Jacqueline L. Nelsen, "Social Licence to Operate," *International Journal of Mining, Reclamation and Environment* 20, 3 (2006): 161–162, https://doi.org/10.1080/17480930600804182

corporate sustainability and risk-management practices and theory more generally. In referencing the social licence to operate, the UN Framework seeks to stimulate firms' appreciation of the economic and societal costs associated with business-related human rights abuse. The UN Framework report and some of its extensive supporting studies make the implications for companies tangible: companies may suffer economically, for example through loss of customers or reduced investments and access to capital, if they cause adverse social impacts.[16] To prevent this, the UN Framework argues that they should have policies and adopt processes to meet their responsibility to respect, including through impact assessments and adequate follow-up.[17] Risk-based due diligence is a management process for that purpose. The UNGPs operationalise this through their extensive guidance for how companies should develop and apply due diligence to identify and manage actual or potential adverse human rights impacts.[18]

Neither the UN Framework nor UNGPs establish new human rights. Rather, they explain the implications for businesses and governments of already existing human rights, with a particular focus on adverse business impacts. Both documents refer to the International Bill of Human Rights and the International Labour Organisation (ILO)'s fundamental labour conventions as the minimum standards that should inform business responsibilities for human rights. The former comprises the UDHR,[19] the International Covenant on Economic, Social and Cultural Rights (ICESCR)[20] and the International Covenant on Civil and Political Rights (ICCPR).[21] The latter comprises eight ILO conventions on the abolition and elimination of slavery, forced labour and child labour, on the protection of labour unions and the right to organise and engage in collective negotiation, and on freedom from discrimination in the workplace. As those human rights instruments are only the minimum baseline, according to the UN Framework and UNGPs, companies may need to observe other instruments or standards as well, such as the ILO Convention No. 169 on Indigenous and Tribal Peoples (1989) (ILO C169),[22] and the UN Declaration on the Rights of Indigenous Peoples (2007) (UNDRIP),[23] which incorporate the principle of Free, Prior and Informed Consent (FPIC).[24]

---

16 Compare David B. Spence, "Corporate Social Responsibility in the Oil and Gas Industry: The Importance of Reputational Risk," *Chicago-Kent Law Review* 86, 1 (2011): 59–85.
17 UN Framework, paras 60–64.
18 See UNGPs 15, 17–22 and commentaries.
19 UN General Assembly, Universal Declaration of Human Rights, UNGA Res A/RES/217(III), December 10, 1948.
20 International Covenant on Economic, Social and Cultural Rights 1966 (ICESCR).
21 International Covenant on Civil and Political Rights 1966 (ICCPR).
22 Indigenous and Tribal Peoples Convention 1989, ILO Convention 169, 1989.
23 UN General Assembly, Declaration on the Rights of Indigenous Peoples, UNGA Res 61/295, September 13, 2007.
24 See also Wilson, this volume; and Johnstone, this volume (on free, prior and informed consent).

84 *Karin Buhmann*

3 Risk-based due diligence

The UN Framework introduced a new conceptual terminology for how companies should act in order to identify and manage adverse human rights impacts: human rights due diligence. A standard of conduct,[25] human rights due diligence is concerned with reducing and managing risks caused *by* a company *to* society. The direction of this due diligence process differs from that which informs the financial or legal liability due diligence concept that is well-known to managers, corporate lawyers and accountants. Conventional due diligence is focused on reducing and managing risks *to* the company *by* factors in society, for example in the context of corporate mergers or acquisitions.

Dubbed "risk-based due diligence" because of the direction of the process, the novel due diligence approach has been adopted by several other transnational business governance instruments.[26] Perhaps the most wide-reaching of these are the OECD Guidelines for Multinational Enterprises, which since their 2011 revision have applied the approach to most of the issue areas covered by the Guidelines (including human rights, labour, environment, anti-corruption, and consumer concerns).[27] The OECD Guidelines apply the term "risk-based due diligence" as they expand requirements on due diligence to identify and manage adverse impacts from human rights to include also environment, labour and industry issues, consumer concerns and some other topics. Implementation of the Guidelines is supported by detailed sectoral due diligence guidance instruments issued by the OECD based on the Guidelines as well as a general due diligence guidance issued in 2018.[28] The risk-based due diligence approach has also been adopted by regional instruments, such as the EU's Conflict-Minerals Regulation[29] (as a process to be undertaken) and the Non-Financial Reporting Directive[30] (as a process to be reported on). At the national level, uptake of risk-based due diligence is on

25 See John Ruggie and John F. Sherman III, "The Concept of 'Due Diligence' in the UN Guiding Principles on Business and Human Rights: A Reply to Jonathan Bonnitcha and Robert McCorquodale," *European Journal of International Law* 28, 3 (2017): 921–928 (on human rights due diligence as a standard of conduct rather than a standard of result).
26 Karin Buhmann, "Business and Human Rights."
27 OECD, *OECD Guidelines for Multinational Enterprises*, 2011 edition (Paris: OECD Publishing, 2011).
28 In addition to a general due diligence guidance for all sectors, adopted in 2018, the OECD has issued sector guidance for the financial sector, responsible supply chains for textiles and apparel, minerals from high risk and conflict affected areas, agricultural products, and for meaningful stakeholder engagement in the extractive sector. See OECD, *Due Diligence Guidance for Responsible Business Conduct*.
29 EU Regulation 2017/821 of the European Parliament and of the Council of 17 May 2017 laying down supply chain due diligence obligations for Union importers of tin, tantalum and tungsten, their ores, and gold originating from conflict-affected and high-risk areas (2017) OJ 2017 L130/1.
30 EU Directive 2014/95/EU of the European Parliament and of the Council of 22 October 2015 amending Directive 2013/34/EU as regards disclosure of non-financial and diversity information by certain large undertakings and groups (2014) OJ 2014 L330/1.

the rise and has so far been integrated as a standard of conduct in the UK and Australian Modern Slavery acts, a Dutch act on child labour due diligence, and the French *loi de vigilence* (a statute requiring risk-based due diligence regardless of sector). Guidelines issued by the Chinese business organisation for the mining and minerals sectors, applying to mining sector investment and minerals supply chains, also embrace risk-based due diligence as a process to be undertaken.[31] Given China's economic and political interest in Arctic sources of minerals, this fact is not without relevance, even if the Chinese guidelines are primarily adopted with "conflict minerals" mined or traded out of the Central African region in mind.[32]

Whereas conventional due diligence is static in the sense that once a decision is made, any resulting risk or liability is also accepted, the risk-based due diligence process should be ongoing until the very end of an activity. Although the UNGPs recognise that prioritisation may be necessary when a company is unable to address all problems at once, ideally no harm (whether potential or actual) should arise.

Risk-based due diligence is a complex process involving a number of steps that are connected by the objective of identifying, preventing, mitigating and remedying potential or actual harms, and accounting for the actions and decisions made by the company as part of that process. In line with the UN Framework's focus on avoiding harm caused by companies, risk-based due diligence entails a strong preventive aspect. Whereas lawyers may tend to emphasise ex-post facts such as harm caused, and ex-ante accountability-related actions such as monitoring, enforcing, sanctioning, risk-based due diligence calls on managers to engage in a series of steps to prevent proactively harm from occurring. The provision of access to remedy is meant to ensure that remedy is available when rights are perceived to be infringed upon nevertheless. Along with the communicative aspect of accounting for decisions and actions taken, access to remedy is an ex-post element of the corporate responsibility to respect in that these actions occur after harm has occurred, and after the decisions and actions to identify and manage risks or actual impacts have taken place.

A UN-issued interpretive guide on the corporate responsibility to respect human rights[33] notes that the human rights due diligence process should, for example, uncover risks of non-legal as well as legal complicity and generate

---

31 China Chamber of Commerce of Metals, Minerals & Chemicals, *Guidelines for Social Responsibility in Outbound Mining Investment* (Beijing: CCCMC, 2014), https://cdn.globalwitness.org/archive/files/library/cccmc%20guidelines%20for%20social%20resposibility%20in%20outbound%20mining%20investments%20oct%202014%20ch-en.pdf; China Chamber of Commerce of Metals, Minerals & Chemicals, *Chinese Due Diligence Guidelines for Responsible Mineral Supply Chains* (Beijing: CCCMC, 2015), https://mneguidelines.oecd.org/chinese-due-diligence-guidelines-for-responsible-mineral-supply-chains.htm
32 Buhmann, Karin, "Chinese Mineral Sourcing Interests and Greenland's Potential as a Source of 'Conflict-Free' Minerals," *Arctic Yearbook* 6/7 (2018), https://arcticyearbook.com/arctic-yearbook/2018
33 UN Office of the High Commissioner for Human Rights, *The Corporate Responsibility to Respect Human Rights: An Interpretive Guide*, UN Doc. HR/PUB/12/02, 2012, 6, www.ohchr.org/Documents/Publications/HR.PUB.12.2_En.pdf

appropriate responses. Adequate responses vary according to whether there is a risk that adverse impact may occur, or whether actual impact has occurred. Actual impact requires remediation. Potential impact requires action to prevent a human rights risk from materialising, or at least to mitigate (reduce) as far as possible the extent to which it may do so. Where some residual impact on human rights is unavoidable, this in turn requires remediation.[34]

By reducing its harmful social impact, a company may also reduce the risk to itself that may flow from reputational damage or economic sanctions by stakeholders. Thus, a well-performed human rights due diligence process may also serve as a risk management tool for the company in reducing risks of reputational damage and potential economic loss,[35] thereby protecting its social licence to operate.

Stakeholder engagement is a key step in risk-based due diligence. It connects both to the proactive and reactive elements of the concept: it should take place to help identify potential or actual harm; and to ensure adequate remedy where harm does occur. Meaningful engagement with potential or actual victims is a core source of information for enterprises to understand about their impact and its implications for those potentially or actually affected. Without such understanding, the enterprise may overlook important information to allow it to identify, prevent, mitigate, remedy and account for its impacts. The UN Framework, UNGPs, and OECD Guidelines apply the terms "affected stakeholders." Obviously, many "affected stakeholders" are also rights-holders. There are no indications that the term "affected stakeholders" was adopted to exclude or overlook the rights-holder status of victims. Rather, the adopted language appears to be selected to stay in line with the general stakeholder-orientation that permeates much management literature related to the social responsibilities of corporations. Applying well-known language ("stakeholders") and qualifying it ("affected") enables managers, who are the ones to adopt and exercise risk-based due diligence, to relate to the term in a more direct manner than they might have to the "rights-holders" term.[36] The UNGPs recommend that companies work with human rights experts, for example on the impact assessment process.[37] Doing so would support a process of identifying the rights of "affected stakeholders."

The UNGPs explain that to enable business enterprises to assess their human rights impacts accurately, they should seek to understand the concerns of potentially affected stakeholders by consulting them directly in a manner that takes into account language and other potential barriers to effective engagement. In situations

---

34 See also, ibid., 19.
35 See also, UN Human Rights Council, "Clarifying the Concepts of 'Sphere of Influence' and 'Complicity,'" UN Doc. A/HRC/8/16, May 15, 2008 (authored as a companion report to the UN Framework report).
36 See Karin Buhmann, *Changing Sustainability Norms through Communicative Processes: The Emergence of the Business & Human Rights Regime as Transnational Law* (Cheltenham: Edward Elgar, 2017) (for a general analysis of strategic communication as part of the construction of the UN Framework and UNGPs).
37 UNGPs, Principle 18.

where such consultation is not possible, business enterprises should consider reasonable alternatives such as consulting credible, independent expert resources, including human rights defenders and others from civil society. Hence, the process of risk-identification through stakeholder engagement should involve "meaningful" consultation with affected stakeholders.[38] This point connects directly to participation, not least to participation in decision-making relating to one's life-situation, as discussed in the following section.

4 Participation as an aspect of risk-based due diligence

Public participation in decision-making is an integrated element in international human rights law. Recent decades have seen an increasing emphasis on the fact that public participation in decision-making on issues affecting one's own life and the community in which one lives is not only a matter of regular, free elections of policy-makers, but also a matter of involvement in decision-processes at the local level.[39] The shift to emphasise the dual aspects has been clear if not much debated in the literature at least since the 1992 Rio Declaration and Agenda 21[40] and the 1993 Vienna Declaration and Programme of Action.[41] The former is the end document from the global summit on sustainable development; the latter a lead policy document emerging from a global summit on human rights. Both summits were organised by the UN and formed part of a series of global high-level meetings that took place during the 1990s on a range of environmental and social issues related to the UN's overall objectives. The participative aspects of the Rio Declaration have been elaborated through the Aarhus Convention.[42]

Agenda 21 recognises, amongst other things, that one of the fundamental prerequisites for the achievement of sustainable development is broad public participation in decision-making, and that this includes the need of individuals, groups and organisations to participate in decisions, particularly those that affect the communities in which they live. The Rio Declaration and Agenda 21 also make explicit references to vulnerable and indigenous peoples in several other contexts,

---

38 Ibid.
39 George (Rock) Pring and Susan Y. Noé, "The Emerging International Law of Public Participation Affecting Global Mining, Energy, and Resources Development," in *Human Rights in Natural Resource Development: Public Participation in the Sustainable Development of Mining and Energy Resources*, eds Donald M. Zillman, Alastair Lucas and George (Rock) Pring (Oxford Scholarship Online, 2002), doi: 10.1093/acprof:oso/9780199253784.003.0002; Gillian Triggs, "The Rights of Indigenous Peoples to Participate in Resource Development: An International Legal Perspective," in *Human Rights in Natural Resource Development: Public Participation in the Sustainable Development of Mining and Energy Resources*, doi: 10.1093/acprof:oso/9780199253784.003.0004
40 United Nations Conference on Environment and Development. *Agenda 21, Rio Declaration, Forest Principles.* New York: United Nations, 1992.
41 UN World Conference on Human Rights, Vienna Declaration and Programme of Action, *International Legal Materials* 32, 1661 (1993) (Vienna Declaration).
42 See Wilson, this volume.

thereby contributing to underscoring the importance of including these groups in participatory initiatives.[43]

The Vienna Declaration and Programme of Action states that:

> States should ensure the full and free participation of indigenous people in all aspects of society, in particular in matters of concern to them (…);
>
> Great importance must be given to the promotion and protection of the human rights of persons belonging to groups which have been rendered vulnerable, including migrant workers, the elimination of all forms of discrimination against them, and the strengthening and more effective implementation of existing human rights instruments. States have an obligation to create and maintain adequate measures at the national level, in particular in the fields of education, health and social support, for the promotion and protection of the rights of persons in vulnerable sectors of their populations and to ensure the participation of those among them who are interested in finding a solution to their own problems (…);
>
> It is essential for States to foster participation by the poorest people in the decision-making process by the community in which they live, the promotion of human rights and efforts to combat extreme poverty (…);
>
> Measures to be taken, where appropriate, should include facilitation of [the] full participation [by national, ethnic, religious and linguistic minorities] in all aspects of the political, economic, social, religious and cultural life of society and in the economic progress and development in their country. (…)
>
> Equally important is the assistance to be given to the strengthening of the rule of law, the promotion of freedom of expression and the administration of justice, and to the real and effective participation of the people in the decision-making processes.[44]

Moreover, the Vienna Declaration urged states to ensure the full and free participation by vulnerable or underprivileged groups, including indigenous people, in all aspects of society, in particular in matters of concern to them.

The Rio and Vienna Declarations are political texts. However, the implementation and monitoring mechanisms of such texts have made observers argue that they can be likened to soft or even in some contexts hard law as to states' commitments.[45] The Rio and Vienna Declarations were and remain important documents. The Rio Declaration established the political foundations for much of the action that has since been undertaken in regard to ensuring public participation in environmental decision-making, including the Aarhus Convention. The Vienna Declaration's pronouncement of all human rights being mutually

---

43 Ibid., articles 22 and 23.
44 Ibid., I, paras 20 and 25, II paras 26, 27 and 67.
45 Dinah Shelton, "Introduction," in *Commitment and Compliance: The Role of Non-Binding Norms in the International Legal System*, ed. Dinah Shelton (Oxford: Oxford University Press, 2000), 1–18.

interdependent, interrelated and indivisible contributed significantly to bridging the gap between countries or regions insisting on civil and political or economic, social and cultural rights having prominence (partly but not only a Cold War legacy). For the current purposes, both declarations were also important in bringing the focus of participation in decision-making closer to the lives of affected individuals and highlighting the need for special attention to be paid to special groups, including indigenous peoples.

Adopted in 1948 and 1966 respectively, the Universal Declaration and the International Covenant on Civil and Political Rights emphasise "the right to take part in the government" of one's country or "the conduct of public affairs," in both cases "directly or through freely chosen representatives."[46] Adopted several decades later, the Rio and Vienna Declarations testify to a realisation that there is more to public participation than the exercise of government and public affairs, and that participation at the community level is an essential aspect of the right. Hence, the Declarations draw the attention of signatory states to the fact that decision-making processes must provide for real and effective participation.

The UNGPs emphasise meaningful stakeholder consultation as an element in the exercise of due diligence to identify and manage adverse impact, clearly stating that this is in order for the views of affected stakeholders to be taken into account.[47] The OECD Guidelines refer to effective stakeholder engagement and provide examples of the process (e.g. "meetings, hearings or consultation proceedings") and contexts (e.g. "the planning and decision-making concerning projects or other activities involving, for example, the intensive use of land or water, which could significantly affect local communities").[48]

Having adopted the risk-based due diligence approach, the OECD Guidelines and their general and sector-specific guidance texts complement the UNGPs' provisions. Being recommendations that adhering states undertake to make to companies operating in or from their states, the Guidelines apply to a large number of the world's companies active in the extractive sectors. Russia is the only Arctic country that is not an OECD member and does not separately adhere to the Guidelines. It is currently not clear whether the Guidelines apply directly within Greenland but a case can be made for the Greenlandic government to expect companies operating in Greenland to observe the Guidelines.[49] Companies

---

46 UDHR, article 21(1); "1. Everyone has the right to take part in the government of his country, directly or through freely chosen representatives. 2. (....)... 3. The will of the people shall be the basis of the authority of government; this will shall be expressed in periodic and genuine elections which shall be by universal and equal suffrage and shall be held by secret vote or by equivalent free voting procedures." ICCPR, article 25: "Every citizen shall have the right and the opportunity, without any of the distinctions mentioned in article 2 and without unreasonable restrictions: (a) To take part in the conduct of public affairs, directly or through freely chosen representatives (...)."
47 UNGPs, Principle 3, commentary, and Principle 21 with commentary.
48 OECD Guidelines, chapter II, commentary para. 25.
49 Greenland is not an independent member of OECD but at a general level involved in the organization by virtue of Denmark's membership. In line with the Act on Greenlandic Self-Government, Greenland accedes or adheres to OECD agreements of its

among the large number of multinationals in the extractive sector that are based in OECD countries or the currently 12 other countries that adhere to the Guidelines would be subject to such expectations. Moreover, companies in countries that do not explicitly adhere to the Guidelines can be subject to similar expectations. For example, Chinese companies involved in minerals supply chains or investment in the mining sector are covered by Chinese guidelines on responsible conduct that are designed to be in line with the UNGPs, the OECD Guidelines and the OECD Guidance for responsible minerals supply chains.[50] There is no doubt that the UN Framework and UNGPs apply throughout the Arctic, albeit (as in the case of the OECD Guidelines) without binding effect unless they are incorporated into a corporate contract.

As part of its efforts to help explain the practical implications of its Guidelines, the OECD has issued a due diligence guidance for meaningful stakeholder engagement in the extractive sector.[51] The guidance explains that meaningful stakeholder engagement refers to ongoing engagement with stakeholders that is two-way, conducted in good faith, and responsive. Two-way engagement means, amongst other things, that parties express opinions, share perspectives and listen to alternative viewpoints to reach mutual understanding,

---

own accord. Greenland's authorities engage in collaboration with OECD in several areas, such as exchange of information on matters of financial accounts and taxation, and territorial reviews for strengthening the economy and ensuring sustainable development of fisheries. On this basis, an argument can be made that as long as Greenland has not explicitly made a declaration to adhere to OECD's Guidelines for Multinational Enterprises, they will not be considered to apply in Greenland as a result of national adherence. This can be said to be reflected in the fact that the 2012 statute establishing the Danish NCP exempts its competence from applying in Greenland unless a specific decree is made to expand the competence to Greenland. Yet an argument can also be made that the OECD Guidelines already apply to Greenland. A statement submitted to Greenland's Self-Government in response to a public consultation concerning the Danish government's proposal to establish the Danish NCP with a statutory basis, Transparency Greenland (the Greenland chapter of Transparency International) made that point. The reasoning was that as Denmark ratified the Convention on the Organisation for Economic Co-operation and Development in 1961, thereby becoming a member of the OECD, which was established the same year, and as no reservation was made at that time as regards the Convention's application to Greenland, nor has such a reservation been made at a later stage. In 1976 Denmark acceded to the Investment Declaration which includes the Guidelines in an Annex, and again did not make a reservation to the application to Greenland, nor has such a reservation been made at a later stage. See Transparency Greenland, *Consultation Response to Public Consultation on Danish Bill on the Mediation- and Complaints Handling Institute for Responsible Business Conduct as to Its Application to Greenland*, 2012, www.transparency.gl/wp-content/uploads/Mæglings-og-klageinstitution-20.01.2012.pdf

50 See China Chamber of Commerce of Metals, Minerals & Chemicals, *Guidelines for Social Responsibility in Outbound Mining Investment*; China Chamber of Commerce of Metals, Minerals & Chemicals, *Chinese Due Diligence Guidelines*; and Buhmann, Karin, "Chinese Mineral Sourcing Interests."

51 OECD, *Due Diligence Guidance for Meaningful Stakeholder Engagement in the Extractive Sector* (Geneva: OECD, 2017).

and that steps are taken towards a joint decision-making process. Good faith engagement depends on the participants on both sides of the engagement. It means that the parties engage with the genuine intention to understand how stakeholder interests are affected by enterprise activities. Responsive engagement requires a follow-through on outcomes of stakeholder engagement activities through implementation of commitments that the parties have agreed to. As part of this, it must be ensured that adverse impacts on stakeholders are appropriately addressed. This includes the provision of remedies when enterprises have caused or contributed to such impacts, and that stakeholder views are taken into account in project decisions.[52]

The guidance further explains why meaningful stakeholder engagement is an important means of implementing due diligence. It is an effective activity for identifying and avoiding potential adverse impacts, appropriately mitigating and remedying impacts when they do occur, and ensuring that potential positive impacts are optimised for all stakeholders. If stakeholder engagement is not properly carried out, its function of helping identify and acting on impacts as part of the due diligence process may not be realised and adverse impacts may not be avoided or addressed. Moreover, poor stakeholder engagement can give rise to actual or perceived adverse impacts.[53] The launch of the process as such, or inviting stakeholders to share their views and perceptions of needs to be addressed, raises expectations that stakeholders' views will be taken seriously and acted upon. If the stakeholder engagement process is not thorough, impacts may be overlooked and stakeholders may lose trust in the process or the company.

The guidance also makes it clear that even within one sector, there is no one-size-fits-all. As a result, the stakeholder engagement and due diligence required for a particular project may depend on the specificities and differences between mining and oil and gas extraction in regard to methods of extraction, processing and transport; the location of resources; licensing and relations to governments; project life-spans; and organisation.[54] The diversity of tasks carried out in the context of planning an activity, executing it, closing down a project, and following-up for example to fill a mine, may all require different steps to be taken for meaningful stakeholder engagement. The diversity of roles of staff may also affect the specific stakeholder engagement and the degree to which it is meaningful to the stakeholders.[55] The guidance stresses that asking the right questions is crucial for stakeholder engagement to be meaningful and generate the type of information needed for the due diligence process. The process requires both cultural sensitivity and awareness of the relevant national and international legal frameworks, including, if relevant to or expected by indigenous peoples, a process conforming to free, prior and informed consent (FPIC).[56]

52 Ibid., 18.
53 Ibid.
54 Ibid., 20–22.
55 Ibid., 24–26.
56 See ibid., 29–112 (for details).

However, what meaningful stakeholder consultation or stakeholder engagement actually entails in particular situations is neither prescribed by the UNGPs nor the OECD Guidelines. Guidance from cases handled by remedial institutions for those guiding instruments can contribute relevant direction for companies. National Contact Points (NCPs) under OECD's Guidelines are established to promote the Guidelines and handle grievances concerning alleged infringements of the Guidelines. For practical purposes, NCPs also serve as a key remedial institution for the UNGPs.[57] The following section recounts some NCP jurisprudence related to meaningful consultation with affected stakeholders.

5 NCP statements on participation as part of a risk-based due diligence process

Although NCPs do not have powers to issue enforceable judgments, they fill a remedy gap for transnational business operations and their social impacts. As state-based non-judicial remedy institutions established in countries that adhere to the OECD Guidelines, NCPs have extraterritorial powers in that an alleged violation occurring in a country without an NCP may be examined by the NCP of the company's home state. This provides NCPs with extraterritorial reach that courts rarely enjoy. Some NCPs use their power to issue final statements at the end of the handling of a case to make clear assessments on how company conduct diverted from the standard of conduct entrenched in the Guidelines. Some also issue recommendations for conduct to be in accordance with the Guidelines.

Like courts' jurisprudence, NCP statements are a source of insights into what constitutes conduct in line with particular normative directives.[58] Since risk-based due diligence became incorporated into the Guidelines based on the UNGPs, there has been a rise in complaints to NCPs on various aspects of due diligence, including stakeholder engagement. In some instances, NCPs applied the UN Framework's due diligence approach even before it was integrated into the OECD Guidelines. This occurred in the case *Survival International v. Vedanta*,[59] which was handled by the NCP of the United Kingdom. The complaint concerned allegations of inadequate stakeholder engagement by mining company Vedanta for a projected bauxite mine in India. The NCP final statement explained that Vedanta had failed to put in place an adequate and timely consultation mechanism to

57 UN Framework, para. 98; Buhmann, "Business and Human Rights."
58 Basak Baglayan, "Searching for Human Rights Norms for Corporate Conduct in Domestic Jurisprudence: A Bottom-Up Approach to International Law, *Nordic Journal of Human Rights* 36, 4 (2018): 371–389; Karin Buhmann, "Analysing OECD National Contact Point Statements for Guidance on Human Rights Due Diligence: Method, Findings and Outlook," *Nordic Journal of Human Rights* 36, 4 (February 2018): 390–410, https://doi.org/10.1080/18918131.2018.1547526; Larry Catá Backer, "Rights and Accountability in Development (Raid) v. Das Air and Global Witness v. Afrimex – Small Steps towards an Autonomous Transnational Legal System for the Regulation of Multinational Corporations," *Melbourne Journal of International Law* 10, 1 (2009): 258–307.
59 *Survival International v. Vedanta Resources plc*, UK NCP (September 25, 2009).

engage fully with an indigenous community that would be affected by the impact of its operations on the environment and health and safety. The NCP found that the company has also failed to use other mechanisms to assess the implications of its activities on the community, such as a human rights impact assessment. The statement contributed to ongoing elaboration of what is entailed in exercising meaningful stakeholder consultation as part of due diligence.

Specific steps to be taken in stakeholder engagement to involve victims was an issue in the case *GCM Resources*,[60] a complaint that was handled by the UK NCP after the 2011 revision of the Guidelines. The complaint concerned displacement of local populations and environmental degradation resulting from a coalmine project in Bangladesh, and the alleged failure of the company to respect the rights of communities in that area. The final statement urged the company to identify appropriate ways to re-engage with affected communities, increase the information available to them, and take account of their views. Thus, the NCP underscored the need for effective stakeholder engagement to identify and understand the views and concerns of potential or actual victims, and offered guidance for re-establishing soured relations with affected stakeholders with a view to enabling meaningful stakeholder engagement in future.

Involving a question on whether a company should exercise FPIC, the *Statkraft*[61] case concerned corporate activities in northern Sweden in regard to the construction of a wind farm. The complaint, which was handled by the Swedish and Norwegian NCPs in collaboration, was based on allegations that the Norwegian energy company Statkraft had taken insufficient account of the interests of a Saami village and failed to respect the human rights of the villagers, including with regard to consultation. The reindeer herding collective lodging the complaint acknowledged that Statkraft had consulted with the community during the planning stages of the wind power plant, but contended that "meaningful engagement" had not taken place. They alleged non-observance of the right of indigenous peoples to FPIC, with reference to ILO C169. The two collaborating NCPs did not find that Statkraft had failed to comply with the OECD Guidelines, but issued recommendations for actions the company might consider, including to observe clearly indigenous peoples' rights. This statement complements the normative baseline of the UNGPs and OECD Guidelines by clarifying that a company can go beyond that normative baseline and include additional human rights instruments in its due diligence process; highlighting the particular relevance of ILO C169 to indigenous or tribal areas.

In regard to an NGO complaint lodged against the company Eurasian Natural Resources Corporation (ENRC)[62] concerning its activities in the Democratic Republic of Congo (DRC), the UK NCP found that ENRC had not engaged

---

60 *IAC & WDM v. GCM Resources plc*, UK NCP (November 20, 2014).
61 *Jijnjevaerie Saami Village and Statkraft*, NCP of Sweden and Norway (August 2, 2016)
62 *Eurasian Natural Resources Corporation* (*RAID v. ENRC*), NCP of the United Kingdom (March 14, 2016).

effectively with two stakeholder communities on the concession and had not taken adequate steps to address impacts on the communities that arise from taking forward mining projects. In the final statement the UK NCP observed that in order to identify and address any risks of adverse effects, establishing good communication channels with local stakeholders should be a priority for the company according to the NCP.

Published NCP statements that criticise company conduct explicitly or do so implicitly through recommendations for changed conduct may cause reputational damage for the company. This can affect their social licence to operate and their general economic situation, thus directly impacting the core foundations for a company. The desire to avoid such criticism can therefore act as a driver for companies to act in accordance with the Guidelines. This is not a single solution to problems of inadequate stakeholder consultation, but it may complement other measures to inform corporate conduct and help increase the quality of consultation with affected stakeholders, so that the process is perceived as meaningful by those who are potentially or actually impacted by corporate activities, for example in the extractive industries.

6 Conclusion and outlook: implications for companies involved in extractives activities in the Arctic

Spurred by concerns with the adverse impacts that economic activities can cause to communities and general society, political support at international level and in some regional and national contexts has led to the issuance of governmental guidance for responsible business conduct.

The UN Framework, UNGPs and OECD Guidelines are leading international sources of norms for such conduct. They institutionalise risk-based due diligence as a standard of conduct expected by companies, and prescribe that meaningful consultation with affected stakeholders is a core element in the process to adequately identify and manage risks to individuals and groups.

The UN instruments have global applicability and therefore apply in all Arctic countries. As the OECD Guidelines apply to companies operating in or out of adhering states (which in addition to all OECD countries include several non-OECD states), the Guidelines *de facto* apply to a large number of companies active in the extractives sector in the Arctic, either because they are based in an adhering country, or because the host country adheres to the Guidelines. National guidance instruments, including some issued by the Chinese minerals- and mining sector, also apply risk-based due diligence.

Despite these normative instruments not being legally binding, non-observance is not without consequence for companies. Because companies need to make profits and raise capital to function, economic losses and other events that negatively affect their financial situation can have significant implications for the situation of a company in the short and longer term. The theory of the social licence to operate has evolved on this foundation, based on observations in the mining sector and expanding to other sectors. Reputational damage, whether caused by media or civil society reports or critical statements from NCPs, has the potential to affect a company's social licence to operate. As a result, companies may suffer financially if they do not engage in adequate stakeholder engagement to fully identify and manage the adverse impacts that they (or their business partners) may cause.

Meaningful stakeholder consultation is closely related to the right to participation in decision-making relating to the communities in which individuals live. Meaningful stakeholder consultation as a standard of conduct, as defined in the UNGPs and related instruments, can be considered a further extension of the right to participation as endorsed by the Rio and Vienna Declarations. The two Declarations highlighted states' duties to ensure participation in decision-making, including at the community level. The Business & Human Rights regime has institutionalised a recognition that companies too have responsibilities for human rights. Under the State Duty to Protect, states have obligations to implement their duties through appropriate means, such as legislation, adjudication and guidance, including guidance for companies on what exactly risk-based due diligence entails in a particular context. Under the Corporate Responsibility to Respect human rights, companies should incorporate meaningful stakeholder consultation as an element in the due diligence process.

The extractive sectors – both in regard to fossil and living resources – have been prominent in drawing attention to the adverse impacts that local communities and their individual members may suffer when companies neglect to engage in due diligence or stakeholder consultation that is meaningful to affected stakeholders. The emergent jurisprudence of NCPs testifies to this and also helps suggest improved practices for companies. The problems may vary in different local contexts, but as the cases noted above show, communities' perceptions that stakeholder engagement processes are inadequate are not limited to any particular region, and this and other chapters in this book show that there are plenty of examples in the Arctic. As many communities affected by mining, other natural resource extraction or renewable energy activities are indigenous, it is particularly interesting that the Norwegian and Swedish NCPs have highlighted that companies should consider going beyond the minimum normative baseline suggested by the UNGP (the International Bill of Rights and ILO core labour standards) and explicitly observe indigenous peoples' rights in accordance with ILO C169. UNDRIP observance could be considered as well.

References

Backer, Larry Catá. "Rights and Accountability in Development (Raid) v. Das Air and Global Witness v. Afrimex: Small Steps towards an Autonomous Transnational Legal System for the Regulation of Multinational Corporations." *Melbourne Journal of International Law* 10, 1 (2009): 258–307.

Baglayan, Basak. "Searching for Human Rights Norms for Corporate Conduct in Domestic Jurisprudence: A Bottom-up Approach to International Law." *Nordic Journal of Human Rights* 36, 4 (2018): 371–389.

Buhmann, Karin. "Business and Human Rights: Understanding the UN Guiding Principles from the Perspective of Transnational Business Governance Interactions." *Transnational Legal Theory* 6, 2 (2015): 399–434. doi:10.1080/20414005.2015.1073516

Buhmann, Karin. *Changing Sustainability Norms through Communicative Processes: The Emergence of the Business & Human Rights Regime as Transnational Law*. Cheltenham: Edward Elgar, 2017.

Buhmann, Karin. "Analysing OECD National Contact Point Statements for Guidance on Human Rights Due Diligence: Method, Findings and Outlook." *Nordic Journal of Human Rights* 36, 4 (2018): 390–410. doi:10.1080/18918131.2018.1547526

Buhmann, Karin. "Chinese Mineral Sourcing Interests and Greenland's Potential as a Source of 'Conflict-Free' Minerals." *Arctic Yearbook* 6/7 (2018). https://arcticyearbook.com/arctic-yearbook/2018

China Chamber of Commerce of Metals, Minerals & Chemicals. *Chinese Due Diligence Guidelines for Responsible Mineral Supply Chains*. Beijing: CCCMC, 2015. https://mneguidelines.oecd.org/chinese-due-diligence-guidelines-for-responsible-mineral-supply-chains.htm

China Chamber of Commerce of Metals, Minerals & Chemicals. *Guidelines for Social Responsibility in Outbound Mining Investment*. Beijing: CCCMC, 2014. https://cdn.globalwitness.org/archive/files/library/cccmc%20guidelines%20for%20social%20resposibility%20in%20outbound%20mining%20investments%20oct%202014%20ch-en.pdf

EU Directive 2014/95/EU of the European Parliament and of the Council of 22 October 2015 amending Directive 2013/34/EU as regards disclosure of non-financial and diversity information by certain large undertakings and groups (2014). OJ 2014 L330/1.

EU Regulation 2017/821 of the European Parliament and of the Council of 17 May 2017 laying down supply chain due diligence obligations for Union importers of tin, tantalum and tungsten, their ores, and gold originating from conflict-affected and high-risk areas (2017). OJ 2017 L130/1.

Eurasian Natural Resources Corporation (*RAID v. ENRC*), NCP of the United Kingdom. March 14, 2016.

Hasenclever, Andreas, Peter Mayer, and Volker Rittberger. *Theories of International Regimes*. Cambridge: Cambridge University Press, 1997.

IAC & WDM v. GCM Resources plc, UK NCP. November 20, 2014.

ILO Convention 169 (1989). "Indigenous and Tribal Peoples Convention. Adopted 27 June 1989, entered into force 5 September 1991." *International Legal Materials* 28, 1382.

International Covenant on Civil and Political Rights 1966. United Nations Treaty Series 999, 171.

International Covenant on Economic, Social and Cultural Rights 1966. United Nations Treaty Series 993, 3.

Jijnjevaerie Saami Village and Statkraft, NCP of Sweden and Norway. August 2, 2016.

Krasner, Stephen D. "Structural Causes and Regime Consequences: Regimes as Intervening Variables." *International Organization* 36, 2 (1982): 185–205. doi:10.1017/s0020818300018920

Monash University. *Human Rights Translated 2.0: A Business Reference Guide*. Geneva: OHCHR, 2017. https://www.ohchr.org/documents/publications/HRT_2_0_EN.pdf

Nelsen, Jaqueline L. "Social Licence to Operate." *International Journal of Mining, Reclamation and Environment* 20, 3 (2006): 161–162. doi:10.1080/17480930600804182

OECD. *Due Diligence Guidance for Meaningful Stakeholder Engagement in the Extractive Sector*. Geneva: OECD, 2017. https://mneguidelines.oecd.org/stakeholder-engagement-extractive-industries.htm

OECD. *Due Diligence Guidance for Responsible Business Conduct.* Paris: OECD, 2018. https://www.oecd.org/investment/due-diligence-guidance-for-responsible-business-conduct.htm

OECD. *OECD Guidelines for Multinational Enterprises, 2011 Edition.* Paris: OECD, 2011.

Owen, John R. and Deanna Kemp. "Social Licence and Mining: A Critical Perspective." *Resources Policy* 38, 1 (2012): 29–35.

Pring, George (Rock) and Susan Y. Noé. "The Emerging International Law of Public Participation Affecting Global Mining, Energy, and Resources Development." In *Human Rights in Natural Resource Development: Public Participation in the Sustainable Development of Mining and Energy Resources,* edited by Donald M. Zillman, Alastair Lucas, and George (Rock) Pring. Oxford Scholarship Online, 2002. doi:10.1093/acprof:oso/9780199253784.003.0002

Prno, Jason and D. Scott Slocombe. "Exploring the Origins of 'Social License to Operate' in the Mining Sector: Perspectives from Governance and Sustainability Theories." *Resources Policy* 37, 3 (2012): 346–357. doi:10.1016/j.resourpol.2012.04.002

Ruggie, John and John F.ShermanIII. "The Concept of 'Due Diligence' in the UN Guiding Principles on Business and Human Rights: A Reply to Jonathan Bonnitcha and Robert McCorquodale." *European Journal of International Law* 28, 3 (2017): 921–928.

Ruggie, John. *Guiding Principles on Business and Human Rights: Implementing the United Nations "Protect, Respect and Remedy" Framework.* UN Doc. A/HRC/17/31. March 21, 2011.

Ruggie, John. *Protect, Respect and Remedy: A Framework for Business and Human Rights. Report of the Special Representative on Human Rights, Transnational Corporations and Other Business Enterprises.* UN Doc. A/HRC/8/5. April 7, 2008.

Seppala, Nina. "Business and the International Human Rights Regime: A Comparison of UN Initiatives." *Journal of Business Ethics* 87, S2 (2009): 401–417. doi:10.1007/s10551-009-0297-4

Shelton, Dinah. "Introduction." In *Commitment and Compliance: The Role of Non-Binding Norms in the International Legal System,* edited by Dinah Shelton, 1–18. Oxford: Oxford University Press, 2000.

Spence, David B. "Corporate Social Responsibility in the Oil and Gas Industry: The Importance of Reputational Risk." *Chicago-Kent Law Review* 86, 1 (2011): 59–85.

Survival International v. Vedanta Resources plc, UK NCP. September 25, 2009.

Transparency Greenland. *Consultation Response to Public Consultation on Danish Bill on the Mediation- and Complaints Handling Institute for Responsible Business Conduct as to Its Application to Greenland.* 2012. www.transparency.gl/wp-content/uploads/Mæglings-og-klageinstitution-20.01.2012.pdf

Triggs, Gillian. "The Rights of Indigenous Peoples to Participate in Resource Development: An International Legal Perspective." In *Human Rights in Natural Resource Development: Public Participation in the Sustainable Development of Mining and Energy Resources,* edited by Donald M. Zillman, Alastair Lucas, and George (Rock) Pring. Oxford Scholarship Online, 2002. doi:10.1093/acprof:oso/9780199253784.003.0004.

UN Conference on Environment and Development. *Agenda 21, Rio Declaration, Forest Principles.* New York: United Nations, 1992.

UN General Assembly. Universal Declaration of Human Rights, UNGA Res A/RES/217 (III). December 10, 1948.

UN General Assembly. Declaration on the Rights of Indigenous Peoples, UNGA Res 61/295. September 13, 2007 (UNDRIP).

UN Office of the High Commissioner for Human Rights. *The Corporate Responsibility to Respect Human Rights: An Interpretive Guide.* UN Doc. HR/PUB/12/02. 2012. www.ohchr.org/Documents/Publications/HR.PUB.12.2_En.pdf

UN World Conference on Human Rights. "Vienna Declaration and Programme of Action." *International Legal Materials* 32, 1661 (1993).

Part II
Participation in practice

5 Youth as a resource in extractive industry decision-making processes
A case study using social media and visual methods to engage young Greenlanders

Anna-Sofie Skjervedal

Introduction: (The lack of) youth engagement in extractive industry development

Although climate change is impacting peoples' cultures and livelihoods globally, the Arctic is a centre for some of the most rapid climate change effects.[1] The changing climate is making the Arctic more accessible, and along with changes to sea-ice, glaciers and landscapes, social, cultural, economic and political changes also pose new risks and opportunities for people living in the Arctic. The changes challenge the future livelihoods of people in these northern communities who will have to anticipate new futures for themselves – to rethink their ways of life, how they perceive themselves and organise their societies.[2]

The changing climate has also generated a renewed interest in exploration and exploitation of mineral resources, including hydrocarbons, in Greenland. To sustain the current living-standards and to create prosperity and wealth for the future generations to come – along with hopes of one day becoming a fully independent nation state – the Government of Greenland places great emphasis on developing the mineral resource sector, including hydrocarbons, into one of the country's primary and principal business sectors.[3]

---

1 ACIA, "Impacts of a Warming Arctic: Arctic Climate Impact Assessment," in *ACIA Overview Report* (Cambridge: Cambridge University Press, 2004), 8; Mark Nuttall, "Anticipation, Climate Change, and Movement in Greenland," *Etudes/Inuit/Studies* 34, no. 1 (2010): 22.
2 Frank Sejersen, *Rethinking Greenland and the Arctic in the Era of Climate Change: New Northern Horizons* (London and New York: Routledge, 2015), 1.
3 Rune Langhoff, *Med Folkets Mandat? Høringsprocesser og Borgerinddragelse på Råstofområdet* [With the People's Authorisation? Hearing Processes and Public Participation within the Area of Natural Resources] (Nuuk and Copenhagen: Inuit Circumpolar Council (ICC) and the World Wide Fund for Nature (WWF), August 2013), 5. http://inuit.org/fileadmin/user_upload/File/2013/Reports/Med_folkets_mandat_DK_19_august_2013.pdf; Committee for Greenlandic Mineral Resources to the Benefit of Society, *To the Benefit of Greenland* (Nuuk and Copenhagen: University of Greenland and University of Copenhagen, 2014), 8. http://greenlandperspective.ku.dk/this_is_greenland_perspective/background/report-papers/To_the_benefit_of_Greenland.pdf; Government of Greenland, "Guidelines on the Process and Preparation of the SIA Report for Mineral Projects," (Nuuk: ProGrafisk Aps, 2016), 4. https://www.govmin.gl/images/stories/minerals/sia_guide

In the Arctic context, even small projects can carry risks of major social impacts at local and national scales, and may have the potential to affect the ways of life of the local communities severely.[4] Greenlandic society has already undergone a rapid transformation as development in the extractive sector has gained speed within the last decade, and, regardless of how the mineral resources are exploited, Greenlanders can expect further profound changes in the years to come.[5]

The rapid expansion of the extractive sector stirs both high hopes for the future and anxieties among Greenlanders. In Greenland there are strong interrelations between the human and natural environments, as both traditional and modern ways of life are tied closely to the use of the country's living natural resources for food, employment and recreation.[6] Whether people make a living as hunters or fishers or use the sea and land for recreational purposes, sustainable management of the natural resources is fundamental to sustain and improve living standards, and for people to be able to adapt to the changes and take advantage of the new opportunities. Strikingly, young people, who have a greater stake in the future outcomes of current decisions and developments than most (and are therefore sometimes referred to as "future stakeholders"),[7] generally pose a seldom-heard voice in public participation processes and public debates about future development. According to researchers in youth engagement, such as Kurt-Shai[8] and Marot and Mali,[9] youth constitutes the population group most likely to experience and have to cope with both the negative and positive impacts of societal changes. Although youth engagement – parallel to a growing recognition of the

line/SIA_guideline.pdf; Government of Greenland, *Oliestrategi 2019–2023* [Oil strategy 2019–2023] (Nuuk: Prografisk Aps, 2019), 6, https://naalakkersuisut.gl/~/media/Na noq/Files/Hearings/2019/Oliestrategi%20for%202019_2023/Documents/Oliestrategi %202019-2023%20DK%204.pdf

4 See Johnstone and Hansen, this volume.

5 Mark Nutall, "Imagining and Governing the Greenlandic Resource Frontier," *The Polar Journal* 2 (2012); Anna-Sofie Hurup Olsen and Anne Merrild Hansen, "Perceptions of Public Participation in Impact Assessment: A Study of Offshore Oil Exploration in Greenland," *Impact Assessment and Project Appraisal* 32 (2014): 72; Anne Merrild Hansen, Frank Vanclay, Peter Croal, and Anna-Sofie Hurup Skjervedal, "Managing the Social Impacts of the Rapidly-Expanding Extractive Industries in Greenland," *The Extractive Industries and Society* 3 (2016): 25.

6 Anna-Sofie Hurup Olsen, "Public Participation in Environmental and Social Impact Assessment: Exploring the Human Dimension of Oil Exploration in Greenland," Master's thesis, Aalborg University, 2012, p. 73; Olsen and Hansen, "Perceptions of Public Participation"; Anna-Sofie Hurup Skjervedal, "Towards Meaningful Youth Engagement: Breaking the Frame of the Current Public Participation Practice in Greenland," Ph.D. diss., Ilisimatusarfik – The University of Greenland and Aalborg University, 2018, p. 43.

7 Naja Marot and Barbara C. Mali, "Youth and Regional Development – Participation by Future Stakeholders in Today's Decisions on Post-Mining Regions," in *Post-Mining Regions in Central Europe – Problems, Potentials, Possibilities*, ed. Peter Wirth, Barbara C. Mali, and Wolfgang Fischer (Munich: Oekom, 2012), 195–212.

8 Ruthanne Kurt-Schai, "The Roles of Youth in Society: A Reconceptualization," *The Educational Forum* 52, no. 2 (1988): 113.

9 Marot and Mali, "Youth and Regional Development – Participation."

importance of participatory planning for community development in project development – has been endorsed by various international agencies, governments, and NGOs in the last 50 years, youth participation is in general seldom applied. In practice, this leaves youth as an often unused potential in development planning, despite being the population group most likely to experience the greatest impact of the societal changes.[10]

The lack of focus on including youth has great consequences for young Greenlanders, as they miss out both on having a say about project development and on getting a fair chance to adapt to and plan for the future. Further, they lack information about how extractive industry development may affect their current and future lives, as well as proper information about education and job opportunities related to the expanding extractive sector.[11]

Ideally, public participation contributes to ensuring a more democratic decision-making process, where transfer of power from government to the citizens enables the public to influence a development.[12] The expected benefits of public participation include, among other things, conflict risk mitigation, information exchange and mutual learning, while also avoiding costly delays, providing access to local knowledge, concerns, and preferences, enabling the potentially affected community to gain a better understanding of the proposed project and plans, and hence improving their ability to develop an informed opinion.[13] However,to realise this

---

10 David Driskell, *Creating Better Cities with Children and Youth: A Manual for Participation* (Abingdon: Taylor & Francis Ltd, 2002); Barry Checkoway and Lorraine Gutiérrez, *Youth Participation and Community Change* (New York: Routledge, 2011); Marot and Mali, "Youth and Regional Development – Participation."
11 Skjervedal, *Towards Meaningful Youth Engagement*, 65.
12 Lone Kørnøv, "Public Participation," in *Tools for Sustainable Development*, eds Lone Kørnøv, Mikkel Thrane, Arne Remmen, and Henrik Lund (Aalborg: Aalborg Universitetsforlag, 2007), 719–738; Matthew Cashmore, Alan Bond, and Dick Cobb, "The Role and Functioning of Environmental Assessment: Theoretical Reflections upon an Empirical Investigation of Causation," *Journal of Environmental Management* 88 (2008): 1233–1248; Basilio Verduzco Chavéz and Antonio Sanchéz Bernal, "Planning Hydroelectric Power Plants with the Public: A Case of Organizational and Social Learning in Mexico," *Journal of Impact Assessment and Project Appraisal* 26, no. 3 (2008): 163–176; Stewart Lockie, Maree Franetovich, Sanjay Sharma, and John Rolfe, "Democratisation versus Engagement? Social and Economic Impact Assessment and Community Participation in the Coal Mining Industry of the Bowen Bassin, Australia," *Journal of Impact Assessment and Project Appraisal* 26, no. 3 (2008): 177–188; Gwen Ottinger, "Changing Knowledge, Local Knowledge and Knowledge Gaps: STS Insights into Procedural Justice," *Science, Technology and Human Values* 38, no. 2 (2013): 250–270.
13 Joe Weston, "Consultation and the Conflict of Interests in the EIA Process," in *Planning and Environmental Impact Assessment in Practice*, ed. Joe Weston (Harlow: Longman, 1997), 93–120; Ron Bisset, "Methods of Consultation and Public Participation," in *Environmental Assessment in the Developing and Transitional Countries: Principles, Methods and Practice*, eds Norman Lee and Clive George (Chichester: Wiley, 2000), 149–160; Clive George, "Comparative Review of Environmental Assessment Procedures and Practice," in *Environmental Assessment in the Developing and Transitional Countries*, 35–70; Ilan Kapoor, "Towards Participatory

potential in practice often proves difficult.[14] Although public participation in Greenland is purportedly on a level with international best practice,[15] a gap exists between formal guidelines and public participation in practice, and Greenland's public participation processes have been subject to much criticism from various sources. In a recent report with contributions from research experts within a wide range of fields on future scenarios for the development of Greenland, it was stated that "insufficient, late and overly narrow public participation are major themes in the decision phase of the natural resource projects."[16] The call for formal, strengthened practices and processes of public participation in relation to extractive industry development has so far prompted only minor changes, leaving room for improvements to close the gap between Greenland's public participation potential and the implementation of meaningful participation in practice. This has led to dissatisfaction and frustration among stakeholders both directly and indirectly involved in the process, including industry proponents, civil society, and the wider Greenlandic public.[17]

An explanation for the failure to facilitate meaningful and effective participation in Greenland is that the most prevalent form of participation is the public consultation meeting. These provide the main forum within which the potentially affected local public may utter their concerns and fears as well as hopes and aspirations regarding project planning and decision-making within the extractive sector. Public meetings appear to attract only a narrow range of people within the

Environmental Management?" *Journal of Environmental Management* 63, no. 3 (2001): 269–279; John Glasson, Riki Therivel, and Andrew Chadwick, "Participation, Presentation and Review," in *Introduction to Environmental Impact Assessment*, 3rd edn, eds John Glasson, Riki Therivel, and Andrew Chadwick (London and New York: Routledge, 2005), 165–194; Lone Kørnøv, "Public Participation;" Ciaran O'Faircheallaigh, "Public Participation and Environmental Impact Assessment: Purposes, Implications, and Lessons for Public Policy Making," *Environmental Impact Assessment Review* 30, no. 1 (2010): 19–27.

14 Anne Shepherd and Christi Bowler, "Beyond the Requirements: Improving Public Participation in EIA," *Journal of Environmental Planning and Management* 40, no. 6 (1997): 725–738; Michael Hibbard and Susan Lurie, "Saving Land but Losing Ground: Challenges to Community Planning in the Era of Participation," *Journal of Planning Education and Research* 20, no. 2 (2000): 187–195; Judith E. Innes and David E. Booher, "Reframing Public Participation: Strategies of the 21st Century," *Planning Theory and Practice* 5, no. 4 (2004): 419–436; Brian W. Head, "Community Engagement: Participation in Whose Terms?" *Australian Political Science* 42, no. 3 (2007): 441–454; Aniekan Udofia, Bram Noble, and Greg Poelzer, "Meaningful and Efficient? Enduring Challenges to Aboriginal Participation in Environmental Impact Assessment," *Environmental Impact Assessment Review* 65 (2017): 164–174.

15 See, e.g., Government of Greenland, "Guidelines on the Process and Preparation of the SIA Report for Mineral Projects."

16 Committee for Greenlandic Mineral Resources to the Benefit of Society, "To the Benefit of Greenland."

17 HS Analyse, *Befolkningen om borgermøder om råstoffer* [Public opinions at public meetings about natural resources] (Nuuk: WWF – World Wide Fund for Nature, 2014), http://awsassets.wwfdk.panda.org/downloads/hs_analyse_borgermoder.pdf; Olsen and Hansen, "Perceptions of Public Participation," 7.

local communities, with the typical format being a presentation by planners, extractive industry representatives, decision-makers and other experts with subsequent time for feedback and questions. Further, research investigating multiple stakeholders' perceptions and approaches to the very concept, process and practice of public participation reveals discrepancies between understandings and recognitions of what public participation can or should do, and how to do it. These divergences direct attention to a lack of transparency in the decision-making processes, difficulties in accessing available information, a lack of adequate information, too much one-way communication (from proponents to affected stakeholders); all challenges shared across nations worldwide.[18]

Prerequisites for active and meaningful participation arguably include a clear definition of the purpose of participation as well as early exchange of knowledge and experience through mutual dialogue between project proponents, government authorities, and the potentially affected communities, so as to manage expectations, guarantee learning, establish trust, and promote sustainable development through resilience and capacity building, as well as involvement in the project planning, assessment, and decision-making process. Further, one thing is to discuss public participation and extractive industry development with individuals, who work with these matters on a daily basis; another is to approach ordinary citizens and have a meaningful dialogue around these subjects. In my experience, approaching people in the local communities asking them to provide their perspective on "extractive industry development" – or even the issue of "public participation" itself – many will simply shrug their shoulders or answer that they know too little to have a "qualified" opinion on such matters. For ordinary citizens, issues that relate to their everyday lives are much higher on the agenda and much more relatable. Thus, the information presented must be framed in such a manner that it takes as the point of departure their everyday lives and the visions they hold for their children and their grandchildren. Moreover, young people will have specific perspectives and will respond differently to various approaches to elicit their concerns and priorities.

As a basis for understanding how the Greenlandic youth think about, live in and act in accordance to the world around them, and how they orient themselves toward the future, this chapter contributes to our understanding of the social and cultural effects of a changing Arctic by shedding light on young Greenlanders' perceptions of future challenges and possibilities in light of the current development of the extractive industry in Greenland. In doing so, it addresses and highlights the needs and priorities of the Greenlandic youth that are of relevance to both local and regional decision-making.

---

18 Mark Nuttall, "Imagining and Governing the Greenlandic Resource Frontier," *The Polar Journal* 2 (2012): 113–124; Hansen et al., "Managing the Social Impacts," 30; Skjervedal, *Towards Meaningful Youth Engagement*, 57–61.

Potential and challenges for youth engagement

As mentioned in the introduction, difficulties in engaging youth constitute a wide-reaching challenge in public participation both within and beyond the extractive sector, in Greenland and other nations across the world – this in spite of the fact that the importance of acknowledging young people as stakeholders, along with the benefits of youth participation, have been explicitly recognised in the political arena since the 1970s.[19] This formal recognition was supported by the World Commission on Environment and Development in its report *Our Common Future*,[20] where youth is acknowledged as the population group most likely to be affected by decisions of both environmental and societal character. The role of youth as stakeholders is further supported by the UN Convention on the Rights of the Child,[21] emphasising the right of youth to engage in decision-making processes according to the competences and abilities they hold. Moreover, the 21st principle of the Rio Declaration of 1992[22] and Agenda 21[23] state that young people ought to participate actively in all levels of decision-making that may affect their current lives and hold consequences for their future.[24]

The very concept of youth participation may be defined as a process of real influence and involvement of young people in decisions that affect their lives.[25] For the purpose of this research, youth are defined as being between 15 and 30 years of age.[26] Inspired by the UN youth definitions,[27] this age range was established as an adjustment to the Greenlandic context, taking its point of departure in the age division employed by Statistics Greenland[28] and the comprehensive "SLiCA" survey of Arctic Living Conditions.[29] In Greenland, this population group counts approximately 13,500 individuals, and thus makes up 24 per cent of the Greenlandic population, with a fairly equal division between males (6,627 individuals) and females (6,631 individuals). The vast majority, more specifically 86 per cent, live in the bigger cities, with the remaining youth living in the smaller settlements.[30]

---

19 Driskell, *Creating Better Cities*.
20 Gro Brundtland, *Report of the World Commission on Environment and Development: Our Common Future*. UN Doc. A/42/427, August 4, 1987.
21 Convention on the Rights of the Child 1989.
22 "Rio Declaration on Environment and Development 1992," *International Legal Materials* 31 (1992): 876.
23 United Nations Conference on Environment and Development, *Agenda 21, Rio Declaration, Forest Principles*. New York: United Nations, 1992.
24 Marot and Mali, "Youth and Regional Development-Participation."
25 Checkoway and Gutiérrez, *Youth Participation*.
26 Skjervedal, *Towards Meaningful Youth Engagement*.
27 UN Youth, "Definition of Youth," accessed October 7, 2019, www.un.org/esa/socdev/documents/youth/fact-sheets/youth-definition.pdf
28 Statistics Greenland, "Greenland in Figures 2018," May 2018, www.stat.gl/publ/kl/GF/2018/pdf/Greenland%20in%20Figures%202018.pdf
29 Birger Poppel, "Living Conditions and Perceived Quality of Life Among Indigenous Peoples in the Arctic," in *Global Handbook of Quality of Life: Exploration of Well-Being of Nations and Continents*, eds Wolfgang Glatzer, Laura Camfield, Valerie Møller, and Mariano Rojas (New York: Springer, 2015), 715–747.
30 Statistics Greenland, "Greenland in Figures 2018."

A strikingly low educational level counts as one of the primary challenges in Greenland compared to other countries and in terms of the otherwise high political ambitions for – and the resources spent on – this area. For instance, statistical analysis in Greenland shows that half of the 25–34 year-olds have no further education beyond completing the municipal primary and lower secondary school. Too many leave school with poor qualifications and bleak prospects for continuing further up the education system. For young people, this means missing out on opportunities for a satisfying work life and for being self-supporting. For society, high employment and income constitute vital features for societal prosperity and financing of the welfare state. Nevertheless, there has not been much progress throughout the last ten years.[31] This development is problematic for active public participation, as a certain degree of literacy is necessary to assess critically, analyse and give feedback on the information made available by planners and decision-makers in relation to project development in the extractive sector.

The missing voice of young Greenlanders leaves many important questions unanswered: *What are their hopes and fears for their future as well as the future extractive industry development in Greenland? How do they view their role in this development? What knowledge do young Greenlanders hold of impacts that the extractive industry development may cause and how these impacts may affect their lives? And how do they imagine the future development in Greenland in general?*

The case study: Facebook and visual methods as tools for meaningful youth engagement

Methods

The case study draws upon a qualitative explorative study, henceforth referred to as the "Photo Forum" study, which took place in Greenland in May and June 2015. The research sought specifically to test Facebook and photo-elicitation as alternative tools for targeting and meaningfully engaging the hitherto scarcely represented Greenlandic youth and to capture their interests, values, fears, hopes and aspirations for the future along with their thoughts on future extractive development in Greenland. The social media network Facebook was used as an interactive data collection platform along with the visual method of photo-elicitation (also called photo-interviewing). I took as the starting point my own Facebook network as owing to the endless pool of entangled "friendship" networks, Facebook proved an efficient means of recruitment through "snowballing," fostering a continuously growing sample size through both direct personal invitations and as new "friends" became aware of and requested to join the Photo Forum group. Further, through the Facebook profiles of

---

31 Økonomisk Råd, *Nunatta aningaasaqarnera – Grønlands Økonomi* [Greenland's Economy], October, 2018, https://naalakkersuisut.gl/~/media/Nanoq/Files/Attached%20Files/Finans/DK/Oekonomisk%20raad/2018%20-%20%C3%B8konomisk%20r%C3%A5ds%20rapport%20dk.pdf

the research participants, it was often possible to extract other relevant information, such as gender, age, and location.[32]

A total of 80 young Greenlanders, 30 (37.5 per cent) males and 50 (62.5 per cent) females, between the age of 15 and 30 years were recruited as Photo Forum group members. Twenty-one (26 per cent) of them qualified as active participants in the Photo Forum study and a subsequent online survey. To qualify as an active participant the group members were to contribute with at least one photo and annotation during the data collection period of four consecutive weeks. Fifty-nine per cent of the respondents were partly passive, having made no contributions to the study but who had been following the activity and input shared within the Photo Forum group. Three per cent were passive: group members who had made no contributions to the study nor followed the activity within the group. Nine of the active participants also agreed to separate, more in-depth, semi-structured online interviews with the researcher, where the interview took the photos produced by each participant as its point of departure.

The young Greenlanders were from cities and settlements all over Greenland, from Qaqortoq in Southwest Greenland to Uummannaq in Northwest Greenland, and from Tasiilaq in East Greenland to Maniitsoq in West Greenland, and also included a small number of Greenlandic students studying in Denmark. Most of the respondents, however, resided in Nuuk.

Why Facebook?

Evans-Cowley and Hollander have highlighted the value of internet-based participation tools in creating an interactive and networked environment for decision-making, which is appropriate to this study as a way to build a "common language" and as a means to elicit young peoples' concerns and priorities.[33]

Statistics show that 61 per cent of the Greenlandic population – approximately 34,000 out of a total of 55,860 people – are registered on Facebook and use this social medium on a daily basis.[34] Similarly, Facebook proved to be the most widely used social media platform among the young participants. Representing a widely used, low-cost, simple, and familiar tool, this social media network proved particularly useful in cutting across the vast distances between the widely scattered cities and settlements of Greenland. As one of the young participants put it,"when people live this far from each other, as people do here in Greenland, a 'place' like Facebook is a useful tool to keep each other updated about what's going on in our lives." Although (high-speed) web access is not equally available to the poorest members of society and the more remote

---

32 Michael Kosinski, Michal, Sandra C. Matz, Samuel D. Gosling, Vesselin Popov, and David Stillwell, "Facebook as a Research Tool for the Social Sciences: Opportunities, Challenges, Ethical Considerations, and Practical Guidelines," *American Psychological Association* 1, no. 6 (2015), 543–556.

33 Jennifer Evans-Cowley and Justin Hollander, "The New Generation of Public Participation: Internet-based Participation Tools," *Planning Practice and Research* 25, no. 3 (2010).

34 *Greenland Today*, "Facebook Connects Greenland," September 13, 2016, http://greenlandtoday.com/facebook-connects-greenland/?lang=en

settlements, it was – in line with other case studies – possible through the use of Facebook to raise awareness of the project and across wide distances reach people who might otherwise not have become aware of the study and enable them to join it, thereby establishing remote involvement. Further, the common use of Facebook "posts" – the sharing of photos with a short text attached – was suitable to combine with the initial stages of the method of photo-elicitation, enabling engagement in a prompt and straightforward manner in their own time.

Photo-elicitation – a collaborative approach to youth engagement

Photo-elicitation is a visual method widely applied within the social sciences, and particularly common in youth studies, where drawings, photos, collages, timelines and other respondent-generated visual data are utilised with the purpose of eliciting in-depth understandings of respondents' views and experiences on various phenomena. Emphasised for its collaborative and more versatile qualities, photo-elicitation may prompt unique, in-depth knowledge compared to what is possible to convey through standard verbal interview procedures alone.[35]

This more creative approach appealed to the young research participants, encouraged engagement and enhanced empowerment of this frequently marginalised group in society. With their self-produced visual representations, they attached a short annotation explaining in writing what they wished to express through the visual images. In this way, the young participants conveyed information about their "interests and values," "hopes and dreams," "fears and worries" and "visions for the future" – themes highly relevant to planners and decision-makers seeking to improve opportunities for "future stakeholders" within areas such as education, work, family life, health and leisure.[36] The key themes detected on the basis of the collected photos and annotations were thematically analysed and are presented and discussed below.

---

35 Susan A. Tucker and John V. Dempsey, "Photo-Interviewing: A Tool for Evaluating Technological Innovations," *Evaluation Review* 15 (1991), 639–654; Marcus Banks and Howard Morphy, *Rethinking Visual Anthropology* (New Haven CT: Yale University Press, 1997); Marcus Banks, *Visual Methods in Social Research* (London: Sage, 2001); Sarah Pink, *Visual Ethnography* (London: Sage, 2001); Gillian Rose, *Visual Methodologies* (London: Sage, 2001); Douglas Harper, "Talking about Pictures: A Case for Photo-Elicitation," *Visual Studies* 17, no. 1 (2002), 13–26; Malcolm Collier, "Approaches to Analysis in Visual Anthropology," in *Handbook of Visual Analysis*, eds Theo Van Leeuwen and Carey Jewitt (London: Sage, 2008).
36 Nora Didkowsky, Michael Ungar, and Linda Liebenberg, "Using Visual Methods to Capture Embedded Processes of Resilience for Youth across Cultures and Contexts," *Journal of the Canadian Academy of Child and Adolescent Psychiatry* 19 (2010), 12–18; Gillian Symon and Cathy Cassell, *Qualitative Organizational Research: Core Methods and Current Challenges* (Los Angeles: Sage, 2012); Dawn Lyon and Giulia Carabelli, "Researching Young People's Orientations to the Future: The Methodological Challenges of Using Arts Practice," *Journal of Qualitative Research* 16, no. 4 (2015), 430–445; Giulia Carabelli and Dawn Lyon, "Young People's Orientations to the Future: Navigating the Present and Imagining the Future," *Journal of Youth Studies* 19, no. 8 (2016).

Priorities and concerns as perceived by the Greenlandic youth

Social relations, education and work

The primary "values and interests," as defined by the young research participants, were by far their social relations (family, spouses and friends), along with education and work. Responses strongly indicated that family and friends not only have great influence on where the young participants choose to settle in the future but also constitute a determining factor in how far they progress through the education system. For the majority of the participants, being close to family and friends was further considered a main criterion for whether the participants saw a future for themselves in Greenland or elsewhere. The future aspirations of the young Greenlanders involved, in particular, pursuing their dream education and/or dream job, and support from "mentors" and/or from home, especially from parents or grandparents, was highlighted as a great motivational factor for achieving these goals. From the perspective of the young participants, education means more freedom in the sense that getting an education gives you more freedom to do what you love. It constitutes a "window to the world," which allows the young people to travel, explore and gain new experiences, all of which were also highlighted as important ways to obtain quality of life and wellbeing (see Figures 5.1 and 5.2).

The young participants further viewed education not only as a means to their own independence, but also as a means to an independent Greenland. As stated by one of the young participants in an interview: "The education level is slowly rising, whether it be electricians or academics. I think it is great. There is a need for all of them. It contributes to making Greenland more independent and free." Alongside issues of inadequate housing, inequality, and the vast social problems such as violence, exploitation and abuse, several of the young participants emphasised the low level of education as among some of the greatest ongoing contemporary challenges faced in Greenland. Simultaneously, the young Greenlanders emphasised a heightened education level as a key to overcome many of these challenges.

Wellbeing and quality of life

Along with the goals of pursuing their preferred education and jobs, the young Greenlanders who participated in the Photo Forum study expressed an overall aspiration to be happy. Above all else, the participants seemed concerned with quality of life and wellbeing for themselves and their family. One of the sources of quality of life and wellbeing mentioned by participants was the nature of Greenland, in which many of the participants considered themselves deeply rooted as part of their identity as Greenlanders. As stated by a participant during one of the in-depth photo-interviews:

> It is a kind of therapy. I like just sitting in the nature, watching it, taking it all in. Or walking. The nature is a part of me; I carry it with me. Like, when I go

Figure 5.1 "The most important things in my life are my son (him with the branches in the stroller) and my freedom. The freedom to do what I want: study, draw, or go make discoveries with my son."
Source: Photo and annotation: Young Greenlandic woman, 26 years old, May 2015.

for a walk in the wintertime here in Denmark, in the slush, and come across a spot of snow that sounds just "right," has the right kind of sound as you step on it. It takes me back to Greenland.

Going sailing, fishing, hiking, hunting, or picking berries with family and friends were all activities highly cherished by the young Greenlanders. Further, being with loved ones and having the opportunity to encounter new challenges and experiences were considered prerequisites for a "good" life.

Culture and identity

The responses elicited from the young participants also disclosed features of identity and belonging. Some stressed their deep-seated ties to Greenland as

Figure 5.2 "In 10 years I will be a nurse, live in Nuuk and have a family of my own. Up till then I will have had an internship in Tanzania and Vietnam, worked as a nurse at Doctors Without Borders and in a war zone. The picture symbolises the road forward at the only 'highway' in Greenland: The ice by Uummannaq."
Source: Photo and annotation: Young Greenlandic woman, 24 years old, May 2015.

being due to a sense of strong connection with the Arctic nature, their family and upbringing and Greenlandic foods. Several participants mentioned the importance of preserving the Greenlandic language and also expressed a wish to preserve Greenland's culture and traditions. Along with social relations, how strong they considered their ties to Greenlandic culture and Greenland as a place of "home" was often linked to whether they planned to stay or return to Greenland in later years.

One challenge in pursuing a higher education, as emphasised by the participants who were Greenlandic students living in Denmark at the time when the Photo Forum study was conducted, was the sense of having a "divided identity," being "Danish" and "Greenlandic" concurrently. When asked about their "fears and concerns," many responded that they were concerned about not wanting to return to Greenland, as they feared they would not feel welcome in their own home country. Several of the young participants expressed a frustration with the often prominent "them" and "us" discourse flourishing within Greenlandic society. For instance, some of the young people felt discriminated against, due to their non-Greenlandic appearance or inability to speak "Kalaallisut" (West Greenlandic) fluently. It was also a concern among those with children, or those wanting to have children in the future, that their children might be discriminated against or looked down upon for not being "true Greenlanders," for instance because they might not speak the native language or have the "right" appearance. The young

Figure 5.3 "My family, my friends and the experiences I gather are most important in my life. This picture also shows my passion for physical activities, both indoors and outdoors."
Source: Photo and annotation: Young Greenlandic man, 22 years old, May 2015.

Figure 5.4 "The most important thing for me is my work, travelling, new challenges, new experiences, proving to myself that I can do even better, nature and my family."
Source: Photo and annotation: Young Greenlandic woman, 27 years old, May 2015.

participants highlighted these reasons as obstacles to a future for themselves or their family in Greenland. Such concerns are displayed in the following quote, from an interview with a Greenlandic student in Denmark:

> I believe that all who wish to work for our country, and who feel at home here, should be thought of as Greenlanders. We all need that – it should not be "them" and "us" [...] Though I do understand and speak Greenlandic, I am constantly reminded that I am not "Greenlandic" enough. It makes me feel "less" Greenlandic than those who fully master the language.

However, the participants also expressed a belief or hope that this would not be the case and that people in general receive a warm welcome and a chance to be a part of the local community. Language featured as a recurring theme among the young participants, with "Kalaallisut" as both a value to be maintained and passed on to the future generations and as an important – but often challenging – part of Greenlandic culture and of being a Greenlander. One participant explained in an interview that:

> It is difficult to hold on to and keep up with the Greenlandic language. But I will at least try, for the sake of myself, but also for the sake of my daughter. It is important that she at least has knowledge of the Greenlandic language and is able to understand it. It has to do with having this sense of community, connectedness with your origin.

Another respondent expressed that "[language] means a lot in Greenland. In Greenland, many view the language as a defining factor of who you are, whether you are Danish or Greenlandic. [...] It is like you have 'betrayed' the country, not learning it [Greenlandic] as a child, or not having maintained it."

On the other hand, language was also mentioned as a source of power, in the sense that being able to master multiple languages provides more opportunities. In that connection, Danish and English were mentioned as key to succeeding in the education system, based on the claim that it is very difficult to get through the education system without being fluent in these two languages.

Perspectives on Greenlandic independence and the extractive industry development in Greenland

An independent Greenland, and the road towards becoming independent, was also a recurring theme. As expressed by two of the interview participants below, an independent Greenland is a subject addressed with mixed feelings, being both something to aspire to in the future as well as a great source of concern:

> My biggest worry is the question of the autonomy of Greenland. I share the aspiration for Greenland to become independent. But the "here-and-now-at-

Figure 5.5 "In my home I have two shelves with things that remind me of my origin, my home. Greenland has changed through the years I have lived abroad, so I am not sure what to expect when I return. I hope I will be able to feel at home. I am consistently fighting against these objects becoming 'tourist artefacts' in my own home, trying to keep the traditions they represent alive through me."
Source: Photo and annotation: Greenlandic woman, 29 years old, May 2015.

Figure 5.6 "I have a wish and expectation that I one day will return to my home town with my boyfriend and our daughter. In the mean-time my daughter learns about Greenland through Greenlandic books."
Source: Photo and annotation: Greenlandic woman, 29 years old, May 2015.

whatever-cost" way of thinking scares me. If we, and those who lead our country, do not think about this thoroughly, it can go horribly wrong.

I think any country would want independence. I think that it is possible for Greenland to gain independence, but it is a matter of when it is ready for it. In a divided country with a divided population, independence may bring people back together, but it could also destroy the country. So, I am not sure that is what Greenland needs right now. The financial situation must be improved, and the people have to be able to stand together more as a nation than what I see at the moment.

The importance of stepping out of the passive role of "victims" and instead taking on a more active role, was emphasised by the young participants. They believe that everybody must take responsibility for their own lives and create a good life for themselves and their children, before Greenland can become truly ready for independence. However big or small their contribution is, everybody can play a part in improving Greenlandic society. On the path towards independence, it is also important to be allowed to "think big," to be creative and innovative, and to enable new businesses to grow. From the perspective of some of the participants, it is very difficult to gain both general as well as financial support to make this happen.

Uncertainty regarding the extractive industry development in Greenland was also revealed in the findings. A few of the young participants stated that they feared poor management of the extractive sector, which could have severe consequences for Greenland at a local, regional, and national level. The majority, however, did not feel sufficiently informed about opportunities and risks pertaining to an expansion of the extractive industry in Greenland to have an "independent opinion" on the matter. Most of the young participants vaguely stated that they welcomed more mineral and petroleum activities – "What choice does Greenland have besides that opportunity?" – but emphasised that the development had to take place in the most sustainable manner possible, fearing a potential oil spill would destroy the vulnerable and beautiful environment, which they consider an important part of Greenland's culture as well as a brand in relation to the outside world.

Many stated that if Greenland is to go down the path towards becoming a mining nation, it is of vital importance that people are properly informed and know of the positive as well as negative impacts of expanding the extractive sector. The responsibility to ensure a proper and fair management of the extractive development is placed with the Greenlandic politicians, but, at the same time, the young Greenlanders doubt that the government will be able to properly handle the development and thus ensure the best possible benefits for Greenland. As expressed by one of the interviewees:

I hope that people living in Greenland are more well-informed about the subject than I am, and that the politicians look thoroughly into the matter. When they do, they are also responsible for sharing this knowledge with the population. If something goes wrong, everyone will suffer from the consequences. I hope that they put their heads together to make reasonable decisions.

Others believed that there should not be a mining industry in Greenland at all and that Greenland should "stay clean" and instead ought to broaden the scope and consider new sources of income, for instance through developing the unrealised tourism potential, or by giving greater priority to the living resources, such as new sources of food, the fishing industry, and alternative energy sources like hydropower.

Reflective concluding remarks

The Photo Forum youth case study shows the potential to start filling the gap between formal guidelines and meaningful participation in practice, both within and outside Greenland and across sectors. The explorative case study that has unfolded in this chapter has shed light on some of the challenges and opportunities for applying the social media network Facebook and a visual approach – photo-elicitation – as alternative and supplementary participatory means to engage the often marginalised group of youth and capture their interests, values, fears,

Figure 5.7 "This is a picture of a block of flats, 'Blok P,' which was torn down in 2012. The flag on the building symbolises change and expectations attached to the implementation of self-rule in Greenland. One of my fears for the future is that the economic situation, and the problem with housing, does not improve, and that the social inequalities become even bigger so that even more people decide to emigrate. Many, especially young people, lack a proper home, which can make it hard for them to focus on studies and their future. Having a roof over their head is a vital prerequisite for young people to grow as humans, learn and prepare for their future."
Source: Photo and annotation: Young Greenlandic man, 30 years old, May 2015.

hopes and aspirations for the future along with their thoughts on future extractive development.

The new digital technologies and media, such as social media networks, have revolutionised communication and information conveyance. Mobile technology is a part of the everyday lives of today's youth, allowing easy and instant communication on a global scale, social interaction and participation "on the go," diminishing the issue of location in many respects.[37] Facebook as a communicative platform proved effective in engaging young Greenlanders as it served not only as a flexible, familiar and commonly applied medium among youth for receiving and providing information across vast distances between the cities, settlements, and across national borders; it also functioned as a safe forum for engagement.[38] However, the high percentage of non-participant Photo Forum group members suggests that one should not exaggerate the influence of online participation tools for active engagement. Facebook is exactly that, a tool. Although social media may provide an opportunity for providing input and having a say, it does not guarantee active participation. Participation requires action and this power lies with the young people themselves.[39]

Combined with the visual approach, however, the empowerment of youth is arguably enhanced, proving potential for active engagement among the young participants by serving as familiar means of information sharing and communication. The use of photos motivated engagement by capturing the interest of youth and allowing them to express themselves in a non-verbal way which strongly resembled their everyday use of Facebook. Arguably, the use of visual representations further prompted reflection on and critical thinking about issues central and relevant to the lives of the young individuals, placing an emphasis on the potential of the photo-elicitation method to reveal different perspectives and views from the often taken-for-granted assumptions about the ways the young participants perceive their futures.[40]

The study indicates that online and visual participation forms may work best as part of a broader participatory process, which enables face-to-face interaction and "real" commitment among participants. Rather than competitive fora of traditional public participation, the use of Facebook and visual images as a frame for youth engagement may thus serve as complementary forms of participatory means to supplement the more traditional approaches.[41]

At any rate, the findings emphasise the importance of project proponents and planners being aware of reaching and engaging youth on their own terms by the appliance of tools that the young people are already using. The study's findings

---

37 Caroline Wang and Mary A. Burris, "Photovoice: Concept, Methodology, and Use for Participatory Needs Assessment," *Health Education and Behaviour* 24 (1997), 369–387.
38 Ibid.; Nina Eliasoph, *The Politics of Volunteering* (Cambridge: Polity Press, 2013).
39 Jacqueline Briggs, *Young People and Political Participation: Teen Players* (London: Palgrave Macmillan, 2017).
40 Skjervedal, *Towards Meaningful Youth Engagement*.
41 Evans-Cowley and Hollander, "The New Generation of Public Participation."

certainly prove that young people do have a lot on their hearts and minds and can contribute with valuable, otherwise hidden knowledge and perspectives, revealing features which to a greater or lesser degree have relevance for understanding what guides their actions, the choices they make for their lives, as well as how they imagine the future, including the future of the extractive industry in Greenland.

From the findings of the youth case study, it is particularly interesting that none of the participants perceived the extractive industries as a sector in which they themselves would take part. When the subject of extractive industry development was broached, it was talked about as something that takes place outside young Greenlanders' sphere of involvement. Further, when discussing the benefits and challenges that the future extractive industry development might bring, the young participants talked more of how they might impact Greenland rather than how such developments might have a direct impact on their own lives. Their responses moreover revealed a lack of trust in the ability of the Greenlandic government properly to manage the social impacts of the future development, which also resembles a recurring theme within the general criticism of public participation practices in Greenland.[42]

The responses of the young Greenlanders are particularly interesting as they stand in stark contrast to the great role that is commonly assigned to Greenlandic youth as "future bearers of hope" in securing local content in the extractive projects, deemed the main way of ensuring positive benefits to Greenlandic society.[43] Rather, many of the young Greenlanders who took part in the Photo Forum study seemingly feel disconnected from their home country, or have other plans for their future than working in the extractive industry. Judging from the themes brought up by the Greenlanders studying in Denmark at the time of this study, many of the young participants are currently marked by a fear that they are not welcome in their own home country, and similarly fear discrimination against their children if they stay or return to Greenland. Many of the participants expressed frustration at the fervent ongoing "nationalistic" debates that focus on what makes a "true" Greenlander,[44] causing a division in society at a time when a united Greenland is highly needed. Rather than actively engaging in this development, the young Greenlanders take the role of spectators of the extractive industry development, stating that they have other ideas of what they want to do for a living rather than work in the industry or in other ways take part in developing the extractive sector. The young participants seemed more concerned with how to maintain and improve their quality of life and wellbeing, including being close to loved ones and close to nature, and being able to pursue their goals in education and jobs of their own choice; to create "the good life" for themselves and their (future) children, rather than to follow the objective for the young generation in Greenland set forth by the Greenlandic government.

42 Olsen and Hansen, "Perceptions of Public Participation," 7; Hansen et al., "Managing the Social Impacts," 27; Skjervedal, *Towards Meaningful Youth Engagement*, 202.
43 Skjervedal, *Towards Meaningful Youth Engagement*, 202, 208.
44 Kuupik Vandersee Kleist and Rebekka Johanne Knudsen, "Sitting on Gold: A Report on the Use of Informally Acquired Skills in Greenland" (Copenhagen: A Greenland Perspective Publication – University of Copenhagen, 2016), 18.

So, what can we learn from the inputs and perspectives put forth by the young stakeholders for future improvements of the participation process and practice in relation to extractives?

Certainly the study shows that by adapting participatory approaches and methods to the specific target group, otherwise marginalised "future stakeholders" such as the Greenlandic youth, that group can be empowered to engage actively in current discussions about development to the benefit of both the decision-makers and the future generations. The case of the Greenlandic youth speaks to the necessity to break the framework of current public participation practices and develop new approaches to ensure active and meaningful engagement and enhance the mutual dialogue and learning that are vital for a sustainable future development.[45] The young Greenlanders hold valuable perspectives on and opinions about the current development, which are highly relevant to and should be included in discussions about where Greenland is headed in the future.

The Photo Forum youth study grew out of the recognition that if one approaches people in local communities and asks them to provide their perspective on "extractive industry development" or "public participation" they will frequently reply that they know too little to have a valid opinion. To make these discussions relevant to ordinary citizens the framing of the questions must be relevant to their everyday lives. It is thus advantageous to consider broadening the range of forms of public participation, providing opportunities for including a broader representative voice among the local communities, through tailoring the participation form(s) to the specific project, local context, and target group, with a focus on creating a "safe forum" for active and collaborative engagement.[46] In the case of the youth study in Greenland, Facebook served as this "safe forum" – a familiar platform used by the young participants on a frequent basis for communication. The visual dimension added to this by serving as a common language between the researcher and the participants, and as a means to elicit valuable knowledge about young peoples' concerns, needs, and priorities for change in decision-making.

The case study emphasises the necessity of not neglecting the human factor in the extractive industry development. The participants treasured an opportunity to have their voices heard on matters which they consider important, while voicing their otherwise hidden stories – stories about identity and belonging, of values and strong ties to both family and nature, and how these features influence the way they think and act. More knowledge of the benefits of youth participation may aid to heighten awareness among planners and decision-makers – as well as among youth themselves – and enable them to have a better and clearer view of young people as resources and hence improve the real involvement and influence of young people in planning processes and decisions that affect their lives.[47]

45 Skjervedal, *Towards Meaningful Youth Engagement*, 204.
46 Ibid., 206.
47 Barry Checkoway, Kameshwari Pothukuchi, and Janet Finn, "Youth Participation in Community Planning: What are the Benefits?" *Journal of Planning, Education and Research* 14, no. 2 (1995): 134–139.

References

ACIA. "Impacts of a Warming Arctic: Arctic Climate Impact Assessment." In *ACIA Overview Report*. Cambridge: Cambridge University Press, 2004.

Banks, Marcus and Howard Morphy. *Rethinking Visual Anthropology*. New Haven CT: Yale University Press, 1997.

Banks, Marcus. *Visual Methods in Social Research*. London: Sage, 2001.

Bisset, Ron. "Methods of Consultation and Public Participation." In *Environmental Assessment in the Developing and Transitional Countries: Principles, Methods and Practice*, edited by Norman Lee and Clive George, 149–160. Chichester: Wiley, 2000.

Briggs, Jacqueline. *Young People and Political Participation: Teen Players*. London: Palgrave Macmillan, 2017.

Brundtland, Gro. *Report of the World Commission on Environment and Development: Our Common Future*. UN Doc. A/42/427. August 4, 1987.

Carabelli, Giulia and Dawn Lyon. "Young People's Orientations to the Future: Navigating the Present and Imagining the Future." *Journal of Youth Studies* 19, no. 8 (2016): 1110–1127.

Cashmore, Matthew, Alan Bond, and Dick Cobb. "The Role and Functioning of Environmental Assessment: Theoretical Reflections upon an Empirical Investigation of Causation." *Journal of Environmental Management* 88 (2008): 1233–1248.

Chavéz, Basilio Verduzco and Antonio Sanchéz Bernal. "Planning Hydroelectric Power Plants with the Public: A Case of Organizational and Social Learning in Mexico." *Journal of Impact Assessment and Project Appraisal* 26, no. 3 (2008): 163–176.

Checkoway, Barry and Lorraine Gutiérrez. *Youth Participation and Community Change*. New York: Routledge, 2011.

Checkoway, Barry, Kameshwari Pothukuchi, and Janet Finn. "Youth Participation in Community Planning: What Are the Benefits?" *Journal of Planning, Education and Research* 14, no. 2 (1995): 134–139.

Collier, Malcolm. "Approaches to Analysis in Visual Anthropology". In *Handbook of Visual Analysis*, edited by Theo Van Leeuwen and Carey Jewitt, 35–60. London: Sage, 2008.

Committee for Greenlandic Mineral Resources to the Benefit of Society. *To the Benefit of Greenland*. Nuuk and Copenhagen: University of Greenland and University of Copenhagen, 2014. http://greenlandperspective.ku.dk/this_is_greenland_perspective/background/report-papers/To_the_benefit_of_Greenland.pdf

Convention on the Rights of the Child 1989. United Nations Treaty Series 1577, 3.

Didkowsky, Nora, Michael Ungar, and Linda Liebenberg. "Using Visual Methods to Capture Embedded Processess of Resilience for Youth across Cultures and Contexts." *Journal of the Canadian Academy of Child and Adolescent Psychiatry* 19 (2010): 12–18.

Driskell, David. *Creating Better Cities with Children and Youth: A Manual for Participation*. Abingdon: Taylor & Francis, 2002.

Eliasoph, Nina. *The Politics of Volunteering*. Cambridge: Polity Press, 2013.

Evans-Cowley, Jennifer and Justin Hollander. "The New Generation of Public Participation: Internet-based Participation Tools." *Planning Practice and Research* 25, no. 3 (2010): 397–408.

George, Clive. "Comparative Review of Environmental Assessment Procedures and Practice." In *Environmental Assessment in the Developing and Transitional Countries: Principles, Methods and Practice*, edited by Norman Lee and Clive George, 35–70. Chichester: Wiley, 2000.

Glasson, John, Riki Therivel, and Andrew Chadwick. "Participation, Presentation and Review." In *Introduction to Environmental Impact Assessment*, 3rd edn, edited by John Glasson, Riki Therivel and Andrew Chadwick, 165–194. London and New York: Routledge, 2005.

Government of Greenland. "Oliestrategi 2019–2023" [Oil strategy 2019–2023]. Nuuk: Prografisk Aps, 2019. https://naalakkersuisut.gl/~/media/Nanoq/Files/Hearings/2019/Oliestrategi%20for%202019_2023/Documents/Oliestrategi%202019-2023%20DK%204.pdf

Government of Greenland. *Guidelines on the Process and Preparation of the SIA Report for Mineral Rrojects*. Nuuk: ProGrafisk Aps, 2016. https://www.govmin.gl/images/stories/minerals/sia_guideline/SIA_guideline.pdf

Greenland Today. "Facebook Connects Greenland." September 13, 2016. http://greenlandtoday.com/facebook-connects-greenland/?lang=en

Hansen, Anne Merrild, Frank Vanclay, Peter Croal, and Anna-Sofie Hurup Skjervedal. "Managing the Social Impacts of the Rapidly-Expanding Extractive Industries in Greenland." *The Extractive Industries and Society* 3 (2016): 25–33.

Harper, Douglas. "Talking about Pictures: A Case for Photo-Elicitation." *Visual Studies* 17, no. 1 (2002): 13–26.

Head, Brian W. "Community Engagement: Participation in Whose Terms?" *Australian Political Science* 42, no. 3 (2007): 441–454.

Hibbard, Michael and Susan Lurie. "Saving Land but Losing Ground: Challenges to Community Planning in the Era of Participation." *Journal of Planning Education and Research* 20, no. 2 (2000): 187–195.

HS Analyse. *Befolkningen om borgermøder om råstoffer* [Public opinions at public meetings about natural resources]. Nuuk: World Wide Fund for Nature, 2014. http://awsassets.wwfdk.panda.org/downloads/hs_analyse_borgermoder.pdf

Innes, Judith E. and David E. Booher. "Reframing Public Participation: Strategies of the 21st Century." *Planning Theory and Practice* 5, no. 4 (2004): 419–436.

Kapoor, Ilan. "Towards Participatory *Environ Manag*?" *Journal of Environmental Management* 63, no. 3 (2001): 269–279.

Kleist, Kuupik Vandersee and Rebekka Johanne Knudsen. *Sitting on Gold: A Report on the Use of Informally Acquired Skills in Greenland*. A Greenland Perspective Publication. Copenhagen: University of Copenhagen, 2016.

Kørnøv, Lone. "Public Participation." In *Tools for Sustainable Development*, edited by Lone Kørnøv, Mikkel Thrane, Arne Remmen, and Henrik Lund, 719–738. Aalborg: Aalborg Universitetsforlag, 2007.

Kosinski, Michael, Sandra C. Matz, Samuel D. Gosling, Vesselin Popov, and David Stillwell. "Facebook as a Research Tool for the Social Sciences Opportunities, Challenges, Ethical Considerations, and Practical Guidelines." *American Psychological Association* 1, no. 6 (2015): 543–556.

Kurt-Schai, Ruthanne. "The Roles of Youth in Society: A Reconceptualization." *The Educational Forum* 52, no. 2 (1988): 113–132.

Langhoff, Rune. *Med Folkets Mandat? Høringsprocesser og Borgerinddragelse på Råstofområdet* [With the People's Authorisation? Hearing Processes and Public Participation within the Area of Natural Resources]. Nuuk and Copenhagen: Inuit Circumpolar Council (ICC) and the World Wide Fund for Nature (WWF), August 2013. http://inuit.org/fileadmin/user_upload/File/2013/Reports/Med_folkets_mandat__DK__19_august_2013.pdf

Lockie, Stewart, Maree Franetovich, Sanjay Sharma, and John Rolfe. "Democratisation versus Engagement? Social and Economic Impact Assessment and Community Participation in the Coal Mining Industry of the Bowen Bassin, Australia." *Journal of Impact Assessment and Project Appraisal* 26, no. 3 (2008): 177–188.

Lyon, Dawn and Giulia Carabelli. "Researching Young People's Orientations to the Future: The Methodological Challenges of Using Arts Practice." *Journal of Qualitative Research* 16, no. 4 (2015): 430–445.

Marot, Naja and Barbara C. Mali. "Youth and Regional Development: Participation by Future Stakeholders in Today's Decisions on Post-Mining Regions." In *Post-Mining Regions in Central Europe: Problems, Potentials, Possibilities*, edited by Peter Wirth, Barbara C. Mali, and Wolfgang Fischer, 195–212. Munich: Oekom, 2012.

Nuttall, Mark. "Anticipation, Climate Change, and Movement in Greenland." *Etudes/Inuit/Studies* 34, no. 1 (2010): 21–37.

Nuttall, Mark. "Imagining and Governing the Greenlandic Resource Frontier." *The Polar Journal* 2 (2012): 113–124.

O'Faircheallaigh, Ciaran. "Public Participation and Environmental Impact Assessment: Purposes, Implications, and Lessons for Public Policy Making." *Environmental Impact Assessment Review* 30, no. 1 (2010): 19–27.

Økonomisk Råd. *Nunatta aningaasaqarnera – Grønlands Økonomi* [Greenland's Economy]. October 2018. https://naalakkersuisut.gl/~/media/Nanoq/Files/Attached%20Files/Finans/DK/Oekonomisk%20raad/2018%20-%20%C3%B8konomisk%20r%C3%A5ds%20rapport%20dk.pdf

Olsen, Anna-Sofie Hurup and Anne Merrild Hansen. "Perceptions of Public Participation in Impact Assessment: A Study of Offshore Oil Exploration in Greenland." *Impact Assessment and Project Appraisal* 32 (2014): 72–80.

Olsen, Anna-Sofie Hurup. "Public Participation in Environmental and Social Impact Assessment – Exploring the Human Dimension of Oil Exploration in Greenland." Master's thesis, Aalborg University, 2012.

Ottinger, Gwen. "Changing Knowledge, Local Knowledge and Knowledge Gaps: STS Insights into Procedural Justice." *Science, Technology and Human Values* 38, no. 2 (2013): 250–270.

Pink, Sarah. *Visual Ethnography*. London: Sage, 2001.

Poppel, Birger. "Living Conditions and Perceived Quality of Life Among Indigenous Peoples in the Arctic." In *Global Handbook of Quality of Life: Exploration of Well-Being of Nations and Continents*, edited by Wolfgang Glatzer, Laura Camfield, Valerie Møller, and Mariano Rojas, 715–747. New York: Springer, 2015.

"Rio Declaration on Environment and Development 1992." *International Legal Materials* 31 (1992): 876.

Rose, Gillian. *Visual Methodologies*. London: Sage, 2001.

Sejersen, Frank. *Rethinking Greenland and the Arctic in the Era of Climate Change: New Northern Horizons*. London and New York: Routledge, 2015.

Shepherd, Anne and Christi Bowler. "Beyond the Requirements: Improving Public Participation in EIA." *Journal of Environmental Planning and Management* 40, no. 6 (1997): 725–738.

Skjervedal, Anna-Sofie Hurup. "Towards Meaningful Youth Engagement: Breaking the Frame of the Current Public Participation Practice in Greenland." Ph.D. dissertation, Ilisimatusarfik: University of Greenland and Aalborg University, 2018.

Statistics Greenland. "Greenland in Figures 2018." May 2018. www.stat.gl/publ/kl/GF/2018/pdf/Greenland%20in%20Figures%202018.pdf

Symon, Gillian and Cathy Cassell. *Qualitative Organizational Research: Core Methods and Current Challenges*. Los Angeles CA: Sage, 2012.

Tucker, Susan A. and John V. Dempsey. "Photo-Interviewing: A Tool for Evaluating Technological Innovations." *Evaluation Review* 15 (1991): 639–654.

Udofia, Aniekan, Bram Noble, and Greg Poelzer. "Meaningful and Efficient? Enduring Challenges to Aboriginal Participation in Environmental Impact Assessment." *Environmental Impact Assessment Review* 65 (2017): 164–174.
UN Youth. "Definition of Youth." Accessed October 7, 2019. www.un.org/esa/socdev/documents/youth/fact-sheets/youth-definition.pdf
UN Conference on Environment and Development. *Agenda 21, Rio Declaration, Forest Principles*. New York: United Nations, 1992.
Wang, Caroline and Mary A. Burris. "Photovoice: Concept, Methodology, and Use for Participatory Needs Assessment." *Health Education and Behaviour* 24 (1997): 369–387.
Weston, Joe. "Consultation and the Conflict of Interests in the EIA Process." In *Planning and Environmental Impact Assessment in Practice*, edited by Joe Weston, 93–120. Harlow: Longman, 1997.

6 Comparative expectations of resource development in selected Greenland communities

Rachael Lorna Johnstone and Anne Merrild Hansen

Introduction

The level and intensity of mineral exploration in Greenland has been increasing in recent years. After a temporary setback during the global financial crisis, the number of licences in 2019 was at the same level as prior to the crisis. In October 2019, there were 6 active exploitation licences and 60 small-scale licences, 12 active prospecting licences, and 60 exploration licences granted. Several more were under application.[1] Viewed in light of Greenland's small population of approximately 56,000 inhabitants,[2] this level of activity represents one active licence for every thousand people. Most of the activity pertains to minerals, with a significant fall in the investment in hydrocarbon development.[3]

Extractive industries around the world have high impacts on the natural environments and people in the surrounding areas. Therefore, this level of activity creates the potential for serious and irreversible consequences for nature and Greenlanders' lifestyles, cultures and wellbeing. The Government of Greenland acknowledges the social risk and opportunities related to extractive industries. With the aim of securing that extractive projects contribute to sustainable development, attempts are made to balance national interests and protection of local values whenever projects are planned and implemented. During the application processes for licences to extract minerals and conduct exploration drilling for hydrocarbons, companies are required to undertake environmental and social impact assessments and these include mandatory public participation processes. However, recent studies have found that extractive projects bring changes at the early stages of exploration which can provoke anxiety and unrest at both individual and community level.[4] The social impacts are already present long before the impact assessments are conducted. Recent research

---

1 Greenland Minerals Authority, "List of Mineral and Petroleum Licences in Greenland," Mineral Licence and Safety Authority, October 16, 2019, 21, https://govmin.gl/images/Documents/Current_Licences_and_Activities/List_of_Licences_16-10-2019.pdf
2 "Population," Statistics Greenland, accessed August 16, 2019, www.stat.gl/dialog/topmain.asp?lang=en&sc=BE
3 Greenland Minerals Authority, "List of Mineral and Petroleum Licences in Greenland," Greenland Minerals Authority, Mineral Licence and Safety Authority, July 1, 2019, Section V.
4 Anne Merrild Hansen and Pelle Tejsner, "Identifying Challenges and Opportunities for Residents in Upernavik as Oil Companies Are Making a First Entrance into Baffin

indicates that people start adapting to potential changes as soon as they know that there is commercial interest in exploiting resources nearby and they begin to form opinions regarding the development.[5]

As there is no formal consultation or public participation at these early stages in the planning process, we investigate how people relate to potential developments and what their expectations are in this regard. We hope that our work can help improve the participatory processes in Greenland, both by informing the government of potential improvements that might be introduced and assisting the general public to understand and engage with the processes available in a more satisfactory manner.

In this chapter we present a study carried out in Greenland between May 2017 and October 2019. The aim of the study is to explore how people in different regions of Greenland relate to former, existing and planned exploration and extraction projects in their areas. This may inform companies and authorities on how to engage with people in the given areas prior, during and after development and about how to mitigate negative impacts and enhance potential benefits. The chapter begins with an explanation of the methodology and ethical considerations, followed by a short description of extractive industries in Greenland, the basic regulatory framework and an introduction to the towns and settlements included in the study. The results section follows, broken down into three main sections on visions, decision-making and influence, as well as a short discussion of issues frequently raised by the citizens not directly related to extractive industries. A subsequent analysis identifies common interests and concerns, as well as regional differences. The chapter continues with interpretations of some of the results before concluding with a brief account of the implications of the study for improving participation in Greenland.

Methodology and ethical considerations

The study drew on theoretical approaches of Beck and Giddens regarding risk, modernity and risk perception.[6] In light of the government's ambitious resource development strategy, we sought to understand people's perceptions, hopes and concerns for the future and the role that extractive industries played in shaping them.

Our central research question was:

How do people perceive the impact of extractive projects around Greenland on their future?

Bay," *Arctic Anthropology* 53, no. 1 (2016): 84–94, https://doi.org/10.3368/aa.53.1.84
5 Ibid.; Anne Merrild Hansen and Rachael Lorna Johnstone, "In the Shadow of the Mountain: Assessing Early Impacts on Community Development from Two Mining Prospects in South Greenland," *The Extractive Industries and Society* 6, no. 2 (2019): 480–88, https://doi.org/10.1016/j.exis.2019.01.012
6 Hansen and Johnstone, 2019. See also, e.g., Ulrich Beck, *A Critical Introduction to Risk Society* (London: Pluto Press, 2004); and Anthony Giddens, *Runaway World: How Globalization Is Reshaping Our Lives* (New York: Routledge, 2003).

Our sub-research questions were:

1 Visions: what risks and opportunities do the citizens foresee in relation to extractive industries locally and in Greenland in general?
2 Decision-making: how are decisions made and do the citizens consider the allocation of risk and responsibility to be just?
3 Influence: how do the citizens consider that extractive projects affect their prospects and preparations for the future?

We use the term "citizen" to refer to the people with whom we spoke during our fieldwork. We choose this term in preference to the more passive "interviewee" to indicate the agency of the people that contributed to our research. They did not simply answer questions that we presented to them but contributed with their own insights and often led the dialogue. Many of them are also active in local or national debates regarding extractive industries and other issues. The term "citizen" is used in a social sense, rather than a strictly legal sense, as we did not inquire into people's legal nationality but considered all residents of an area as "citizens."

While a great deal of research has been conducted in the Narsaq area, the site of the Kuannersuit (Kvanefjeld) rare earth element and uranium project, and many researchers visit the capital city, Nuuk, we surmised that there was limited attention paid to people living in other settlements around Greenland, particularly those that are difficult to reach. We therefore applied a comparative approach to our findings for each settlement to discern if there were notable differences around Greenland and what factors might explain these differences. Thus, we introduced a fourth sub-research question:

1 Comparisons: are there notable regional differences in perceptions of extractive industries around Greenland, and what factors can explain these differences?

A total of 92 citizens joined us in the study, representing 16 settlements. A summary of the fieldwork and brief introduction to the settlements is presented below. We initially sought citizens through direct email and telephone contact as well as calling for citizens on local Facebook pages. We relied in addition on personal contacts through the university where we both work, as well as personal friendships and acquaintanceships. We relied on a "snowball" approach, asking our citizens directly if they could recommend others who might be interested in speaking to us, and we also struck up spontaneous conversations. We sought citizens from a broad pool, including local and central government, small business, farming, education, social services, tourism, NGOs, police and community services.

The interviews were held in a mixture of West Greenlandic, English and Danish. Citizens sometimes switched language mid-interview in order to express themselves more comfortably. Written notes were taken but a decision was taken early on not to record the discussions as people were more willing to speak freely when the recording device was switched off. Shortly after the interviews, the notes were typed up and we reflected together on what we had learned.

South Greenland, especially Narsaq, has been inundated with researchers and journalists seeking to learn more about the Kuannersuit project, and for this reason we were conscious of "interview fatigue." The conversations were therefore relatively unstructured, giving the citizens the opportunity to speak freely about their own hopes and concerns regarding development rather than sticking to a strict list of questions. During a brainstorming session at the beginning of the project, we developed a number of questions to which we would return in interviews if we believed that a citizen might wish to say more about a particular topic. These were inspired by existing literature in the field but did not follow any single study. As we sought to understand people's perceptions, we did not challenge any views presented or fact-check any statements after the meetings.

Neither of us identifies as indigenous, although Anne grew up in South Greenland in a mixed family and speaks West Greenlandic (Kalaallisut). We endeavoured to uphold principles of relationships, respect, responsibility and reciprocity in our research with Inuit and other Greenlanders, though we acknowledge that we may not understand these in the same way as indigenous people.[7] To establish a personal relationship, we allowed each person to introduce themselves according to their own terms before we did the same, sharing our own background, before explaining the aims of the research project. We demonstrated respect by listening to our citizens, allowing them to steer the conversation to a large extent and waiting for them to identify the issues they considered most important rather than leading with a narrow list of questions pertaining only to our research on extractive industries. (Nevertheless, we recognise that identifying ourselves as working for an Oil and Gas Research Centre and describing our research project would itself influence the citizen's contribution.) Later, based on our notes, we categorised responses according to our research framework. In terms of responsibility, we sought explicit consent to use the citizens' comments in developing our work and in particular, for the reproduction of any photographs on our project website. We agreed not to identify any citizens by name (or other designation, such as farm-holding, that would make identification very easy). (On rare occasions, we sought explicit permission to cite someone on a specific point and asked him or her to confirm their satisfaction with a draft text before publishing.) However, we could not guarantee that readers from Greenland would not be able to guess individual identities based on context, given the very small size of some of the communities we visited and the public profiles of some of the citizens whose views may already be well known. We ensured that each was comfortable with this approach before going further. We reviewed the notes from each of the meetings and analysed the contributions of the citizens according to the three

---

7 Leola Roberta Rainbow Tsinnajinnie, Robin Starr Zape-tah-hol-ah Minthorn, and Tiffany S. Lee, "K'é and Tdayp-Tday-Gaw, "Embodying Indigenous Relationality in Research Methods," in *Applying Indigenous Research Methods: Storying with Peoples and Communities*, eds Sweeney Windchief and Timothy San Pedro (New York: Routledge, 2019), 40.

sub-research questions. We also noted common issues that were raised repeatedly that did not relate directly to extractive industries but were considered important by the citizens. We then examined the responses by region to look for similarities and differences in visions, decision-making and influence. These three broad themes are interwoven so a number of points might be presented in more than one category.

As for reciprocity, we published short briefing notes of two-to-three pages shortly after each of our fieldwork expeditions, which summarised our initial findings. These were published in English, Danish and Greenlandic and we advised the participating citizens when they were available online. We stayed in local hotels or guesthouses (with the exception of the North Greenland trip where Anne stayed on the *Arctic Command* vessel), ate in local restaurants and (on payment) with local families. We shopped in local stores, and gave small gifts to the citizens to thank them for their contribution.

We reject the (non-indigenous) view of interviewees as research subjects from whom we should obtain data and with whom the relationship ends at the end of the research period.[8] We have remained in contact with many of the citizens, through, for example, email, social media and personal meetings. Furthermore, we reject the notion that our research is objective in the sense of being separable from all its contributors and the relationships that we have established through the process.

Extractive industries in Greenland

Greenland is a country within the Kingdom of Denmark (the Realm) which, since 2009, has enjoyed self-government and, as of 2010, has had exclusive responsibility regarding extractive projects on the territory and in surrounding maritime zones.[9] Its economy and the maintenance of the standard of living to which most Greenlanders aspire, is dependent on the annual block grant from Denmark.[10] There is a great deal of attention paid internationally to Greenland's moves towards full independence as a sovereign state and this topic often rises to the fore during election campaigns.[11]

---

8 Sweeney Windchief and Timothy San Pedro, "Preface," in *Applying Indigenous Research Methods: Storying with Peoples and Communities* (New York: Routledge, 2019), xxi–xxii.
9 Danish Parliament, Act no. 473 of 12 June 2009 on Greenland Self-Government; Greenland Parliament, Act of 7 December 2009 on Mineral Resources and Mineral Resource Activities (Mineral Resources Act); "Fields of Responsibility Assumed by the Greenland Home Rule Government (I and II) and Greenland Self-Government (III) Respectively," accessed August 16, 2019, www.stm.dk/multimedia/GR_oversigt_sagsomr_270110_UK.pdf
10 Rasmus Gjedssø Bertelsen, Jens C. Justinussen, and Coco Smits, "Energy as a Developmental Strategy: Creating Knowledge-Based Energy Sectors in Iceland, the Faroe Islands, and Greenland," in *Handbook of the Politics of the Arctic*, eds Leif Christian Jensen and Geir Hønneland (Cheltenham: Edward Elgar, 2015).
11 See, e.g., Shafi Musaddique, "Greenland Eyes Independence from Denmark after Election Vote," *CNBC*, April 25, 2018, https://www.cnbc.com/2018/04/25/greenland-eyes-independence-from-denmark-after-election-vote.html; Arne Finne, "Greenland's Smallest Government Party, Partii Naleraq, Wants Full Independence from Denmark from 2021," *High North News*, March 23, 2018, https://www.highnorthnews.

130 *Rachael Lorna Johnstone and Anne Merrild Hansen*

Therefore, from outside of Greenland at least, extractive industries are often viewed as a means towards independence. However, within Greenland, economic development is welcomed for its own sake, to contribute to stability, growth and improved living conditions irrespective of larger constitutional questions.[12] We did not inquire directly into the citizens' views on independence, but in our discussions they were keen to promote economic growth and stability, good employment opportunities, stable populations and a higher standard of living for their own sakes. In other words, they were interested in increasing the economic independence of the country without necessarily seeking political independence.

Inuit traded iron and talc before the colonial period.[13] Commercial mining goes back over 200 years, with coal mining in the Disko area in the 1700s.[14] Copper, cryolite, zinc, lead, precious metals and precious gems have all been targeted historically.[15] The Danish government examined the potential uranium deposits in the 1960s, as part of its (then) strategy of developing nuclear power for its domestic energy needs, but abandoned nuclear energy in the 1980s and with it, its interest in the Greenland deposits.[16] However, the government has in recent years been promoting extractive

　　com/en/wants-independent-greenland-2021; Ragnhild Grønning, "Future Independence, Arctic Minister and Social Issues on the Agenda as Greenland Goes to Polls in Danish Elections," *High North News*, June 3, 2019, https://www.highnorthnews.com/en/future-independence-arctic-minister-and-social-issues-agenda-greenland-goes-polls-danish-elections
12 See, e.g., Naalakkersuisut Coalition Agreement 2014, "Koalitionsaftale, Fællesskab, Tryghed og Udvikling," accessed December 13, 2018, https://naalakkersuisut.gl/~/media/Nanoq/Files/Attached%20Files/Naalakkersuisut/DK/Koalitionsaftaler/SIUMUT_DEMOKRAATIT_ATASSUT_Isumaqatigiissut%20atuuttoq_04122014_dk_endelig.pdf; Naalakkersuisut Coalition Agreement 2016; Siumut, Inuit Ataqatigiit, Partii Naleraq, "Lighed, Tryghed og Udvikling," accessed December 13, 2018, https://naalakkersuisut.gl/~/media/Nanoq/Files/Attached%20Files/Naalakkersuisut/DK/Koalitionsaftaler/Koalitionsaftale_S_IA_PN_2016_2018.pdf, and Naalakkersuisut Coalition Agreement 2018; Siumut, Partii Naleraq, Atassut, Nunatta Qitornai, "Koalitionsaftale 2018, Nunarput – i fællesskab – i udvikling – med plads til alle," accessed August 16, 2019, https://naalakkersuisut.gl/~/media/Nanoq/Files/Attached%20Files/Naalakkersuisut/DK/Koalitionsaftaler/040518%20Siumut_Naleraq_Atassut_Nunatta%20qitornai_Final_da.pdf
13 Bo Sandroos, *The Greenland Mineral Resources Act: The Law and Practice of Oil, Gas and Mining in Greenland* (Copenhagen: Djøf Publishing, 2015), 55.
14 Janina Priebe, "A Modern Mine? Greenlandic Media Coverage on the Mining Community of Qullissat, Western Greenland, 1942–1968," *The Polar Journal* 8, no. 1 (February 2018): 141–62, https://doi.org/10.1080/2154896x.2018.1468620
15 Bent Ole Gram Mortensen, "The Quest for Resources – The Case of Greenland," *Journal of Military and Strategic Studies* 15, no. 2 (2014): 93–128; Frank Sejersen, *Efterforskning og udnyttelse af råstoffer i Grønland i historisk perspektiv*. Report, Committee for Greenlandic Mineral Resources to the Benefit of Society, January 2014, https://greenlandperspective.ku.dk/this_is_greenland_perspective/background/report-papers/Efterforskning_og_udnyttelse_af_r_stoffer_i_Gr_nland_i_historisk_perspektiv.pdf. See also Sandroos, 56–57 (for a list of projects from the 1850s to 2014).
16 P. Kalvig, *Preliminary Mining Assessment of the Uranium Resource at Kvanefjeld, the Ilímaussaq Intrusion, South Greenland*. Report (Roskilde, Denmark: Risø National Laboratory, 1983); Cindy Vestergaard and Gry Thomasen, "Governing Uranium in

industries at a level unprecedented for the country.[17] Development has been much slower than that anticipated in the government's 2014–18 mineral strategy, but is nonetheless viewed as a pillar of the future economy of Greenland.

Hydrocarbon exploration has a shorter and more erratic history, with five wells having been drilled between 1976 and 1977, then a pause before explorations recommenced in 2000 but have never reached the exploitation stage.[18] Evidence of extensive hydrocarbon deposits on and around Greenland is strong but their commercial viability is another matter. Since the collapse in the Brent crude price in 2014–15 and with an increasing interest globally in the transition to cleaner energy forms, Greenland's potential as a hydrocarbon exporter may never become more than theoretical. Nevertheless, the Greenland government has not "given up" on hydrocarbons and is waiting for an upturn in the oil price.[19]

The map below at Figure 6.1 displays the main geological formations and mineral deposits in Greenland.

Outline of the regulatory framework

Exploration and exploitation of natural resources is known to contribute to major changes at individual, community and national levels.[20] Under the Greenland Mineral Resources Act, developers must conduct an environmental impact assessment (EIA) and a social sustainability assessment, known more commonly in the literature as a social impact assessment (SIA).[21] The government may, and invariably does in practice, require an agreement on social sustainability and other socio-economic issues, i.e., an Impacts and Benefit Agreement (IBA), with local communities to promote equitable development.[22] The provisions in the Mineral Resources Act on EIA and SIA are brief but are developed further in a number of topic-specific Guidelines.[23] Although these latter are not legally binding in a formal sense, it is unlikely that the government will grant a licence in cases where the developer has not met, if not exceeded, the requirements in the Guidelines.

the Realm From Zero Tolerance to Uranium Producer," Danish Institute for International Studies, January 18, 2016. https://www.diis.dk/en/research/governing-uranium-in-the-realm

17 *Our Mineral Resources – Creating Prosperity for Greenland: Greenland's Oil and Mineral Strategy 2014–2018* (Nuuk: Naalakkersuisut, Government of Greenland, 2014), http://naalakkersuisut.gl/~/media/Nanoq/Files/Publications/Raastof/ENG/Greenland_oil_and_mineral_strategy_2014-2018_ENG.pdf

18 See Sandroos, 53–54 (for a summary of activity from 1970 to 2014).

19 Male citizen, Nuuk, April 12, 2018.

20 Lucia Mancini and Serenella Sala, "Social Impact Assessment in the Mining Sector: Review and Comparison of Indicators Frameworks," *Resources Policy* 57 (2018): 98–111, https://doi.org/10.1016/j.resourpol.2018.02.002

21 Mineral Resources Act, Parts 15 and 16.

22 Ibid., Part 16, section 78a.

23 See, "Acts, Regulations and Guidelines," Naalakkersuisut: Government of Greenland, accessed August 16, 2019, https://govmin.gl/licensing/acts-regulations-and-guidelines/ (for the most recent versions of the guidelines).

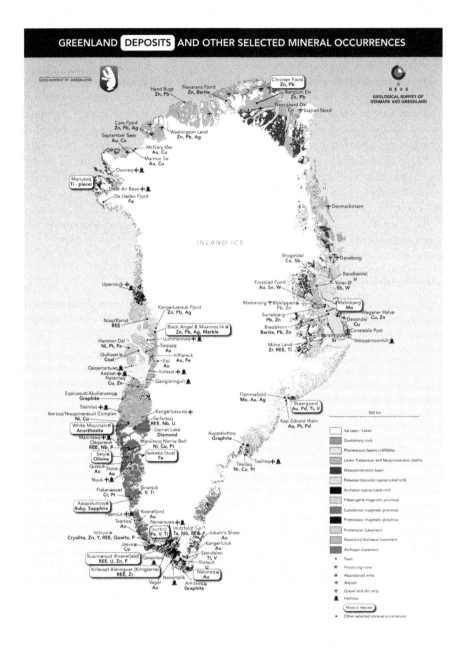

Figure 6.1 Greenland geology and selected mineral occurrences
Source: Reproduced with permission of Geological Survey of Denmark and Greenland (GEUS).

However, SIAs need not be conducted for hydrocarbon projects until companies are applying for exploration drilling permits, or in the case of mining, not until the company applies for a production licence. This is very often many years into the prospecting and exploration processes, which have their own social impacts, sometimes quite profound. After years of studies and exchanges of information and negotiations between the companies, the government and state run scientific bodies such as the Institute for Natural Resources, the formal public consultation period is only eight weeks.[24]

Summary of the towns and settlements included in the study

The fieldwork was conducted between May 2017 and October 2019. We talked with a total of 92 Greenlanders from all five municipalities in Greenland and visited 16 towns and settlements. Table 6.1 provides an overview of the fieldwork, indicating the settlements visited, the region in which they are located, the main industries, and the number of citizens who took part.

The settlements range in size from the capital Nuuk (population 17,984) to a farm in South Greenland (population 7). Moriusaq is a settlement that has been abandoned by its residents. The buildings are presently being used by a mining company exploring for titanium sand. In most cases, meetings were arranged in advance but spontaneous conversations also contributed to the study. A scheduled trip to Sisimiut and Ilulissat was cancelled owing to weather conditions, though a short visit to Ilulissat was included later. Some interviews pertaining to other places in Greenland were held in Nuuk and a few also in Iceland. No interviews were conducted in the Qeqertalik municipality, which was carved out of the southern end of the former Qaasuitsup region in 2018 (the rest of the former region became Avannaata). However, some of the citizens had connections to the Qeqertalik region. In many cases, a citizen had strong connections with more than one area, but in Table 6.1 we identify the citizens according to the region that was discussed most in the conversations.

In the study we identified four regions, based on culture, in preference to the municipalities defined by the government. There are major differences within individual municipalities and this is especially true for the Sermersooq municipality, created in 2009. It stretches from Nuuk in the West right across the icecap to Ittoqqortoormiit and Tasiilaq on the East. West and East Greenland are very different, historically, culturally, economically and even linguistically, as explained in Chapter 3 of this volume, so we have considered them separately. We defined the regions based on common demographic characteristics such as dialects/language, main industries and employers, and resources available including traditional foods. The regions are further characterised by their individual geographical features and distinct landscapes. The reason why we decided to distinguish between

---

24 "Social Impact Assessments (SIA)," Naalakkersuisut: Government of Greenland, accessed August 16, 2019, https://www.govmin.gl/en/socio-economics/social-impact-assessment-sia/

Table 6.1 Summary of fieldwork, 2017–2019

Town or settlement	Geographic region (Greenland municipality)	Population	Main industries and employers	Interviews
Ittoqqortoormiit	East Greenland (Sermersooq)	311	Hunting; tourism	4
Nerlerit Inaat	East Greenland (Sermersooq)	transient	Airport and helipad; tourism	4
Tasiilaq	East Greenland (Sermersooq)	2,006	Education; tourism; social services	13
Ilulissat	North Greenland (Avannaata)	4,563	Seat of Avannaata municipality; tourism; fishing; trading; handicrafts; education; social services	3
Innarsuit	North Greenland (Avannaata)	175	Fishing; hunting	2
Kullorsuaq	North Greenland (Avannaata)	436	Fishing; hunting	3
Moriusaq	North Greenland (Avannaata)	0	Settlement closed in 2010 when last inhabitants moved to Qaanaaq. Now subject to exploration mining.	2
Nutaarmiut	North Greenland (Avannaata)	43	Fishing; hunting	1
Nuussuaq	North Greenland (Avannaata)	186	Fishing; hunting	3
Qaanaaq	North Greenland (Avannaata)	628	Hunting; social services	4
Savissivik	North Greenland (Avannaata)	60	Hunting	5
Upernavik	North Greenland (Avannaata)	1,067	Fishing; hunting	2
Farm near Narsarsuaq[a]	South Greenland (Kujalleq)	7	Sheep farming; tourism	2
Narsaq	South Greenland (Kujalleq)	1,365	Fishing; sealing; farming; tourism; education	10
Qaqortoq	South Greenland (Kujalleq)	3,093	Seat of Kujalleq municipality; fishing; sealskin processing; education; healthcare; tourism; social services	7
Settlement near Qaqortoq[a,b]	South Greenland (Kujalleq)	8	Reindeer herding; tourism	2
Maniitsoq	West Greenland (Qeqqata)	2,534	Fishing; hunting	19

(Continued)

Table 6.1 (Cont.)

Town or settlement	Geographic region (Greenland municipality)	Population	Main industries and employers	Interviews
Nuuk	West Greenland (Sermersooq)	17,984	Capital city of Greenland (seat of government and parliament); seat of Sermersooq municipality; fishing; education; healthcare; shipping; tourism; retail; social services	6

[a] These places are not named in this chapter to protect the identity of those interviewed.
[b] This place was not visited personally by either of the authors.

the regions in Greenland in this manner was based on the expectation that peoples' values and perceptions are influenced by these contexts. Giddens highlights how time- and place-based contextual factors are important structures influencing social action and decision-making.[25]

As explained in Chapter 3 of this volume, North and East Greenland were colonised much later than South and West Greenland. They remained socially and politically isolated until the late nineteenth century. Their spoken dialects (or languages) differ from Kalaallisut as spoken on the west coast, and the culture is still deeply rooted in myths and legends. In the East, the landscape is characterised by young and steep mountains. Approximately 3,500 people live in the region. The largest town is Tasiilaq with 2,000 inhabitants. Most of East Greenland is connected to the rest of Greenland and to Iceland by planes between Kangerlussusaq and Kulusuk, supplemented by helicopter or boat transfers. However, for most of the year it is only possible to travel to Ittoqqortoormiit via Iceland, by plane, then helicopter. There is limited access in summer by boat. The distances are huge. Tasiilaq and Ittoqqortoormiit are 842 km apart with no direct transport links – Tasiilaq is closer to Reykjavík, and Ittoqqortoormiit closer to Akureyri in North Iceland than the towns are to one another. East Greenland is in Kalaallisut called *Tunu* which can be translated as the "back" or the "other side."

We define North Greenland as that part of the west coast located north of the Polar Circle. North Greenland is characterised by the midnight sun in summer when the sun does not set and the polar night where the sun does not rise above the horizon. Along the North Greenland coastline, stretching thousands of miles, lie small communities based on hunting and fishing. Dog sledding is only possible and allowed north of the Polar Circle, which means in the North region and in East Greenland. Livelihoods in North Greenland are characterised by tourism, fishing and subsistence hunting. The Ilulissat Icefjord has been a UNESCO World Heritage Site since 2004 and has experienced a rapid increase in tourism over the

---

25 Anthony Giddens, *The Constitution of Society: Outline of the Theory of Structuration* (Cambridge: Polity Press, 2016), 282.

past decade, becoming the most popular tourist destination in Greenland, with over 20,000 visitors each year.[26] Further north, fisheries are dominant and in the northernmost settlements people live primarily as hunters. The landscape in the North is diverse, with lush tundra, barren rocky mountains and deep icefjords. North Greenland is called *Avannaa* in Kalaallisut, which means "what lies North of somewhere."

Greenland's capital Nuuk is located in West Greenland, within the aforementioned giant municipality of Sermersooq. Nuuk is the home of most educational institutions in Greenland, the seat of the Government and Parliament and related offices, the largest municipal administration and the main offices of financial institutions, employers' and workers' associations, as well as the offices of the largest fishing companies in Greenland. Nuuk represents a mix of traditional and modern culture in Greenland. West Greenland is called *Kitaa* in Kalaallisut, which can be translated as "what lies to the west" or the "outer coast."

South Greenland is the most verdant in Greenland, with soil, vegetation and freshwater, which allows for agriculture. A Norse settlement history intersects with modern Greenlandic fishing and hunting communities. Approximately 50 sheep farms are located in the region today and people in the south refer to the region as the "food chamber" (direct translation of the term used, which corresponds to "bread basket") of Greenland. The landscape in South Greenland is dominated by old mountains and, natural hot springs and blue ice in the water. South Greenland has its own distinct culture, with ties to the history of the North Atlantic and nearly 15,000 hectares of the area is recognised as a UNESCO World Heritage Site based on its unique geographical, historical and cultural importance.[27] South Greenland is called *Kujataa*, which means "what lies south of somewhere."

Findings

Each settlement in Greenland is unique and even settlements that are relatively close together and appear superficially similar can have very different experiences of and expectations for resource development. Inequality in living conditions became clear during the study, particularly in respect of housing and sanitation, with people in some settlements within the same municipality living in social housing that residents of Nuuk would frankly not tolerate. The people of Tasiilaq did not consider themselves connected to Ittoqqortoomiit more than to any other part of Greenland, though both settlements are located in East Greenland and part of the Sermersooq municipality, and citizens of Tasiilaq certainly did not think of the Jameson Land explorations as a "local" matter. Even in the geographically smallest municipality, Kujalleq, we found significant differences between two towns that are superficially similar – Narsaq and Qaqortoq. Each of these towns is

---

26 "Ilulissat Today," *Ilulissat Kangia*, February 18, 2019, www.kangia.gl/Fakta_om_isf jorden/Ilulissat_i_ dag?sc_lang=en
27 UNESCO, "Kujataa Greenland: Norse and Inuit Farming at the Edge of the Ice Cap," UNESCO World Heritage Centre, accessed October 23, 2019, https://whc.unesco.org/en/list/1536/

close to a mining project, which has been at the exploration stage for many years.[28] These differences relate both to the nature of the extractive project but also the wider social circumstances of the towns concerned as well as each settlement's unique cultural history and mythology.

During the fieldwork conducted for this study, we experienced that the further from Nuuk we travelled, the more closely attached the citizens are to the land and traditional activities, especially hunting. This was especially pronounced in the North and the East, which have, as noted, significantly different histories and experiences of colonisation. However, the human–environmental relationship was also stronger in South Greenland than in Nuuk.

Unsurprisingly, we also found that those who lived close to an extractive project had more defined views both about that project and extractive industries in general than those who did not live near a development. Also, people living close to projects would use a vocabulary and refer to the regulation related to extractives in a manner that made it clear that they had gained insight and built knowledge about the management system and the physical implications both in relation to potential environmental impacts and the derived social effects.

Visions: what risks and opportunities do the citizens foresee in relation to extractive industries locally and in Greenland in general?

All the people we talked to expressed a strong attachment to their homes and communities and wanted to see them thrive in the future. The citizens articulated a strong connection to *their* land, especially the farmers and those engaged in hunting. They not only want to continue with their traditional activities, they want to continue them *in the same places*. Only one of the ninety-two citizens indicated that he would be content to be bought out and would relocate his business elsewhere. This person, an immigrant to Greenland, expressed a different relationship to the land, one more reflecting dominion over the land as a commodity, than the other citizens, whether or not they were Inuit, Greenland-born of European origin, or immigrants. The subsistence and sharing culture are still very important, both socially and economically, especially in the East and throughout the North.

Some citizens lived in fear that their settlement would close altogether. This must be viewed in light of the deliberate closure of smaller settlements in the 1950s and 1960s, as well as the gradual depopulation and eventual demise of other settlements in the following decades.[29] In Narsaq, this fear was connected to

---

28 See also Johnstone and Hansen, 2019 (for an in-depth examination of these two towns and the neighbouring mining projects).
29 See, e.g., Søren Rud, *Colonialism in Greenland: Tradition, Governance and Legacy* (Cham, Switzerland: Palgrave Macmillan, 2017), 122–124; Anne Merrild Hansen, Frank Vanclay, and Anna-Sofie Hurup Skjervedal, "Managing the Social Impacts of the Rapidly-Expanding Extractive Industries in Greenland," *The Extractive Industries and Society* 3, no. 1 (2016): 28, https://doi.org/10.1016/j.exis.2015.11.013; and Tony Dzik, "Settlement Closure or Persistence: A Comparison of Kangeq and Kapisillit, Greenland," *Journal of Settlements and Spatial Planning* 7, no. 2 (2016).

the Kuannersuit mining project: some people believed that the mine would stabilise the community, but at least one person believed that there was a deliberate policy to depopulate and eventually close the town to allow the project to proceed unhindered by local concerns.[30] Elsewhere, concerns about the existential stability of communities did not relate directly to extractive industries. However, there were concerns that a settlement might become dependent on an extractive project – and thus collapse at the project's end. Some recalled the town of Qullissat, a town established around a coal mine in the Disko area; once the sixth largest town in Greenland, it was closed down in 1972 after the coal mine was considered to be insufficiently profitable.[31] Citizens discussed the importance of diversification to prevent any settlement being dependent on a single company.

The recent history of Maniitsoq also coloured views towards extractives locally. Around 2006, Alcoa had extensive plans for an aluminium smelter in the rapidly depopulating and struggling town and promised it a glorious revival.[32] However, Alcoa gradually lost interest in the project, leaving a great deal of disillusionment and scepticism in its wake. Maniitsoq has since experienced a significant upturn owing to heavy investment in top quality fish processing, but its people are now wary of large-scale investors and more self-confident (owing to the successful fish factories) about finding their own ways forward.

Some citizens opposed extractive industries *per se* and did not believe it was the right way to develop Greenland's economy. They disagreed in principle with extracting and exporting raw materials and anticipated high levels of leakage of the benefits to the corporate interests outside of Greenland in the manner of a developing country economy. However, some who strongly opposed exploitation of uranium (for example, at the Kuannersuit project), were not opposed to mining in general.

Where support was expressed for extractive industries, it was *always* conditional. None of the citizens expressed the opinion that development could come at any cost. They all sought assurances regarding environmental and social sustainability, non-interference with hunting grounds, and positive impacts on the local community (not just for the national budget). Concern was expressed that old mines had not been properly cleaned up and they wanted assurances that future developments would be better handled, and include a proper clean-up. Employment and business opportunities were of particular importance. Many citizens anticipated that jobs would be created, but had mixed views about who would take these jobs. We heard that a few locals were working on the Jameson Land project near (by Greenland standards) Ittoqqortoormiit, usually as hunters to defend camps from polar bears, but those jobs required people to be away from their homes for four to six months at a stretch. However, there were hopes in the town that mining and hydrocarbon developments would provide secure, well-paid jobs for some Ittoqqortoormiit residents and

---

30 See also, Hansen and Johnstone, 2019.
31 Priebe; and Rachael Lorna Johnstone, "The Impact of International Law on Natural Resource Governance in Greenland" *Polar Record*, 2019.
32 Martin Breum, *The Greenland Dilemma* (Copenhagen: Royal Danish Defence College, 2015), 51–60.

therefore bring more stability and money into the community. One young citizen in South Greenland compared mining work positively with his current work on a fishing vessel, as he could be home every night instead of missing his home for weeks or months at a time. Many saw jobs in extractives as compatible with traditional lifestyles, even as a kind of "subsidy" to the traditional lifestyle, by making it economically viable. There were, however, concerns that work in extractives would be temporary, resulting in unemployment in the medium-term, and worries that extractive jobs would offer better salaries, competing with local employers for limited skilled labour. Others saw potential in supply-chain services, including provision of traditional food to camps.

In Ittoqqortoormiit and Nerlerit Inaat, there were both hopes and fears regarding the potential of extractive projects to improve services, in particular transport. Should projects bring investment into the Nerlerit Inaat airport, this might increase and improve services for local people. However, there was a fear that companies would prefer to invest in expansion of the Mestersvig airport (206 km north of Ittoqqortoormiit and 172 km north of Nerlerit Inaat), in which case the service to Nerlerit Inaat, and hence the helicopter and boat connections to the settlement, could be significantly reduced. One citizen saw potential for extractive companies to improve waste management in the town, since they would have to take care of their own garbage and the human waste of their workers. He saw a possibility for an IBA to require a company to share their facilities (whether plans to ship out waste or to manage it onsite) with the people of Ittoqqortoormiit.

There was not a high degree of concern amongst the citizens regarding an "influx" of foreign workers beyond a preference that incomers not take jobs that Greenlanders could do, though one citizen was concerned that migrant workers would not respect the environment or local culture. Maniitsoq has a number of Chinese workers at the fish factories, and local people expressed very positive attitudes regarding their contribution to the workplace and the local community. Although they are not very socially integrated, the citizens from Maniitsoq spoke very positively about, for example, the stability they bring to the fish processing operations and hence to the Greenlanders' jobs. Concerns about the social impacts of large migrant workforces might be overstated, though more examples would require to be studied.

Some citizens preferred extractive projects to be far from settlements or believed that permission was more likely to be forthcoming if there was no settlement nearby because of low social impact. However, others believed that there would be significantly higher social benefits if extractives were close to communities, with one citizen suggesting that Greenlanders would be "spectators to their own development" if extractives only took place in isolated locations.[33] Those who were more sceptical about the social benefits of the projects suspected that they would be "spectators" in any case, as the decision-making and benefits would happen elsewhere, though the "spectacle" (in the pejorative sense) would be closer to home.

33 Male citizen, Narsaq, personal communication, May 23, 2017.

At a political level and in many English-language media reports on Greenland, extractive industries are often tied to the question of the political independence of Greenland. However, this was a secondary matter for the majority of our citizens. Everyone favoured economic development in principle (whether or not through extractive industries) to boost health, educational and social services, general wellbeing, incomes, and stability. However, they did not necessarily view extractives primarily as a means to the goal of achieving independence from Denmark, but rather as a potential business development opportunity locally. The national economy and independence from Denmark is not what concerns people in their daily lives: they want to know that *their* settlement will be enhanced by a project since they are the ones who bear the risk.

Decision-making: how are decisions made and do citizens consider the allocation of risk and responsibility to be just?

Most citizens were anxious to get more information. This was true irrespective of the distance to the nearest project, but the kind of information sought differed accordingly and those who lived closer to projects were more likely to have made a concerted effort to obtain information. Nevertheless, in Ittoqqortoormiit, even the most active and well-informed citizens found it difficult to get reliable information about activities in the neighbouring areas.

People wanted to know what was in the mountains surrounding them even, or perhaps especially, when there was no visible exploration underway. They also wanted to learn more about the mining industry and the practical processes of mining. When scientists showed up, citizens wanted to hear about what they were looking for and what they found. Whether there are no commercially-interesting deposits or just no commercial interest in deposits was disputed – for example, people in Tasiilaq discussed the potential in their mountains but we were told by a Sermersooq municipal representative in Nuuk that there was nothing. (In fairness, the representative in Nuuk had no mandate regarding extractive projects.) A perceived lack of interest in the potential of East Greenland, together with the lack of information, contributed to the feeling of being "left behind."

The people we talked to in general wanted information earlier but they also wanted it in a more accessible form. Online materials were of limited use when many people do not have internet access at home (owing to the high cost) or cannot read English or Danish well, especially complex technical and scientific reports. They found it difficult to distinguish between reliable and unreliable information on the internet. One citizen from Ittoqqortoormiit also described his town as a "silent zone" regarding the nearby Jameson Land onshore oil explorations, and told us that he had learned about drilling plans from the national newspaper.

The citizens did not feel that the companies or government agencies reached out to them but rather that they always had to seek out information and they always had the burden of going to them. This included attending public meetings, which was impossible for farmers as it would require an overnight stay away from their flocks. In North Greenland, we heard that meetings were held in the hunting season and during the national annual dog sledge championship. A public meeting regarding a mining project had been held in Ittoqqortoormiit shortly before the research visit, but attendance had been low as it was held at the same time as the twice-yearly departure of the supply ship, which is celebrated with a family fireworks show. Although the mining company representatives remained in Ittoqqortoormiit for a further two days owing to weather conditions, they did not hold another meeting. One local citizen would have liked to have been left with some printed material and/or the use of a Facebook site to discuss the developments. (Given the cost of internet in the small settlements, Facebook is more widely used and more accessible, through cellphones, than websites with complex graphics.[34])

In South Greenland, where prominent projects had been in the exploration stage for over a decade, there was a great deal of frustration regarding the length of time to get a decision and the lack of any timetable for a decision. Naturally, people wanted to know if the mining project would go ahead or not, but they also wanted to have an idea about *when* they might get an answer so they could make plans around it. A citizen in Tasiilaq was equally critical of the length of time taken to make decisions regarding the Kuannersuit project, even though he was not personally affected.

The citizens indicated the importance of informal pathways to try to influence projects and to obtain information. While they might have limited confidence in the impact they might make through formal processes, they would contact members of the community whom they considered to be influential. Strong families take leadership positions in communities and they act as a conduit for information and feedback. However, in depopulating settlements such as Narsaq, which are especially losing the better-educated and well-connected members, it is not so clear that these pathways will remain effective. A government lawyer told us that the only formal complaints come from the companies themselves, not from individuals, suggesting that citizens do not view legal processes as the most effective way to secure the outcomes they want. He believed that they would go directly to politicians to push for a solution rather than litigate.

The experience of Maniitsoq in responding to the interest and later abandonment of Alcoa confirms the importance of strong local leadership in getting the most from a development – even when it does not happen. We were told that initially there was significant opposition to the Alcoa investment but that local people were persuaded to support it because they felt involved and because there was strong local leadership. At that time, Maniitsoq was an independent municipality (before the formation of the Qeqqata municipality). One citizen also compared the preparation for the merger of Sisimiut and Maniitsoq into the Qeqqata municipality and the importance of the hiring of an anthropologist to help the towns understand one another and prepare. She believed there was potential for a similar approach for large-scale developments.

34 See also Skjervedal, this volume.

Citizens expressed concerns about the early impacts of prospecting and exploration and sought more information and greater involvement. One explicitly mentioned the need for the Impact-Benefit Agreement (IBA) to be negotiated sooner[35] especially because such a low proportion of projects ever reach the exploitation stage. Another argued that rather than an IBA to transfer some of the benefits, an agreement should be made for local involvement and participation in management. Along with a third citizen, they expressed doubts about the suitability of direct cash transfers and preferred ongoing commitment and investment, rather than a one-off transfer.

We heard frustration regarding apparent domination of the debate by "outsiders" – mining or oil companies on the one hand and international non-governmental organisations (INGOs) on the other – who focus only on arguments for or against the extractive venture but are not perceived to offer alternatives. Citizens felt used by outside interest groups, with one citizen stating strongly, "They don't care about us" with reference to the mining companies;[36] but we heard similar opinions about the INGOs. There was a great deal of mistrust in the information provided by both groups of external actors.

Locally, the debate was not always considered to be respectful. Some people felt ridiculed if they expressed concern about developments; others feared social retaliation if they spoke against a popular view, or a view held by influential local actors. In our interviews as well as in a workshop on participation held in Nuuk, social media was highlighted as a forum for bullying connected to opinions on developments.[37]

Most citizens sought greater local involvement in decision-making and local benefits, especially in the very large regions of Sermersooq and Avannaata. Feelings were more mixed regarding uranium: some thought that it should be a decision for local people irrespective of their personal views, while others thought it was a question of strategic national importance that needed to be decided at national level, possibly through a referendum. There have been many calls for a national referendum to be held on the principle of whether extraction of uranium should be permitted within the country.[38] There was a widespread acceptance that it was reasonable for the Self-Government authorities in Nuuk to have the final say as to whether a project should go ahead, even if many citizens wanted to have more local input into the decision-making process. However, citizens expressed

---

35 Male citizen, Nuuk, May 19, 2017.
36 Female citizen, Narsaq, May 23, 2017.
37 See, Anne Merrild Hansen and Rachael Lorna Johnstone, "Improving Public Participation in Greenland Extractive Industries," in *Current Developments in Arctic Law*, V, eds Kamrul Hossain and Anna Petrétei, 17–19. Rovaniemi, Finland: Arctic Law Thematic Network, 2018, https://www.ulapland.fi/news/Volume-5-of-the-Current-Developments-in-Arctic-Law-is-out!/38394/26bee361-9cee-4d63-9804-64607438a0fb
38 See, e.g., Aaja Chemnitz Larsen et al.,"Opinion: Requiring Referendum on Uranium," *High North News*, February 12, 2016, https://www.highnorthnews.com/en/opinion-requiring-referendum-uranium; and Jane George, "Greenland's IA Party Wants Referendum in Wake of Uranium Export Laws," *Nunatsiaq News*, June 13, 2016, https://nunatsiaq.com/stories/article/65674new_uranium_export_laws_prompt_greenlands_ia_to_seek_uranium_vote/

doubts about the competence of the civil service owing to lack of experience, a rapid turnover of staff in key positions, and a shortage of experts.[39] One citizen doubted that the Self-Government were negotiating firmly enough with outside investors. In smaller towns and settlements, there was concern that the benefits of projects would be captured by the Self-Government in Nuuk or spread too widely within enormous municipalities for local people to benefit. One believed that the national grant to the Southern municipality of Kujalleq would be reduced in accordance with any income that municipality received directly from a mining project and thus it would be no better off.

Influence: how do the citizens consider that extractive projects affect their prospects and preparations for the future?

Unsurprisingly, those who lived relatively close to a large-scale extractive project considered that such projects had more impact on their lives than those who lived at some distance. In most cases where there was no project nearby, extractives did not have a significant impact on their planning, with the exception of one person who had made the decision to go to mining school.

Proximity to projects, especially long-delayed projects, led to uncertainty which in turn led to paralysis. We described this phenomenon elsewhere as "Narsaq on hold."[40] Citizens had ambitions but were unwilling to act to realise them while they were waiting for a decision as to whether the mining project would go ahead or not. Many preferred a "wrong" decision just to have certainty and to be able to move on. One citizen from East Greenland hypothesised that the uncertainty also contributed to alcohol abuse because people did not feel like they had alternatives, at least in the short term. We found that the principal outside actors (mining companies and large INGOs) do not offer alternatives, local people did have alternative visions for their own personal development and that of their settlements but they were unable to pursue these as long as the uncertainty regarding the mine remained. For example, one tourism operator would not invest in expanding his business in case the mine deterred future visitors.

The polarisation we witnessed in Narsaq, the town beside the controversial Kuannersuit project, was much stronger than anything we saw elsewhere. Where developments remain fairly hypothetical (and especially where they do not involve radioactive materials), people could disagree without it reaching a level of personal antipathy and leaking into other areas of social life and community organisation. In Narsaq today, a consensus approach to mineral development appears impossible. Opinions were entrenched as all or nothing and it was extremely difficult for people to offer conditional support. The venture has caused deep social divisions that take time and attention away from other important local issues.[41] One citizen from Maniitsoq (the

39 See also, Hansen et al., 27 (on citizens' lack of confidence in the government's ability and necessary resources to bargain effectively with large companies).
40 Hansen and Johnstone, 2019.
41 See also, ibid.

town of the abandoned Alcoa project) explained the need for a settlement to be strong *before* investment by extractive companies: this allows the community to be less dependent and to be better prepared to benefit from the opportunity.

Greenland's tourism industry is growing in all regions but citizens had different views about whether mining posed a threat to it or could potentially be compatible. In Narsaq, there were strong fears that a mine would devastate the tourist industry, though the presence of uranium is a likely factor in this concern. However, one of the citizens from South Greenland had well-considered practical plans to work alongside a mining company to expand his tourism operations, for example, by encouraging the mining company to build roads, ports and energy supplies that could be shared. In Tasiilaq and Ittoqqortoormiit, even among those working directly in the tourism industry, there was a belief that extractive industries and tourism could go hand in hand. The mountains were large enough for a mine not to trouble tourist, hiking or hunting trails, and one citizen envisaged trips to take tourists to seek out surface minerals under a small-scale licence.

During the period of Alcoa's interest in Maniitsoq, the town established "citizen councils." These remain active to this day and are fora for citizens to express their views on all kinds of developments, not just heavy industry or extractives. Based on wide consultation through workshops, the town council drew up a report to show Alcoa how they saw the future of the town. Alcoa may have left but the council still have the plan containing those visions to provide the basis for future town planning.[42]

Other common concerns not related to extractive industries

During our conversations, we discussed many issues that were not directly related to extractive projects. Some themes arose repeatedly and we include the most important here, as they provide context for the debate on extractives and are relevant to future planning in Greenland.

The 2009 municipal mergers that reduced the number of Greenland municipalities from eighteen to four (now five) came in for repeated criticism in Narsaq and Tasiilaq, with feelings particularly strong in Tasiilaq. In these former municipal centres, citizens complained of the loss of quality jobs, lack of access to services, cultural misunderstandings and, in East Greenland, linguistic differences. We heard also that families had relocated to Nuuk from Ittoqqortoormiit following centralisation of their jobs. One citizen from North Greenland also criticised the mergers for similar reasons. Citizens from smaller settlements all over Greenland also complained about the lack of access to professional services, for example, banking.

Hunting management loomed large for many North Greenland and Ittoqqortoormiit citizens who did not have confidence in the quota system and believed that their local expertise was overlooked. This was despite the fact that one citizen involved in the regulatory side found that the (Western) scientific data was poor in the North. One citizen believed that management was still based on Western/

---

42 Berit Steenstrup et al., "Visjonsrapport: Maniitsoq" (Tromsø: 70°N arkitektur AS, 2010).

Danish principles that did not take into account local conditions and which prioritised the wildlife over the people who lived amongst it.

People in smaller centres felt abandoned by both the national government and by their municipal centres, though this view was also expressed in the more closely culturally connected South[43]. In one Northern settlement, this was expressed as: "They forget those who are most important to remember"[44]. Others, especially from the North and East, indicated that decision-makers rarely visit and do not understand the culture outside of Nuuk. People were proud of their different traditions. East Greenlanders recounted prejudice that they had experienced from West Greenlanders, and we also heard negative comments about the East from people in Nuuk who had never visited East Greenland, comments that did not bear any relation to our own experiences on fieldwork. Prejudice against East Greenlanders goes back many decades.[45] North Greenlanders told similar stories, of people ashamed to speak their own language or feeling looked down on by people in Nuuk, notwithstanding the North's essential contribution to the national economy through fisheries.

A number of structural challenges were also raised, such as the welfare and housing policies that make it difficult to accept paid work and permit only the resource-strong families to move to Nuuk[46]. Poor and expensive telecommunications especially in the East and North compound some of the problems of obtaining information across the huge new municipalities, further complicated by the linguistic divisions. The delivery system was also criticised, which remains based on a colonial model where everything is first shipped to Nuuk and then shipped (back) again to the settlement where it is needed.

Common interests, expectations, hopes and concerns

All the citizens want their own settlement to thrive and continue. Normally this would not need stating, but Greenland's twentieth-century history of settlement closures and forced relocations has left lasting trauma and fears that this will reoccur. While we are not aware of any plan to close settlements deliberately, the capital Nuuk expects to double its population by 2030, increasing its national population share from 30 per cent to 50 per cent, and it is unlikely that such a rapid increase can come from natural population growth, the return of Greenlanders living abroad and new immigrants.[47] People are particularly attached to

43 Female citizen, Qaqortoq, May 25, 2017.
44 Male citizen, Kullorssuaq, July 22, 2018.
45 Robert Petersen, "On the West Greenlandic Cultural Imperialism in East Greenland," in Cultural Imperialism and Cultural Identity. Proceedings of the 8th Conference of Nordic Ethnographers/Anthropologists, ed. Carola Sandbacka, 187–95 (Helsinki, Finland: Finnish Anthropological Society, 1977); and Astrid Nonbo Andersen, "Restorative Justice and the Greenlandic Reconciliation Process," Yearbook of Polar Law 11 (2019) (in press).
46 Female citizen, Qaqortoq, May 25, 2017.
47 Kevin McGwin, "A Strategy to Double Nuuk's Population Begins with a New Housing District," The Arctic Journal, February 9, 2017, https://www.arctictoday.com/a-strategy-to-double-nuuks-population-begins-with-a-new-housing-district/

their home territories; they would not be satisfied with a relocation elsewhere to somewhere that, to outside eyes, might be superficially similar. We heard repeatedly that nature and family bring people back. However, we also heard from some people in the North and the East that they did not want their children to come back because they did not see opportunities for them.

Although they had shared views on their desire to stay in their homes, citizens had different views on whether extractive industries would facilitate or hinder that objective. Some feared extractives would force people away, in particular in Narsaq, owing to concerns regarding contamination from uranium. Others believed that the mine would keep people in the area and encourage others to return, by providing quality jobs.

The strong attachment people expressed towards their homes has policy implications that go beyond extractives: the data demonstrate that populations of the smallest settlements are decreasing, especially of young people.[48] However, they want to go back, so what is stopping them? Perhaps the picture is brighter than the statistics indicate: young people may leave for education and training but aim to return in their 30s or 40s, especially to raise their own families – *if* the opportunities are there.

Citizens of Greenland want development; but they want it without negative impacts on their communities. There was a strong, urgent need expressed to defend traditions, more pronounced in East and North Greenland. One of the citizens from Ittoqqortoormiit described his town's traditions as the "ways of Ittoqqortoormiit" that were quite distinct from those of other settlements.[49] He was keen to pass them on to future generations.

There was a broad openness towards foreign workers, especially in Maniitsoq, which had recent experience of a significant immigrant Chinese workforce in the fish factories. However, while citizens sought stability and retention of the population, they did not necessarily want population *growth* – some were quite happy with things as they are.

A common theme throughout the fieldwork was the importance of informal pathways of communication. Strong families and influential individuals were mentioned as the conduit through which to seek to influence developments, in preference to formal consultation processes. Young people talked of going through seniors to be heard while taking limited part in formal hearings.[50] Lack of formal participation does not necessarily mean *no* participation or lack of interest. However, in depopulating towns and settlements, the strong families are more likely to leave and thus important communication pathways can be broken. The strong social networks also present social risks for those who are perceived to transgress the general consensus or the views of the stronger members. Social exclusion, ridicule or bullying were mentioned as risk factors in speaking up with an unpopular view. (Informal communication strategies may be seen as reducing this risk.) Social exclusion is not only psychologically damaging, it can also have serious economic consequences in a subsistence and sharing economy.

48 "Population," Statistics Greenland.
49 Male citizen, Ittoqqortoormiit, March 3, 2019.
50 See Skjervedal, this volume (on the absence of youth in formal participation proceedings).

Some differences between settlements

As already noted, in those settlements that were close to an extractive project, citizens had stronger views. However, irrespective of distance, we also found that the towns and settlements that were more stable (e.g. Nuuk, Qaqortoq, Tasiilaq, Maniitsoq and Ilulissat) there was less interest. We hypothesise that this is because there are a number of alternative possibilities for local development. Although both Narsaq and Qaqortoq are close to mining prospects, the TANBREEZ project next to Qaqortoq does not define the town in the same way that the Kuannersuit project overshadows Narsaq.[51]

As soon as prospecting begins, there are social impacts – including social division. While plans are in the early stages and development is largely theoretical, local views are less defined and people are more able to find a middle ground, for example, setting a number of conditions before they would consider offering support. Uranium is particularly divisive throughout Greenland, but the Kuannersuit project is also located next to a struggling town and this is as much of a factor. It is easy for citizens either to blame the mining company for their troubles or to see it as a potential saviour. Where there is insecurity and there is a project nearby, the insecurity is attributed to that project. Where there is similar insecurity but no project, another explanation is given. In Tasiilaq, we found that many problems were attributed to the municipal merger.

In North and East Greenland, there is a very strong Inuit identity and emphasis on continuation of traditional activities, especially hunting. This was a much more pressing topic for many of the citizens than extractives. To the extent that extractives were considered, they were viewed in light of their potential impact on hunting – primarily as a risk factor, especially offshore hydrocarbons. We were reminded that hydrocarbon and mining projects are transient but that hunting and fishing are long-term. However, some in the North and Ittoqqortoormiit do see positive opportunities from extractives and others who did not want to see extractive industries in the North did not object to developments elsewhere in Greenland, especially if far from fishing and hunting grounds. All prioritised hunting. Table 6.2 summarises broadly the prevailing attitudes in each region.

Hypotheses regarding Greenland culture and its integration into extractive planning

Building on our fieldwork results in light of our wider familiarity with Greenland culture and theories of extractive industries, we present two hypotheses for further consideration and study.

The first hypothesis is that attachment to land in Greenland is not principally economic. This is important for foreign companies working in Greenland more used to working in countries in which land is principally regarded as a commodity, and one that to some extent can be substituted with another piece of land. The

---

51 Hansen and Johnstone, 2019.

Table 6.2 Perceptions of opportunities, risks, decision-making process and influence of extractive industries in four regions of Greenland

	North	South	East	West
Opportunities	Job opportunities in mining. Extractives to supplement income. Possibility of coupling seasonal work for industry and hunting/fishing.	Job opportunities and supply-chain services to stabilise local population and economy and encourage workers to come (back) from elsewhere in Greenland. Mining projects as potential 'saviour' of struggling town.	Job opportunities in mining and hydrocarbons. Tourism and mineral development could go hand in hand. Interest in small scale mining – local ownership.	Extractives to boost economy.
Risks	Fears of contamination from oil, especially offshore; impacts on hunting and fishing – and hence culture. Pollution from oil considered irreversible. Fewer fears related to mining. Fears of radical social change – e.g. significant increase in sizes of settlements.	Contamination, particularly from uranium. Collapse of farming and fishing industries. Collapse of tourism owing to contamination fears or unsightliness.	Pollution. Impacts on recreational hunting.	Risk of dependency on a single industry.
Decision-making	Government in Nuuk should decide, but listen more to local voices.	Government in Nuuk should decide in conjunction with municipality and local voices. Need for more information, earlier, more accessible and from an impartial source.	Government in Nuuk should decide, but listen more to local voices. Need for more information about potential and existing projects.	Government in Nuuk should decide in conjunction with municipality and local voices. Potential for Maniitsoq citizens' councils as a means to encourage broad participation and communicate views.
Influence	Limited immediate impact on personal or business plans.	People feel unable to make life decisions and business investments while they wait for decision on mining. Existential fear in Narsaq that town will close – Kuannersuit mine viewed as "saviour" or conversely as "death knell."	Little immediate impact on personal or business plans.	Little immediate impact on personal or business plans. Degree of scepticism in Maniitsoq following Alcoa involvement; people reluctant to wait for heavy industry to provide solutions.

close and personal relationship between Greenlanders and the land increases in relation to involvement in traditional activities (especially hunting) and distance from Nuuk, and decreases in line with settlement size.

For many Greenlanders, the prospect of leaving their home is tragedy. For those who do leave for work or study, there is a strong draw to return home. There is very little conception that one could simply move to another town or region and start over without there being a very high personal cost. Young people who move away for education and training plan to return home in the medium-term, once they have developed their skills. Yet, we know from the statistics that many *do not* return notwithstanding a strong will to do so. Even if they return to Greenland, they may not return to their home settlement.[52] It is important to understand why they do not do so.[53] We hypothesise that besides the common conjectures regarding employment opportunities, the quality of housing available in some of the outlying settlements may also be a factor: after living in a modern apartment building in Nuuk or in a European town, it is difficult to move back to a draughty house with mould and no flushing toilet.

The Greenlanders most involved in traditional activities do not want to be modernised or industrialised.[54] They want to maintain the skills and have the opportunities to provide for themselves and stay where they are, living as they do. Extractive industries are only relevant to them to the extent that they can help them do that. We therefore suggest that investors consider seasonal work for Greenlanders that does not interfere with peak hunting and fishing times, perhaps employing migrant labour in the hunting and fishing periods.

Our second hypothesis builds on the concept of "sacrifice zones," which are usually understood as physical locations where it is agreed to damage the environment, often irreparably, to pursue a project.[55] They are justified for the overall benefit of a community or country. In the Western conception, the opposite of a sacrifice zone is a wilderness area. An area is considered "unspoilt" or a wilderness if no one is in it – and that is regarded as a value that is worth protecting for its own sake. Therefore, wilderness areas are not usually regarded as suitable sacrifice zones.[56] The Western approach sees human contact as already spoiling nature, so a large-scale project in or nearby a populated area is less objectionable from this perspective. One problem with this view is that it puts the pressure on the peoples that have damaged the environment least to continue to protect it, at the cost of

52 "2017 Bopælsland Efter Fuldført Uddannelse," Statistics Greenland, accessed August 16, 2019, www.stat.gl/dialog/main.asp?lang=da&sc=UD&version=201805
53 See, e.g., Anja Rosa, "Derfor Kommer Vi ikke Hjem" [That is why we do not return home], *Sermitsiaq*, March 6, 2017, https://sermitsiaq.ag/node/194656
54 See also, Hansen et al., 28 (on the close connection to land and the choice to continue traditional activities not being principally "economic").
55 See, e.g., Berit Skorstad, Brigt Dale, and Ingrid Bay-Larsen, "Governing Complexity. Theories, Perspectives and Methodology for the Study of Sustainable Development and Mining in the Arctic," in *The Will to Drill: Mining in Arctic Communites*, eds Brigt Dale, Ingrid Bay-Larsen, and Berit Skorstad (Cham, Switzerland: Springer, 2018) 19–21.
56 See, e.g., Mary Sweeters, "5 Reasons the World Needs an Arctic Sanctuary," *Greenpeace*, December 22, 2014, https://www.greenpeace.org/usa/five-reasons-protect-arctic/

their own economic development, to "save the world," while those countries that have already polluted can continue to do so as their environment is "not worth saving."

The separation of humans and nature is incongruent with the Inuit worldview that considers humans as *part of* nature, not as domineering over it. Humans are part of the equilibrium. Humans *can* spoil nature of course but human habitation or seasonal hunting or berry-picking in an area does not spoil nature but is simply part of nature, keeping the ecosystem in balance. Whether an area is spoilt or wilderness is not necessarily connected to human contact. Indigenous people around the world have an excellent record in protecting the environments *of which they are a part* (not *in which they live*).[57]

Greenland has such an enormous territory, with a vast "untouched" wilderness, that for many Greenlanders it is more acceptable to have extractives far from settlements. They do not accept that settlements should become sacrifice zones for development – instead they fear they will become a "sacrifice community." They are more willing to accept a development that can take place in a limited and contained area, far away from human activity, precisely because there is so much of it. Recognising the place of Inuit as part of nature, especially those most connected to traditional activities, requires Western developers to consider new paradigms as to what makes an area worth protecting. They need to listen to Greenlanders about this and not be swayed unduly, for example, by the assumptions of well-funded international campaign groups.[58]

Concluding remarks and reflections on participation

In the light of the present level and intensity of development of extractive projects in Greenland, and based on the recognition that extractive projects can have mayor impact on the future life, wellbeing and business development in communities, it is very important that developers and government alike be sensitive to the personal connection that citizens have with the land and appreciate the importance of traditional activities in their lives.

---

57 See, "UN Report: Nature's Dangerous Decline 'Unprecedented'; Species Extinction Rates 'Accelerating' – United Nations Sustainable Development," United Nations Sustainable Development Goals, United Nations, accessed August 16, 2019, https://www.un.org/sustainabledevelopment/blog/2019/05/nature-decline-unprecedented-report/ (concluding that "Three-quarters of the land-based environment and about 66% of the marine environment have been significantly altered by human actions. On average these trends have been less severe or avoided in areas held or managed by Indigenous Peoples and Local Communities").
58 At the time of writing, Greenpeace's "Save the Arctic" petition had approximately 8,800,000 signatures: over double the popluation of the entire Arctic. WWF had over 5 million paid-up members.

The capital, Nuuk, may be tiny by global standards but it is an "urban giant" in Greenland and people living elsewhere, particularly in the North and East, feel misunderstood or overlooked at best and discriminated against at worst. Settlements in Greenland, especially the smaller ones and those furthest from Nuuk, are not urban and planning cannot be based on models drawn from a small, metropolitan, European country. The citizens who live in them choose to be there. They do not want to be "modernised" or urbanised but want to retain their cultures and traditions while accepting some of the advantages of modernisation on their own terms – but not wholesale transformation into city-living.

This calls for context-adapted strategies for engagement of citizens and improved information exchange. The study presented in this chapter points to some issues for consideration both by government and industry involved in the extractive sectors, when engaging with people in potentially affected communities.

The study showed amongst other things that citizens in all regions of Greenland are mostly open *in theory* to extractive industries but must be convinced that they can be compatible, even support, traditional ways of living and community values. Seasonal contracts with extractive companies that fit around hunting, fishing, and berry-picking times, might be one way to encourage more local involvement and provide more local benefit. Trust towards companies and authorities promoting extractive industries has not yet been established, primarily due to a lack of dialogue with the citizens. Communication therefore needs considerable improvement if people in impacted communities are to accept projects in their region. Citizens want information earlier: to know about the mineral potential of the mountains amongst which they live and hunt, and certainly before foreign prospectors show up. Information needs to be more accessible – not internet-dependent and in the appropriate language. It should also not focus exclusively on technical analysis but also on social considerations.

The study further identified local frustrations related to development of extractives when it came to the decision-making processes. Delays in decision-making regarding projects were at least as much of a concern as fear of contamination should a project go ahead. It therefore seems that the structures around decision-making processes could be more streamlined and more clearly communicated. At the very least, citizens need a timeline that tells them accurately *when* they might expect a decision, to enable them to plan around it. (This would be equally welcome to investing companies.) Decision-making and benefit-sharing agreements also need to emphasise the local. While all opinions are valid, those of the people who bear the risk should be given more weight.

Participation is not always taking place through the formal consultation processes. Informal channels of communication, for example, talking with community leaders, chatting in the supermarket or at kindergarten pick-up, seeking out information online, and sharing views on social media, are important means of exchanging information and opinions. However, the informal channels risk being destabilised in towns and settlements with high outmigration. Consultation strategies could recognise and use informal pathways. For example, companies sometimes employ a local representative as a permanent conduit of information.

The risk of ridicule or social exclusion discourages people from participating in formal processes and may also make it difficult to use informal pathways if their opinion differs from that of influential citizens. Consultation strategies should ensure safe ways to submit opinions and information.[59] It is important that extractive projects do not create deep divisions in communities as was seen in Narsaq.[60] Earlier sharing of information and the creation of spaces for the respectful exchanges of opinions before views become entrenched in the many years of prospecting and exploration might have prevented some of the social damage to the community.

The work of Maniitsoq Council (now part of Qeqqata municipality) in establishing citizens' councils to discuss visions for the future, by which they developed a town plan and continue to base decisions, also demonstrates the benefit of holding consultation more broadly, and not just when a large-scale venture is on the horizon. A longer-term strategy of consultation brings in a wider range of participants and allows citizens to consider alternative opportunities for development and seek out improvements in unrelated areas. It creates a strong community network with a good level of public trust already in place to negotiate should an extractive company come into town. An approach like this in Narsaq might have allowed the community to find more points of commonality, unrelated to the Kuannersuit project, and use these as a starting point on which to seek consensus or at least hold mutually respectful discussions about how best to handle the commercial interest in the mountain.

Acknowledgment

We would like to express our sincere thanks to all the citizens who contributed to this study. We would also like to thank the Government of Greenland who funded the research project.

References

"2017 Bopælsland Efter Fuldført Uddannelse." Statistics Greenland. Accessed August 16, 2019. www.stat.gl/dialog/main.asp?lang=da&sc=UD&version=201805

"Acts, Regulations and Guidelines." Naalakkersuisut: Government of Greenland. Accessed August 16, 2019. https://govmin.gl/licensing/acts-regulations-and-guidelines/

Beck, Ulrich. *A Critical Introduction to Risk Society*. London: Pluto Press, 2004.

Bertelsen, Rasmus Gjedssø, Jens C. Justinussen, and Coco Smits. "Energy as a Developmental Strategy: Creating Knowledge-Based Energy Sectors in Iceland, the Faroe Islands, and Greenland." In *Handbook of the Politics of the Arctic*, edited by Leif Christian Jensen and Geir Hønneland, 3–25. Cheltenham: Edward Elgar, 2015.

Breum, Martin. *The Greenland Dilemma*. Copenhagen: Royal Danish Defence College, 2015.

Danish Parliament Act no. 473 of 12 June 2009 on Greenland Self-Government.

---

59 Hansen and Johnstone, 2018.
60 Hansen and Johnstone, 2019.

Dzik, Tony. "Settlement Closure or Persistence: A Comparison of Kangeq and Kapisillit, Greenland." *Journal of Settlements and Spatial Planning* 7, no. 2 (2016): 99–112.

"Fields of Responsibility Assumed by the Greenland Home Rule Government (I and II) and Greenland Self-Government (III) Respectively." Accessed August 16, 2019. www.stm.dk/multimedia/GR_oversigt_sagsomr_270110_UK.pdf

Finne, Arne. "Greenland's Smallest Government Party, Partii Naleraq, Wants Full Independence from Denmark from 2021." *High North News*, March 23, 2018. https://www.highnorthnews.com/en/wants-independent-greenland-2021

George, Jane. "Greenland's IA Party Wants Referendum in Wake of Uranium Export Laws." *Nunatsiaq News*, June 13, 2016. https://nunatsiaq.com/stories/article/65674new_uranium_export_laws_prompt_greenlands_ia_to_seek_uranium_vote/

Giddens, Anthony. *Runaway World: How Globalization Is Reshaping Our Lives*. New York: Routledge, 2003.

Giddens, Anthony. *The Constitution of Society: Outline of the Theory of Structuration*. Cambridge: Polity Press, 2016.

Greenland Minerals Authority. "List of Mineral and Petroleum Licences in Greenland." Mineral Licence and Safety Authority, July 1, 2019.

Greenland Minerals Authority. "List of Mineral Licences in Greenland." Mineral Licence and Safety Authority, October 16, 2019. https://govmin.gl/images/Documents/Current_Licences_and_Activities/List_of_Licences_16-10-2019.pdf

Greenland Parliament Act of December 7, 2009 on mineral resources and mineral resource activities (Mineral Resources Act).

Grønning, Ragnhild. "Future Independence, Arctic Minister and Social Issues on the Agenda as Greenland Goes to Polls in Danish Elections." *High North News*, June 3, 2019. https://www.highnorthnews.com/en/future-independence-arctic-minister-and-social-issues-agenda-greenland-goes-polls-danish-elections

Hansen, Anne Merrild, and Pelle Tejsner. "Identifying Challenges and Opportunities for Residents in Upernavik as Oil Companies Are Making a First Entrance into Baffin Bay." *Arctic Anthropology* 53, no. 1 (2016): 84–94. https://doi.org/10.3368/aa.53.1.84

Hansen, Anne Merrild and Rachael Lorna Johnstone. "Improving Public Participation in Greenland Extractive Industries." In *Current Developments in Arctic Law, V*, edited by Kamrul Hossain and Anna Petrétei, 17–19. Rovaniemi, Finland: Arctic Law Thematic Network, 2018. https://www.ulapland.fi/news/Volume-5-of-the-Current-Developments-in-Arctic-Law-is-out!/38394/26bee361-9cee-4d63-9804-64607438a0fb

Hansen, Anne Merrild and Rachael Lorna Johnstone. "In the Shadow of the Mountain: Assessing Early Impacts on Community Development from Two Mining Prospects in South Greenland." *The Extractive Industries and Society* 6, no. 2 (2019): 480–488. https://doi.org/10.1016/j.exis.2019.01.012

Hansen, Anne Merrild, Frank Vanclay, Peter Croal, and Anna-Sofie Hurup Skjervedal. "Managing the Social Impacts of the Rapidly-Expanding Extractive Industries in Greenland." *The Extractive Industries and Society* 3, no. 1 (2016): 25–33. https://doi.org/10.1016/j.exis.2015.11.013

"Ilulissat Today." *Ilulissat Kangia*, February 18, 2019. www.kangia.gl/Faktaomisfjorden/Ilulissatidag?sc_lang=en

Johnstone, Rachael Lorna. "The Impact of International Law on Natural Resource Governance in Greenland." *Polar Record*, 2019. Forthcoming.

Kalvig, P. *Preliminary Mining Assessment of the Uranium Resource at Kvanefjeld, the Ilímaussaq Intrusion, South Greenland*. Report. Roskilde, Denmark: Risø National Laboratory, 1983.

Larsen, Aaja Chemnitz, Christian Juhl, Rasmus Nordqvist, Mikkel Myrup, Hans Pedersen, Mariane Paviassen, Christian Ege, and Niels Henrik Hooge. "Opinion: Requiring Referendum on Uranium." *High North News*, February 12, 2016. https://www.high northnews.com/en/opinion-requiring-referendum-uranium

Mancini, Lucia and Serenella Sala. "Social Impact Assessment in the Mining Sector: Review and Comparison of Indicators Frameworks." *Resources Policy* 57 (2018): 98–111. https://doi.org/10.1016/j.resourpol.2018.02.002

McGwin, Kevin. "A Strategy to Double Nuuk's Population Begins with a New Housing District." *The Arctic Journal*, February 9, 2017. https://www.arctictoday.com/a-stra tegy-to-double-nuuks-population-begins-with-a-new-housing-district/

Mortensen, Bent Ole Gram. "The Quest for Resources – The Case of Greenland." *Journal of Military and Strategic Studies* 15, no. 2 (2014): 93–128.

Musaddique, Shafi. "Greenland Eyes Independence from Denmark after Election Vote." *CNBC*, April 25, 2018. https://www.cnbc.com/2018/04/25/greenland-eyes-indep endence-from-denmark-after-election-vote.html

Mythen, Gabe. *Ulrich Beck: A Critical Introduction to the Risk Society*. London: Pluto Press, 2004.

Naalakkersuisut Coalition Agreement 2014. "Koalitionsaftale, Fællesskab, Tryghed og Udvikling." Accessed December 13, 2018. https://naalakkersuisut.gl/~/media/Na noq/Files/Attached%20Files/Naalakkersuisut/DK/Koalitionsaftaler/SIUMUT_ DEMOKRAATIT_ATASSUT_Isumaqatigiissut%20atuuttoq_04122014_dk_endelig.pdf

Naalakkersuisut Coalition Agreement 2016; Siumut, Inuit Ataqatigiit, Partii Naleraq. "Lighed, Tryghed og Udvikling." Accessed December 13, 2018. https://naalakkersui sut.gl/~/media/Nanoq/Files/Attached%20Files/Naalakkersuisut/DK/Koalitionsafta ler/Koalitionsaftale_S_IA_PN_2016_2018.pdf

Naalakkersuisut Coalition Agreement 2018; Siumut, Partii Naleraq, Atassut, Nunatta Qitornai. "Koalitionsaftale 2018, Nunarput – i fællesskab – i udvikling – med plads til alle." Accessed August 16, 2019. https://naalakkersuisut.gl/~/media/Nanoq/Files/ Attached%20Files/Naalakkersuisut/DK/Koalitionsaftaler/040518%20Siumut_Naleraq_ Atassut_Nunatta%20qitornai_Final_da.pdf

Nonbo Andersen, Astrid. "Restorative Justice and the Greenlandic Reconciliation Process." *Yearbook of Polar Law* 11 (2019) (in press).

Our Mineral Resources: Creating Prosperity for Greenland: Greenland's Oil and Mineral Strategy 2014–2018. Nuuk: Naalakkersuisut, Government of Greenland, 2014. http://naalakkersuisut.gl/~/media/Nanoq/Files/Publications/Raastof/ENG/Greenland oil and mineral strategy2014-2018_ENG.pdf

Petersen, Robert. "On the West Greenlandic Cultural Imperialism in East Greenland." In *Cultural Imperialism and Cultural Identity. Proceedings of the 8th Conference of Nordic Ethnographers/Anthropologists*, edited by Carola Sandbacka, 187–195. Helsinki, Finland: Finnish Anthropological Society, 1977.

"Population." Statistics Greenland. Accessed August 16, 2019. www.stat.gl/dialog/topmain.asp?lang=en&sc=BE

Priebe, Janina. "A Modern Mine? Greenlandic Media Coverage on the Mining Community of Qullissat, Western Greenland, 1942–1968." *The Polar Journal* 8, no. 1 (February 2018): 141–162. https://doi.org/10.1080/2154896x.2018.1468620

Rosa, Anja. "Derfor kommer vi ikke hjem" [That is why we do not return home]. *Sermitsiaq*, March 6, 2017. https://sermitsiaq.ag/node/194656

Rud, Søren. *Colonialism in Greenland: Tradition, Governance and Legacy*. New York: Springer International, 2018.

Sandroos, Bo. *The Greenland Mineral Resources Act: The Law and Practice of Oil, Gas and Mining in Greenland*. Copenhagen, Denmark: Djøf Publishing, 2015.

Sejersen, Frank. *Efterforskning og udnyttelse af råstoffer i Grønland i historisk perspektiv*. Report. Committee for Greenlandic Mineral Resources to the Benefit of Society, January 2014. https://greenlandperspective.ku.dk/this_is_greenland_perspective/background/report-papers/Efterforskning_og_udnyttelse_af_r_stoffer_i_Gr_nland_i_historisk_perspektiv.pdf

Skorstad, Berit, Brigt Dale, and Ingrid Bay-Larsen. "Governing Complexity. Theories, Perspectives and Methodology for the Study of Sustainable Development and Mining in the Arctic." In *The Will to Drill: Mining in Arctic Communities*, edited by Brigt Dale, Ingrid Bay-Larsen, and Berit Skorstad, 13–32. Cham, Switzerland: Springer, 2018.

"Social Impact Assessments (SIA)." Naalakkersuisut: Government of Greenland. Accessed August 16, 2019. https://www.govmin.gl/en/socio-economics/social-impact-assessment-sia/

Steenstrup, Berit, Gisle Løkken, Irene Wilner Bergholt, Joar Lillerust, Amgdalena Haggard, Michele R. Widerøe, and Petra Schnutenhaus. *Visjonsrapport: Maniitsoq*. Tromsø, Norway: 70°N Arkitektur AS, 2010.

Sweeters, Mary. "5 Reasons the World Needs an Arctic Sanctuary." Greenpeace, December 22, 2014. https://www.greenpeace.org/usa/five-reasons-protect-arctic/

Tsinnajinnie, Leola Roberta Rainbow, Robin Starr Zape-tah-hol-ah Minthorn, and Tiffany S. Lee. "K'é And Tdayp-Tday-Gaw: Embodying Indigenous Relationality in Research Methods." In *Applying Indigenous Research Methods: Storying with Peoples and Communities*, edited by Sweeney Windchief and Timothy San Pedro, 37–54. New York: Routledge, 2019.

"UN Report: Nature's Dangerous Decline 'Unprecedented'; Species Extinction Rates 'Accelerating' – United Nations Sustainable Development." United Nations Sustainable Development Goals.United Nations. Accessed August 16, 2019. https://www.un.org/sustainabledevelopment/blog/2019/05/nature-decline-unprecedented-report/

UNESCO. "Kujataa Greenland: Norse and Inuit Farming at the Edge of the Ice Cap." UNESCO World Heritage Centre. Accessed October 23, 2019. https://whc.unesco.org/en/list/1536/

Vestergaard, Cindy and Gry Thomasen. "Governing Uranium in the Realm From Zero Tolerance to Uranium Producer." Danish Institute for International Studies, January 18, 2016. https://www.diis.dk/en/research/governing-uranium-in-the-realm

Windchief, Sweeney and Timothy San Pedro. "Preface." In *Applying Indigenous Research Methods: Storying with Peoples and Communities*, xvi–xxv. New York: Routledge, 2019.

7 "Our consent was taken for granted"
A relational justice perspective on the participation of Komi people in oil development in northern Russia

Julia Loginova and Emma Wilson

Introduction

The Pechora River valley lies to the west of the Ural Mountains in the Komi Republic in northern Russia. The Komi people of this region have increasingly been contesting the way that oil extraction takes place in the north of the republic, namely in Izhma and Usinsk districts.[1] Lacking legal protection of their rights as indigenous people from the Russian government, one of their concerns includes the lack of involvement in decision-making about oil projects that affect them. This chapter illustrates the experiences of northern Komi communities regarding consultation and engagement prior to industrial activities carried out close to the communities and the areas that they depend on for their livelihoods. The Russian oil company Lukoil-Komi has been at the heart of the issues we discuss, and it is the only oil company currently operating in Izhma district, although several other companies operate in neighbouring Usinsk district. We use a relational justice approach[2] as the analytical lens to place emphasis on the "relations" and "processes" of community engagement and consultation.

International law and industry standards include requirements to seek the consent of indigenous communities that are likely to be affected by industrial

---

1 Simone Pierk and Maria Tysiachniouk, "Structures of Mobilization and Resistance: Confronting the Oil and Gas Industries in Russia," *The Extractive Industries and Society* 3, no. 4 (2016) 997–1009; Emma Wilson, "What Is the Social Licence to Operate? Local Perceptions of Oil and Gas Projects in Russia's Komi Republic and Sakhalin Island," *The Extractive Industries and Society* 3, no. 1 (2016): 73–81; Denisse Rodriguez and Julia Loginova, "Navigating State-Led Extractivism in Ecuador and Russia: Fluid Identities and Agendas of Socio-Environmental Movements," in *The Right to Nature: Social Movements, Environmental Justice and Neoliberal Natures*, eds Elia Apostolopoulou and Jose A. Cortes-Vazquez (Abingdon: Routledge, 2018).
2 Mirella Cobeleanschi Gavidia and Deanna Kemp, "Company–Community Relations in the Mining Context: A Relational Justice Perspective," in *Natural Resources and Environmental Justice: Australian Perspectives*, eds Sonia Graham, et al. (Clayton South, VIC: CSIRO Publishing, 2017); Deanna Kemp, John R. Owen, Nora Gotzmann, and Carol J. Bond, "Just Relations and Company–Community Conflict in Mining," *Journal of Business Ethics* 101, no. 1 (2011): 93–109. https://doi.org/10.1007/s10551-010-0711-y; Gail Whiteman, "All My Relations: Understanding Perceptions of Justice and Conflict between Companies and Indigenous Peoples," *Organization Studies* 30, no. 1 (2009): 101–120, https://doi.org/10.1177/0170840608100518

development.[3] Free, prior and informed consent (FPIC) is a mechanism by which indigenous people can exercise their right to self-determination and other human rights.[4] The FPIC concept reflects the need for indigenous people to protect the integrity of their lands, and a strong belief that states and companies ought to respect the decision-making authority of indigenous peoples in relation to whether resource development should take place – and how – within their traditional territories.[5] The application of FPIC can be confusing and contentious. This may be due to poor understanding of the underlying socio-cultural issues, the level at which FPIC should be applied and who represents community interests in the engagement, and a lack of prior agreement on the values underlying the engagement, the processes to be followed, the expected outcomes and how they will be agreed upon.[6] In addition to FPIC, requirements in international hard and soft law pertaining to states' "duty to consult" with indigenous (and non-indigenous) communities, "public participation in decision-making" and "meaningful consultation and engagement" are equally significant.[7]

Resource development projects frequently fall short of meaningful community engagement, consultation and consent.[8] Indigenous and non-indigenous local communities often fight simply to have their voices heard by governments and companies that are failing to observe key international indigenous and human rights principles. There are potential direct reputational and financial impacts for companies, and the loss of a social licence to operate may lead to costly conflicts and revenue losses.[9] A particular challenge is presented where the status of indigeneity itself is legally unresolved,[10] as is the case with the Komi people.

3 James Anaya, *Report of the Special Rapporteur on the Rights of Indigenous Peoples, James Anaya: Extractive Industries and Indigenous Peoples*, 2013. UN Human Rights Council, UN Doc. A/HRC/24/41; Cathal Doyle and Jill Cariño, *Making Free, Prior and Informed Consent a Reality: Indigenous Peoples and the Extractive Sector* (London: Indigenous Peoples Links/PIPLinks; Middlesex University School of Law; The Ecumenical Council for Corporate Responsibility, 2013); Asia Pacific Forum of National Human Rights Institutions and the Office of the United Nations High Commissioner for Human Rights, *The United Nations Declaration on the Rights of Indigenous Peoples: A Manual for National Human Rights Institutions* (Geneva: APF and OHCHR, 2013); Emma Wilson, *What Is Free, Prior and Informed Consent?* (Ájluokta/Drag, Norway: Árran Lule Sami Centre, 2016).
4 Matthias Åhrén, *Indigenous Peoples' Status in the International Legal System* (Oxford: Oxford University Press, 2016).
5 Anaya, *Report of the Special Rapporteur*.
6 Wilson, "What Is Free, Prior and Informed Consent?"; see also Wilson, this volume, and Johnstone, this volume.
7 See Wilson, this volume.
8 Anthony J. Bebbington and Jeffrey Bury, *Subterranean Struggles: New Dynamics of Mining, Oil, and Gas in Latin America*, vol. 8 (Austin TX: University of Texas Press, 2013); Andrea Behrends, Stephen P. Reyna, and Günther Schlee, *Crude Domination* (Oxford: Berghahn Books, 2011).
9 Daniel M. Franks et al., "Conflict Translates Environmental and Social Risk into Business Costs," *Proceedings of the National Academy of Sciences* 111, no. 21 (December 2014): 7576–7581, https://doi.org/10.1073/pnas.1405135111
10 See also Wilson, this volume.

In the north of the Komi Republic, reindeer herding, cattle breeding, fishing, hunting, and gathering of mushrooms and berries in forests and tundra remain critically important for households despite radical changes in the local economy caused by the transition from the collective farms established during the Soviet era to a more market-based economy. These nature-based livelihoods not only provide sources of food and income but they have been central to the essence of living in the area. The traditional way of life of northern Komi communities has been increasingly challenged by the oil industry that started up in the Timan-Pechora oil and gas province in the 1960s and has been expanding ever since.[11] Relations between the industry and affected rural communities have been increasingly contentious, compounded by power imbalances in community–company relations.[12]

Russian law defines "Indigenous small-numbered peoples" (*korennye malochislennye narody*) as peoples under 50,000 persons who practise traditional livelihoods and customs on traditional lands and recognise themselves as an independent ethnic community.[13] Forty ethnic groups residing in the north are legally recognised as "Indigenous small-numbered peoples of the North, Siberia and the Far East" (*korennye malochislennye narody Severa, Sibiri i Dal'nego Vostoka*, referred to hereafter as KMNS).[14] These peoples have rights guaranteed by the state set out in the Russian Constitution, and national and regional legislation. The Komi people are not included in the list of KMNS as their population of around 300,000 exceeds the established limit, and, therefore, they are not eligible for the related legal protection.[15] The northern group of Komi, including those who live in the villages of the Pechora River valley, are known as the Izhma Komi, Komi-Izhma (Komi-Izhemtsy) or Izvatas. They number just 40,000 and have in the past sought to secure indigenous status on their own, based on their practice of reindeer herding and their unique dialect of the Komi language. They have been recognised as an indigenous people by the United Nations (UN) and other international institutions based on the principle of self-determination, but to date have had little success within Russia.[16]

11 Lenfrid Borozinets et al., *Istoriya Stanovleniya I Razvitya Neftegazovogo Kompleksa Komi Kraya* [History of the Establishment and the Development of the Oil and Gas Industry of the Komi Region] (Ukhta: Ukhta State Technical University, 2004).
12 Pierk and Tysiachniouk, "Structures of Mobilization"; Rodriguez and Loginova, "Navigating State-Led Extractivism."
13 Russia, Law N 82-FZ "On Guarantees of the Rights of Indigenous Peoples of the Russian Federation" [*O Garantiyakh Prav Korennykh Malochislennykh Narodov Rossiyskoy Federatsii*] (1999).
14 Russia, Decree of the Government of the Russian Federation of N 536-r "On the Approval of the List of Indigenous Small-numbered Peoples of the North, Siberia and the Far East of the Russian Federation" [*Ob utverzhdenii perechnya korennykh malochislennykh narodov Severa, Sibiri i Dal'nego Vostoka Rossiyskoy Federatsii*] (2006).
15 Maxim Zadorin, "The Status of Unrecognized Indigenous Communities and Rural Old-Residents of the Russian Arctic," *The Yearbook of Polar Law* 5, no. 1 (2013): 669–74.
16 Kim Hye Jin, Yuriy P. Shabaev, and Kirill V. Istomin, "Lokalnaya Gruppa V Poiske Identichnosti (Komi-Izhemtsy: Dinamika Kulturnyh Transformatsy)" [A Local Group in Search for Identity (Komi-Izhma: Dynamics of Cultural Transformations)], *Sociological Issledovaniya* [Sociological Studies] 8, no. 376 (2015).

Lacking legal protection, northern Komi communities have been increasing their awareness about the extractive industry and its adverse impacts, their own rights in relation to resource extraction, and the routines of community consultation and engagement.[17] They are aware that domestic and foreign companies operating in Russia have been expanding their practices of corporate social responsibility (CSR) in response to gaps in the implementation of international norms and national legislation.[18] However, there remains little understanding of the ways in which community–company relations unfold in northern Komi.

The people of northern Komi feel that their consent is taken for granted by the government agencies granting oil licences and the oil companies developing the deposits. Decisions are made without adequate consultation or engagement, either in the early stages of project planning and impact assessments, or in later phases of development. The failure to engage meaningfully with the communities regarding oil activities has resulted in a sustained local protest against the industry, which has partly undermined the authority of companies and the state in the region.[19] Local residents have not necessarily been opposed to the oil industry uniformly. But they have been turned against the proponents of oil development in the region by high levels of environmental damage and the failure to communicate effectively with local residents.[20]

This study analyses the community–company relations through the lens of relational justice, considering the *processes* as well as the *outcomes* of engagement. It establishes a case to argue that communities affected by resource extraction projects experience power imbalances as a result of industrial development with inadequate legal safeguards, and this can be compounded if the indigenous status of local populations is not legally recognised. We also argue that meaningful engagement prior to project development can be beneficial for balancing power relations. For industry, more balanced power relations can provide a more solid foundation for a company's or industry's social licence to operate, and can help to avoid the loss or weakening of a social licence in challenging circumstances. If power imbalances are not addressed by the companies and the authorities,

---

17 Timo Pauli Karjalainen and Joachim Otto Habeck, "When The Environment Comes to Visit: Local Environmental Knowledge in the Far North of Russia," *Environmental Values* 13, no. 2 (January 2004): 167–186, https://doi.org/10.3197/0963271041159877; Florian Stammler and Aitalina Ivanova, "Confrontation, Coexistence or Co-Ignorance? Negotiating Human-Resource Relations in Two Russian Regions," *The Extractive Industries and Society* 3, no. 1 (2016): 60–72, https://doi.org/10.1016/j.exis.2015.12.003

18 Laura A. Henry, et al., "Corporate Social Responsibility and the Oil Industry in the Russian Arctic: Global Norms and Neo-Paternalism," *Europe-Asia Studies* 68, no. 8 (2016): 1340–1368, https://doi.org/10.1080/09668136.2016.1233523; Ilan Kelman, et al., "Local Perceptions of Corporate Social Responsibility for Arctic Petroleum in the Barents Region," *Arctic Review of Law and Politics* 7, no. 2 (2016), https://doi.org/10.17585/arctic.v7.418

19 Pierk and Tysiachniouk, "Structures of Mobilization"; Rodriguez and Loginova, "Navigating State-Led Extractivism."

20 Wilson, "What Is the Social Licence to Operate?"

communities may be compelled to act on their own terms, potentially further undermining or destroying the social licence to operate.

After presenting the methodology for the study, this chapter introduces a relational justice approach to examine relational processes of community engagement in resource development. It further describes the peculiarities of community engagement across northern Russia. The analysis of empirical data reveals the experiences of communities in Izhma and Usinsk districts during the planning and implementation of oil projects.

Methodology

This study was based on ethnographic fieldwork and desk-based research. The empirical data were gathered by both authors in separate field research projects. The authors met once in the field in June 2015. Loginova collected data primarily during fieldwork in the Komi Republic in summer 2015, although further visits took place subsequently. Geographically, it covered the villages and oil fields in the Pechora River valley in the north of the Komi Republic as well as the capital Syktyvkar in the south of the republic. The fieldwork included interviews with community members (n=15) in Shelyaur, Shelyabozh and Ust'-Usa, members of civil society (n=5) in Izhma, Kolva and Syktyvkar, representatives of local (n=6) and regional governments (n=10) and oil companies (n=7) in Usinsk, Syktyvkar and Moscow.

Wilson's analysis draws primarily on interviews carried out in collaboration with a Komi research partner between 2013 and 2015.[21] The field data were gathered during three 10–15-day visits to the north of the Komi Republic in November 2013, March 2014 and June 2015. The researchers spoke to a total of 50 stakeholders, including 33 interviews of 1–2 people (and one village group meeting) in Usinsk district (Usinsk, Kolva, Ust'-Usa, Novikbozh and Mutnii Materik), Izhma district (Izhma, Shelyaur, Krasnobor and Vertep), Syktyvkar and Moscow. The locations of the villages visited by the two authors are shown on the map in Figure 7.1.

Both authors took handwritten notes during interviews and meetings, and subsequently transcribed and coded them for the analysis. The interviews were supplemented by participant observation during the fieldwork, including discussions with hotel or hostel residents, such as researchers or oil workers, in Usinsk and Izhma. Documents were considered a useful source of evidence to supplement information collected through interviews, enabling triangulation and greater reliability. These included official laws and policies, company annual reports, agreements of cooperation and the documents of civil society groups. Some of these were available openly online whereas others were provided by the research participants during the interviews.

---

21 Emma Wilson and Kirill Istomin, "Beads and Trinkets? Stakeholder Perspectives on Benefit Sharing and Corporate Responsibility in a Russian Oil Province," *Europe-Asia Studies* (2019), https://doi.org/10.1080/09668136.2019.1641585

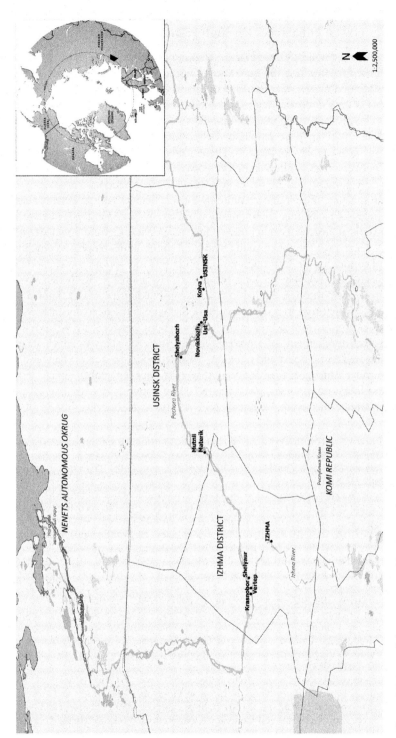

Figure 7.1 Map of the Komi Republic (top right) and settlements in Izhma and Usinsk districts mentioned in the study

Addressing power imbalances through relational justice

In the literature on resource extraction and community–company relations, a justice lens is often used to scrutinise the outcomes of resource development. Much of the research has focused on the *distributional* aspects of justice, emphasising the inequitable burdens of environmental degradation and their health effects.[22] For example, scholars of "energy justice" suggest that injustices are embodied in the production of energy.[23] A few scholars have emphasised the importance of *relational* injustices embedded in resource development.[24] These studies argue that "processes" and "relations" between communities and more powerful actors influence the outcomes of resource development, and are therefore critical for investigation.

Indeed, in practice, meaningful community engagement requires a dynamic and relational process of facilitating communication, involvement and exchange between a community and an organisation in order to achieve specific social and organisational outcomes.[25] These processes of engaging with local communities emphasise ongoing dialogue and continuing work through various trade-offs and options toward finding common ground and possibly reaching consensus.[26] Relational justice is defined as the justice produced through equitable relationship-building processes, known as "just relations," which may include negotiation, dialogue and agreement-making.[27] In this way it captures formal and informal interactions between actors prior to, during and after development of a project, considering the extent to which stakeholders are treated with respect and honesty.[28] Just relations are seen as channels for negotiating and balancing power relations that exist between global capital, state authority and local communities, given that a lack of community consultation and engagement defines the inequitable distribution of impacts and benefits. Just relations

---

22 Dara O'Rourke and Sarah Connolly, "Just Oil? The Distribution Of Environmental and Social Impacts of Oil Production and Consumption," *Annual Review of Environment and Resources* 28, no. 1 (2003): 587–617, https://doi.org/10.1146/annurev.energy.28.050302.105617

23 Noel Healy, Jennie C. Stephens, and Stephanie A. Malin, "Embodied Energy Injustices: Unveiling and Politicizing the Transboundary Harms of Fossil Fuel Extractivism and Fossil Fuel Supply Chains," *Energy Research and Social Science* 48 (2019): 219–234, https://doi.org/10.1016/j.erss.2018.09.016; Darren McCauley, et al., "Energy Justice in the Arctic: Implications for Energy Infrastructural Development in the Arctic," *Energy Research and Social Science* 16 (2016): 141–146, https://doi.org/10.1016/j.erss.2016.03.019; Roman Sidortsov and Benjamin Sovacool, "Left out in the Cold: Energy Justice and Arctic Energy Research," *Journal of Environmental Studies and Sciences* 5, no. 3 (February 2015): 302–307, https://doi.org/10.1007/s13412-015-0241-0

24 Gavidia and Kemp, "Company–Community Relations"; Kemp, et al., "Just Relations and Company–Community Conflict in Mining"; Whiteman, "All My Relations."

25 Kim A. Johnston, "Toward a Theory of Social Engagement," in *The Handbook of Communication Engagement*, eds Kim A. Johnston and Maureen Taylor (Hoboken NJ: Wiley, 2018), 23.

26 Layla Hughes, "Relationships with Arctic Indigenous Peoples: To What Extent Has Prior Informed Consent Become a Norm?" *Review of European, Comparative and International Environmental Law* 27, no. 1 (2018), https://doi.org/10.1111/reel.12232

27 Kemp, et al., "Just Relations and Company–Community Conflict in Mining."

28 Whiteman, "All My Relations."

provide opportunities for indigenous and non-indigenous people affected by resource projects to establish a stronger bargaining position in decision-making about resource development that tends to prioritise large-scale investment over local livelihoods.[29]

Relational injustices are contextual, yet still embedded within international, national and regional legal rules, voluntary norms and informal practices. These are explained in the next section in relation to resource extraction industries and community–company relations in northern Russia.

Legal and voluntary aspects of consultation and community engagement in extractive industries in northern Russia

The Russian Constitution (1993) establishes the rights of all Russian citizens to a favourable environment and access to environmental information (Article 42) and participation in decision-making (Article 32). Article 69 guarantees the rights of KMNS in accordance with generally accepted principles and norms of international law and international treaties of the Russian Federation.[30] In 1973, the then-Soviet Union ratified the International Covenant on Economic, Social and Cultural Rights (ICESCR) and the International Covenant on Civil and Political Rights (ICCPR).[31] Article 1 of both covenants upholds the right of all peoples to self-determination, meaning to freely determine their political status and freely pursue their economic, social and cultural development, and it states that in no case may people be deprived of their means of subsistence. These ratifications remain in effect for the Russian Federation.

In 1995, Russia ratified the Convention on Biological Diversity, which calls on governments to require environmental impact assessments (EIA) and ensure public participation in decision-making about projects likely to have an impact on biodiversity (Article 14), while also protecting customary use of biological resources (Article 10).[32] Russia has not ratified the International Labour Organisation (ILO) Convention 169 on the Rights of Indigenous and Tribal Peoples (1989) (ILO C169), and it abstained in the vote on the UN Declaration on the Rights of Indigenous Peoples (UNDRIP) in 2007.[33] However, these instruments are frequently referred to by activists, scholars, lawmakers and legal advisers developing

---

29 Kemp, et al., "Just Relations and Company–Community Conflict in Mining."
30 Constitution of the Russian Federation, 1993.
31 International Covenant on Civil and Political Rights 1966 (ICCPR); International Covenant on Economic, Social and Cultural Rights 1966 (ICESCR).
32 Convention on Biological Diversity 1992 (CBD). See also, Convention on Biological Diversity, *Akwé:Kon Voluntary Guidelines for the Conduct of Cultural, Environmental and Social Impact Assessment Regarding Developments Proposed to Take Place on, or Which Are Likely to Impact on, Sacred Sites and on Lands and Waters Traditionally Occupied or Used by Indigenous and Local Communities* (Montreal: Secretariat of the Convention on Biological Diversity, 2004) (developed and officially endorsed by the Parties to the CBD, including Russia).
33 Indigenous and Tribal Peoples Convention 1989, ILO Convention 169, 1989; UN General Assembly, Declaration on the Rights of Indigenous Peoples, UNGA Res 61/295, September 13, 2007 (UNDRIP).

national and regional legislation, who refer to Article 69 of the Constitution regarding Russia's acknowledgement of international treaties (see above).[34]

In 2011, the UN Human Rights Council unanimously approved the (non-binding) UN Guiding Principles on Business and Human Rights (UNGPs).[35] These principles define states' and businesses' responsibilities to protect and respect human rights. Notably, they call on businesses to incorporate "meaningful consultation" into their due diligence processes (including impact assessments). The UN Global Compact, a voluntary corporate responsibility network founded in 2000, has close links with the UNGPs, and has received a broad uptake in Russia in recent years.[36]

The basic requirement for public consultation in the context of industrial projects in Russian law is set by the 1995 law N 174-FZ "On the ecological expert review." It requires that project documentation (including EIAs[37]) passes through the process of state ecological expert review.[38] Public consultation is required at all stages of EIA and can take several forms, including distribution of EIA documentation by project proponents in libraries and public surveys, "open days" for the public to come and ask project proponents questions, and "public hearings" (*obschestvennye slushaniya*). The latter are public meetings during which the project plans and EIA are presented by project proponents and discussed by the public.

In 2007, the obligation to conduct a state ecological expert review was reduced to oil projects with potential substantial impact, for example, taking place offshore or within nature reserves. However, for the majority of oil-related infrastructure on land, there is still a requirement for public hearings set by the Town Planning Code in relation to the general state expert review of project documentation.[39] Specific ways to carry out public hearings are regulated by municipal authorities and vary from region to region, but they commonly include voting (secret or open) when participants vote to approve the project at the end of the meeting. In some cases, as illustrated in our case study, a public hearing can be declared invalid

---

34 Natalia I. Novikova, *Okhotniki i neftyaniki: issledovaniya v yuridicheskoy antropologii* [Hunters and Oil Workers: Research in Legal Anthropology] (Moscow: Nauka, 2014).

35 John Ruggie, *Guiding Principles on Business and Human Rights: Implementing the United Nations "Protect, Respect and Remedy" Framework*, UN Doc. A/HRC/17/31, March 21, 2011 (UNGPs).

36 UN Global Compact, "The Ten Principles of the UN Global Compact," accessed October 10, 2019, https://www.unglobalcompact.org/what-is-gc/mission/principles

37 See Russia, Law N 7-FZ "On Environmental Protection" [*Ob okhrane okruzhayushchey sredy*] (2002) (for the Russian version of environmental impact assessment (*Otzenka vozdeistviia na okruzhayushuyu sredu (OVOS)*) which is required prior to the commencement of environmentally hazardous activities that have a significant environmental and economic impact.)

38 Russia, Law N 174-FZ "On the Ecological Expert Review" [*Ob ekologicheskoy ekspertize*] (1995), article 14.

39 Russia, Town Planning Code of the Russian Federation [*Gradostroitel'nyy kodeks Rossiyskoy Federatsii*] (2004), article 49; Russia, Decree of the Government of the Russian Federation N 145 "On the Procedure for Organizing and Conducting State Expertise of Project Documentation and Results of Engineering Surveys" [*O poryadke organizatsii i provedeniya gosudarstvennoy ekspertizy proyektnoy dokumentatsii i rezul'tatov inzhenernykh izyskaniy*] (2007).

by participants, forcing the project proponents to respond to public demands and organise a further public hearing. Nonetheless, the outcomes of public consultation and public hearings only have the weight of recommendations to the state commission that grants approvals to projects. In general, public consultation in Russia has been found to have an informative rather than consultative function.[40]

Participation in decision-making regarding land use in areas where industrial projects might compete with indigenous peoples' traditional land use is also subject to the 1999 law N 82-FZ "On guaranteeing the rights of indigenous small-numbered peoples of the Russian Federation." It allows indigenous people to "possess and use their lands, free of charge, in places of traditional habitation and economic activities in the pursuit of traditional economic activities."[41] The 2001 law N 49-FZ "On territories of traditional natural resource use of the indigenous small-numbered peoples of the North, Siberia and the Far East" regulates the establishment of areas for traditional natural resource use.[42] However, implementation of the rights to possess and use traditional lands has been patchy across indigenous communities in Russia, with no clear "mechanisms-in-practice," while policymakers at regional and local levels frequently fail to prioritise traditional resource use when it competes with extractive industry projects.[43]

Article 1 of the N 174-FZ law "On the ecological expert review" calls for consideration of socio-economic impacts of a project, although this requirement is undermined by the lack of adequate procedures for assessing socio-economic or cultural impacts.[44] The law N 82-FZ "On guaranteeing the rights of indigenous small-numbered peoples of the Russian Federation" contains a reference to indigenous peoples' right to take part in an *etnologicheskaya ekspertiza* (anthropological expert review),[45] which is similar to a socio-cultural impact assessment.

40 Nicole Kovalev and Johann Koeppel, "Introduction to the Environmental Impact Assessment System and Public Participation in the Russian Federation," *Journal of Environmental Assessment Policy and Management* 5, no. 3 (2003): 321–338, https://doi.org/10.1142/s146433320300136x
41 Russia, Law N 82-FZ "On Guarantees of the Rights of Indigenous Peoples of the Russian Federation," article 8.
42 Russia, Law N 49-FZ "On Territories of Traditional Natural Resource Use of the Indigenous Small-Numbered Peoples of the North, Siberia and the Far East" [*O territoriyakh traditsionnogo prirodopol'zovaniya korennykh malochislennykh narodov Severa, Sibiri i Dal'nego Vostoka Rossiyskoy Federatsii*] (2001), article 2
43 Gail Fondahl and Anna Sirina, "Rights and Risks: Evenki Concerns Regarding the Proposed Eastern Siberia–Pacific Ocean Pipeline," *Sibirica* 5, no. 2 (January 2006), https://doi.org/10.3167/136173606780490720; Emma Wilson and Krystyna Swiderska, "Extractive Industries and Indigenous Peoples in Russia: Regulation, Participation and the Role of Anthropologists," IIED Working Paper (London: IIED, 2009); Natalia Yakovleva, "Oil Pipeline Construction in Eastern Siberia: Implications for Indigenous People," *Geoforum* 42, no. 6 (2011): 708–719, https://doi.org/10.1016/j.geoforum.2011.05.005
44 Olga A Murashko, "What Is the Etnologicheskaia Ekspertiza in Russia?" *Sibirica* 5, no. 2 (2006): 77–94; Law N 174-FZ "On the Ecological Expert Review," article 1.
45 Russia, Law N 82-FZ "On Guarantees of the Rights of Indigenous Peoples of the Russian Federation," article 7.

There has been considerable progress in developing this concept and related methodologies but *etnologicheskaya ekspertiza* has not received a wide application across all Russian regions yet.[46]

However, these guarantees and mechanisms do not apply to communities that practise traditional livelihoods but lack legal recognition as KMNS.[47] These include the Komi, Sakha and other ethnic groups whose populations exceed 50,000 people. The Republic of Sakha (Yakutia) has, however, recently developed regional legislation on the *etnologicheskaya ekspertiza*;[48] yet in practice the lack of clarity on methods and procedures, and the domination of federal legislation over regional, mean that there is still no strong obligation for companies to carry out an *etnologicheskaya ekspertiza* in the region.[49]

Scholars have highlighted the importance of international corporate responsibility standards in managing relations between communities and companies in Russia.[50] In part to address formal governance gaps, and in response to the demands of indigenous and local communities as well as investors and lenders, meaningful stakeholder engagement and FPIC have been increasingly incorporated into the standards and practices of corporations operating in northern Russia. For example, the Yamal liquefied natural gas (LNG) project in Western Siberia has carried out an extensive FPIC process with local nomadic reindeer herding communities, and the Forest Stewardship Council (FSC) has been implementing FPIC processes as part of its certification of Russian forestry products.[51] Yet, despite the fact that FPIC processes have been applied to local Komi communities in the FSC certified areas in the south of the Komi Republic (the Komi Model Forest Project in Priluzje), no FPIC processes have taken place in the northern oil-producing districts, because there has been

---

46 Natalia I. Novikova and Emma Wilson, *Anthropological Expert Review: Socio-Cultural Impact Assessment for the Russian North* (Ájluokta/Drag, Norway: Arran Lule Same Centre, 2017); Tatiana Roon, "Globalization of Sakhalins Oil Industry: Partnership or Conflict? A Reflection on the Etnologicheskaia Ekspertiza," *Sibirica* 5, no. 2 (January 2006).
47 Zadorin, "The Status of Unrecognized Indigenous Communities."
48 Russia, Decree of the Government of the Republic of Sakha "On the Procedure for Organizing and Conducting Ethnological Expert Review in Places of Traditional Residence and Traditional Economic Activities of Indigenous Minorities of the North of the Republic of Sakha (Yakutia)" [*O Poryadke organizatsii i provedeniya etnologicheskoy ekspertizy v mestakh traditsionnogo prozhivaniya i traditsionnoy khozyaystvennoy deyatel'nosti korennykh malochislennykh narodov Severa Respubliki Sakha (Yakutiya)*] (2011).
49 Novikova and Wilson, "Anthropological Expert Review."
50 Henry, et al., "Corporate Social Responsibility"; Douglas Rogers, "The Materiality of the Corporation: Oil, Gas, and Corporate Social Technologies in the Remaking of a Russian Region," *American Ethnologist* 39, no. 2 (2012): 284–96.
51 Emma Wilson, *Evaluating International Ethical Standards and Instruments for Indigenous Rights and the Extractive Industries* (Ájluokta/Drag, Norway: Árran Lule Sami Centre, 2016), https://tinyurl.com/IndigenousStandards; Maria S. Tysiachniouk, *Transnational Governance through Private Authority: The Case of the Forest Stewardship Council Certification in Russia*, vol. 7 (Wageningen, Netherlands: Wageningen Academic Publications, 2012), 307.

no external driver to do so, even though the contexts are comparable. The next section reports empirical findings on the experiences of residents of the northern villages in Izhma and Usinsk districts in relation to engagement with the oil industry.

Komi people and oil development: relational injustices

Life with oil

The Izhma Komi have long relied on their traditional livelihoods of reindeer herding, hunting, fishing, and gathering mushrooms and berries. In the 1960s, large oil deposits were discovered in the middle reaches of the Kolva River, which flows into the Pechora River. The town of Usinsk was established as a centre of oil production in the Timan-Pechora oil and gas province, which covers over 600,000 square kilometres with deposits of 2.4 billion tonnes of oil and gas.[52]

The rapid and poorly regulated development of the Soviet oil industry catalysed profound complex changes in the local environment, affecting the reindeer pastures of the collective farms, which adjusted their migration routes accordingly.[53] The impact of industrial development was amplified in the 1990s when Russia experienced dramatic changes in its political and economic systems while transitioning from Soviet-led development. Insecure access to lands and environmental degradation were triggered by inadequate policy and planning regulations and their poor implementation. One of the world's largest onshore oil spills happened in 1994 close to the Kolva River, forever changing the state of the environment – and environmental consciousness – in the Pechora River valley.[54] The Russian multinational company Lukoil acquired the assets of the state-owned Komineft' that had presided over the 1994 spill, and the subsidiary Lukoil-Komi was established in 1999. Although Lukoil-Komi contributed to the post-1994 cleanup, oil spills and pipeline leakage have continued in the region.[55] Although comprehensive medical statistics are lacking, since 1994, people have observed an increase in the occurrence of asthma, skin problems and cancer, as well as weakened immune systems, especially among children. For example, the incidence of asthma among children in

---

52 Borozinets, et al., *Istoriya Stanovleniya*.
53 Mark J. Dwyer and Kirill V. Istomin, "Komi Reindeer Herding: The Effects of Socialist and Post-Socialist Change on Mobility and Land Use," *Polar Research* 28, no. 2 (2009): 282–97; Mark J. Dwyer and Kirill V. Istomin, "Mobility and Technology: Understanding the Vulnerability of Two Groups of Nomadic Pastoralists to Reindeer Losses," *Nomadic Peoples* 10, no. 2 (2006): 142–165; Joachim Otto Habeck, "How to Turn a Reindeer Pasture into an Oil Well, and Vice Versa: Transfer of Land, Compensation and Reclamation in the Komi Republic," in *People and the Land. Pathways to Reform in Post-Soviet Siberia*, ed. Erich Kasten (Berlin: Reimer, 2002), 125–147.
54 Karjalainen and Habeck, "When 'the Environment' Comes to Visit."
55 Wilson and Istomin, "Beads and Trinkets?"

Izhma and Usinsk districts increased threefold between 1995 and 2008.[56] These health issues have been linked to the polluting effects of the oil industry.[57]

In the 2000s, new territories have been increasingly explored for oil, as existing deposits in Usinsk district have become depleted while the demand for oil has continued to increase. The first oil exploration well in Izhma district was drilled in 2000 on the territory of the Sebys nature reserve by the private Russian-Cypriot-British-American company Pechoraneftegaz. The development met with strong opposition because local people were not informed about the project before the drilling began (even though community consultation was required by law). As communities learned about the operations, they objected to oil exploration taking place in an area that had been in use for subsistence practices by many generations.[58] In a move to safeguard their societal security, they took legal action against the regional government and defended the Sebys reserve from the oil industry.[59] Nonetheless, in 2003, Lukoil-Komi did manage to start operations elsewhere in Izhma district and has since been developing a few small and medium-sized deposits.

Previous studies have explored relations between Lukoil-Komi and local communities in Izhma and Usinsk districts, illustrating the ways in which the company's CSR practices have evolved, and different types of social partnership and benefit-sharing agreements have emerged in the region.[60] In practice, the Usinsk authorities have had more influence on the trajectory of oil development in the area than the Izhma authorities because Usinsk district has a township designation with more flexibility and greater decision-making autonomy than the rural

---

56 Stuvøy, "Human Security, Oil and People"; Irina S. Bodnar and Vladimir G. Zainullin, "*Ekologo-meditsinskaya Otsenka Zabolevayemosti Naseleniya Respubliki Komi*" [Ecological and Medical Assessment of the Morbidity of the Population of the Komi Republic], *Proceedings of the Komi Science Center, Ural Branch of the Russian Academy of Sciences* 1, no. 9 (2012): 35–40.

57 Kirsti Stuvøy, "Human Security, Oil and People: An Actor-Based Security Analysis of the Impacts of Oil Activity in the Komi Republic, Russia," *Journal of Human Security* 7, no. 2 (2011): 5–19, 14.

58 Ernest Mezak, "*Izhemskie Muzhiki Vyigrali Sud U Glavy Respubliki Komi*" [Izhma Men Won the Court with the Head of the Komi Republic]," *Lesnye novosti* [Forest News], March 2001.

59 Julia Loginova, "Achieving Human and Societal Security in Oil Producing Regions: A Komi-Izhma Community Perspective from Pripechor'e, Russia," in *Human and Societal Security in the Circumpolar Arctic*, eds Kamrul Hossain, José Miguel Roncero Martin, and Anna Petretei (Leiden: Brill Nijhoff, 2018), 209.

60 Minna Pappila, Soili Nysten-Haarala, and Ekaterina Britcyna, "Participation in Benefit-Sharing Arrangements in the Komi Republic," in *Russian Analytical Digest No. 202: Oil Company Benefit Sharing in the Russian North* (Centre for Security Studies: ETH Zurich, 2017); Maria S. Tysiachniouk and Andrey N. Petrov, "Benefit Sharing in the Arctic Energy Sector: Perspectives on Corporate Policies and Practices in Northern Russia and Alaska," *Energy Research and Social Science* 39 (2018): 29–34; Emma Wilson, "Rights and Responsibilities: Sustainability and Stakeholder Relations in the Russian Oil and Gas Sector," in *Northern Sustainabilities: Understanding and Addressing Change in the Circumpolar World*, eds Gail Fondahl and Gary N. Wilson (New York: Springer International, 2017).

settlements of Izhma district (including the district centre, Izhma). Moreover, because of the long legacy of the oil industry in Usinsk district, where oil company headquarters are based, the district authorities have been more supportive of oil projects than the local leadership in Izhma district, where the district administration and the movement of Komi-Izhma people, known as *Izvatas*, are both influential within local society. The next section uncovers how recent oil projects have developed in both districts and how Lukoil-Komi and local authorities have engaged with local people based on the experiences of our fieldwork communities.

"When we saw a truck passing by ..."

In interviews, village residents described their experiences of consultation and engagement before and during the planning and development of oil projects. For them, seeing machinery, hearing the noise, and the smell of burning gas are the signs that oil activities are about to commence or have already commenced. For example, one interviewee in Shelyaur (Izhma district) explained how one day in 2014 he was woken up by the noise of tractors and all-terrain vehicles passing the house.[61] He followed the trucks into the forest and discovered a river crossing and creeks covered with logs and branches; much wood had been cut and there were several technical roads with heavy machinery stuck and drowning in mud. It was a drilling site under construction within walking distance from the village.[62]

Once news about the new drilling site spread throughout the community, people were angered. After the incident in the Sebys nature reserve (described earlier), this was another intervention into their territory without provision of information to the community or any public consultation. The feeling of frustration accompanied the anger because these activities seemed to be legal for the operating company. Our exploration of this issue, including discussion with representatives of Lukoil-Komi in Usinsk, revealed that an expert review, including public consultation, is required for oil wells and pipeline installation, but not for technical roads, huts, storehouses, work camps, seismic testing, pipeline upgrades and repairs.[63] According to the Lukoil-Komi representatives, the accompanying infrastructure can be built before the public is consulted, while the approval of the project documentation is granted separately by the state committee.[64] Acting in accordance with this interpretation of the law, Lukoil-Komi has been conducting seismic testing and its contractors were developing sites for extraction without prior consultation or engagement with communities.

In Krasnobor (Izhma district), we encountered an entrepreneur and private hunter whose hunting ground had been destroyed when trees were cut down for seismic testing. According to him, he had not been aware of the proposed testing

---

61 Employee of an agricultural education institution, hunter, male, Komi, personal communication, Shelyaur, June 2015/
62 Ibid.
63 Employee, Lukoil-Komi, personal communication, Usinsk, June 2015.
64 Ibid.

and felt angry and frustrated not only because of the lost hunting grounds but because no one warned or discussed with him the plans for the site.[65] It was only later, when Lukoil-Komi was found to be in violation of the law by failing to carry out public consultation prior to drilling an actual well, that he was able to throw his considerable influence behind a local protest against the company (see below).

In retrospect, these community members perceived that they had expected to face some negative impacts from the oil industry; they were aware of how environmentally damaging oil-related activities can be.[66] Oil spills frequently occur in neighbouring Usinsk district, which has hosted the oil industry for longer, and several oil spills had already occurred in Izhma district itself, near Shelyaur, in 2010 and 2014.[67] However, the villagers had not expected to deal with such poor communication and engagement prior to the development of the projects.[68] Despite the legality of their actions, the failure of Lukoil-Komi to engage with communities prior to building infrastructure close to villages and on hunting grounds, added to the recurring instances of environmental pollution, undermined the reputation of the company among rural residents and turned potentially supportive community members against oil activities.[69] The next section explains how these processes have contributed to relational injustices experienced by the communities.

Relational injustices

Community members that we engaged with in the course of our fieldwork perceived as unfair the fact that they were not consulted (or even informed) prior to seismic testing, the construction of infrastructure, and the preparation of drilling sites for oil extraction on the territories they rely on for their livelihoods and other resource-use activities.[70] Additionally, they did not receive any compensation for impacts on traditional livelihoods or for the loss of hunting grounds.[71] These were common grievances against Lukoil-Komi and the local authorities by individual community members and whole villages, indicating wider relational injustices that derive from a legal framework that does not adequately protect their livelihoods.

As explained earlier, Komi people lack legal recognition as KMNS, and therefore are not formally guaranteed rights as an indigenous people. The Komi Republic has no regional legislation to compensate for this gap (such as, for

65 Entrepreneur, male, Komi-Izhma, Krasnobor, June 2015.
66 Two entrepreneurs, male and female, Komi-Izhma, Kolva, November 2013.
67 Member of a socio-environmental movement, personal communication, Shelyaur, June 2015.
68 Employee in a diary unit, female, Komi-Izhma, personal communication, Shelyaur, June 2015; Reindeer herder, male, Komi-Izhma, personal communication, Shelyaur, June 2015.
69 Two entrepreneurs, male and female, Komi-Izhma, Kolva, November 2013.
70 Entrepreneur, male, Komi-Izhma, Krasnobor, June 2015; Teacher, female, Komi-Izhma, Vertep, June 2015.
71 Activist, male, Komi-Izhma, Novikbozh, November 2013; Entrepreneur, male, Komi-Izhma, Krasnobor, June 2015.

example, the regulations about the *etnologicheskaya ekspertiza* in the Sakha Republic). The lack of legal recognition of their indigenous status means that the territories used for nature-based activities by the Komi people cannot be formally registered as territories of traditional resource use. The absence of this status prevents affected resource users from enjoying the right to prior consultation and from receiving fair compensation for damage to their traditional livelihoods as a result of industrial projects. This challenge also concerns non-Komi residents of northern villages, who also practise natural resource-based activities such as hunting, fishing and gathering, and whose families may have done so for generations.

Another aspect of relational injustice in northern Komi is poor access to information. A lack of timely project information prevents communities from understanding the potential impacts of projects and from making informed decisions. A teacher from Shelyabozh explained this aspect:

> When I wanted to see what is going on in our [Pechora River] valley with the oil industry, it was challenging to gain any information on specific projects. I could not travel very far, but we do not know anything about the scale, technology, time frames, etc. I understand these are highly technological developments, and [the company does not see] why do I even need to understand. And this is what scares me.[72]

Lack of information about environmental impacts, especially in the case of serious pollution incidents, is another challenge experienced by communities. A community member in Shelyabozh explained during an interview:

> The most difficult thing to deal with is the lack of any environmental data we can work with. We experience pollution, but it is hard to know at what scale and what are the concrete impacts on the land, water, or our health. There is minimal monitoring, organised by the government, but operated by companies. And we cannot have the data. They just say that everything is within the norms.[73]

For instance, in November 2012, an industrial accident took place at the oil facilities in the middle reaches of the Kolva River in Usinsk district. The river was covered with ice at the time, and the incident was kept quiet. However, in May 2013 between 20 and 200 tonnes of oil came floating down the Kolva River with the ice during the spring thaw, affecting local fisheries and animal grazing on the river banks. The Russian-Vietnamese company Rusvietpetro eventually took responsibility for the spill. However, the damage in terms of broken trust with local communities extended beyond that single company, to the industry more widely and the local and regional authorities.[74]

---

72 Employee of a school, female, Russian, personal communication, Shelyabozh, June 2015.
73 Fisher, hunter, male, Komi-Izhma, personal communication, Shelyabozh, June 2015.
74 Wilson, "What Is the Social Licence to Operate?"

A representative of the Izhma nature protection office explained that a lack of environmental data prevents government agencies estimating the scope of damage done to the environment and calculating the amount of compensation for the environmental damage.[75] Recently, government offices have developed and applied methodologies for evaluating the damage to the environment.[76] As a result, Lukoil-Komi has been increasingly penalised for damage to forest resources or soils. The fines are directed to the regional and federal budgets (depending on the designation of the resources that have been damaged) but not to communities. The sums are minimal and do not encourage companies to enhance their standards and investments into the project design and performance.[77] As a representative of Usinsk town administration explained, more evidence of localised environmental pollution – often provided by local people – is needed to justify compensation: this is all about "negotiating the social partnership."[78]

Companies operating in the region – in this case Lukoil-Komi – have also failed to carry out meaningful community engagement or seek communities' consent to activities that directly affect and frequently harm their traditional livelihoods. They have not deemed this necessary either in order to respect international norms, or as a strategy to mitigate social risk. As a result, local communities feel that Lukoil-Komi and the authorities have been taking their consent for granted when making decisions relating to oil drilling projects and other related infrastructure. Communities feel that their rights to the land that they depend on for their livelihoods and other nature-based activities are considered to be less important than the rights granted to extraction companies, more so because their rights as indigenous people are not recognised by the state.

These aspects of relational injustice bring to light existing power imbalances. Formal procedures, or the lack thereof, have significant implications for the ways oil projects are planned and developed. The next section explains how community members have attempted to address the existing power imbalances.

Balancing power relations

As described in the previous section, relational injustice characterises community–company relations in developing oil projects in northern Komi. Given the failure of Lukoil-Komi and the authorities to establish a meaningful dialogue with local communities, community members, individually and collectively, have been seeking ways to challenge power imbalances in order to address their grievances. Oil projects in Izhma district have become the locus of resistance.

---

75 Senior administrator, Izhma nature protection office, personal communication, Izhma, June 2015.
76 Ibid.
77 Senior administrator, Usinsk town administration, personal communication, Usinsk, June 2015.
78 Senior administrator, Usinsk town administration, personal communication, Usinsk, March 2015.

In early 2014, given the lack of public consultation prior to actual drilling in Shelyaur, Izhma district, local residents immediately protested and activism promptly became a viable way to challenge the existing powers. Community members engaged in protest rallies, social media and newspaper activism, and demanded an environmental referendum.[79] From 2014, protest rallies proliferated across Izhma district (including Izhma, Shelyaur, Krasnobor and Vertep) and Usinsk district (including Shelyabozh, Ust-Usa, Novikbozh, Mutnii Materik and Kolva) and were well-attended. The protests were in response to oil spills and other pollution-related incidents; a lack of information sharing, community consultation and meaningful engagement; and political action and inaction at the local and regional level (for instance, the abolition of the Komi Republic's Ministry of Natural Resources and Environmental Protection). During the protests, communities contested the prevailing managerial approaches and technological solutions applied by the companies and approved by the authorities.[80]

The protestors urged local residents to reject the oil projects if there should be no proper communication and dialogue. The protest resolutions, which protestors showed to Loginova during fieldwork, contained demands for broader responsibility for socio-ecological protection of the Pechora River basin and the traditional way of life of the Izhma Komi people, and for support to rural development and specific projects (a bakery, a waste utilisation facility, bridge repair, hospital equipment, and public transport for low-income groups). The resolutions went further to demand the transfer of certain government functions from the regional level to the municipal level (Usinsk and Izhma districts). Additionally, the resolutions evoked justice claims by stating that development of the industry and its impacts are unjust and come at the expense of a few villages, the unique local culture and ways of life.

The protests targeting Lukoil-Komi and the different levels of government were not covered in local or regional TV, radio or newspapers. The Save Pechora Committee approached a broader audience and received media support from some independent federal TV and radio channels and international organisations.[81] They strengthened their cooperation with Greenpeace Russia and organised a number of round table discussions, press and bloggers' tours, and expeditions to Izhma and Usinsk districts. They reached out to significant people in federal and regional politics and the industry, conveying stories and images of environmental degradation and the impacts of oil activities on traditional livelihoods and language in the Komi Republic and the Arctic region more widely.

---

79 Rodriguez and Loginova, "Navigating State-Led Extractivism."
80 IWGIA, Russia, "Komi in Usinsk District Declare 'the End of our Patience has Come,'" June 6, 2014, https://www.iwgia.org/en/russia/2064-russia-komi-in-usinsk-district-dec lare-the-end-of
81 IWGIA, Russia, "We Izhma Komi are Indigenous People and this Is Our Land," April 14, 2014, https://www.iwgia.org/en/russia/2012-russia-we-izhma-komi-are-indi genous-people-and-thi; 350.org, "Striking: Indigenous Komi People in Russia Are Fed Up with Oil," April 16, 2014, https://350.org/komi-are-fed-up-with-oil/

Activism resulted in counter-responses from the oil industry and the authorities. For example, in 2015 a new state-sponsored environmental organisation was formed at the Republic level, called *Zelenaya Respublika* (Green Republic). The organisation promoted the image of a sustainable oil industry in Usinsk district on official local and regional TV and radio channels and social media to cover up the "dirty" side exposed by the environmentalists and rural residents of Izhma district. In a fieldwork interview with a representative of the Komi Republic government, it was explained that *Zelenaya Respublika* received government support to create a positive reputation for the region.[82] Additionally, activism resulted in pressure on the activists, but did not result in criminal proceedings against them, as increasingly happens in other parts of Russia.[83]

The protests have intensified in northern Komi at a time of increasing domestic and international tension in Russia as a result of the conflict over the Crimean Peninsula that escalated in 2014. Among various initiatives to protect government policy, the Russian Government enacted greater enforcement of laws against so-called "foreign agents"[84] and audited various non-governmental organisations (NGOs) on the presence of foreign funding and their influence on political processes. A range of NGOs was forced to cease their activities across Russia.[85] The NGOs active in the oil fields in northern Komi felt that they had to resist not only the irresponsible activities of the oil industry but also fight to gain the trust from the state that questioned their intentions.[86]

The protests across northern villages turned quickly into an organised movement, building on the individual and collective frustrations that had accumulated over the years. As part of the movement, communities made efforts to establish a dialogue with representatives of Lukoil-Komi and government agencies at various levels. In March 2014, more than 150 residents from 12 villages in Izhma and Usinsk districts gathered in the House of Culture in Krasnobor. They invited multiple stakeholders, and the meeting was attended by representatives of the environmental prosecutor's office, heads of the municipalities, deputies of rural

---

82 Senior administrator, Regional Ministry of Natural Resources and Environment Protection, personal communication, Syktyvkar, June 2015.
83 See, e.g., Mikhail Matveev, "'Kechimov's Case': Everyday Conflict or Clash of Civilizations?" [*"Delo Kechimova": Bytovoy Konflikt Ili Stolknoveniye Tsivilizatsiy?*], Activatica.org (2015) (for the case of the Khant shaman, an activist, Sergey Kechimov in Ugra, who was formally charged for killing the dog of an oil worker while defending his traditional land and sacred lake).
84 Russia, Law N 121-FZ "On Amendments to Legislative Acts of the Russian Federation regarding the Regulation of the Activities of Non-profit Organisations Performing the Functions of a Foreign Agent" [*O vnesenii izmeneniy v otdel'nyye zakonodatel'nyye akty Rossiyskoy Federatsii v chasti regulirovaniya deyatel'nosti nekommercheskikh organizatsiy, vypolnyayushchikh funktsii inostrannogo agenta*] (2012).
85 Maria Tysiachniouk, Svetlana Tulaeva, and Laura A. Henry, "Civil Society under the Law 'On Foreign Agents': NGO Strategies and Network Transformation," *Europe-Asia Studies* 70, no. 4 (2018): 615–637.
86 Member of a socioenvironmental movement, personal communication, Izhma, June 2015.

councils, and leaders of environmental and ethnic movements. Lukoil-Komi abstained from participation.

At the meeting, participants announced that they were no longer willing to tolerate the poor engagement by the company and its contractors and questioned the interests of the municipal government in these practices. Moreover, since the legislation does not protect their rights as indigenous peoples, communities urged Lukoil-Komi to change the ways of developing oil projects and engaging with local communities by respecting their rights as indigenous peoples. People insisted that any activities on the territory of Izhma district could proceed only once the requirement for legitimate public consultation had been met.

Public hearings for two of the new proposed sites were promptly scheduled soon after the meeting by the district's municipal administration. One public hearing about the development of the Yuzhno-Sedmesskoe oil field at a distance of 25 kilometres from Izhma was organised in Izhma in December 2014. About 40 people took part. After heated discussions about the project design, Lukoil-Komi failed to provide detailed information about how drilling would affect the freshwater supply in the village.[87] Moreover, project documentation did not contain all required stamps and signatures.[88] The company did not have any strategy to address public demands from the March meeting.[89] As a result, the public hearing was declared failed and invalid by a majority of votes.

Declaring the public hearing failed and invalid was a strategic response to offset the lack of prior consultation and deficient engagement with communities. In a fieldwork interview, a resident of Shelyaur who took part in the 2014 public hearing in Izhma explained that rejection of the oil project at the public hearing would not prevent the state commission from approving the project documentation since the outcomes of public hearings are only advisory.[90] The oil projects would proceed. However, if a public hearing is declared invalid, then the company needs to make the changes demanded by the public and organise a further public hearing.[91] According to the interviewee, this was a way for communities to ensure that Lukoil-Komi employed the best available technological solutions to minimise the impact and respect communities' opinions.[92] However, there were disputes among community members regarding this strategy. In particular, community members working for Lukoil-Komi and its contractors were unsupportive of these actions.[93]

A follow-up public hearing for the Yuzhno-Sedmesskoe oil field was announced in Izhma several months later. However, the meeting was cancelled at the last

---

87 Senior administrator, Izhma Rayon Administration and Rural Council, personal communication, Izhma, June 2015.
88 Ibid.
89 Member of ethnic movement leadership, personal communication, Izhma, June 2015.
90 Reindeer herder, male, Komi-Izhma, personal communication, Shelyaur, June 2015.
91 Senior administrator, Izhma Rayon Administration and Rural Council, personal communication, Izhma, June 2015.
92 Member of ethnic movement leadership, personal communication, Izhma, June 2015.
93 Ibid.

minute, leaving communities frustrated and angry.[94] They gathered in the administration building and were informed by a representative of the Izhma administration that Lukoil-Komi had been operating beyond the terms and conditions of the licences given for the oil fields, violating the time frames for exploration and extraction activities. These issues of non-compliance with the licences, legislation and technological design of the projects were acknowledged in 2015 by the regional government in its report on the State of the Environment.[95] However, it cost Lukoil-Komi little investment of money and time to renew the licences and proceed with the drilling.

Yet it was clear that Lukoil-Komi's social licence to operate had been seriously undermined in Izhma district, where the industry had not been operating as long as in Usinsk district, and which did not have the historical dependency on the industry and the strong support base that the industry has in Usinsk. When Lukoil-Komi had initially started working in Izhma district, the company had entered an agreement with the Izhma municipal administration to contribute to the socio-economic development of the district, provided funds to support local hospitals and schools, and donated funds for charity projects in culture and sports. The company installed banners in villages promoting its corporate social responsibility, attended public events and held media and outreach campaigns (for example, in the newspaper *Severnye Vedomosti*, in schools and online social networks). However, these activities have not had a significant impact on overall living conditions, and any positive impact has been undermined by the lack of meaningful engagement and environmental care around oil activities.[96] And while a significant number of positions were opened for seasonal and shift-based jobs, local people had to compete with applicants from across Russia, often more competent and experienced with work in technologically complex operations. Moreover, not everyone in communities favoured these job opportunities. For instance, one man from Shelyaur worried that "these jobs keep men away from families and traditional way of life, destroying social and cultural ties."[97]

Another way for local people to balance power relations has been through direct negotiation with Lukoil-Komi. Community representatives wanted to progress in establishing a dialogue with the managers of Lukoil-Komi and local and regional government officials, who, however, were found to be reluctant and constraining the dialogue. In Izhma district, representatives of the ethnic movement of Komi-Izhma people *Izvatas* had engaged directly with Lukoil-Komi when it started its activities in the early 2000s, but this direct engagement had been discontinued in the 2010s with the greater focus by the company on the

94 Ibid.
95 Komi Republic, *Report of the Government of the Komi Republic, State of the Environment in the Komi Republic in 2015* [*Gosudarstvennyy doklad o sostoyanii okruzhayushchey sredy Respubliki Komi v 2015 godu*] (Syktyvkar: Komi Republic, 2016) http://mpr.rkomi.ru/left/gosdoklad/
96 See also, Wilson and Istomin, "Beads and Trinkets?"
97 Employee of an agricultural education institution, hunter, male, Komi-Russian, personal communication, Shelyaur, June 2015.

district administration.[98] *Izvatas* thus took up the lead on negotiations following the recent wave of protests. The company had to respect the position of the movement as a representative body of the local people.[99]

Feeling that decisions about the contribution of Lukoil-Komi to rural development were made in the rooms of bureaucrats, *Izvatas* engaged with the oil company to challenge this. As explained by its representative, the movement represents the development aspirations of Komi-Izhma people, their livelihoods, culture and language in Izhma district and beyond.[100] Since Lukoil-Komi had established itself in the region, it was important for *Izvatas* that the company's contribution strengthened traditional livelihoods rather than weakening them (as they believed was the case with many oil jobs).[101] The movement was determined to negotiate with Lukoil-Komi the support needed for the benefit of the local people and the wellbeing of local society as a whole.

The agreement negotiated in summer 2015 centred on support for the education of rural youth in skills needed in the community. It was seen as a challenge to the parallel conventional negotiations between Lukoil-Komi and the Izhma district administration.[102] Lukoil-Komi accepted the request and provided the required funds. *Izvatas* gained the opportunity to allocate the funds among families. However, not everyone agreed with the decisions made as community members who were not part of the movement felt excluded and questioned why only certain families would benefit. Moreover, this agreement between *Izvatas* and Lukoil-Komi raised questions among environmentalists. At the time, environmentalists questioned whether the negotiators representing the community had gone too far, suggesting people should focus more on protesting oil spills and promoting better public consultation, rather than accepting financial support.[103] The challenge of negotiating while also retaining the power of protest[104] is exhibited clearly here and is an unresolved element of the Komi protests. However, it is also worth noting that both oil spills and public protest have continued since our fieldwork visits.[105]

98 Civil society leader, personal communication, Izhma, June 2015.
99 Member of ethnic movement leadership, personal communication, Izhma, June 2015.
100 Ibid.
101 Civil society leader, personal communication, Izhma, June 2015.
102 Senior administrator, Izhma District Administration and Rural Council, personal communication, Izhma, June 2015.
103 Member of a socioenvironmental movement, personal communication, Shelyaur, June 2015; Environmentalist, Moscow, personal communication, June 2015.
104 Ciaran O'Faircheallaigh, "Extractive Industries and Indigenous Peoples: A Changing Dynamic?" *Journal of Rural Studies* 30 (2013): 20–30, https://doi.org/10.1016/j.jrurstud.2012.11.003
105 Thomas Nilsen, "Locals Blame Lukoil after Disastrous Oil Spill," *Independent Barents Observer*, May 9, 2016, https://thebarentsobserver.com/en/ecology/2016/05/locals-blame-lukoil-after-disastrous-oil-spill; Elena Solovieva, "Protestors in Komi Village Demand an Apology from the President of Lukoil Vgit Alekperov," *Independent Barents Observer*, May 19, 2017, https://thebarentsobserver.com/ru/node/2380; Elena Solovieva, "A Journey Across Russia's Desolate Oil Region," *Greenpeace*, February 19, 2019, https://www.greenpeace.org/international/story/21011/a-journey-across-russias-desolate-oil-region/

Discussion and conclusion

This chapter has taken a relational justice perspective to uncover how oil companies in the northern Komi Republic consult and engage with the local Komi communities most affected by oil and gas developments in the area, who lack the legal status of indigenous peoples. The community–company–government relations are characterised by inherent power imbalances. It is evident that neither the authorities nor the companies involved in oil exploration and extraction in northern Komi have sought to address these power imbalances in their engagement with local communities. This could have been done through meaningful consultation and engagement processes, going beyond the minimum legal requirements.

Instead, in recent years, the companies and the government have drawn closer together and alienated the rural communities still further, focusing engagement on the district administrative centres and away from the rural villages. The lack of a legal imperative for companies to consult meaningfully with communities prior to a whole range of industrial activities, from seismic testing to drilling site preparation, has further underscored the impression of communities that the industry treats them with a lack of respect. This impression is compounded by repeated environmental disruptions, such as oil spills and negligent waste management, and a lack of information about project plans or even about serious pollution incidents when they take place. The accumulated frustrations were such that, when communities encountered an actual legal violation (a failure to consult a community prior to drilling a well), this was enough to trigger a widespread public protest, which is still to be resolved.

Our research in Izhma and Usinsk districts suggests that if companies and authorities had made more effort to engage consistently and meaningfully with local communities, they might have reduced or avoided local frustrations and the ensuing unrest. Many of our respondents expressed strong opposition to the way that the industry was being developed in the region, but did not oppose the oil industry per se. They appreciated that it was a historically legitimate economic activity in the region (especially in Usinsk district) and had the potential to create local jobs and support wider economic development – if operating cleanly and in close dialogue with local communities. However, in the absence of efforts by the authorities and the companies to establish or maintain such a dialogue, it was left to local residents to seek to balance power relations themselves. This has proven costly to the industry, both reputationally and in terms of its ability to continue its activities.

The rural communities asserted that support to socio-economic development negotiated between oil companies and the municipal administration is an insufficient form of benefit sharing, in light of the sacrifices made by the communities. They felt that practices of consultation and engagement are unfair and disrespectful of the rights and interests of community members. These arguments were used by the communities to challenge the prevailing practices, in their efforts to rebalance power relations. The informal representative structures of communities – notably the *Izvatas* movement and the networks of activists working with the Save

Pechora Committee – have been influential in mitigating some of the power asymmetries and finding ways of expressing dissent. For example, communities developed a practice of declaring public hearings invalid in order to force companies and authorities to organise legitimate processes of consultation.

Effectively, the organised movement of rural people has instituted a form of local oil politics oriented to achieving relational justice. They have successfully recruited outsider communities to this movement, by using social and personal networks, social media and international scrutiny, to challenge efforts to limit media coverage locally. They have linked the plight of the northern Komi oil communities to wider global issues about the sustainability of the Arctic. Ultimately, the demands made to Lukoil-Komi and the authorities also remain deeply rooted in the unresolved status of indigeneity of Komi people and related claims to territorial control. However, by opening up debates beyond this vexed question to wider issues of sustainability and justice, they have succeeded in drawing considerable attention to their cause. As a result, Lukoil-Komi has started to make changes to the ways that it engages with local people. The agreement negotiated with *Izvatas* was a tentative start to a more meaningful local dialogue, albeit one which has still not fully resolved local issues several years later.

In the past decade, resource development has accelerated in northern Russia. Companies continuously employ innovative advanced technologies to access remote parts and tame harsh northern environments. However, many of these companies remain old-fashioned in ignoring the voices and interests of indigenous and non-indigenous rural communities who rely on the environment in multiple ways to maintain and develop their livelihoods and cultures. In the past, this has been possible, given the isolation of such places, but social media and international campaigns are starting to change this. Meaningful consultation and engagement need to become the new norm for the companies operating in northern Russia, both for the sake of communities themselves and in order for the industries to continue to operate in the modern age. This requires a combination of national and regional legislation, international standards and voluntary approaches. Going beyond the law is increasingly proving to be a wise risk-mitigation strategy for companies, while sticking strictly to the law has proven to be a high-risk strategy, as our case study suggests. At the same time, advances also need to be made in national and regional laws that minimise the relational injustices currently prevailing in regions affected by the extraction of natural resources.

References

350.org. "Striking: Indigenous Komi People in Russia Are Fed Up with Oil." April 16, 2014. https://350.org/komi-are-fed-up-with-oil/

Åhrén, Matthias. *Indigenous Peoples' Status in the International Legal System*. Oxford: Oxford University Press, 2016.

Anaya, James. *Report of the Special Rapporteur on the Rights of Indigenous Peoples, James Anaya: Extractive Industries and Indigenous Peoples, 2013*. UN Human Rights Council. UN Doc. A/HRC/24/41.

Asia Pacific Forum and OHCHR. *The United Nations Declaration on the Rights of Indigenous Peoples: A Manual for National Human Rights Institutions.* Sydney and Geneva: Asia Pacific Forum of National Human Rights Institutions/Office of the United Nations High Commissioner for Human Rights, 2013. www.ohchr.org/Documents/Issues/IPeoples/UNDRIPManualForNHRIs.pdf

Bebbington, Anthony J. and Jeffrey Bury. *Subterranean Struggles: New Dynamics of Mining, Oil, and Gas in Latin America*, vol. 8. Austin TX: University of Texas Press, 2013.

Behrends, Andrea, Stephen P. Reyna, and Günther Schlee, *Crude Domination*. Oxford: Berghahn Books, 2011.

Bodnar, Irina S. and Vladimir G. Zainullin. "Ekologo-meditsinskaya Otsenka Zabolevayemosti Naseleniya Respubliki Komi" [Ecological and Medical Assessment of the Morbidity of the Population of the Komi Republic]. *Proceedings of the Komi Science Center, Ural Branch of the Russian Academy of Sciences* 1, no. 9 (2012): 35–40.

Borozinets, Lenfrid, et al. *Istoriya Stanovleniya I Razvitya Neftegazovogo Kompleksa Komi Kraya* [History of the Establishment and the Development of the Oil and Gas Industry of the Komi Region]. Ukhta: Ukhta State Technical University, 2004.

Convention on Biological Diversity 1992. United Nations Treaty Series 1760, 79.

Convention on Biological Diversity. *Akwé:Kon Voluntary Guidelines for the Conduct of Cultural, Environmental and Social Impact Assessment Regarding Developments Proposed to Take Place on, or Which Are Likely to Impact on, Sacred Sites and on Lands and Waters Traditionally Occupied or Used by Indigenous and Local Communities.* Montreal: Secretariat of the Convention on Biological Diversity, 2004.

Doyle, Cathal and Jill Cariño. *Making Free, Prior and Informed Consent a Reality: Indigenous Peoples and the Extractive Sector.* London: Indigenous Peoples Links/PIPLinks; Middlesex University School of Law; The Ecumenical Council for Corporate Responsibility, 2013. www.ecojesuit.com/wp-content/uploads/2014/09/Making-FPIC-a-Reality-Report.pdf

Dwyer, Mark J. and Kirill V. Istomin. "Komi Reindeer Herding: The Effects of Socialist and Post-Socialist Change on Mobility and Land Use." *Polar Research* 28, no. 2 (2009): 282–297. https://doi.org/10.1111/j.1751-8369.2009.00108.x

Dwyer, Mark J. and Kirill V. Istomin. "Mobility and Technology: Understanding the Vulnerability of Two Groups of Nomadic Pastoralists to Reindeer Losses." *Nomadic Peoples* 10, no. 2 (2006): 142–165. https://doi.org/10.3167/np.2006.100209

Fondahl, Gail and Anna Sirina. "Rights and Risks: Evenki Concerns Regarding the Proposed Eastern Siberia–Pacific Ocean Pipeline." *Sibirica* 5, no. 2 (2006). https://doi.org/10.3167/136173606780490720

Franks, D.M., R. Davis, A. Bebbington, S. Ali, D. Kemp, and M. Scurrah. "Conflict Translates Environmental and Social Risk into Business Costs." *Proceedings of the National Academy of Sciences* 111, no. 21 (2014): 7576–7581. https://doi.org/10.1073/pnas.1405135111

Gavidia, Mirella Cobeleanschi and Deanna Kemp. "Company–Community Relations in the Mining Context: A Relational Justice Perspective." In *Natural Resources and Environmental Justice: Australian Perspectives*, edited by Sonia Graham, Libby Robin, Jennifer McKay, and Steven Schilizzi. Clayton South VIC: CSIRO Publishing, 2017.

Habeck, Joachim Otto. "How to Turn a Reindeer Pasture into an Oil Well, and Vice Versa: Transfer of Land, Compensation and Reclamation in the Komi Republic." In *People and the Land. Pathways to Reform in Post-Soviet Siberia*, edited by Erich Kasten, 125–147. Berlin: Reimer, 2002.

Healy, Noel, Jennie C. Stephens, and Stephanie A. Malin. "Embodied Energy Injustices: Unveiling and Politicizing the Transboundary Harms of Fossil Fuel Extractivism and Fossil Fuel Supply Chains." *Energy Research and Social Science* 48 (2019): 219–234. https://doi.org/10.1016/j.erss.2018.09.016

Henry, Laura A., Soili Nysten-Haarala, Svetlana A. Tulaeva, and Maria Tysiachniouk. "Corporate Social Responsibility and the Oil Industry in the Russian Arctic: Global Norms and Neo-Paternalism." *Europe-Asia Studies* 68, no. 8 (2016): 1340–1368. https://doi.org/10.1080/09668136.2016.1233523

Hughes, Layla. "Relationships with Arctic Indigenous Peoples: To What Extent Has Prior Informed Consent Become a Norm?" *Review of European, Comparative & International Environmental Law* 27, no. 1 (2018). https://doi.org/10.1111/reel.12232

ILO Convention 169 (1989). "Indigenous and Tribal Peoples Convention. Adopted 27 June 1989, entered into force 5 September 1991." *International Legal Materials* 28, 1382.

International Covenant on Civil and Political Rights 1966. United Nations Treaty Series 999, 171.

International Covenant on Economic, Social and Cultural Rights 1966. United Nations Treaty Series 993, 3.

IWGIA, Russia. "Komi in Usinsk District Declare 'The End of Our Patience Has Come.'" June 6, 2014. https://www.iwgia.org/en/russia/2064-russia-komi-in-usinsk-district-declare-the-end-of

IWGIA, Russia. "We Izhma Komi Are Indigenous People and This Is Our Land." April 14, 2014. https://www.iwgia.org/en/russia/2012-russia-we-izhma-komi-are-indigenous-people-and-thi

Johnston, Kim A. "Toward a Theory of Social Engagement." In *The Handbook of Communication Engagement*, edited by Kim A. Johnston and Maureen Taylor. Hoboken NJ: Wiley, 2018.

Karjalainen, Timo Pauli and Joachim Otto Habeck. "When The Environment Comes to Visit: Local Environmental Knowledge in the Far North of Russia." *Environmental Values* 13, no. 2 (2004): 167–186. https://doi.org/10.3197/0963271041159877

Kelman, Ilan, Julia Stephanie Perelstein Loe, and Elana Wilson Rowe. "Local Perceptions of Corporate Social Responsibility for Arctic Petroleum in the Barents Region." *Arctic Review of Law and Politics* 7, no. 2 (2016). https://doi.org/10.17585/arctic.v7.418

Kemp, Deanna, John R. Owen, Nora Gotzmann, and Carol J. Bond. "Just Relations and Company–Community Conflict in Mining." *Journal of Business Ethics* 101, no. 1 (2011): 93–109. https://doi.org/10.1007/s10551-010-0711-y

Komi Republic. *Report of the Government of the Komi Republic, State of the Environment in the Komi Republic in 2015* [*Gosudarstvennyy doklad o sostoyanii okruzhayushchey sredy Respubliki Komi v 2015 godu*]. Syktyvkar: Komi Republic, 2016. http://mpr.rkomi.ru/left/gosdoklad/

Kovalev, Nicole and Johann Koeppel. "Introduction to the Environmental Impact Assessment System and Public Participation in the Russian Federation." *Journal of Environmental Assessment Policy and Management* 5, no. 3 (2003): 321–338. https://doi.org/10.1142/s146433320300136x

Loginova, Julia. "Achieving Human and Societal Security in Oil Producing Regions: A Komi-Izhma Community Perspective from Pripechor'e, Russia." In *Human and Societal Security in the Circumpolar Arctic*, edited by Kamrul Hossain, José Miguel Roncero Martin, and Anna Petretei. Leiden: Brill Nijhoff, 2018. https://doi.org/10.1163/9789004363045_010

Matveev, Mikhail. "'Kechimov's Case': Everyday Conflict or Clash of Civilizations?" [*"Delo Kechimova": Bytovoy Konflikt Ili Stolknoveniye Tsivilizatsiy?*] Activatica.org, 2015.

McCauley, Darren, Raphael Heffron, Maria Pavlenko, Robert Rehner, and Ryan Holmes. "Energy Justice in the Arctic: Implications for Energy Infrastructural Development in the Arctic." *Energy Research and Social Science* 16 (2016): 141–146. https://doi.org/10.1016/j.erss.2016.03.019

Mezak, Ernest. "Izhemskie Muzhiki Vyigrali Sud U Glavy Respubliki Komi" [Izhma Men Won the Court with the Head of the Komi Republic]. *Lesnye novosti* [Forest news]. March 2001.

Murashko, Olga A. "What Is the Etnologicheskaia Ekspertiza in Russia?" *Sibirica* 5, no. 2 (2006): 77–94.

Nilsen, Thomas. "Locals Blame Lukoil after Disastrous Oil Spill." *Independent Barents Observer*, May 9, 2016. https://thebarentsobserver.com/en/ecology/2016/05/locals-blame-lukoil-after-disastrous-oil-spill

Novikova, Natalia I. *Okhotniki i neftyaniki: issledovaniya v yuridicheskoy antropologii* [Hunters and Oil Workers: Research in Legal Anthropology]. Moscow: Nauka, 2014.

Novikova, Natalia I. and Emma Wilson. *Anthropological Expert Review: Socio-Cultural Impact Assessment for the Russian North*. Ajluokta/Drag, Norway: Arran Lule Same Centre, 2017.

O'Faircheallaigh, Ciaran. "Extractive Industries and Indigenous Peoples: A Changing Dynamic?" *Journal of Rural Studies* 30 (2013): 20–30. https://doi.org/10.1016/j.jrurstud.2012.11.003

O'Rourke, Dara and Sarah Connolly. "Just Oil? The Distribution of Environmental and Social Impacts of Oil Production and Consumption." *Annual Review of Environment and Resources* 28, no. 1 (2003): 587–617. https://doi.org/10.1146/annurev.energy.28.050302.105617

Pappila, Minna, Soili Nysten-Haarala and Ekaterina Britcyna. "Participation in Benefit-Sharing Arrangements in the Komi Republic." In *Russian Analytical Digest No. 202: Oil Company Benefit Sharing in the Russian North*, 6–9. ETH Zurich: Centre for Security Studies, 2017.

Pierk, Simone and Maria Tysiachniouk. "Structures of Mobilization and Resistance: Confronting the Oil and Gas Industries in Russia." *The Extractive Industries and Society* 3, no. 4 (2016): 997–1009. https://doi.org/10.1016/j.exis.2016.07.004

Rodriguez, Denisse and Julia Loginova. "Navigating State-Led Extractivism in Ecuador and Russia: Fluid Identities and Agendas of Socio-Environmental Movements." In *The Right to Nature: Social Movements, Environmental Justice and Neoliberal Natures*, edited by Elia Apostolopoulou and Jose A. Cortes-Vazquez. Abingdon: Routledge, 2018.

Rogers, Douglas. "The Materiality of the Corporation: Oil, Gas, and Corporate Social Technologies in the Remaking of a Russian Region." *American Ethnologist* 39, no. 2 (2012): 284–296. https://doi.org/10.1111/j.1548-1425.2012.01364.x

Roon, Tatiana. "Globalization of Sakhalins Oil Industry: Partnership or Conflict? A Reflection on the Etnologicheskaia Ekspertiza." *Sibirica* 5, no. 2 (2006). https://doi.org/10.3167/136173606780490702

Ruggie, John. *Guiding Principles on Business and Human Rights: Implementing the United Nations "Protect, Respect and Remedy" Framework*. Geneva and New York: United Nations, 2011 (UNGPs). UN Doc. A/HRC/17/31. March 21, 2011.

Russia. Constitution of the Russian Federation, 1993.

Russia. Decree of the Government of the Russian Federation of N 536-r "On the Approval of the List of Indigenous Small-numbered Peoples of the North, Siberia and the Far East of the Russian Federation" [*Ob utverzhdenii perechnya korennykh malochislennykh narodov Severa, Sibiri i Dal'nego Vostoka Rossiyskoy Federatsii*] (2006).

Russia. Decree of the Government of the Russian Federation N 145 "On the Procedure for Organizing and Conducting State Expertise of Project Documentation and Results of Engineering Surveys" [*O poryadke organizatsii i provedeniya gosudarstvennoy ekspertizy proyektnoy dokumentatsii i rezul'tatov inzhenernykh izyskaniy*] (2007).

Russia. Decree of the Government of the Republic of Sakha (Yakutia). "On the Procedure for Organizing and Conducting Ethnological Expert Review in Places of Traditional Residence and Traditional Economic Activities of Indigenous Minorities of the North of the Republic of Sakha (Yakutia)" [*O Poryadke organizatsii i provedeniya etnologicheskoy ekspertizy v mestakh traditsionnogo prozhivaniya i traditsionnoy khozyaystvennoy deyatel'nosti korennykh malochislennykh narodov Severa Respubliki Sakha (Yakutiya)*] (2011).

Russia. Law N 121-FZ "On Amendments to Legislative Acts of the Russian Federation regarding the Regulation of the Activities of Non-profit Organisations Performing the Functions of a Foreign Agent" [*O vnesenii izmeneniy v otdel'nyye zakonodatel'nyye akty Rossiyskoy Federatsii v chasti regulirovaniya deyatel'nosti nekommercheskikh organizatsiy, vypolnyayushchikh funktsii inostrannogo agenta*] (2012).

Russia. Law N 174-FZ "On the Ecological Expert Review" [*Ob ekologicheskoy ekspertize*] (1995).

Russia. Law N 49-FZ "On Territories of Traditional Natural Resource Use of the Indigenous Small-Numbered Peoples of the North, Siberia and the Far East" [*O territoriyakh traditsionnogo prirodopol'zovaniya korennykh malochislennykh narodov Severa, Sibiri i Dal'nego Vostoka Rossiyskoy Federatsii*] (2001).

Russia. Law N 7-FZ "On Environmental Protection" [*Ob okhrane okruzhayushchey sredy*] (2002).

Russia. Law N 82-FZ "On Guarantees of the Rights of Indigenous Peoples of the Russian Federation" [*O Garantiyakh Prav Korennykh Malochislennykh Narodov Rossiyskoy Federatsii*] (1999).

Russia. Town Planning Code of the Russian Federation [*Gradostroitel'nyy kodeks Rossiyskoy Federatsii*] (2004).

Russia. *Report of the Government of the Komi Republic, State of the Environment in the Komi Republic in 2015* [*Gosudarstvennyy doklad o sostoyanii okruzhayushchey sredy Respubliki Komi v 2015 godu*]. Syktyvkar, Komi Republic, 2016. Retrieved from http://mpr.rkomi.ru/left/gosdoklad/

Sidortsov, Roman, and Benjamin Sovacool. "Left Out in the Cold: Energy Justice and Arctic Energy Research." *Journal of Environmental Studies and Sciences* 5, no. 3 (2015): 302–307. https://doi.org/10.1007/s13412-015-0241-0

Solovieva, Elena. "A Journey Across Russia's Desolate Oil Region." Greenpeace, February 19, 2019. https://www.greenpeace.org/international/story/21011/a-journey-across-russias-desolate-oil-region/

Solovieva, Elena. "Protestors in Komi Village Demand an Apology from the President of Lukoil Vgit Alekperov." *Independent Barents Observer*, May 19, 2017. https://thebarentsobserver.com/ru/node/2380

Stammler, Florian and Aitalina Ivanova. "Confrontation, Coexistence or Co-Ignorance? Negotiating Human-Resource Relations in Two Russian Regions." *The Extractive Industries and Society* 3, no. 1 (2016): 60–72. https://doi.org/10.1016/j.exis.2015.12.003

Stuvøy, Kirsti. "Human Security, Oil and People." *Journal of Human Security* 7, no. 2 (2011): 5–19. https://doi.org/10.3316/jhs0702005

Tysiachniouk, Maria S. and Andrey N. Petrov. "Benefit Sharing in the Arctic Energy Sector: Perspectives on Corporate Policies and Practices in Northern Russia and Alaska."

Energy Research and Social Science 39 (2018): 29–34. https://doi.org/10.1016/j.erss.2017.10.014

Tysiachniouk, Maria S. *Transnational Governance through Private Authority: The Case of the Forest Stewardship Council Certification in Russia, vol. 7.* Wageningen, Netherlands: Wageningen Academic Publishers, 2012.

Tysiachniouk, Maria, Svetlana Tulaeva, and Laura A. Henry. "Civil Society under the Law 'On Foreign Agents': NGO Strategies and Network Transformation." *Europe-Asia Studies* 70, no. 4 (2018): 615–637. https://doi.org/10.1080/09668136.2018.1463512

UN General Assembly. Declaration on the Rights of Indigenous Peoples, UNGA Res 61/295. September 13, 2007 (UNDRIP).

UN Global Compact. "The Ten Principles of the UN Global Compact." Accessed October 10, 2019. https://www.unglobalcompact.org/what-is-gc/mission/principles

Whiteman, Gail. "All My Relations: Understanding Perceptions of Justice and Conflict between Companies and Indigenous Peoples." *Organization Studies* 30, no. 1 (2009): 101–120. https://doi.org/10.1177/0170840608100518.

Wilson, Emma and Kirill Istomin. "Beads and Trinkets? Stakeholder Perspectives on Benefit Sharing and Corporate Responsibility in a Russian Oil Province." *Europe-Asia Studies* (2019) https://doi.org/10.1080/09668136.2019.1641585

Wilson, Emma and Krystyna Swiderska. "Extractive Industries and Indigenous Peoples in Russia: Regulation, Participation and the Role of Anthropologists." *IIED Working Paper* (London: IIED, 2009).

Wilson, Emma. "Rights and Responsibilities: Sustainability and Stakeholder Relations in the Russian Oil and Gas Sector." In *Northern Sustainabilities: Understanding and Addressing Change in the Circumpolar World*, edited by Gail Fondahl and Gary N. Wilson, 177–188. New York: Springer International, 2017.

Wilson, Emma. "What Is the Social Licence to Operate? Local Perceptions of Oil and Gas Projects in Russia's Komi Republic and Sakhalin Island." *The Extractive Industries and Society* 3, no. 1 (2016): 73–81. https://doi.org/10.1016/j.exis.2015.09.001

Wilson, Emma. *Evaluating International Ethical Standards and Instruments for Indigenous Rights and the Extractive Industries.* Ájluokta/Drag, Norway: Árran Lule Sami Centre, 2016. https://tinyurl.com/IndigenousStandards

Wilson, Emma. *What Is Free, Prior and Informed Consent (FPIC)?* Ájluokta/Drag, Norway: Árran Lule Sami Centre, 2016.

Yakovleva, Natalia. "Oil Pipeline Construction in Eastern Siberia: Implications for Indigenous People." *Geoforum* 42, no. 6 (2011): 708–719. https://doi.org/10.1016/j.geoforum.2011.05.005

Zadorin, Maxim. "The Status of Unrecognized Indigenous Communities and Rural Old-Residents of the Russian Arctic." *The Yearbook of Polar Law* 5, no. 1 (2013): 669–674.

8 Local views on oil development in a village on the North Slope of Alaska

Anne Merrild Hansen and Panigruaq Ipalook

Introduction

Many communities throughout the Arctic have experienced both undesired social impacts as well as benefits of oil and gas development.[1] Typically, impacts and benefits are debated and negotiated prior to project development and the concerns of citizens are recorded and addressed during mandatory impact assessment processes.

Companies applying for licenses to extract oil and gas in any Arctic country are met with legal requirements to conduct environmental and social impact assessments.[2] Often companies must meet further supplementary impact assessment requirements from international investment institutions such as the World Bank and the European Investment Bank if they are to finance activities.[3] The

---

1 Anne Merrild Hansen and Ross Virginia, "The Future of Hydrocarbon Development in Greenland: Perspectives from Residents of the North Slope of Alaska," *ARCTIC* 71, no. 4 (2018): 365–374, doi: 10.14430/arctic4750; Brigt Dale, Siri Veland, and Anne Merrild Hansen, "Petroleum as a Challenge to Arctic Societies: Ontological Security and the Oil-Driven 'Push to the North,'" *The Extractive Industries and Society* 6, no. 2 (2019): 367–377, doi: 10.1016/j.exis.2018.10.002; Florian Stammler and Vladislav Peskov, "Building a 'Culture of Dialogue' among Stakeholders in North-West Russian Oil Extraction," *Europe-Asia Studies* 60, no. 5 (2008): 831–849, doi: 10.1080/09668130802085182; Julia S.P. Loe and Ilan Kelman, "Arctic Petroleum's Community Impacts: Local Perceptions from Hammerfest, Norway," *Energy Research and Social Science* 16 (2016): 25–34, doi: 10.1016/j.erss.2016.03.008; Dara O'Rourke and Sarah Connolly, "Just Oil? The Distribution of Environmental and Social Impacts of Oil Production and Consumption," *Annual Review of Environment and Resources* 28 (2003): 287–617, doi: 10.1146/annurev.energy.28.050302.105617
2 Anne Merrild Hansen, Sanne Vammen Larsen, and Bram Noble, "Social and Environmental Impact Assessments in the Arctic," in *The Routledge Handbook of the Polar Regions*, eds Mark Nuttall, Torben Christensen, and Martin Siegert, chapter 29 (New York: Routledge, 2018).
3 European Investment Bank, "EIB Environmental Assessment," accessed October 15, 2019, https://www.eib.org/attachments/strategies/environmental-assessment.pdf; World Bank, Independent Evaluation Group, *World Bank Group impact Evaluations: Relevance and Effectiveness* (Washington DC: World Bank Group, 2012), https://openknowledge.worldbank.org/bitstream/handle/10986/13100/757230PUB0EPI00013000Pubdate0209013.pdf?sequence=1&isAllowed=y

purpose of the impact assessment processes is to identify and mitigate negative impacts and enhance desired outcomes of development in order to promote sustainable development.

Public participation activities are mandatory in the impact assessment processes, and arenas, such as public meetings and workshops, etc., are set up to foster dialogues. In these arenas, debates take place between proponents, authorities and citizens of the impacted communities regarding the proposed projects and community development.[4] Methodologies, approaches, timing, effect and issues raised in the public participation processes have been subject to various studies.[5] Companies must record and analyse public opinion, knowledge and concerns in order to understand how undesired impacts can be avoided and benefits gained.

However, debates are also taking place outside of the arenas formally provided during participation processes in relation to impact assessments, and the dialogue amongst the locals continues after the planning and implementation of projects. While the ongoing dialogues in the community are informal, they are neither structured nor recorded and the content of the debates does not necessarily reach the companies or the public authorities. In this chapter, we present the findings from an exploratory study of post impact assessment debates related to oil and gas development in the case of a village, Nuiqsut, on the North Slope of Alaska.

The study is based on semi-structured interviews with 82 people living on the North Slope and qualitative interviews with 26 persons representing authorities, researchers, companies and native organisations in Utqiaġvik (formerly known as Barrow) and Nuiqsut in 2016. The semi-sturctured interviews were not always set up in advance but instead sometimes developed from spontaneous meetings with people we met during field work, such as a young woman working in a catering company in Prudhoe Bay, who offered a ride from the airport to a cafe during a stopover. We have also reviewed debates on Facebook between locals from Nuiqsut about oil development. The chapter further draws on the personal observations and experiences of one of the authors (Panigruaq), who is an oral historian. Panigruaq was born in Fairbanks and raised on the North Slope between the villages of Utqiaġvik and Nuiqsut. He has been involved in public

---

4 Lone Kørnøv, "Public Participation," in *Tools for Sustainable Development*, eds Lone Kørnøv, Mikkel Thrane, Arne Remmen, and Henrik Lund (Aalborg: Aalborg Universitetsforlag, 2007), 719–738; Ilan Kapoor, "Towards Participatory Environmental Management?" *Journal of Environmental Management* 63, no. 3 (2001): 269–279, doi: 10.1006/jema.2001.0478

5 Anna-Sofie Hurup Olsen and Anne Merrild Hansen, "Perceptions of Public Participation in Impact Assessment: A Study of Offshore Oil Exploration in Greenland," *Impact Assessment and Project Appraisal* 32 (2014): 72–80; Jennifer M.P. Stewart and A. John Sinclair, "Meaningful Public Participation in Environmental Assessment: Perspectives from Canadian Participants, Proponents and Government," *Journal of Environmental Assessment Policy and Management* 9, no. 2 (2007), 161–183; Ron Bisset, "Methods of Consultation and Public Participation," in *Environmental Assessment in Developing and Transitional Countries*, eds Norman Lee and Clive George (Chichester: Wiley, 2000), 149–160.

meetings and engaged in various debates on management of oil projects and oil related funds for the past ten years.

To set the scene, this chapter first introduces how the oil-economy of Alaska has evolved and describes how the funds from oil are distributed. The Alaskan village of Nuiqsut and the local situation regarding oil and gas development are then explained. Three themes identified in the local debates around oil development are presented before concluding remarks are made.

Oil and money on the North Slope

Oil exploration on the North Slope of Alaska goes back almost 150 years when oil seeps were identified in Cook Inlet in the 1850s.[6] In 1968, the first commercial hydrocarbon discovery in Alaska was made onshore in Prudhoe Bay on the northern coast of the North Slope. Expectations of the reserves in the area were high and the discovery sparked what is commonly referred to as "The Black Gold Rush" with reference to the historical gold rush in Klondike.[7] In 1969, the state authority held an oil lease auction. Alaska owned the land and drilling rights went to the highest bidders. This sale earned the state over 900 million USD.[8]

To get the oil from Prudhoe Bay to market, a group of oil companies established a venture named "Alyeska Pipeline Company."[9] The Alyeska project involved building a 1300-kilometre pipeline across Alaska to the port of Valdez on Prince William Sound. The pipeline crossed lands that were at the time still under the cloud of unsettled aboriginal title.[10] The question of Alaska Native land claims therefore had to be resolved expeditiously to ensure certainty in investments by oil producers and others.[11] The US Secretary of the Interior imposed a land freeze that prevented any pipeline construction until the claims were settled. This happened subsequently in 1971 when President Richard Nixon signed the Alaska Native Claims Settlement Act of 1971 into law.[12] As part of the settlement, the Alaska Native Claims Settlement Act divided Alaska into geographic regions.[13]

---

6 Claus M. Naske and Herman E Slotnick, *Alaska: A History* (Oklahoma: University of Oklahoma Press: 2014).

7 Ibid.

8 "The State of Alaska Has Collected More than $160 Billion from Oil & Gas since 1959," Alaska Oil and Gas Association, accessed October 18, 2019, https://www.aoga.org/industry/history-1960s

9 H.C. Jamison, L.D. Brockett, and R.A. McIntosh, *Prudhoe Bay – a 10-year Perspective* (Tulsa OK: The American Association of Petroleum Geologists, 1980). See also, "About Us," Alyeska Pipeline Service Company, accessed October 18, 2019, https://www.alyeska-pipe.com/AboutUs

10 Dixie Dayo and Gary Kofinas, "Institutional Innovation in Less than Ideal Conditions: Management of Commons by an Alaska Native Village Corporation," *International Journal of the Commons* 4, no. 1 (2010): 142–159.

11 Ibid.

12 A.J. McClanahan, "The Alaska Native Claims Settlement Act of 1971," *Cultural Survival Quarterly* 27, no. 3 (2003), 20–22.

13 "Alaska Native Corporations," Resource Development Council, accessed October 15, 2019, https://www.akrdc.org/alaska-native-corporations

Alaska Natives then organised a regional corporation for each region. Those corporations were authorised to select lands that would become their property in fee simple. Each region also contains numerous smaller "village corporations." Altogether 12 regional corporations and 225 village corporations were established and received fee title to 40 million acres of land and a cash settlement of 962.5 million USD in exchange for the concession of claims to all other lands in Alaska.[14] Today the Arctic Slope Regional Corporation owns nearly 5 million acres of surface and subsurface lands on the North Slope.[15]

The pipeline from Prudhoe Bay was completed in 1976 and the oil development in Alaska took off. The boom in Prudhoe Bay fuelled a huge increase in state spending and sparked the creation of the "Alaska Permanent Fund," a state-managed, public trust in 1976.[16] The Permanent Fund revenues are primarily invested in stocks and real estate. In 1982, the fund paid the first annual dividend to all residents who had lived in the state more than six months. The first dividend was 1,000 USD per person.[17] Alaskans continue to receive dividends from the fund today.

Stocks in native corporations, established under the Alaska Native Claims Settlement Act, were issued only to Natives born before or on December 18, 1971 and who could demonstrate that they were at least one-quarter Alaska Native by blood.[18] The Alaska Native Claims Settlement Act was amended in 1988 to provide for enrolment of "new natives" born after 1971 as voting stockholders in the regional corporations. The individual corporation boards of the village corporations hold the right to decide if the corporation wants to offer people born after 1971 shares or if they want only to have the original shares. In 1990, the Arctic Slope Regional Corporation became the first of only four Alaska Native corporations to enrol shareholders born after 1971. The Arctic Slope Regional Corporations included qualifying Alaskan North Slope Iñupiat born after 1971, and each receives 100 shares on birth.[19] The shares from 1971 can be passed on by inheritance to the next generations but the new shares are personal and are extinguished on the death of the holder.[20] Today, nearly 70 per cent of Arctic Slope Regional Corporation shareholders were born after 1971.[21]

The influence of oil development on the Alaskan economy is vast, as more than 17 billion barrels of oil have been produced on the North Slope since the discovery of the Prudhoe Bay oil field. Oil production is referred to as the engine of

14 Ibid.
15 "Nuiqsut," Official website of the North Slope Borough, accessed October 15, 2019, www.north-slope.org/our-communities/nuiqsut
16 Naske and Slotnick, *Alaska: A History*.
17 Alaska Permanent Fund Corporation, accessed October 15, 2019, www.apfc.org/home/Content/home/index.cfm
18 Ibid.
19 Lee Huskey, *The Economy of Village Alaska* (Anchorage: University of Alaska, 1992).
20 Maude Blair, "Issuing New Stock in ANCSA Corporations," *Alaska Law Review* 33 (2016): 273–286.
21 See also, "Arctic Slope Regional Corporation (ASRC)," Alaskan Natives, accessed October 15, 2019, https://www.alaskan-natives.com/75/arctic-slope-native-association (for further information).

economic growth in Alaska and has funded up to 90 per cent of the state's unrestricted General Fund revenues in most years since and has accounted for over 180 billion USD in total revenue since statehood. Even during periods of low oil prices, oil revenues accounted for approximately 70 per cent of unrestricted General Fund revenues in Alaska. The oil industry further accounts for one-third of Alaskan jobs and constitutes about half of the overall economy in the state.[22]

While the economic impact of oil development in Alaska as described is profound, Alaskan production has actually been in long-term decline since peaking in 1988 when the state accounted for 25 per cent of US domestic production, producing 2,017,000 barrels of crude oil per day. In 2017, Alaska provided approximately 7 per cent of the domestic production which equals 497,000 barrels of crude oil per day.[23] With an estimated 40–50 billion barrels of conventional oil remaining to be developed on the North Slope and offshore areas of the Alaskan Arctic, it is not for a lack of resource that production has declined. The majority of the remaining reserves are located on federal lands and offshore areas where access has not been permitted. There is, however, increased interest from the Federal State authorities in the opening of new areas in Alaska for oil development, and new discoveries are still being made on native lands.

Nuiqsut, a native village surrounded by oil fields

The North Slope of Alaska is one of the most extreme environments in which people live and work.[24] The social organisation of Alaskan Natives centres on group subsistence activities and on an extensive network that shares the subsistence harvest. Cultural knowledge and practices have been refined over many generations.[25] Most of the Borough's 9,000 residents live in the eight communities of Anaktuvuk Pass, Atqasuk, Utqiaġvik, Kaktovik, Point Hope, Point Lay, Wainwright and Nuiqsut. Utqiaġvik serves as the Borough seat of government. The Iñupiat Community is an Alaska Native tribe, which represents and is selected by the Iñupiat people of the Arctic Slope region.[26]

Resources in the area

The native village of Nuiqsut is located south of the Colville River Delta at the Beaufort Sea and southeast of Utqiaġvik, 50 miles west of Prudhoe Bay on the

---

22 "Alaska's Oil & Gas Industry," Resource Development Council, accessed October 15, 2019, https://www.akrdc.org/oil-and-gas
23 "Alaska Field Production of Crude Oil," U.S. Energy Information Administration, accessed October 15, 2019, https://www.eia.gov/dnav/pet/hist/LeafHandler.ashx?n=PET&s=MCRFPAK2&f=A
24 John Kruse, Judith Kleinfeld, and Robert Travis, "Energy Development Effects on Alaska's North Slope: Inupiat Population," *Human Organization* 41, no. 2 (1982): 97–106, doi: 10.17730/humo.41.2.t823308164w76158
25 "Nuiqsut," Official website Of The North Slope Borough.
26 Ibid.

North Slope. The area has traditionally been a gathering and trading place for the Iñupiat and is still today considered a good area for hunting and fishing. A village corporation for Nuiqsut (Kuukpik Corporation) was established in 1973 under the provisions of the Alaska Native Claims Settlement Act. Twenty-seven families who had traditionally lived in the area and who had close cultural ties to the land moved from Utqiaġvik and settled in the area, while the Arctic Slope Regional Corporation funded construction of the village of Nuiqsut, which is Iñupiaq for "something beautiful over the horizon." Today (2018), Nuiqsut is home to a population of approximately 450 people, of whom 87 per cent are Iñupiat. Like other North Slope villages, Nuiqsut's economy is still based primarily on subsistence hunting, fishing, and whaling. Nearby subsistence species include bowhead whales, caribou, seals, moose and waterfowl. Fish caught for subsistence include whitefish, burbot, arctic char and grayling. The public sector employed 54 per cent of the workers in Nuiqsut, and other employment opportunities are with the Kuukpik Village Corporation and the construction industry. Some residents sell local arts and crafts, including skin masks and boats, fur mittens, parkas and carved ivory.

Besides being rich in resources for hunting and gathering, the Colville River Delta is also the site of the Alpine oil field, operated by ConocoPhillips Alaska. Alpine is the fifth largest oil discovery on the North Slope and the first on Native-owned lands. Production from the Alpine started in late 2001. Subsistence hunting remains the integral way of life for the people of Nuiqsut. A surface-use agreement was negotiated between Kuukpik and ConocoPhillips, which amongst other things led to the establishment of a panel named the Kuukpik Subsistence Oversight Panel. This panel provides ongoing local input and oversight for the protection, promotion and health of the subsistence resources in the area.[27] Nuiqsut is today surrounded by land leased for development by oil companies. More than 50,000 barrels of oil, or roughly a tenth of the state's oil production, is produced each day from oil fields owned by ConocoPhillips.

Culture and identity

The significance of Nuiqsut's subsistence is not in food gathering alone but with the intertwining of food gathering and the sociocultural identification of a traditional and unique lifestyle.[28] This Iñupiat lifestyle gives the natives of the region a sense of pride, identity, distinction, and unity.[29] The whaling culture complex of Utqiaġvik and the previously mentioned cultural complexes of Nuiqsut and Kaktovik are of great symbolic value. The preservation of the Iñupiat language is also an important part of the native culture. Aside from the pride and distinction of

27 "About Us," Kuukpik Corporation, accessed October 18, 2019, https://www.kuukpik.com/corporation/about-us/
28 Aaron Wernham, "Inupiat Health and Proposed Alaskan Oil Development: Results of the First Integrated Health Impact Assessment/Environmental Impact Statement for Proposed Oil Development on Alaska's North Slope," *EcoHealth* 4, no. 4 (2007): 500–513.
29 Ibid.

having their own language, the Iñupiat language is highly functional. Nelson lists 94 Inuit words which are used to convey concepts about ice age, thickness, condition, movement, and topography.[30] Any influence which erodes the use and understanding of the Iñupiat language concurrently undermines the ability of subsistence hunters to perform their tasks. Conversely, the erosion of subsistence will concurrently erode language and knowledge, making it possible that future generations will not be effective subsistence hunters.

The subsistence lifestyle has been developing and changing since the first non-Iñupiat contact. The subsistence hunters today use new tools, such as snowmobiles, high powered rifles, outboard motors, harpoons with explosive heads, etc. Yet there is still a continuity with the traditional practices and, for example, the whale hunt is still connected to various spiritual activities (like singing the whales in, when the catch is brought to shore) and social structures related to sharing of meat, blanket toss parties celebrating the harvest, etc. The subsistence lifestyle in this way still forms the basis for their way of life even though the hunters today need to engage in urban processes to acquire, maintain, and use the modern technological tools. An integral part of traditional subsistence living is therefore that it is dynamically changing. However, the people of Nuiqsut seem to expect that the subsistence lifestyle will continue at a significant level for future generations.[31]

Three themes from debates in Nuiqsut on oil development

During our conversations with people in Nuiqsut, all expressed strong opinions about oil development and the related impacts which were obviously experienced as very present in their everyday lives. Overall, people were divided on the question of whether or not oil development should proceed and expand in the Coldville River area. There were shared concerns and shared anticipations expressed, but also great variation in the nuances in opinions and attitudes.

People's attitudes were clearly influenced by what they perceived as essential for sustainable development of their community and hence whether they perceived oil development as an activity which could provide opportunities to improve living standards, or as a risk of the opposite. They did, however, not always agree on what improving living standards and quality of life entailed. Certain themes were nevertheless recurrently brought up, and the arguments motivating people's opinions and attitudes towards oil development centred around these. The three themes were: (1) pace and intensity of development; (2) language and cultural preservation; and (3) influence on decision-making. The three themes are further elaborated in the following sections, and an overview is presented below in Table 8.1

---

30 Richard K. Nelson, *Hunters of the Northern Ice* (Chicago: University of Chicago Press, 1969).
31 *Nuiqsut Comprehensive Development Plan 2015–2035, Final Draft* (Alaska: Community Planning and Real Estate Division and NSB Department of Planning & Community Services, 2016) www.north-slope.org/assets/images/uploads/NUI_Final_Draft_Jan2016.pdf

Table 8.1 Overview of themes and questions raised in debates about oil and gas in Nuiqsut

Theme	Questions discussed
Pace and intensity of development	Should any oil development be accepted, anywhere, anytime at any cost? Where do we draw the line? Can development happen too fast/slow? Can activities be too place- or time-crowding? When is the location acceptable? Can it be too close to town?
Cultural preservation	Does oil development provide funds, which make it possible to uphold traditional living? Does oil development compromise culture and destroy heritage? Do mitigation funds promote preservation rather than allowing for culture to be dynamic and develop? Is culture by itself developing with oil as it has before with resources available?
Rights to participate and influence decision-making	Who has the (informal) right to be involved in participation processes and decision-making? Is it legitimate to be critical about oil development if you receive and accept money from mitigation funds? Is it possible to oppose to oil development if you are a shareholder in regional corporations who receive taxes from oil development? Is it legitimate to have an opinion if you were not born on the land, not affected by the development, or do not have family ties there? Is decision-making transparent enough? Is it okay to oppose drilling if there are no proven, direct, negative impacts on people or the environment? Can you be pro-oil if you are indigenous and have ties to the land? Can you be pro-oil if you are concerned about preserving your culture? Can board members in corporations be trusted to protect the interests of the whole community?

Theme 1: pace and intensity of development

Though people in Nuiqsut in general expressed acceptance of oil development in the area, they still discussed whether development might happen too quickly and if it would be better to get the extraction "over with" and move on, or rather to stretch it out to secure a more continuous money flow. Some of the people with whom we talked thought that too many licences were active at the same time and that new projects were being implemented before people had a chance to adapt to the change caused by earlier developments. There were also expressions of concern that if development is too fast then the resources would be quickly depleted and the area left dry, with a sudden collapse of the local economy. There were also some who hoped for a rapid development, to have the basins emptied in order to get access to the funds from the development and to be able to continue life in the village without further worries.

People who worried about the pace of development explained how oil development had caused dramatic and, to some extent, irreversible changes to the surrounding landscape without allowing people the time needed to adapt to these changes. They found that the physical infrastructure related to development was located and designed in ways that had unexpected negative aesthetic and cultural consequences, and that they had not foreseen or expected the level of impact it had on their well-being. They noted that the scenic values of large areas and the feeling of solitude when going out on the land had been compromised, and with this the value of the tundra. One explained that areas where she used to go camping on the land with her grandmother in the summer, which were previously relatively inaccessible tundra, are now easily accessed by car. During a ride to the area, she pointed out how today a bridge and pipelines run through the area. "It is not that I am against development," she explained, "it is just that it is so overwhelming. This was our place where we would go to be alone, then the road and pipelines were suddenly there. It changed the area."

Besides the pace of development, some Nuiqsut residents also expressed concerns about the intensity of activities and the proximity to the homes in the village. They would discuss whether a location was acceptable and if it might be too close to town. "People are divided on the question of where they draw the line," as one noted. Our attention was drawn to debates on Facebook in relation to this theme. In a public discussion, Nuiqsut residents were talking about the proximity to town of a particular new project being planned. One wrote: "There are many many benefits; yet this is too close to home ... this one right here is three miles away. It is the most concerning one to the village." In response to this, other Nuiqsut residents came forward. Some agreed, others did not. Some stated that the person raising this concern was himself receiving money from mitigation funds and the question was raised whether someone should express scepticism towards increased development while accepting money from the industry. Others questioned if the person raising the concern had the legitimacy to be critical and thereby potentially compromise development if he did not have strong family ties to the area. Some highlighted the family relations when they stated their opinion, to legitimise their arguments:

> We continue to lose our traditional lands as we speak. Putu, the most recent historical site that is now being trampled by a joint drilling rig ... extending south to the other historical site of Kayuqtusiluk, where Simmonds and Ericklook families have memories of their moments living in sod-houses, and towards downriver near the site of Nigliagvik, where Amy Taalak's historical camp is no longer used because of the existing pipeline that ruins the beauty of camping.

The issue of proximity of projects is linked to another concern in the community, namely health concerns regarding pollution. This is also a subject to which national news media have paid attention.[32] All community members we talked to expressed worries about increasing respiratory problems amongst the population and particularly amongst youth, and some feared that this was related to emissions from nearby oil fields. They were afraid that health problems would increase if the oil fields were expanded and came even closer to the town. As one stated: "The development has proceeded too rapidly, without enough care for the health of the people from an air quality and subsistence perspective ... And now we are virtually surrounded." Some pointed to a health study from 2012 finding that 7 per cent of adults in Nuiqsut experience chronic breathing problems such as asthma, emphysema or a persistent cough.[33] While companies active in the area have set up a number of continuous air and water quality monitoring programmes to ensure that any changes in local air or water quality are discovered, and some health experts point to non-communicable diseases, mould in houses and tobacco smoking as the main explanation behind the alarming numbers, the locals did not feel confident that changes in air quality are being reported if found. One person with whom we talked pointed to the "other explanations" as "all being related to oil development anyway" referring to more people moving to the area and therefore more people living in houses causing increased humidity and more mould, more people being exposed to smoke in their houses, and imported foods increasing with the development.

Theme 2: cultural preservation

The second theme identified in the debates around oil development in Nuiqsut is related to the impact on culture and in particular the preservation of language as an important cultural marker and the derived social implications. While our talks with people left the impression that the residents appreciated the support of the local formal economy provided through mitigation funds, dividend payments, jobs, etc., there was still disagreement over whether it simultaneously compromised culture and destroyed heritage.

Some considered the support from industrial activities as a prerequisite for upholding a high living standard while also living a traditional lifestyle involving subsistence hunting and the sharing culture. Mitigation funds have been set up to alleviate and compensate for undesired impacts. Yet some people still found that the development has undesired and unforeseen impacts. They primarily pointed to socio-cultural and health issues. They expressed worries about what might happen to Nuiqsut in the future, with or without oil. Most people in the community appreciated that the funds provided to mitigate negative impacts together with the support for the school and for the preservation of nature, yet felt that parallel processes of preserving culture (particularly language) are threatened by oil

---

32 Sabrina Shankman, "Surrounded by Oil Fields, an Alaska Village Fears for Its Health," *InsideClimate News*, December 13, 2018, https://insideclimatenews.org/news/01082018/alaska-north-slope-oil-drilling-health-fears-pollution-risk-native-village-nuiqsut

33 See, *Nuiqsut Comprehensive Development Plan 2015–2035*, 104.

development. "English is the oil language," as one noted, referring to its use in the sector, by the corporations and in all information materials, etc. Some were afraid that the loss of language, and of culture in general, might demotivate learning and reconciliation. As one explained:

> We are at a vital point in returning back to our roots, our way of life. We are just learning our language and trapping lifestyle but when you have outside forces like oil and gas you are prone to follow regulations and are restricted access to even historical sites.

The Nuiqsut residents found that the oil development interfered with subsistence hunting, since disturbance of animals and landscapes has meant that trappers and hunters need to travel further to get to hunting grounds. They are, however, being compensated for this as they get money from the mitigation funds to cover the costs of the extra fuel and vehicles needed to be able to continue hunting.

Still, concerns are raised. One explained the dilemma this way:

> Don't get me wrong, there are many who are advocates for oil and gas production as it creates feasibility within the economic aspects of this region, creating jobs and a robust economy that is just beginning to be seen across the North Slope. There are great benefits to having oil and gas production, but is it worth losing our cultural value and ties to the land which it has proven to continue to sustain us, our bodies, our cultural traditions?

Theme 3: rights to participate and influence decision-making

Nuiqsut residents also raised issues relating to "who has a legitimate power" to influence decisions regarding oil development in the area and who should have a say. This is also related to an issue of trust regarding who gets to make the decisions in the end and suspicions regarding the negotiations between shareholders in the regional funds and the companies. As one stated:

> These oil fields just keep taking and taking. Whatever happens behind those closed doors meetings is between Conoco and the entities here of Nuiqsut. We have no say in it. Maybe they don't want you all to be shareholders for a reason. Maybe they don't want to get voted out of their seats. Something fishy is going on.

As mentioned earlier in relation to the debate on the theme of pace and intensity, people debating on Facebook were critical about the fact that a person raising concerns was receiving dividends, and questioned whether it was possible to be sceptical towards increased development yet still accept money from the industry. Others questioned the legitimacy of a critical view from a person or persons who lack strong family ties to the area. In these ways, Nuiqsut residents to some extent discuss internally who has the power to influence decisions regarding oil and gas development in the area and who should have a say. Issues on unjust distribution of costs and benefits were also raised, as one for example noted in relation to a new lease in the aforementioned Putu area:

> We all take the impact cheques, because we're not all entitled to be shareholders of Kuukpik and honestly I don't even want to be a part of a crooked corporation that doesn't care about its citizens. Many say no to Putu yet our leaders still approve.

These remarks referred to people who live in Nuiqsut who are not shareholders, having less income and therefore being dependent on the small amounts from the mitigation fund to uphold their way of living. The person who made this statement also expressed a distrust of the local corporation Kuukpik and its ability to represent the interests of the whole community. Another similarly stated that: "The board members benefit the most. While they leave everyone in the dust. Everyone knows this who lives here."

Debates and division

Rooted in the various different and sometimes conflicting perspectives on oil development in the area of Nuiqsut, it seems that internal conflicts emerge and cause division in the community across the topics raised. As one of the residents stated:

> This tears the community apart. It creates differences at a community level. You see the impacts it has between families; you see monetary impacts; and you see families arguing over land ownership rights; who was here first. This is the epitome of the negative factors oil has on our community.

Similarly another noted: "I've lived here my whole life. I have seen all these changes and it has divided us." Disputes in communities between families and even within the families were amongst issues raised by the respondents.

Related to the issue of land rights and ownership and the related right to influence decision-making around oil development, discussions also circle around the topic of who holds the (moral) right to have a say in general. This is connected to talks about who is more "native," pointing back to the family ties to the land. People question which residents in Nuiqsut belong most, and this turns to disputes about who are the right persons to even live in Nuiqsut, thus creating uncertainty on a personal level when an individual's identity is questioned and residents are categorised into groups belonging more or less than others. One explained how other locals had told him that his family did not belong here since they were not Kuukpik shareholders. Another pointed to what she saw as a prerequisite for a sustainable livelihood:

> It's about finding common ground that will help us adapt to change … It is a trying time for Nuiqsut, yet in the end we each take care of each other, we still celebrate as one people from a strong heritage, real strong heritage.

Concluding remarks

The North Slope Borough is the dominant economic force in North Slope communities. Hydrocarbon activities have been and continue to be the primary source of income on the North Slope. Today, after nearly 50 years of oil production, people living on the North Slope have been found in general to be supportive of the hydrocarbon industry. The standard of living of North Slope communities in Alaska relies largely on a continual flow of money from oil activities, yet new developments are presently causing conflicts and fostering divisions between people in affected villages. This is the case in the village of Nuiqsut which is heavily influenced by oil development. The population finds itself divided on the question of whether the development is promoting a desired improvement in the community and if local values are taken into consideration and valued in an appropriate manner in relation to land-use planning.

The study presented found that heavy debates around oil development take place in Nuiqsut today and that these debates are causing conflicts and leading to division in the community. Based on the findings, three main conclusions are reached. First, the topics discussed prior to development, as identified in this study, could be included and addressed in future impact assessment processes. This includes the sensitive issue of who gets to express their opinions and influence decision-making, and on which levels; the topic of the pace and intensity of development; and the future prospects and the carrying capacity of the area not only from an environmental perspective but also from a social perspective. Second, it can be concluded that listening to the voices of the locals also after development can help to identify environmental concerns, point to the roots of social conflicts and provide insights in relation to perceptions of pros and cons related to development. Third, it is important to acknowledge that peoples' concerns and worries are dynamic and change over time, especially as they experience impacts from development in practice. It seems relevant to establish arenas or create systems where people can express their opinions and receive responses, making their voice heard by the authorities and companies, not only through social media or other media, in order to be able to mitigate and manage potential conflicts that emerge.

References

"About Us." Alyeska Pipeline Service Company. Accessed October 18, 2019. https://www.alyeska-pipe.com/AboutUs

"About Us." Kuukpik Corporation. Accessed October 18, 2019. https://www.kuukpik.com/corporation/about-us/

"Alaska Field Production of Crude Oil." U.S. Energy Information Administration. Accessed October 15, 2019. https://www.eia.gov/dnav/pet/hist/LeafHandler.ashx?n=PET&s=MCRFPAK2&f=A

"Alaska Native Corporations." Resource Development Council. Accessed October 15, 2019. https://www.akrdc.org/alaska-native-corporations

Alaska Permanent Fund Corporation. Accessed October 15, 2019. www.apfc.org/home/Content/home/index.cfm

"Alaska's Oil & Gas Industry." Resource Development Council. Accessed October 15, 2019. https://www.akrdc.org/oil-and-gas

"Arctic Slope Regional Corporation (ASRC)." Alaskan Natives. Accessed October 15, 2019. https://www.alaskan-natives.com/75/arctic-slope-native-association

Bisset, Ron. "Methods of Consultation and Public Participation." In *Environmental Assessment in Developing and Transitional Countries*, edited by Norman Lee and Clive George, 149–160. Chichester: Wiley, 2000.

Blair, Maude. "Issuing New Stock in ANCSA Corporations." *Alaska Law Review* 33 (2016): 273–286.

Dale, Brigt, Siri Veland, and Anne Merrild Hansen. "Petroleum as a Challenge to Arctic Societies: Ontological Security and the Oil-Driven 'Push to the North.'" *The Extractive Industries and Society* 6, no. 2 (2019): 367–377. doi:10.1016/j.exis.2018.10.002

Dayo, Dixie and Gary Kofinas. "Institutional Innovation in Less than Ideal Conditions: Management of Commons by an Alaska Native Village Corporation." *International Journal of the Commons* 4, no. 1 (2010): 142–159.

European Investment Bank. "EIB Environmental Assessment." Accessed October 15, 2019. https://www.eib.org/attachments/strategies/environmental-assessment.pdf

Hansen, Anne and Ross Virginia. "The Future of Hydrocarbon Development in Greenland: Perspectives from Residents of the North Slope of Alaska." *Arctic* 71, no. 4 (2018): 365–374. doi:10.14430/arctic4750

Hansen, Anne Merrild, Sanne Vammen Larsen, and Bram Noble. "Social and Environmental Impact Assessments in the Arctic." In *The Routledge Handbook of the Polar Regions*, edited by Mark Nuttall, Torben Christensen, and Martin Siegert, chapter 29. New York: Routledge, 2018.

Huskey, Lee. *The Economy of Village Alaska*. Anchorage: University of Alaska, 1992.

Jamison, H.C., L.D. Brockett, and R.A. McIntosh. *Prudhoe Bay: A 10-year Perspective*. Tulsa, OK: American Association of Petroleum Geologists, 1980.

Kapoor, Ilan. "Towards Participatory Environmental Management?" *Journal of Environmental Management* 63, no. 3 (2001): 269–279. doi:10.1006/jema.2001.0478

Kørnøv, L. "Public Participation." In *Tools for Sustainable Development*, edited by Lone Kørnøv, Mikkel Thrane, Arne Remmen, and Henrik Lund, 719–738. Aalborg: Aalborg Universitetsforlag, 2007.

Kruse, John, Judith Kleinfeld, and Robert Travis. "Energy Development Effects on Alaska's North Slope: Inupiat Population." *Human Organization* 41, no. 2 (1982): 97–106. doi:10.17730/humo.41.2.t823308164w76158

Loe, Julia S.P. and Ilan Kelman. "Arctic Petroleum's Community Impacts: Local Perceptions from Hammerfest, Norway." *Energy Research and Social Science* 16 (2016): 25–34. doi:10.1016/j.erss.2016.03.008

McClanahan, A.J. "The Alaska Native Claims Settlement Act of 1971." *Cultural Survival Quarterly* 27 no. 3 (2003): 20–22.

Naske, Claus M. and Herman E. Slotnick. *Alaska: A History*. Oklahoma: University of Oklahoma Press, 2014.

Nelson, Richard K. *Hunters of the Northern Ice*. Chicago: University of Chicago Press, 1969.

"Nuiqsut." Official website of the North Slope Borough. Accessed October 15, 2019. www.north-slope.org/our-communities/nuiqsut

Nuiqsut Comprehensive Development Plan 2015–2035, Final Draft. Alaska: Community Planning and Real Estate Division and NSB Department of Planning and Community Services, 2016. www.north-slope.org/assets/images/uploads/NUI_Final_Draft_Jan2016.pdf

Olsen, Anna-SofieHurup and Anne Merrild Hansen. "Perceptions of Public Participation in Impact Assessment: A Study of Offshore Oil Exploration in Greenland." *Impact Assessment and Project Appraisal* 32 (2014): 72–80.

O'Rourke, Dara and Sarah Connolly. "Just Oil? The Distribution of Environmental and Social Impacts of Oil Production and Consumption." *Annual Review of Environment and Resources* 28 (2003): 287–617. doi:10.1146/annurev.energy.28.050302.105617

Shankman, Sabrina. "Surrounded by Oil Fields, an Alaska Village Fears for Its Health." *InsideClimate News*, December 13, 2018. https://insideclimatenews.org/news/01082018/alaska-north-slope-oil-drilling-health-fears-pollution-risk-native-village-nuiqsut

Stammler, Florian and Vladislav Peskov. "Building a 'Culture of Dialogue' among Stakeholders in North-West Russian Oil Extraction." *Europe-Asia Studies* 60, no. 5 (2008): 831–849. doi:10.1080/09668130802085182

Stewart, Jennifer M.P. and A. John Sinclair. "Meaningful Public Participation in Environmental Assessment: Perspectives from Canadian Participants, Proponents and Government." *Journal of Environmental Assessment Policy and Management* 9, no. 2 (2007): 161–183.

"The State of Alaska Has Collected more than $160 Billion from Oil & Gas since 1959." Alaska Oil and Gas Association. Accessed October 18, 2019. https://www.aoga.org/industry/history-1960s

Wernham, Aaron. "Inupiat Health and Proposed Alaskan Oil Development: Results of the First Integrated Health Impact Assessment/Environmental Impact Statement for Proposed Oil Development on Alaska's North Slope." *EcoHealth* 4, no. 4 (2007): 500–513.

World Bank, Independent Evaluation Group. *World Bank Group Impact Evaluations: Relevance and Effectiveness*. Washington DC: World Bank Group, 2012. https://openknowledge.worldbank.org/bitstream/handle/10986/13100/757230PUB0EPI00013000Pubdate0209013.pdf?sequence=1&isAllowed=y

9 Land claims agreements in Canada and the promise of enhanced participation

Nigel Bankes[1]

Introduction

Canada's modern land claims agreements between the Crown and Indigenous communities in Northern Canada, Labrador and British Columbia offer the possibility of enhanced participation by Indigenous communities in resource development decisions within the settlement areas of these claims.[2] Section 35 of the *Constitution Act, 1982* affords these agreements or modern treaties constitutional protection.[3] This chapter examines how the agreements and the interpretive case law on the agreements deal with participation issues. Although land claims agreements continue to be negotiated, some of these agreements have been in place for as much as three decades and as a result we now have a significant body of jurisprudence on these agreements, much of it dealing with Indigenous participation issues in one way or another.

The agreements are not identical but they do have common elements. This is particularly true in Yukon, where all of the final agreements are based on the so-called Umbrella Final Agreement. There are 14 Yukon First Nations and 11 have signed final agreements and self-government agreements with Canada and Yukon.[4] All of the

---

1 Thanks to David Wright for comments on an earlier version of this chapter.
2 The northern agreements on which this chapter focuses include James Bay and Northern Quebec Agreement (1977); Inuvialuit Final Agreement/Western Arctic Claim (1984); Gwich'in Comprehensive Land Claim Agreement (1992); Council for Yukon Indians Umbrella Final Agreement (1993) (Yukon UFA); Nunavut Land Claims Agreement (1993) (NFA); Sahtu Dene and Metis Comprehensive Land Claim Agreement (1994); Labrador Inuit Land Claims Agreement (2005) (LILCA); and Tłı̨chǫ Land Claims and Self Government Agreement (2003) (Tłı̨chǫ Agreement). See, Indigenous and Northern Affairs Canada, "Final Agreements and Related Implementation Matters," Government of Canada; Indigenous and Northern Affairs Canada; Communications Branch, June 18, 2018, https://www.aadnc-aandc.gc.ca/eng/1100100030583/1100100030584 (for texts of all agreements).
3 Constitution Act, 1982, Schedule B to the Canada Act 1982 (UK), 1982, c 11; *Beckman v. Little Salmon Carmacks First Nation*, 2010 SCC 53, paras 2 and 62.
4 *Liard First Nation v. Yukon Government and Selwyn Chihong Mining Ltd*, 2011 YKSC 55, para. 6. The outstanding Yukon First Nations are Liard First Nation, Ross River First Nation and White River First Nation all part of the larger Kaska First Nations.

modern land claims agreements contain recitals or operative provisions emphasizing the importance of Indigenous participation in decision-making concerning the use of land water and resources,[5] as well as chapters or articles dealing with land use planning and project-based impact assessment.[6] The chapters dealing with land use planning and impact assessment are well integrated, with the result that in areas with an approved land use plan only projects that conform to the land use plan can proceed to the impact assessment stage.[7] The agreements typically provide a strong institutional basis for these two functions with some form of land use planning commission and impact review board (and in some cases a water board as well to review projects requiring a water licence).[8] These institutions are established as institutions of public government and also as co-management authorities with appointments from both the federal, territorial or provincial governments, and the Indigenous party to the agreement. As institutions of public government they maintain Online Registries to facilitate public access to planning documents and project related documents.[9] Also, as co-management bodies they exercise authority over the entire settlement area of the land claims agreement.

In addition to being constitutionally protected,[10] federal (and in some cases provincial) implementation or ratification legislation also gives the agreements the force of law.[11] Most of the agreements also contemplate that those chapters or sections of the agreement that provide for new institutions will be implemented through new bespoke legislation.[12] In some cases that legislation will be specific to a particular land claims agreement, whereas in others the implementing legislation may take a more territorial or regional approach. For example, the implementing legislation for chapter 12 of the Umbrella Final Agreement (UFA) (Development Assessment) and its associated Final Agreements applies throughout Yukon and it applies regardless of whether or not a First Nation has reached a final agreement.[13] Similarly, the *Mackenzie Valley Resources Management Act* (MVRMA) applies to the Mackenzie Valley as defined in the statute.[14] The MVRMA served to implement the environmental and resource management provisions

---

5 See, e.g., NFA, Preamble; Gwich'in Agreement, section 1.1.7; Yukon UFA section 12.1.1.2.
6 See, e.g., NFA, article 11, Land Use Planning and article 12, Development Impact; and Yukon UFA, chapter 11, Land Use Planning and chapter 12, Development Assessment.
7 NFA, section 12.3. See also, Nigel Bankes, "The Place of Land-Use Planning in the T. F.N. Claim," in *Hinterland or Homeland? Land-Use Planning in Northern Canada*, eds Terry Fenge and William A. Rees (Ottawa, Canadian Arctic Resources Committee, 1987), 95–112.
8 See, e.g., NFA article 12, Water Management; and Yukon UFA, chapter 14, Water Management.
9 *Liard First Nation*, para. 15.
10 Constitution Act 1982, section 35.
11 See, e.g., Canada, Nunavut Land Claims Agreement Act, SC 1993, c 29.
12 See, e.g., Canada, Nunavut Planning and Project Assessment Act, SC 2013, c 14.
13 Canada, Yukon Environmental and Socio-Economic Assessment Act, SC 2003, c 7 (YESAA).
14 Canada, Mackenzie Valley Resource Management Act, SC 1998, c 25. The definition in the statute excludes that part of the geographical valley that is included within the Inuvialuit settlement region as well as Wood Buffalo National Park.

of the Gwich'in, Sahtu and subsequently the Tlicho agreement, but, as implied above, also applies in the traditional territories of Indigenous communities in the southern part of the valley or watershed that have yet to reach a final agreement.

Some agreements may also provide that project proponents must negotiate some form of impact and benefit agreement (IBA) with a local or regional Indigenous organizations.[15] The need to negotiate such agreements provides additional leverage for engagement by Indigenous communities in a wide range of project-related matters, including not only such things as employment, training and contracting opportunities but also such things as project monitoring activities. While such agreements have frequently been treated as confidential in the past, there is some trend towards making them public.[16]

This combination of land use planning, impact assessment procedures and IBAs offers a range of opportunities to enhance Indigenous engagement and participation in resource projects proposed within the settlement areas of Indigenous communities.[17]

The balance of the chapter falls into four parts. The next part examines one key decision dealing with the land use planning provisions of a land claims agreement. The following part is more extensive and engages with a growing body of case law dealing with the project impact assessment (IA) provisions of modern land claims agreements. The penultimate part deals with the interaction between the IA provisions of modern land claim agreements and the duty to consult and accommodate. The final part provides a conclusion.

Case law on the land use planning provisions of modern land claims agreements

The leading decision on the land use planning provisions of a modern land claims agreement is the recent decision of the Supreme Court of Canada in *First Nation of Nacho Nyak Dun v. Yukon*.[18] This decision involved the circumstances surrounding

15 See, for example, NFA article 26, Inuit Impact and Benefit Agreements.
16 See for example the IBAs between the Qikqitani Inuit Association and Baffinland Iron Ore Mines with respect to the Mary River Iron Ore Project. The original IBA was signed on September 6, 2013 and the new "amended and restated agreement" agreement is effective as of October 22, 2018. The parties also made public an arbitral award with respect to the interpretation of the advance royalty provisions of the agreement. Documents available from, "Documents," QIA, accessed October 16, 2019, https://www.qia.ca/documents
17 See, Ginger Gibson, Dawn Hoogeveen, Alistair MacDonald, and the Firelight Group, *Impact Assessment in the Arctic: Emerging Practices of Indigenous-Led Review* (Whitehorse: Gwich'in Council International, 2018), https://gwichincouncil.com/sites/default/files/Firelight%20Gwich%27in%20Indigenous%20led%20review_FINAL_web_0.pdf (for an exploration of these ideas of leverage within such a complex institutional structure).
18 *First Nation of Nacho Nyak Dun v. Yukon*, [2017] 2 SCR 576, 2017 SCC 58 (CanLII) (Supreme Court). The only other decision that I am aware of dealing with the land use planning provisions of an agreement is *Nunatsiavut Government v. Newfoundland and Labrador*, 2013 NLTD(G) 142. The case had some similarities to the Yukon case insofar as the provincial government expressed concerns to the effect

the development and adoption of the Peel Watershed Regional Land Use Plan in Northern Yukon (Peel Plan). The land use planning process adopted in Yukon was negotiated through the Umbrella Final Agreement (UFA) between Yukon First Nations and Canada and Yukon, and then carried forward into final agreements negotiated by individual Yukon First Nations. In this case, the Peel Plan implicated the interests of four First Nations: Nacho Nyak Dun, Tr'ondëk Hwëch'in, Vuntut Gwichin and the Tetlit Gwich'in.[19]

The UFA and the Final Agreements of these First Nations (in common with other land claims agreements) contemplated that land use plans as adopted under the procedures established in the agreements would apply to all lands within that region (i.e. both First Nation and public lands).[20] Regional land use plans in Yukon are developed by individual regional land use planning commissions (RLUPC) established by government and any affected First Nation(s) and comprised of nominees of Yukon, First Nations and other residents of the region.[21] Once the RLUPC has developed a recommended plan, the plan is forwarded to both Yukon and affected First Nations for their approval with respect to those parts of the plan applying to public or First Nation lands respectively. Each of the First Nations and Yukon was afforded the same authority which was, having consulted with the other, to then "approve, reject or propose modifications to that part of the recommended regional land use plan applying" to the lands for which it had responsibility. In the case of Yukon this would be for public lands included in the planning area.[22] Proposed modifications with written reasons are forwarded to the RLUPC for its reconsideration following which, after further consultation Yukon might approve, reject or modify the plan as it applied to public lands (and the First Nations similarly with respect to First Nation lands).[23]

Land use planning for the Peel watershed began in 2004 with the establishment of the Peel Watershed Planning Commission. The Supreme Court described the planning region (covering almost 68,000 square kilometres) as:

> one of the largest intact wilderness watersheds in North America. Its landscape ranges from "rugged mountains to low, flat taiga forests". The

---

that a draft plan did not appropriately balance economic, environmental and social considerations. That led the province to commission another plan. Although the Nunatsiavut Government (representing Labrador Inuit) did not obtain all the relief that it sought, Justice Butler did conclude that it was entitled to a declaration that "the Respondent's actions (in delaying its required consultation with the Applicant and selection of the option under Part 10.6.1 of the Agreement, without keeping the Applicant informed throughout the process of development and implementation of an LUP satisfactory to the Province) did not meet the standard expected of the duty of the honour of the Crown and that the Respondent is in breach of Part 10.6 of the Agreement."

19 *First Nation of Nacho Nyak Dun*, Supreme Court, para. 7.
20 Yukon UFA, section 11.2.1.1.
21 Yukon UFA, section 11.4.2.
22 Yukon UFA, section 11.6.0.
23 Yukon UFA, sections 11.6.3 and 11.6.5.

ecosystem is characterized by its rich water resources and abundant and diverse fish, wildlife, and plant populations. This wilderness character is nearly untouched by contemporary development – there are no permanent residents and few roads in the watershed. As an intact ecosystem, the watershed supports the traditional activities of the First Nations.[24]

The trial judge noted that while there were no operating mines in the watershed "there is considerable interest in mineral development" and many staked mining claims.[25] The Recommended Plan was developed over a four-year period of research and consultation and was presented to Yukon and affected First Nations in 2009. The Recommended Plan proposed that some 80 per cent of the planning region should be afforded a high degree of protection; the balance would be integrated management areas open to mineral and oil and gas development.[26] The parties entered into letters of understanding offering guidance as to the procedures for reviewing and commenting on the Plan.

Yukon provided some detailed comments on the draft Recommended Plan but also indicated more generally that the Commission should amongst other things "Re-examine conservation values, non-consumptive resource use and resource development *to achieve a more balanced plan.*"[27] Yukon did not propose specific modifications to the Recommended Plan with respect to these matters. The Commission considered these comments but in its Final Recommended Plan stuck to its position that 80 per cent of the watershed should be designated as a conservation area where new surface access would not be allowed.[28] Yukon again consulted affected First Nations as required by the relevant Final Agreements, but was evidently of the view that the Plan as proposed did not accommodate its concerns that the Plan allow for additional development opportunities. At this point, Yukon made a number of fundamental changes to the Plan and "approved" it.[29] Justice Veale's assessment at trial was that the Government approved plan for the public lands within the watershed was

> significantly different than the Final Recommended Plan created by the Commission, in that it both changed the land designation system and shifted the balance of protection dramatically. Under the Government approved plan, 71% of the Peel Watershed is open for mineral exploration with 29% protected compared to 80% protected and 20% open for mineral exploration under the Final Recommended Plan.[30]

---

24 *Nacho Nyak Dun*, Supreme Court, para. 12.
25 *First Nation of Nacho Nyak Dun v. Yukon* 2014 YKSC 69 (First Instance), para. 8.
26 Ibid., paras 57–61.
27 Ibid., para. 73 (emphasis added).
28 Ibid., para. 80.
29 Ibid., paras 109–110.
30 Ibid., para. 111.16.

The question for the Court therefore was whether this change amounted to a permissible "modification" and, if not, what might be the consequences.

All three levels of Court concluded that Yukon's treatment of the Final Recommended Plan was not a permissible modification and that Yukon was in breach of the land claims agreements. For the Supreme Court of Canada it was clear that Yukon could not modify the Final Recommended Plan "so significantly as to effectively reject it"[31] or so as "to effectively create a new plan that is untethered from the one developed by the Commission ...".[32] This conclusion was reinforced by the requirements of consultation, a defined term in the Agreements which required Yukon to:

> provide notice in "sufficient form and detail" to allow affected parties to respond to its contemplated modifications to a Final Recommended Plan, then give "full and fair consideration" to the views presented during consultations before it decides how to respond to the Final Recommended Plan in order to comply with the robust definition of "consultation."[33]

The Court was also at pains to emphasize the broader context and objectives of chapter 11 of the Agreement which emphasized public participation and using the knowledge of both First Nations and other residents. Further, the repeated emphasis on consultation was designed to "foster meaningful dialogue."[34] Crucially, the Court also chose to emphasize that the land use planning process was an integral part of the overall package of benefits in the agreement. It was one of the means by which the First Nations would be "able to meaningfully participate in land use management *in all of their traditional territory* ..."[35]

By providing only general comments in round one of the consultation and then introducing much more specific requirements only at the stage of the second round of consultations, Yukon "thwarted the land use plan approval process"[36]

31 *Nacho Nyak Dun*, Supreme Court, para. 39.
32 Ibid., para. 48.
33 Ibid., para. 41.
34 Ibid., paras 42–45.
35 Ibid., para. 46 (emphasis added). The integrated nature of the obligations under a land claims agreement was also emphasized by Justice Hunt in her concurring judgment in *Nunavut Tunngavik Inc v. Canada (Attorney General)*, 2014 NUCA 2. The case involved Canada's failure to establish a general monitoring plan "to collect and analyse information on the long term state and health of the ecosystemic and socio-economic environment in the Nunavut Settlement Area." Justice Hunt commented on the implications of this commitment as follows [109]: "It is manifest from these and other parts of the Agreement that when surrendering their aboriginal claims the Inuit were adamant about ensuring a healthy future for their traditional homeland, where their ownership, decision-making and harvesting rights would be recognized and protected. A general monitoring plan (Monitoring Plan) was part of the agreed strategy for accomplishing this. Without such a plan, the Planning Commission would be unable to fulfill its important mandate and it would be difficult to protect Inuit rights (including harvesting rights) recognized in the Agreement."
36 *Nacho Nyak Dun*, Supreme Court, para. 55.

and its conduct "was not becoming of the honour of the Crown."[37] Yukon's power to modify was limited; it must be based on changes that it had proposed earlier in the process or in response to changing circumstances.[38] That was not the case here and thus Yukon's approval of the plan must be quashed.[39]

That led to the question of the appropriate remedy. The Court of Appeal would have returned the land use planning process back to the point in time that would have allowed Yukon the opportunity to provide detailed modifications to the Draft Plan. The Supreme Court of Canada considered that this was inappropriate for two reasons. First, it would have involved the Court in close judicial management of the land use planning process. By assessing the adequacy of Yukon's participation at that stage in the process even though the First Nations had not sought relief on that point, the Court would have "improperly inserted itself into the heart of the ongoing treaty relationship between Yukon and the First Nations."[40] Second, by failing to participate earlier Yukon had not breached an obligation but had instead failed to exercise a power[41] and "Yukon must bear the consequences of its failure to diligently advance its interests and exercise its right to propose access and development modifications to the Recommended Plan."[42]

The decision in *Nacho Nyak Dun* is significant for a number of reasons. First, it draws attention to the foundational importance of the land use planning provisions of modern land claims agreements. These provisions, as the Court acknowledges, afford the Indigenous party to the agreement the opportunity to have an important say with respect to the uses that may be made of their entire traditional territory, not just the lands for which the Indigenous community has a recognized title. Second, unlike impact assessment processes, the land use planning provisions facilitate planning at a landscape level and represent a proactive response to the cumulative impacts posed by incremental project developments. Land use planning processes offer the opportunity to rule out certain activities on the landscape from the outset. Third, the case emphasizes the importance of good faith implementation of the obligations embedded in the agreement. In the present case this meant that Yukon was not free to interpret the term "modify" as it wished. Instead, that term had to be interpreted in the context of the entire agreement and in a manner that respects the interests of the Indigenous party to the agreement.

The chapter now turns to the more extensive case law dealing with the interpretation of the impact assessment (IA) provision of modern land claims agreements.

---

37 Ibid., para. 57.
38 Ibid., paras 49–54.
39 Ibid., para. 57.
40 Ibid., para. 60.
41 Ibid., para. 61. The Court characterizes it as "a right" but it is more correctly a power.
42 Ibid., para. 61.

Case law on the impact assessment provisions of modern land claims agreements

The project-based impact review procedures included in modern land claims agreements share common themes with IA or environmental impact assessment (EIA) procedures in general legislation.[43] Thus, they must each address such things as triggers to assessment, scoping,[44] different levels of assessment (e.g. screening, full panel review, etc.).[45] But in addition, the IA provisions of modern land claims agreements and the interpretive case law emphasize public and especially Indigenous involvement and the importance of social and community impacts, as well as the traditional concerns with respect to biophysical and environmental impacts. For example, in *De Beers v. Mackenzie Valley Environmental Impact Review Board*[46] De Beers was attempting to quash the Board's decision to conduct a full Environmental Impact Review of De Beers' proposed Kennady Lake Project (a proposed diamond mine). At least part of the reason that the Board had decided to conduct a full Environmental Impact Review was because of concerns expressed by adjacent Indigenous communities. As Justice Charbonneau noted,

> It is apparent from the record that concerns were expressed in all the communities where the workshops were held. These included concerns about the protection of wildlife, protection of the water quality and quantity, issues related to contaminants, the impact of development on communities, among others. Concerns were also expressed about the fact that two culturally and spiritually significant sites had the potential of being affected by the Project.[47]

However, as the Court (following a lengthy analysis of the MVRMA and its related land claims agreements[48]) acknowledged, this emphasis on community interest was entirely appropriate since "Parliament intended public concern to be an important factor in decisions about proposed developments."[49]

---

43 See, *Building Common Ground: A New Vision for Impact Assessment in Canada*, Expert Panel Report (Ottawa: Minister of Environment and Climate Change, 2017), https://www.canada.ca/content/dam/themes/environment/conservation/environmental-reviews/building-common-ground/building-common-ground.pdf (for a recent, general review).
44 *Tlicho Government v. Mackenzie Valley Impact Review Board*, 2011 NWTSC 31, especially para. 38 (noting that a court should consider general jurisprudence on scoping in examining analogous scoping powers under the MVRMA).
45 *De Beers v. Mackenzie Valley Environmental Impact Review Board*, 2007 NWTSC 24.
46 Ibid.
47 Ibid., para. 63.
48 See text accompanying note 14 above.
49 *De Beers*, para. 66. The Court's summary of the legislation reinforces this conclusion at para. 25: "Parliament intended the Review Board to be the main instrument in the assessment of projects for development in the region. Aboriginal people were intended to have meaningful input in this process. Parliament intended that potential environmental impacts and public concern be important factors for the Review Board in making decisions. Parliament also intended that the preservation of social, cultural and

Perhaps the clearest statement of this sentiment is Justice Blanchard's summary in *Ka's'Gee Tu First Nation v. Canada (Minister of Indian Affairs)*[50] considering the same legislation, the MVRMA (this time in the context of an extension of an existing oil and gas development and in the context of a community that was covered by the legislation even though it had yet to negotiate a final agreement):

> A careful review of the Act, the three Comprehensive Land Claim Agreements referred to in the Act and the above-cited passages from Hansard allow me to make the following observations with respect to the scheme of the Act, its object and Parliament's intention. One of the central purposes of the Act was to provide an important role for Aboriginals and other residents in resource management decisions in the Mackenzie Valley. It is apparent that Parliament took great care in its enactment to ensure that Aboriginals and residents of the Mackenzie Valley are well positioned to deal with matters to be treated by the Act and the Land and Water Board and to do so in their own region. The Act repeatedly stresses the importance of providing a process which recognizes the role of the local residents and their way of life in the management of natural resources in the Mackenzie Valley. Numerous provisions are included that provide for consultation with the various affected communities. Further, the Comprehensive Land Claim Agreements provide that the Supreme Court of the Northwest Territories is to have jurisdiction over all matters which could arise under the agreements. In the case of the Tlicho Agreement, that Court is to have exclusive jurisdiction to review on a question of law or jurisdiction. The record establishes that these land claim agreements were the foundation instruments which led to the passing of the Act and are indeed expressly referred to in the preamble to the Act.[51]

Another important early case is *Qikiqtani Inuit Association v. Canada (Attorney General)*[52] which dealt with the Nunavut Agreement. The case involved an application by an operating mine (Nanisivik) to the newly created Nunavut Water Board for a renewal of its water licence. The Board was the successor to the Northwest Territories Water Board and as such had similar powers and responsibilities but, as Justice Reed of the Federal Court noted, with one significant difference, the new Board

> is specifically directed to take into account Inuit culture, customs and knowledge and the *Agreement* expressly states that one of its objectives is to provide for the right of the Inuit to participate in decision-making that relates to the use of land, water and resources.[53]

economic well-being of the residents of the region and the importance of conservation to well-being and way of life of aboriginal people be taken into account."
50 *Ka's'Gee Tu First Nation v. Canada (Minister of Indian Affairs)*, 2007 FC 764, para. 47.
51 Ibid., para. 47.
52 *Qikiqtani Inuit Association v. Canada (Attorney General)*, 1998 CanLII 8617 (FC).
53 Ibid., para. 6 (referencing the Preamble to the NFA).

The Qikiqtani Inuit Association (QIA), a regional Inuit organization under the Nunavut Agreement, argued that the Board's processes, which led it to issue a new licence to Nanisivik Mines for its ongoing lead/zinc mining and milling operations, constituted a breach of the rules of natural justice. The Court acknowledged that the Board was placed in a difficult position. The mine needed a licence to continue its operations and time was short. The new Board was feeling its way. But there were also

> significant expectations that the Board would operate in a different manner than its predecessor and pay more attention to the concerns of the Inuit that would be directly affected by the decisions that were being made than had been done in the past.[54]

In assessing the adequacy of the Board's process, Justice Reed referenced the Preamble to the Nunavut Land Claims Agreement (NFA)[55] as well as specific provisions relating to the water board including the obligation to give "due regard and weight to Inuit culture, customs and knowledge."[56] Justice Reed also cautioned that "the appointment of Inuit members to the Board does not alone mean that in designing its rules of procedure the Board has met the requirement that it give due regard to Inuit culture, customs and knowledge. Nor does it mean that the purposes of the *Agreement* have been met. Participation by the Inuit who will be affected by a particular decision is what is important."[57]

In the end, however, Justice Reed concluded that any deficiencies that were evident in the Board's procedure (and she did conclude that there were some as assessed against the provisions of the Agreement[58]) were cured by the Board's decision to proceed incrementally by issuing a short-term interim licence to Nanisivik along with an extended period for additional submissions pending a final decision on the renewal application.[59] While the Court also rejected QIA's allegations that the Board had ignored certain of the evidence before it, the importance of the decision in this context is simply the emphasis that the Court gives to the participatory interests of QIA. QIA was not trying to shut the mine down but it did want "the best decision possible to protect the present and future health of the residents and the environment within which they live, consistent with that constraint."[60]

54 Ibid., para. 8.
55 Ibid., para. 32 (referencing, inter alia, that the objectives include "*to provide for* certainty and clarity of rights to ownership and use of lands and resources, and of rights for *Inuit to participate in decision-making concerning the use, management and conservation of land, water and resources*, including the offshore" (emphases added by Justice Reed)).
56 NFA, section 13.3.13(b).
57 *Qikiqtani Inuit Association*, 1998, para. 36.
58 Ibid., paras 34–39.
59 Ibid., para. 41.
60 Ibid., para. 65. The evidence however did make it clear that there were problems with the previous assessment of the mine's operations including with respect to: lack of baseline data; the control of tailings (dust) and the disposal of raw sewage.

Another case that illustrates the importance of community interests in IAs under the terms of modern land claim agreements is *Strateco Resources Inc v. Québec (Attorney General)*.[61] The case involved a proposal from Strateco to allow it to proceed with advanced exploration associated with a uranium mining project within Cree territory subject to the James Bay and Northern Quebec Agreement. The adjacent Cree community of Mistissini was resolutely opposed to the project and the responsible Quebec minister eventually refused to grant Strateco the necessary licence on the grounds that the project was not "socially accepted" by the community. The company commenced an action against the government as well as seeking judicial review of the Minister's decision, principally on the grounds that the Minister had exceeded his authority by relying on social acceptability as the basis for denying the licence and that in doing so he had effectively accorded the Cree community a veto. The Court rejected these claims, emphasizing inter alia that the special impact assessment regime in force in the James Bay area, unlike Quebec's general impact assessment regime, specifically referred to assessing "the protection of the environment and social milieu" and "the protection of the Native people, of their societies, communities and economy."[62] In these circumstances it was reasonable for the Minister to conclude that the social acceptability of the project was a relevant and indeed in this case a determinative consideration.

> The spirit and the wording as well of the JBNQA and the Paix des Braves emphasize the importance of considering the local communities before accepting any project that could have environmental and social impacts on the territory concerned. Social acceptability can be taken into account by the decision-maker, and furthermore, it must be so.[63]

The evidence did not show that the Minister had accorded the Cree a veto. Instead he had carefully weighed all the relevant considerations.[64]

The same emphasis on Indigenous participation is apparent in the Yukon UFA, the legislation implementing the IA provisions of the Yukon Agreements, and the related case law.[65] For example, the purposes of the *Yukon Environmental and Socio-Economic Assessment Act* (YESAA) include "to guarantee opportunities for

---

61 *Strateco Resources Inc v. Québec (Attorney General)* [2018] 1 CLNR 159 *Ressources Strateco inc. c. Procureure générale du Québec*, 2017 QCCS 2679 (CanLII (Que SC)). See also *Quebec (Attorney General) v. Moses*, 2010 SCC 17, para. 17 (noting that it was "of great importance to have Cree and Inuit participation in the environmental impact assessment of projects within their respective territories …").
62 *Strateco Resources Inc*, paras 58–60 and 437.
63 Ibid., para. 448. The Paix des Braves, more formally known as an Agreement Respecting a New Relationship Between the Cree Nation and the Government of Quebec, was a 2002 agreement negotiated between the Cree and the Quebec government as a "nation-to-nation" agreement mapping out a global approach affording the Cree greater autonomy. See ibid., para. 63.
64 Ibid., paras 487–497.
65 See, e.g., *White River First Nation v. Yukon*, 2013 YKSC 66.

Land claims agreements in Canada 211

the participation of Yukon Indian persons – and to make use of their knowledge and experience – in the assessment process."[66]

A few cases do emphasize that the rights of participation and the broad application of IA procedures may have to be balanced against other values. One can see this reflected in *Qikiqtani Inuit Association* mentioned earlier, but a clearer example is *North American Tungsten Corp Ltd v. Mackenzie Valley Land and Water Board*.[67] *Tungtsen* involved an application for the renewal of a water licence and the particular question was whether the renewal was subject to an environmental assessment under the terms of the *MVRMA* (which, as noted earlier, was designed to implement elements of the Gwich'in and Sahtu agreements – and subsequently the Tlicho agreement as well) or whether it was grandparented as part of a respect for "vested interests." The Court of Appeal recognized that the *MVRMA* did serve to implement the agreements and that the purpose of establishing land use planning and land and water boards under the terms of that legislation was "to 'enable residents of the Mackenzie Valley to participate in the management of its resources for the benefit of the residents and of other Canadians': s.9.1, *MVRMA*."[68] However, the Court went on to note that:

> both the Comprehensive Agreements and the *MVRMA* also clearly recognize that a full scale environmental review will not be appropriate in respect of certain existing permits, projects and licences. Instead, both reflect that some grandfathering [sic] of existing developments is required to balance competing interests. Those interests include the legitimate goal of protecting land and water resources in the Mackenzie Valley for the benefit of its citizens, on the one hand, while, at the same time, exempting from the full force of new environmental legislation undertakings developed under an earlier legislative regime.[69]

This led the court to conclude that Tungsten's licence renewal application should not trigger an EA requirement although the Court did observe that this did not exempt Tungsten from the application of current regulatory standards. The Court took note of Tungsten's concession to the effect that the Board was not obliged to grant it a new licence and that were it to do so "the Board may impose whatever conditions it considers appropriate in the circumstances in the exercise of its jurisdiction."[70] This decision (and the *Canadian Zinc* case that followed it[71]) seem exceptional and perhaps confined to the transitional provisions of these

---

66 YESAA, section 5(2)(g).
67 *North American Tungsten Corp Ltd v. Mackenzie Valley Land and Water Board*, 2003 NWTCA 5.
68 Ibid., para. 24.
69 Ibid., para. 24.
70 Ibid., para. 34. Two years later, the Court applied the *Tungsten* decision in *Canadian Zinc Corporation v. Mackenzie Valley Land and Water Board*, 2005 NWTSC 48 to grandparent an access road to a mine site.
71 *Canadian Zinc Corporation*.

212 Nigel Bankes

agreements and implementing statutes. The bulk of the case law takes an expansive view of the IA arrangements as a means of ensuring local and community participation in project-based decision-making.

In sum, we now have an extensive body of case law considering the IA provisions of modern land claims agreements from Yukon through the Mackenzie Valley to Nunavut and Northern Quebec. That case law almost universally emphasizes (and respects) the importance that these agreements accorded to the value of public and Indigenous community participation in resource-related decision-making.

The final substantive part of the paper deals with an additional normative source of community and Indigenous participation, that being the duty to consult and accommodate.

The interaction between the IA provisions of modern land claims agreements and the duty to consult and accommodate

Over the last 30 years Canadian courts have developed an important body of jurisprudence dealing with the Crown's duty to consult and accommodate Indigenous peoples "when the Crown has knowledge, real or constructive, of the potential existence of the Aboriginal right or title and contemplates conduct that might adversely affect it."[72] While the early decisions dealt with claims of aboriginal rights and aboriginal title,[73] this was soon extended to decisions that had the potential to interfere with treaty rights.[74] There is a massive body of case law dealing with what the duty requires in any particular case, but we can make two general points. First, there is a consultation spectrum such "that the scope of the duty is proportionate to a preliminary assessment of the strength of the case supporting the existence of the right or title, and to the seriousness of the potentially adverse effect upon the right or title claimed."[75] And second, where the duty requires anything more than consultation at the shallow end (i.e. just notice) then there must be "demonstrable integration" of Indigenous concerns by the ultimate decision-maker. In order to demonstrate this, the decision-maker will need to able to show (through reasons, or changes to the decision, or inclusion of new or amended terms and conditions) how the decision-maker responded to those concerns. The absence of any change in a proposed approval that fails to justify why an articulated Indigenous interest could not be integrated or accommodated will tend to suggest that Indigenous interests were not taken seriously by the decision-maker.[76]

---

72 *Haida Nation v. British Columbia (Minister of Forests)*, [2004] 3 SCR 511, 2004 SCC 73 (CanLII), para. 35.
73 In addition to *Haida Nation*, see also, *Taku River Tlingit First Nation v. British Columbia (Project Assessment Director)*, 2004 SCC 74 (CanLII), [2004] 3 SCR 550; and *Rio Tinto Alcan Inc. v. Carrier Sekani Tribal Council*, 2010 SCC 43 (CanLII), [2010] 2 SCR 650.
74 *Mikisew Cree First Nation v. Canada (Minister of Canadian Heritage)*, [2005] 3 SCR 388, 2005 SCC 69 (CanLII).
75 *Haida Nation*, para. 39.
76 See, *Gitxaala Nation v. Canada*, 2016 FCA 187; and *Tsleil-Waututh Nation v. Canada (Attorney General)*, 2018 FCA 153 (for two recent Federal Court of Appeals

Similarly, and from the early 1990s, the negotiators of most (but not all) modern land claims agreements began to incorporate into their texts reference to an obligation to consult with respect to the exercise of certain specified powers under the terms of the agreements. The agreements have defined "Consult" or "Consultation" as meaning:

to provide:

(a) to the party to be consulted, notice of a matter to be decided in sufficient form and detail to allow that party to prepare its views on the matter;
(b) a reasonable period of time in which the party to be consulted may prepare its views on the matter, and an opportunity to present such views to the party obliged to consult; and
(c) full and fair consideration by the party obliged to consult of any views presented."[77]

Subsequent provisions of the agreement operationalize the concept throughout the text.[78]

As noted, not all modern land claims agreements use the term. For example, the earlier Northern Quebec and Inuvialuit Agreements do not use the term but also neither does the Nunavut Agreement which was concluded at about the same time that the term was being adopted in other agreements such as the Sahtu and Gwich'in agreements and the UFA.

There are also additional complexities mentioned in the introduction to this chapter that have implications for the interaction between land claims agreements and the duty to consult. These include the fact that the implementing legislation for these agreements carries the language of consultation into general law as part of the statute, and further that these statutes may apply to areas covered by multiple agreements but also to traditional territories for which a comprehensive land claims agreement has yet to be negotiated.[79]

This leads to the following sorts of questions. First, if the agreement adopts the language of the duty to consult and applies that duty to particular decisions, is there still room to apply the constitutional or common law duty to consult (and accommodate) with respect to other decisions or powers? Could the general constitutional duty fill that gap (is it a "gap" at all?) or is the agreement a complete code? Second, where the implementing legislation for the agreement applies to territories that are not subject to the agreement, what role does the duty to

decisions, exemplifying this point, quashing pipeline approvals issued following multi-year assessments).

77 Yukon UFA, chapter 1; Gwich'in Agreement, s. 2.1.1.
78 For example, in *Beckman* (n 2) Justice Binnie notes that the LSCFN treaty refers to the duty to consult more than 60 times [58]. However, he also notes [74] that the duty as defined does not include a duty to try to minimize any identified impacts.
79 See text to notes 13–15.

consult and accommodate play? Third, to what extent can the Crown rely on IA procedures to discharge its duty to consult and accommodate?

The complete code argument

In *Beckman v. Little Salmon Carmacks First Nation* the Supreme Court of Canada definitively rejected the complete code argument.[80] The case involved Yukon's decision to make a grant of agricultural land in the traditional territory of the Little Salmon/Carmacks First Nation (LSCFN). The Agreement did not specifically require Yukon to consult with the First Nation with respect to the proposed grant but the Court was of the view that since members of the First Nation have the right to hunt and fish on those lands until they were taken up for another purpose, then "it was obvious that such grants might adversely affect the traditional economic activities" of the First Nation. Therefore, Yukon "was required to consult with the LSCFN to determine the nature and extent of such adverse effects."[81] The duty to consult was "simply part of the essential legal framework within which the treaty is to be interpreted and performed"[82] and consultation is conceived of as a way of helping to "manage the important ongoing relationship between the government and the Aboriginal community in a way that upheld the honour of the Crown."[83] In this case, however, the Court concluded that Yukon had discharged its duty. The Court also concluded that there was no duty to accommodate in this case since the treaty contemplated that the government would be able to take up lands for agricultural purposes.[84]

The Federal Court had to consider the relationship between the duty to consult in an Agreement and the common law or constitutional basis of the duty in *Nunatsiavut Government v. AG Canada*,[85] one of a number of cases dealing with a hydro project known as the Lower Churchill Project in Labrador.[86] The project involves a series of dams and impoundments on the Lower Churchill above a body of water known as Lake Melville. This case was brought by the Nunatsiavut government which was established under the terms of the Labrador Inuit Land

---

80 *Beckman v. Little Salmon Carmacks First Nation*. All members of the Court were of the view as a matter of principle that a land claims agreement could not be assumed to be a complete code. In this case, however, Justice LeBel and Deschamps were of the view that there was no gap in the treaty that needed to be filled. In their view, the assessment process of chapter 12 provided for the First Nation's participation and would result in more extensive consultation than would be required by the common law duty to consult. See, ibid., paras 92 and 121–124. As a result, Justices LeBel and Deschamps concluded that the Court should not add a further duty to consult beyond the duty stipulated in the treaty, para. 91.
81 Ibid., para. 13.
82 Ibid., para. 69.
83 Ibid., para. 73.
84 Ibid., paras 81–83.
85 *Nunatsiavut Government v. AG Canada*, 2015 FC 492.
86 See, *Nunatsiavut v. Newfoundland and Labrador (Department of Environment and Conservation)*, 2015 NLTD(G) 1 (in which the Nunatsiavut Government also contested a subsequent provincial permitting decision).

Land claims agreements in Canada 215

Claims Agreement (LILCA). The project itself lies outside the Labrador Inuit Settlement Area (LISA) but Lake Melville which lies downstream of the dams is within LISA. The Nunatsiavut Government on behalf of the LILCA beneficiaries was particular concerned about the release of methyl mercury in the impounded areas, bioaccumulation of mercury and possible downstream effects including the contamination of fish and marine mammals in Lake Melville, possibly leading to consumption advisories. Nalcor, the proponent, had originally concluded that there would no such downstream effects.

Since the project was not within the LISA it was not subject to review by institutions established by the LILCA but was instead assessed by a joint review panel (JRP) established under federal and provincial legislation. The Nunatsiavut Government participated in that process. The JRP concluded that the project would have a number of significant adverse effects, including on fishing and seal hunting activities in Lake Melville, *should there be* downstream methyl mercury contamination. However, the Panel was not in a position to assess the likelihood of this happening. Recommendation 6.7 of the JRP suggested that prior to impoundment, Nalcor should be required "to carry out a comprehensive assessment of downstream effects, including baseline mercury data collection and revised modelling to predict the fate of mercury in the downstream environment."[87] Canada ultimately issued the necessary approvals for the project under the *Fisheries Act*. While the approvals were subject to a number of conditions, those conditions in the opinion of the Nunatsiavut Government did not go far enough and it thus alleged that Canada had failed to discharge its duty to consult and accommodate Inuit interests.[88]

In assessing the existence of a duty to consult and the scope of any such duty within the context of a modern land claims agreement, Justice Strickland emphasized that it was important to begin with the text of the agreement, but that the Court could (indeed must) apply the common law principles to interpret the text or to supplement the text if the text were silent.[89] The content of the duty might also be coloured by the terms of the agreement.[90] In this case the Court concluded that the duty to consult with respect to possible downstream effects on Inuit harvesting rights fell between the medium and high end of the spectrum given the seriousness of the potential impacts, were there to be downstream contamination.[91] There was also a duty to accommodate.[92]

In the end Justice Strickland concluded that Canada had discharged its obligation to consult and accommodate. On the consultation side of things there was evidence of real engagement even if the Crown did not follow all of the Nunatsiavut Government's recommendations and did not share its assessment of the type of baseline work that needed to be done in order to render the monitoring programme meaningful.[93]

87 *Nunatsiavut Government v. AG Canada*, para. 40.
88 Ibid., para. 90.
89 Ibid., para. 139.
90 Ibid., paras 173–176.
91 Ibid., para. 172.
92 Ibid., paras 275–276.
93 Ibid., paras 264–269.

On the accommodation side of things the Nunatsiavut Government had identified four issues that were of critical importance to it. Those issues were as follows:

> i) its representation on a high-level management structure; ii) funding for it to conduct and lead baseline research and monitoring of the Lake Melville system, including a large scale, comprehensive understanding of the downstream environments (biophysical, cultural, socioeconomic and health impacts); iii) framework language as a condition of permitting to effect a mechanism for compensation should impacts arise, including harvesting losses and loss of cultural practices resulting from events with significant environmental effects on Inuit or Inuit rights that result from the Project, such as an increase in mercury levels; and, iv) full clearing of the reservoir area including trees and the top layer of organic matter.[94]

Justice Strickland considered how the Crown had responded to each of these requests in some detail. In the end, however, she again concluded that while there were failings in terms of the timeliness of Canada's responses there was evidence of responsiveness to the concerns that had been raised and thus concluded that the Crown had discharged its duty.

While this case evidences significant engagement by the Nunatsiavut Government, it also ultimately confirms the limits to the "consult and accommodate" model. This is perhaps particularly apparent with respect to the reservoir clearing issue. One reason for rejecting this proposal was that of cost but there were also other reasons: it was experimental, the JRP itself had not recommended clearing as extensive as that proposed by the Nunatsiavut Government, and the federal government might not have the authority to impose it. But to the extent that cost was an issue Justice Strickland's response was, at one level, somewhat dismissive with respect to such a serious health issue, for she remarked, following *Beckman*, that "the test of accommodation is not a duty to accommodate to the point of undue hardship for the non-Aboriginal population."[95] That said, Justice Strickland also went on to note that if Nalcor's prediction of no significant downstream contamination proved to be incorrect, this might trigger additional accommodation responsibilities on the part of the Crown.[96]

This decision was not the end of the matter. Civil society protests including a hunger strike ultimately led the Government of Newfoundland and Labrador to agree[97] to establish an Independent Expert Advisory Committee to examine,

---

94 Ibid., para. 278.
95 Ibid., para. 332. Justice Orsborn by contrast in the proceedings in the provincial superior court had expressed concerns about the province's summary dismissal of the full clearing option: see *Nunatsiavut v. Newfoundland and Labrador (Department of Environment and Conservation)*, paras 86 and 111–112.
96 *Nunatsiavut Government v. AG Canada*, para. 344.
97 Daniel MacEachern and Andrew Sampson, "Tears, Relief for Hunger Strikers as Muskrat Falls Agreement Ends Fast," *CBC News*, October 26, 2016, https://www.cbc.ca/news/canada/newfoundland-labrador/billy-gauthier-hunger-strikers-muskrat-falls-1.3821743

Land claims agreements in Canada 217

amongst other things the "feasibility, necessity and potential impacts" of further clearing of the reservoir, all in light of the "protection of the health of the Indigenous and local populations."[98] In this case then it may be said that the combined leverage provided by the IA process, the intervention of the Nunatsiavut Government, and the protests of civil society, ultimately led to an approach that was more respectful of local and Indigenous interests that would be affected by this massive project – and yet see few of the benefits.

The duty to consult and accommodate where there is no final agreement

As discussed above there are examples in both Yukon and Northwest Territories of traditional territories being subject to the terms of land claims agreement implementing legislation dealing with impact assessment where the Indigenous communities concerned have yet to negotiate a final agreement. In these cases the court have uniformly concluded that the communities concerned are entitled to the benefit of any statutory consultation obligations in *YESAA* or the *MVRMA* as well as their common law or constitutional rights of consultation and accommodation.[99]

The role of IA processes in fulfilling the duty to consult and accommodate

In two recent decisions the Supreme Court of Canada has clarified that the Crown may be able to discharge its duty to consult and accommodate obligation through an IA process or similar regulatory proceeding.[100] One of these cases, *Clyde River (Hamlet) v. Petroleum Geo-Services Inc*,[101] also engages the Nunavut Agreement. The decision involved an application to the National Energy Board (NEB) by PGSI for the Board's approval for it to conduct some seismic testing in Baffin Bay and Davis Strait. The Hamlet of Clyde River objected on the basis that the seismic activities would have an effect on marine mammals on which the community depended and the Court acknowledged that this could negatively affect harvesting rights under the Nunavut Agreement.[102] The Court accepted that under the circumstances a Board decision to authorize PGSI's project triggered the Crown's duty to consult.[103] It also

---

98 Newfoundland and Labrador Canada, Municipal Affairs and Environment, "Independent Expert Advisory Committee Terms of Reference," March 24, 2017, https://www.mae.gov.nl.ca/env_assessment/projects/Y2010/1305/ieac_tor.pdf
99 See, *Liard First Nation* and *White River First Nation* (for Yukon). See, *Ka'a'Gee Tu First Nation* (for Northwest Territories).
100 Nigel Bankes, "Clarifying the Parameters of the Crown's Duty to Consult and Accommodate in the Context of Decision-Making by Energy Tribunals," *Journal of Energy and Natural Resources Law* 36 (2017): 163–180.
101 *Clyde River (Hamlet) v. Petroleum Geo-Services Inc.*, [2017] 1 SCR 1069, 2017 SCC 40. The other decision is *Chippewas of the Thames First Nation v. Enbridge Pipelines Inc*, 2017 SCC 41.
102 *Clyde River*, para. 3.
103 Ibid., para. 27. In some respects, it is remarkable how readily the Court reaches this conclusion. Whereas previous decisions dealing with land claims agreements have emphasized the importance of starting with the text of the agreement, see *Beckman v.*

concluded that in principle the NEB could discharge the Crown's obligation because it has "a significant array of powers that permit extensive consultation. It may conduct hearings, and has broad discretion to make orders or elicit information .... It can also require studies to be undertaken and impose preconditions to approval ...."[104] It also has authority to accommodate Indigenous concerns by imposing terms and conditions.[105]

However, the Court also concluded that the steps taken by the Board failed to discharge the Crown's obligation. The Crown's duties in this case were onerous and at the deep end of the consultation spectrum. This was because the community had established rights under the Agreement which were extremely important for economic, cultural and spiritual well-being.[106] The Court emphasized this point by quoting from an earlier decision of the Nunavut Court of Justice (also dealing with seismic testing):

> The Inuit right which is of concern in this matter is the right to harvest marine mammals. Many Inuit in Nunavut rely on country food for the majority of their diet. Food costs are very high and many would be unable to purchase food to replace country food if country food were unavailable. Country food is recognized as being of higher nutritional value than purchased food. But the inability to harvest marine mammals would impact more than ... just the diet of Inuit. The cultural tradition of sharing country food with others in the community would be lost. The opportunity to make traditional clothing would be impacted. The opportunity to participate in the hunt, an activity which is fundamental to being Inuk, would be lost. The Inuit right which is at stake is of high significance.[107]

The risk of harm to the treaty right was also high.[108]

The Court gave several reasons for concluding that the Board's procedures in this case failed to discharge the duty. First, the Board's inquiry was mis-directed. It focused on the significance of the environmental impact. While that was, no doubt, an important part of the Board responsibilities a "consultative inquiry is not properly into environmental effects *per se*. Rather, it inquires into the impact on the *right*."[109] The NEB failed to make that inquiry. Second, the Crown never

---

    Little Salmon Carmacks First Nation, Nacho Nyak Dun; Supreme Court, *Quebec v. Moses, Nunatsiavut Government v. AG Canada*; and *Nunatsiavut v. Newfoundland and Labrador (Department of Environment and Conservation)*, in this case the Court references the Agreement generally (para. 2) but does not engage in any analysis of the text and certainly there is no discussion as to the relationship between the terms of the treaty and general constitutional obligations.

104 *Clyde River*, para. 31.
105 Ibid., para. 32.
106 Ibid., para. 43.
107 Ibid., para. 43, quoting from *Qikiqtani Inuit Association v. Canada (Minister of Natural Resources)*, 2010 NUCJ 12 (CanLII), para. 25.
108 *Clyde River*, para. 44.
109 Ibid., para. 45 (emphasis in original).

explained to the community that it intended to rely on the NEB's process to discharge its duty to consult obligations. And third, the process followed by the NEB fell far short of what was required for deep consultation. Basic questions were left unanswered by the proponent, very little of the documentation was translated into Inuktitut and no funding was made available to the community to allow it to do its own scientific investigation. The court quashed the Board's authorization.

In *Clyde River* the NEB was the final decision-maker with respect to the seismic project but in many of the processes established by northern land claim the IA bodies make recommendations rather than final decisions. One of the consequences of this is that in such a case the Crown will likely not be able to rely exclusively on the IA process (even if well executed) to fully discharge its obligations. The decision in *Ka'a'Gee Tu First Nation v. Canada (Attorney General)*[110] illustrates this point. The case involved an oil and gas project in the traditional territory of the KTFN within which KTFN claimed both treaty and aboriginal rights. Part of the Deh Cho First Nation, KTFN has not negotiated a modern land claims agreement although its territory is included within the area of application of the *Mackenzie Valley Resource Management Act*. As such the project in question was reviewed by the Review Board established by the *MVRMA* and the Review Board duly issued a report including a number of conditions. Several of those conditions were directly responsive to concerns raised by KTFN.[111] Under the Act, the Minister as the ultimate decision-maker has a number of options upon receipt of a report. She can adopt the recommendation or refer it back to the Review Board for further consideration; or after consulting the Review Board, reject the recommendation and order an environmental impact review of the proposal or adopt the recommendation with modifications.

This latter option is known as the "consult to modify" option and it was the option that the Minister decided to follow in this case. The Minister made significant changes to a number of the conditions in which KTFN was particularly interested. KTFN sought judicial review of the decision on the basis that the Crown had breached its duty to consult and accommodate. In considering that claim Justice Blanchard distinguished between the process that led to the preparation and submission of the Review Board's report and the process followed during the consult to modify stage. As for the first part, Justice Blanchard concluded that the process had been adequate:

> The consultation process provided for under the Act is comprehensive and provides the opportunity for significant consultation between the developer and the affected Aboriginal groups. As noted above, the record indicates that the Applicants have had many opportunities to express their concerns in

110 *Ka'a'Gee Tu First Nation*. See, *Yellowknives Dene First Nation v. Minister of Aboriginal Affairs and Northern Development*, 2015 FCA 148, paras 55–66 (by way of contrast, in which the court held that the process followed by the Mackenzie Valley Land and Water Board did serve to discharge the Crown's duty to consult obligations).
111 *Ka'a'Gee Tu First Nation*, para. 44.

writing or at public meetings through submissions made by counsel on their behalf or by the Applicants directly. The record also establishes the Applicants were heavily involved in the process and that their involvement influenced the work and recommendations of the Review Board. In essence, the product of the consultation process is reflected in the Review Board's Environmental Assessment Reports. These reports, while not necessarily producing the results sought by the Applicants, do reflect the collective input of all of the parties involved, including the Applicants. The Environmental Assessment Report concerning the Extension Project clearly shows that many of the concerns of the Applicants were taken into account. While the Review Board ultimately endorsed the project, it did so only with significant mitigating measures and suggestions which were supported by the Applicants and which went a long way in addressing their main concerns.[112]

But at the "consult to modify" stage the Crown had not consulted with KTFN at all, on the grounds that this was not required by the statute. The Court held that this was a mistake since it effectively undermined the work undertaken by the Review Board. The Court directed the Crown to engage in a process of meaningful consultation and, if necessary, accommodation.[113]

The same pattern is observable in Yukon. *White River First Nation v. Yukon*[114] dealt with an application to approve a mining project under the terms of the aforementioned *Yukon Environmental and Socio-Economic Assessment Act* (YESAA). YESAA represents the statutory implementation of chapter 12 of the Yukon Agreements. The purposes of YESAA include "to guarantee opportunities for the participation of Yukon Indian persons – and to make use of their knowledge and experience – in the assessment process."[115] Under the legislation Yukon is divided into six assessment districts, each with a "Designated Office." Where a project is submitted to a Designed Office (DO) for review the DO must "give full and fair consideration to scientific information, traditional knowledge and other information provided to it or obtained by it under this Act," and ultimately make a recommendation to the "decision body."[116] In a case in which the DO concludes that a project will have significant adverse environmental or socio-

---

112 Ibid., para. 118.
113 Ibid., paras 120–124. In further litigation KTFN alleged that the Crown had failed to fulfil its good faith consultation obligations resulting from this Order. The Court examined the record and concluded that the Crown had discharged its obligations: *Ka'A'Gee Tu First Nation v. Canada (Attorney General)*, 2012 FC 297. The Paramount project was also the subject of litigation from another First Nation in *Katlodeeche First Nation v. Canada (Attorney General)*, 2013 FC 458 with respect to the issue of a water licence for the project activities. In this case the Court concluded that the Crown had discharged its duty to consult obligations, partly through the Board process and largely through direct meetings. These meetings confirmed that there were no additional concerns that had not already been dealt with by the Board process.
114 *White River First Nation*.
115 *YESAA* section 5(2)(g).
116 *YESAA* section 39.

economic effects that cannot be mitigated, the DO is to recommend that the project should not be allowed to proceed. That was the case here. The mining claims at issue were in the traditional territory of the White River First Nation (WRFN) as well as the Kluane First Nation. There was evidence that the area was used by the Chisana Caribou Herd (CCH) which was of significant cultural interest to WRFN and also designated as a species of special concern under the *Species at Risk Act*.[117] The Evaluation Report prepared by the DO ultimately concluded that

> there is a direct overlap of Project activities with the calving and post-calving areas [of the CCH] year after year at the same time and at the same location as the proposed Project. The auditory and visual disturbances and loss of the calving ground will likely result in reproductive declines [in the herd].[118]

The DO considered possible mitigation options but ultimately concluded that "avoidance of activities that would cause a loss of this critical habitat is the only practical measure that would mitigate for this significant adverse effect."[119]

The Decision Body (in this case the Director, Mineral Resources) rejected that recommendation. While the Director agreed that the project could have significant adverse effects on the CCH the Director concluded that the effects could be mitigated by restricting project activities both spatially and temporally.[120] The principal issue for the Court was whether the Director had discharged his statutory (and common law) duty to consult the WRFN in the course of making that decision.[121] Justice Veale concluded that the Director had:

---

117 Species at Risk Act, SC 2002, c 29. The WRFN had voluntarily stopped hunting the herd in 1994 due to low population numbers before the species was listed: See, *White River First Nation*, para. 34. The cultural implications flowing from the poor health of the herd were summarized in the evaluation report and quoted by Justice Veale as follows, ibid., para. 54:

"The assessment of wildlife determined that effects to caribou would be significant and adverse by jeopardizing the recovery and causing the continued decline of this endangered herd. The latter will have cascading effects to traditional land use and culture by perpetuating, what is already, a two-decade long ban on hunting of the CCH by WRFN. The continued inability of WRFN to hunt the Chisana Caribou widens the gap in the continuity of cultural practices, with implications for younger generations of WRFN members. WRFN members who do not have the opportunity to hunt CCH may not have the same opportunities to utilize traditional ecological knowledge associated with the herd, and will be less likely to have the same personal connection of 'sense of place' attachment to the animals that often comes with use. Further, the continued demise of the herd may result in a multiple generations of WRFN members who do not 'remember' the presence of CCH in areas of its range, or in its former numbers. Effects to the CCH will affect the future subsistence harvesting of these animals, as the project will result in effects that are likely to cause a decline in this endangered herd, with long-term implications for their recovery."

118 Ibid., para. 50.
119 Ibid., para. 51.
120 Ibid., para. 75.
121 As noted above, WRFN does not have a Final Agreement. However, the *YESAA* incorporates the definition of the duty to consult from the UFA and extends the duty

222 *Nigel Bankes*

breached his duty to consult and accommodate the White River First Nation by failing to provide a meaningful process to provide feedback on the government's basis for rejecting the recommendation that the White River Project not proceed. The consultation following a rejection recommendation must be deep and meaningful. While the First Nation has no power to require the Evaluation Report to be accepted, it should have an opportunity to address the government's basis for rejecting it.[122]

In sum, these cases illustrate that the constitutional duty to consult and accommodate serves as a further source of participation rights to supplement the already extensive rights articulated in modern land claims agreements and their implementing legislation.

Conclusions

Canadian courts have yet to endorse the principle of free, prior and informed consent with respect to resource operations in the traditional territories of Indigenous communities in Canada. However, the courts have interpreted modern land claims agreements as requiring significant engagement with Indigenous community interests as part of landscape-level land use planning as well as project approval. They have also been willing to fill any gaps there may be in such agreements by having resort to the constitutional duty to consult and accommodate. The fact that there has been so much litigation perhaps also suggests that governments have not always been willing to live up to their responsibilities under these agreements or at the very least that the parties did not have a shared understanding of the scope of participation rights under the agreements, or the extent to which the agreement might limit the discretionary powers of governments.

References

Bankes, Nigel. "The Place of Land-Use Planning in the T.F.N. Claim." In *Hinterland or Homeland? Land-Use Planning in Northern Canada*, edited by Terry Fenge and William A. Rees, 95–112. Ottawa: Canadian Arctic Resources Committee, 1987.

Bankes, Nigel. "Clarifying the Parameters of the Crown's Duty to Consult and Accommodate in the Context of Decision-Making by Energy Tribunals." *Journal of Energy and Natural Resources Law* 36 (2017): 163–180.

---

to consult to a First Nation "for which no final agreement is in effect." See *YESAA* sections 3 and 64(2) as quoted in *White River First Nation*, paras 88 and 89. In addition, Justice Veale was also of the view that Yukon owed a common law or constitutional duty to consult and accommodate at the more stringent end of the spectrum, ibid., paras 12 and 96–115. See also *Liard First Nation*, para. 123 (in which Justice Veale notes that Liard First Nation is in a similar position in that it stands to benefit from the assessment process negotiated by other Yukon First Nations).

122 *White River First Nation*, para. 128.

Beckman v. Little Salmon Carmacks First Nation, 2010 SCC 53. Canada.
Building Common Ground: A New Vision for Impact Assessment in Canada. Expert Panel Report. Ottawa: Minister of Environment and Climate Change, 2017, https://www.canada.ca/content/dam/themes/environment/conservation/environmental-reviews/building-common-ground/building-common-ground.pdf
Canada. Constitution Act, 1982, Schedule B to the Canada Act 1982 (UK), 1982, c 11.
Canada. Mackenzie Valley Resource Management Act, SC 1998, c 25.
Canada. Nunavut Land Claims Agreement Act, SC 1993, c 29.
Canada. Nunavut Planning and Project Assessment Act, SC 2013, c 14.
Canada. Species at Risk Act, SC 2002, c 29.
Canada. Yukon Environmental and Socio-economic Assessment Act, SC 2003, c 7.
Canadian Zinc Corporation v. Mackenzie Valley Land and Water Board, 2005 NWTSC 48. Canada.
Chippewas of the Thames First Nation v. Enbridge Pipelines Inc., 2017 SCC 41. Canada.
Clyde River (Hamlet) v. Petroleum Geo-Services Inc., 2017 1 SCR 1069, 2017 SCC 40. Canada.
De Beers v. Mackenzie Valley Environmental Impact Review Board, 2007 NWTSC 24. Canada.
"Documents." QIA. Accessed October 16, 2019. https://www.qia.ca/documents
First Nation of Nacho Nyak Dun v. Yukon, 2014 YKSC 69. First Instance. Canada.
First Nation of Nacho Nyak Dun v. Yukon [2017] 2 SCR 576, 2017 SCC 58 (CanLII). Supreme Court. Canada.
Gibson, Ginger, Dawn Hoogeveen, Alistair MacDonald, and The Firelight Group. *Impact Assessment in the Arctic: Emerging Practices of Indigenous-Led Review*. Whitehorse: Gwich'in Council International, 2018. https://gwichincouncil.com/sites/default/files/Firelight%20Gwich%27in%20Indigenous%20led%20review_FINAL_web_0.pdf
Gitxaala Nation v. Canada, 2016 FCA 187. Canada.
Haida Nation v. British Columbia (Minister of Forests) [2004] 3 SCR 511, 2004 SCC 73 (CanLII). Canada.
Indigenous and Northern Affairs Canada. "Final Agreements and Related Implementation Matters." Government of Canada; Indigenous and Northern Affairs Canada; Communications Branch, June 18, 2018. https://www.aadnc-aandc.gc.ca/eng/1100100030583/1100100030584
Ka'A'Gee Tu First Nation v. Canada (Attorney General), 2012 FC 297. Canada.
Katlodeeche First Nation v. Canada (Attorney General), 2013 FC 458. Canada.
Ka's'Gee Tu First Nation v. Canada (Minister of Indian Affairs), 2007 FC 764. Canada.
Liard First Nation v. Yukon Government and Selwyn Chihong Mining Ltd, 2011 YKSC 55. Canada.
MacEachern, Daniel and Andrew Sampson. "Tears, Relief for Hunger Strikers as Muskrat Falls Agreement Ends Fast." *CBC News*, October 26, 2016. https://www.cbc.ca/news/canada/newfoundland-labrador/billy-gauthier-hunger-strikers-muskrat-falls-1.3821743
Mikisew Cree First Nation v. Canada (Minister of Canadian Heritage) [2005] 3 SCR 388, 2005 SCC 69 (CanLII). Canada.
Newfoundland and Labrador Canada, Municipal Affairs and Environment. "Independent Expert Advisory Committee Terms of Reference." March 24, 2017. https://www.mae.gov.nl.ca/env_assessment/projects/Y2010/1305/ieac_tor.pdf
North American Tungsten Corp Ltd v. Mackenzie Valley Land and Water Board, 2003 NWTCA 5. Canada.

Nunatsiavut Government v. AG Canada, 2015 FC 492. Canada.
Nunatsiavut Government v. Newfoundland and Labrador, 2013 NLTD(G) 142. Canada.
Nunatsiavut v. Newfoundland and Labrador (Department of Environment and Conservation), 2015 NLTD(G) 1. Canada.
Nunavut Tunngavik Inc v. Canada (Attorney General), 2014 NUCA 2. Canada.
Qikiqtani Inuit Association v. Canada (Attorney General), 1998 CanLII 8617 (FC). Canada.
Qikiqtani Inuit Association v. Canada (Minister of Natural Resources), 2010 NUCJ 12 (CanLII). Canada.
Quebec (Attorney General) v. Moses, 2010 SCC 17. Canada.
Rio Tinto Alcan Inc. v. Carrier Sekani Tribal Council, 2010 SCC 43 (CanLII), [2010] 2 SCR 650. Canada.
Strateco Resources Inc v. Québec (Attorney General), [2018] 1 CLNR 159 *Ressources Strateco inc. c. Procureure générale du Québec*, 2017 QCCS 2679 (CanLII (Que SC)). Canada.
Taku River Tlingit First Nation v. British Columbia (Project Assessment Director), 2004 SCC 74 (CanLII), [2004] 3 SCR 550. Canada.
Tlicho Government v. Mackenzie Valley Impact Review Board, 2011 NWTSC 31. Canada.
Tsleil-Waututh Nation v. Canada (Attorney General), 2018 FCA 153. Canada.
White River First Nation v. Yukon, 2013 YKSC 66. Canada.
Yellowknives Dene First Nation v. Minister of Aboriginal Affairs and Northern Development, 2015 FCA 148. Canada.

10 Participation in a small archipelago
The Shetland negotiations

James Mitchell

Before the oil

Shetland lies 700 miles north of London, 300 miles north of Edinburgh, and is 200 miles from Bergen. The islands are about 100 miles long and 35 miles across at the widest point. Their history has been "interpreted as a succession of peoples who came by sea, who settled and built up a way of life only to have it replaced by the culture of new arrivals."[1] While other communities had similar experiences, Shetland's unique experience relates to its geography, lying at the crossroads between Scandinavia and the British isles. This history and its remoteness give rise to its cultural, economic and political distinctiveness. As a report commissioned by Shetland Islands Council noted in 1978, "Shetland is different ... It should be said that this difference is first one of perception. Shetlanders see themselves as different, as a unique contained historic community. This perception is supported by geography and history. Shetland is remote."[2] This difference has also been evident in its politics. Orkney and Shetland returned Jo Grimond, one of only 12 Liberal MPs across the UK, in 1950. In the 1975 referendum on European Economic Community membership, Shetland and the Western Isles were the only two local authorities in the UK to vote against membership.

Shetland's population had been in long-term decline before oil was discovered and stood at 17,567 at the 1971 census compared with over 30,000 a century before. In 1971, Shetland consisted of around 25 inhabited islands, ranging from the Shetland mainland with just under 6,000 people to Trondra with twenty people. Each community was different and providing public services, including transport, was challenging. By the late 1960s, its economy was heavily dependent on external support from UK central government. Fishing and fish processing provided about 30 per cent of employment and 20 per cent of Shetland's income, and about 95 per cent of the land was suitable for rough

---

1 James Nicolson, *Shetland and Oil* (London: William Luscombe, 1975), 28.
2 Lord Kilbrandon and the Nevis Institute, *The Shetland Report, a Constitutional Study Prepared for the Shetland Islands Council by The Nevis Institute under the Chairmanship of Lord Kilbrandon* (Edinburgh: Nevis Institute, 1978), 19.

grazing for sheep farming. These industries along with knitwear were the staples of the islands' economy.[3]

As far back as 1953, an academic study had concluded that the islands were "balancing on the knife-edge between solvency and insolvency."[4] One author noted that a

> symptom of Shetland's decline was the stress placed on education; for education was not designed to equip school-leavers to live and work successfully within the islands: it was regarded as a passport to a good job the British mainland. The lack of opportunity at home was reflected in the scores of young people who lined the rails of the passenger vessel *St Clair* on her twice weekly trip to Aberdeen.[5]

However, there was a view that by the early 1970s Shetland had turned a corner. With the support of the Highlands and Islands Development Board, a government regeneration agency established in 1965, the islands had seen its population stabilise and new fish processing and knitwear factories had been set up.

A major overhaul of the system of local government was initiated in the 1960s. A Royal Commission (Wheatley) recommended that Shetland should be incorporated into Highland Region, a huge area with Inverness as the administrative centre lying almost 300 miles away across the North Sea and much of the Highlands. Shetlanders opposed the move, seeing it as leaving the islands on the remote periphery of what they perceived would be a massive proposed new entity – 275 miles across sea and land separated Lerwick from Inverness, the proposed seat of Highland Council – and campaigned against inclusion. There were salutary lessons that would be useful in later campaigns. As one of the key local figures later explained, "For reasons of the Wheatley exercise, and others ... we began in Shetland to understand the power of the media – press, radio and TV – and to develop some ability at least in this form of communication."[6] This was the era when small units of government were deemed unviable, but the campaign by Shetlanders paid off. A new two-tier system of local government across Scotland was created, with smaller District Councils and larger Regional Councils, but a degree of continuity occurred when Westminster bowed to pressure to allow Shetland, along with two other island archipelagoes, to be retained as an island authority with a largely undisturbed range of responsibilities. Lerwick Town Council was merged with Shetland County Council to form the Shetland Islands Council in 1975.

---

3 I. H. McNicoll and G. Walker, *The Shetland Economy 1976/77: Structure and Performance*, unpublished report (Edinburgh: Department of Business Studies, Edinburgh University, 1978), quoted in Kilbrandon, *The Shetland Report*, 22.
4 Thelma Blance, "The Economy of Shetland, 1930–52" (M.A. dissertation, Aberdeen University, 1953), 78.
5 James Nicolson, *Shetland and Oil*, 39.
6 Edward Thomason, "Shetland in the Seventies: A Shetlander's View of Oil," in *Scandinavian Shetland: An Ongoing Tradition?* ed. John R. Baldwin (Edinburgh: Scottish Society of Northern Studies, 1978), 44.

Opportunities, threats and choices

In 1967, oil and gas were discovered in the Norwegian sector of the North Sea. This raised the possibility of similar finds in the UK sector. Shetland would be the nearest landfall for a large part of potential oil development. In 1971, Shell/Esso made a major oil discovery in the East Shetland basin – the Brent field – but only disclosed this in August 1972. Business confidentiality and the desire to have time to make preparations were likely explanations for withholding this discovery. Subsequent discoveries meant that Shetland would indeed become crucial to oil development and the islands' economy and society would be transformed.

Oil companies and the UK Government saw the North Sea as offering great opportunities. North Sea oil wealth was impossible to calculate precisely, not least as new fields kept being discovered, while fluctuating oil prices and the engineering challenges made costs of and profits from extraction uncertain. Geopolitical developments resulted in oil prices quadrupling over the winter of 1973/74. The National Union of Mineworkers (NUM) had gone on strike in 1972 and 1974, adding to the UK Government's energy crisis. The UK had serious balance of payments problems made worse by the need to import oil. In April 1974, the Scottish Secretary wrote to Prime Minister Harold Wilson, who had been returned as Prime Minister in February to head a Labour Government, and noted that the Shetland developments were "extremely important for our oil supplies" with forecasts suggesting that the equivalent of the UK's total consumption of oil would be coming ashore in Shetland by 1982.[7] Adding to the pressure, the Scottish National Party (SNP) won seven seats in the February 1974 election and went on to win a further four in October's election. Lying in second place across much of the rest of Scotland, the SNP posed a major electoral threat, with possibility of Scotland breaking away as an independent state controlling oil in the North Sea.

The need for oil was not just related to the UK's energy needs. There were serious structural problems in the economy that were becoming increasingly obvious around this time, culminating in a major crisis in the mid-1970s. In 1976, Prime Minister Jim Callaghan had to go cap in hand to the International Monetary Fund to borrow $3.9 billion ($17.3 billion in 2018 prices). As Callaghan said the following year, "God has given Britain her best opportunity for one hundred years in the shape of North Sea oil."[8] Getting oil out of the North Sea as quickly as possible would be a priority for the UK Government. Oil companies shared this objective but this would present technological and engineering challenges. It would not be in the interests of the oil companies to reveal details of risk assessments but they were keen to emphasise the dangers, difficulties and costs. The extent of the North Sea bonanza for the oil companies would only become clear in time. But in the early 1970s, the activity of oil companies was evidence that these companies saw the risk as worthwhile. Any knowledge that the oil companies

---

7 William Ross, "Landing of Offshore Oil Shetland," Note to Prime Minister from William Ross, Secretary of State for Scotland, April 11, 1974, National Archives, PREM 16/614.
8 Christopher Harvie, *Fool's Gold* (London: Hamish Hamilton, 1994), 2.

possessed was not likely to be shared with the UK Government or local communities. Given the geopolitical implications of oil with massive multinational companies involved and energy becoming a key issue in global politics, the North Sea was also attracting the interest of the Federal Government in the United States. This was the context in which a small island authority with its various communities would have to contend.

For Shetlanders, however, other considerations were paramount. Oil development would involve massive disruption, challenge traditional ways of life, and potentially damage Shetland's existing fragile economy. In October 1972, the local paper complained, "It is almost pathetic that the Government, pinning its hopes on oil for the economic salvation of Scotland, seems to have left it to a relatively impoverished local authority to wrestle with the enormous infrastructural problems of the oil boom."[9] There were inevitably different views in the islands, covering the

> whole spectrum from excitement to anxiety, while for those who did not wish to see Shetland changed in any way by the oil industry, there was still the comforting thought that so far no oil had been discovered off Shetland, or at least no finds had been announced. It was still possible to dream that the oil men would drill only dry wells.[10]

But others saw an opportunity to secure the islands' future. Others still saw the opportunities in more individualistic terms. Shetland had hardly featured in Whitehall thinking prior to oil. Many years later, a senior Scottish Office civil servant recalled a meeting when a "very senior official" at the Treasury opened the discussion by asking where Shetland was and whether it consisted of one or two islands.[11] The archipelago's far northerly position meant that it appeared on maps of the UK in a box off the east coast of Scotland.[12]

On Christmas day 1971, Shetlanders watched the *Ocean Traveller* drilling rig anchoring outside Lerwick harbour, a visual symbol of impending change. The number of oil service vessel visits to Shetland soared from 79 in 1971 to 1,809 by 1976. Sumburgh airport, in the South of Shetland, was witnessing more activity and there was the beginning of land speculation in the early 1970s.[13] Oil's impact was also evident in the increased number of telephone connections and numbers of television licences acquired, as well as house building: 106 new houses were completed in 1974, rising to 296 the following year and 471 in 1976. As Jonathan Wills, a Labour activist who would later become editor of the local newspaper, later remarked, the largest contracts that the Council had dealt with had

---

9 *Shetland Times*, editorial, October 11, 1972.
10 Nicolson, *Shetland and Oil*, 69.
11 Gavin McCrone, "The Development of North Sea Oil and Gas," held 11 December 1999, *Institute of Contemporary British History* (2002): 84.
12 Ibid.
13 J.M. Fenwick, "The Shetland Experience: A Local Authority Arms Itself for the Oil Invasion," *Scottish Government Yearbook* (1978): 33–50, 34.

been "valued in tens of thousands of pounds" and by the mid-1970s they were dealing with "hundreds of millions."[14] The local council faced a number of challenges:

- aggregating and articulating divergent views in Shetland's communities;
- gaining formal legal powers to manage oil development;
- negotiating with the UK Government and oil companies, requiring expertise in highly technical complex engineering, economic and legal matters;
- addressing the rapid economic and social changes that were occurring due to oil after 1971.

While oil developments would have an impact throughout the archipelago, some places would be more affected than others. Opportunities and threats existed unevenly and would require careful and sensitive responses.

The early 1970s saw intense debate in the islands. Each of its many communities considered the prospects and most were divided. Scalloway, base to the "Shetland bus" Norwegian special operations during World War II, was one example. It had the potential to become a major service base for oil rigs, and Council officials addressed local meetings while a Scalloway Development Trust was set up with all shades of opinion represented. Efforts were made to offer information in various forms to the local community before a referendum was held which resulted in a narrow victory supporting development. However, it was decided to accommodate the views of opponents and the proposed development scheme was altered. This process of deliberation was also evident in other local communities. A local referendum was also held on Unst, part of which was represented by the Council Convener and where the community was divided. The local community of about 1,100 people opposed compulsory land purchase but favoured development and accepted that it could incorporate between 250 and 500 people over a number of years.[15] A petition signed by 95 of 96 households in Unst was sent to the UK Government setting out the view that the oil companies could use the piers but should install massive tanks on hills away from the villages. They also wanted assurances that any land bought by compulsory order that proved unnecessary should be offered for sale back to the previous owner. There was also a desire to have a lengthier period for consultation.[16]

In September 1973, the Council agreed a policy:

> This County Council, recognising that it may be in the national interest that Shetland be used for oil installations, and having sought to devise policies and to provide machinery which recognise the national interest while protecting those of the Shetland Community, will continue to have regard for the

---

14 Jonathan Wills, *A Place in the Sun: Shetland and Oil – Myths and Realities* (St Johns, Newfoundland: Institute of Economic and Social Research, 1991), 14.
15 Nicolson, *Shetland and Oil*, 82–84.
16 Ibid., 90.

national interest but will give no encouragement to developments and will oppose proposals where these developments or proposals put Shetland at unnecessary risk or fail to provide available safeguards and will at no time put commercial or industrial interests before those of the Shetland Community.[17]

In October 1973, public meetings were held in the villages nearest Sullom Voe, which was increasingly seen as the most likely sight of a major oil development. Almost half the villagers turned out. Comments were invited and received, amounting to many pages of about an inch in thickness. Much of the discussion focused on whether a new town should be created or whether an existing village should be extended. An iterative process developed of consultation, deliberation and revised plans. This eventually led to the Sullom Voe District Plan in June 1974 which was approved by the Council in September. It envisaged the biggest oil port in Europe, housing up to 1,000 incoming families. The Council took pride in the process, regarding it as an example of successful public engagement.[18] Brae, for example, grew substantially as the terminal developed but the local community was largely united and a community association was formed to negotiate with the Council and developers. A local referendum resulted in near unanimity in favour of development.[19] Oil had stimulated community activity and forged new associations.

There was considerable potential for divide-and-rule in the community by oil companies, and there were individuals and communities tempted by lucrative side deals. There were also legitimate concerns. Fishing interests were concerned that oil developments would undermine the local fishing industry. Oil spillage, drilling and fleets of oil vessels were feared as likely to damage the industry. There was a sharp fall in fish prices in 1973/74 adding to the industry's precariousness. Unemployment levels were relatively low (2.2 per cent in 1974) but so too were incomes, adding to concerns that traditional industries would struggle to compete with the lure of work in "black gold." The limited pool of local labour meant that existing industries would be drained of labour and there would be an influx of large numbers of workers to service the oil industry. By the end of 1972 when five oil fields had been discovered, it was estimated that there would need to be about 1,000 extra people brought to Shetland.[20] A paper prepared for the Council in 1973 warned that when oil developments waned the "isolation of Shetland will make it difficult to find alternative employment for the redundant workers and the resulting depopulation will have serious psychological as well as more direct economic repercussions." It identified related challenges:

[A]ll of the labour must be imported to the Islands and that in a short time creates further problems which will demand immediate solution. Schools,

17 Quoted in Staerk, *The Development of North Sea Oil and Gas*, 95.
18 Fenwick, "The Shetland Experience," 43.
19 Nicolson, *Shetland and Oil*, 82–84.
20 Nicolson, *Shetland and Oil*, 79.

hospitals, social services, shopping facilities will be required with the earliest influx of population. The incoming workers will have pastimes which are dissimilar to the traditional Shetland pastimes. It is likely that their demands will be more sophisticated and will require capital expenditure of some magnitude. These facilities will take time to provide and their construction will be made the more difficult by the other demands on building labour.[21]

There were also concerns that oil workers would bring trouble – drugs, vandalism, theft, and prostitution.[22]

A Council meeting in December 1973 approved a ten-point plan aimed at responding to local concerns about compulsory purchase. This included a commitment to consult fully before any action was taken by the Council; that good agricultural land would be conserved wherever possible; and that accommodation would be provided in areas of choice where tenants had to be rehoused.

Capacity building

Shetland's southerly archipelago neighbour Orkney had been engaged in similar endeavours. Information gathered by Orkney Council was shared with Jo Grimond MP. In September 1973, senior Orkney officials visited Pembrokeshire County Council and the Amoco Tanker Terminal and Refinery at Milford Haven. The report back to the Council identified key lessons:

1. Harbour powers are essential to exercise strict control over present and future developments to ensure that these are in line with the council's policy.
2. While some oil companies are better than others there are no "good" oil companies and verbal assurances should not be given too much credence. This also includes expert advice submitted by oil companies to persuade a Planning Authority that their proposals with regard to any particular development are the only practical proposals. In this respect an Authority should –
   a. insist that any undertakings given by oil companies are reduced to formal writing, and
   b. seek their own expert advice.
3. In the initial stages of negotiations a Local Authority should extract from any oil company the maximum benefit possible.
4. A Local Authority should ensure that any pollution measures remain the responsibility of individual oil companies and obtain written agreement on this matter.
5. A Local Authority should ensure that at the end of development there should be reinstatement of the land involved with the exception of those buildings and installations which will be of permanent use to the Authority.

---

21 *Zetland County Council Bill – Peculiarities of Shetland*, Lerwick, May 28, 1973, Grimond papers, National Library of Scotland, Dep.363, Box 16(2).
22 Nicolson, *Shetland and Oil*, 79.

6 Properly controlled oil related development is beneficial to a community but such development creates a chain reaction and steps must be taken to ensure that such a reaction does not adversely affect the local economy ...[23]

This advice would be key to how Orkney and Shetland engaged with the oil industry. A related lesson was to ensure that only one terminal, determined by the Council, would be developed and not a series of smaller terminals for each oil company. There was no desire to see what one MP would refer to as the "proliferation of harbour facilities" as at Milford Haven in Wales.[24]

Shetland had been one of the few local authorities in the UK without a development plan before oil was discovered. The Council needed planners as well as other relevant staff. Ian Clark was the Shetland Council's treasurer and later chief executive and played a key leadership role identifying oil's potential benefits for the islands.[25] In 1975, US Consul in Edinburgh Richard Funkhouser described Clark as a "tyrant" in a telegram to the US State Department. Funkhouser referred to Clark having "hornswaggled some of the biggest multinationals and most sophisticated leaders in Britain out of terms for the development of Sullom Voe which would make Scottish nationalists pale with envy." The Council, the US diplomat maintained in this private message released under Freedom of Information, "had forced the majors into giving them a highly profitable partnership for which they had put up no funds and over which they won significant control."[26]

A key appointment was that of John Manson, a Shetlander who had worked in the oil industry as a consultant early in 1972.[27] At different stages, various bodies were consulted including Parliamentary Agents required for private bill legislation to give the Council the powers it needed, merchant bankers, as well as engineers and oil industry specialists who could advise on what was involved in surveying deepwater anchorages, others who specialised in underground storage of oil and gas. It recognised that the highly specialist technical knowledge was required, though not necessarily because it would be directly engaged in this activity but to understand oil, gas and related industries.

The various interests in oil and gas exploration possessed vastly different levels of experience, information and expertise. The lack of a level playing field in negotiations placed the local communities and the Council at a significant disadvantage. Councillors and council officials attended many conferences and

---

23 *Report by County Clerk and General Manager on visit to Pembrokeshire*, September 17–18, 1973, Grimond Papers, National Library of Scotland, Dep. 363 Box 16.
24 Norman Lamont, *Hansard*, House of Commons, April 30, 1973, vol. 855, col. 883.
25 Iain Noble, "The Development of North Sea Oil and Gas," 79.
26 "Oil Notes from All Over," June 30, 1975, Edinburgh to London, Document Number: 1975 EDINBU00150, Department of State Telegrams, The National Archives and Records Administration (NARA), Access to Archival Databases (AAD), Electronic Telegrams, 1975, Central Foreign Policy Files, created 7/1/1973–12/31/1979.
27 Edward Thomason, *Island Challenge* (Lerwick, Shetland: The Shetland Times Ltd, 1997), 53–54.

seminars as well as visits to comparable developments. Consultants were employed and information gathered in an effort to rebalance this asymmetry. In late 1971, Lerwick Town Council, representing a population of about 6,000 people, sent a delegation to learn from the local community's experience in Bantry Bay Gulf Oil complex in County Cork, Ireland. In late 1972, at its annual general meeting the Shetland Civic Society proposed a conference on oil and urged the UK Government to restrict oil developments until a full investigation had been conducted. It was subsequently suggested that the County Council used the two years from the middle of 1972 to "buy its ticket to the dance" by preparing to ensure the islands did not lose out.[28] The community would require new expertise and shrewd leadership. It could not rely on the wholehearted support of the UK Government given divergent interests on the speed of oil extraction.

However, even with new staff, the Council simply was not legally empowered to negotiate with oil companies on many aspects of development or negotiate with the multinational extraction industry. It required new powers and increased capacity, which it pursued through special Parliamentary procedures at Westminster. An early effort was made to identify new powers that would be required to ensure developments were planned to Shetland's advantage by the Council.

Sullom Voe and the Zetland County Council Act

The Council started to prepare to take advantage of new powers it hoped to gain from central government before they were granted. It took advice from the National Ports Council on how it might operate as a harbour authority and appointed a Ports and Harbour Committee. It sought advice from the Department of Trade and Industry on powers governing control of piloting and engaged with firms that would be required for towing purposes. It also contacted Shell to identify the oil company's needs in the event that the legislation was passed. Consultants advised on planning and development. The Council took the view that these preparations could not await passage of legislation permitting it to act. Much of this was done in a short period of time and much was done with less consultation than would be expected a generation later. Much of the information gathered was sensitive though doubtless much was treated as confidential which might have been made public. This contributed to concerns that the Council was being secretive.

It was soon clear that an oil and gas terminal would be required on Shetland. The Council opposed each of the oil companies having its own terminal, having learned this from experience elsewhere, and proposed instead a single terminal where oil and gas would be piped ashore then transported by tanker to be refined. One oil company, Total Oil Marine Ltd, had already bought up land and was particularly unhappy with this decision. A confidential report to the Council by the County Development Manager identified Sullom Voe, an inlet in the north of Shetland's mainland, as the best site. The report noted which land would have to

---

28 Fenwick, "The Shetland Experience," 35.

be acquired.[29] This focus on Sullom Voe was confirmed in July 1972 by a consultancy which found it to be the best natural harbour in the islands for an oil terminal. The consultancy referred to the area as "Nordport," an invented Shetland-sounding name. In August, the Council's Development Office produced the first Shetland Interim Plan, which sought to ensure that developments would occur in an orderly manner and avoid a free-for-all.

In November 1972, the County Council agreed by 23 votes to 5 with 2 abstentions to promote a Provisional Order in Parliament to give it the necessary powers to implement its emerging plans to acquire land for development; exercise harbour jurisdiction and powers in areas likely to be developed; and licence construction works in these areas. There were two different means by which this might be achieved – a Provisional Order or a Private Bill. In March 1973, Parliamentary authorities ruled that the proposals would require the County Council to promote a Private Bill, a more complex, costly and time-consuming process than a Provisional Order. This process required the services of specialist Parliamentary agents. Private Bill procedure allows for legislation that applies to either individuals, groups, communities or corporate entities but would not be generally applicable.[30] So long as no Member of Parliament objected the procedure could avoid normal Parliamentary procedure, but Tam Dalyell, MP for West Lothian in central Scotland, objected in order to force a debate in Parliament even though he was not opposed to the Bill. It was still subject to a public enquiry by an extra-parliamentary panel meeting in Scotland.

Some businessmen set up a private company, adopting the very name that the consultants had proposed for the Sullom Voe area identified for oil development. Nordport Ltd already had options for 40,000 acres of land for oil development and had some support amongst councillors and in some communities. Chris Baur, a financial journalist on the *Scotsman*, the Edinburgh based newspaper, researched the company and discovered that behind the local front of Shetland businessmen was a complex web of companies leading to Edinburgh merchant bankers.[31] This further convinced the Council that it needed to prevent unplanned development. In February 1973, the Council rejected an application from Nordport Ltd for planning permission to develop Sullom Voe as an oil terminal. The Council maintained that Nordport Ltd's proposals contravened its planning policy, the application was premature as the Council was still studying different places for oil development, and that there was insufficient detail in what had been submitted. But this was not the final battle with Nordport Ltd.

29 Michael Stansbury, "Confidential Report on Land for Major Oil Development," County Development Officer, April 6, 1972, Shetland Archives, CO7194/1–2.
30 The UK Private Legislation Procedure (Scotland) Act, 1936 allows for petitions for private legislation to be considered so long as there is no opposition in Parliament. This resulted in an inquiry held in Scotland which made a recommendation to the UK Government. The Government then decided on whether to support an Order in Parliament. With Parliamentary support, this leads to the passage of private legislation without the same Parliamentary stages that would be involved in public legislation.
31 Wills, *A Place in the Sun*, 19.

The Council had a tradition of non-party politics, but these developments provoked the establishment of a pro-Nordport Ltd grouping on the Council calling itself the Shetland Democratic Group with seven councillors. These councillors were led by a local Church of Scotland minister with links to the Conservative Party. It criticised the Council for its secrecy and argued that all major decisions should be made by the full council rather than in committee, but this was defeated by 14 votes to 8. The Council's Convener (the Scottish term for chairperson) at the time took much of the flak and would go down to defeat at the local elections in 1973. The intense nature of debate was evident in the turnout for the local elections: 82 per cent of electors voted in the Council Convener's ward,[32] much higher than occurred in a Westminster general election, not to mention what normally occurred in a local election. The 1973 local elections saw the election of ten Shetland Democratic Group members on a Council of 30. The local managing director of Northport Ltd was elected to the Council but within a year he stood down from Northport Ltd. The Council elected a new Convener and Vice Convener who carried on the policy of their predecessors. The Shetland Democratic Group accepted the result and after some concessions progress was made without as much acrimony as previously.

Jo Grimond, the local MP, assisted in the process of empowering the council though even he, with over 20 years in Parliament, had to be guided through the intricacies of the Private Bill procedure. In introducing the legislation in the Commons, Grimond outlined the impact on the local communities and summed up the legislation's purpose as seeking to "achieve orderly planning."[33] Grimond, local councillors and council officials had consulted widely across Shetland and the local newspaper had played an important role in giving coverage to the various views expressed at meetings. But opposition and the sense that the local communities most affected were not sufficiently consulted were not allayed. Grimond acknowledged that the Bill "aroused understandable anxiety" in Shetland.[34] Some councillors took the view that Shetland should oppose oil development, though the general view was that this could not be avoided as the UK Government desperately needed the oil. Those individuals and communities most likely to be affected were in places where the Council sought powers to buy land by compulsory order. The local Conservative candidate for the general election warned that if there was no right of appeal against compulsory purchase then individual Shetlanders would be left "defenceless."

While debate raged in Shetland, the Government decided to back at least some of the proposals in the Private Bill. It supported the Council becoming the planning and harbour authority but had reservations about the Council having a share in the profits of oil developers. In late March 1973, the Council estimated that it would cost £3.5 million to buy the land needed for development and argued that

---

32 Thomason, *Island Challenge*, 73.
33 Jo Grimond, MP, Speech moving second reading of Zetland County Council Bill, *Hansard*, House of Commons, April 30, 1973, vol. 855, col. 862.
34 Jo Grimond, MP, *Hansard*, House of Commons, April 30, 1973, vol. 855, col. 863.

this needed to come from a share in oil developments. There was also a view in Government that ministers ought to have a supervisory role and not allow the Council complete autonomy in its proposed new powers. This view was shared across the two main parties – Conservative and Labour – at Westminster.[35] Landowners likely to be affected were informed that there was a prospect of their land being compulsorily purchased, creating opposition and tensions in the communities affected. Some local councillors preferred a more open market approach or 'free-for-all' as supporters of Council intervention expressed it. Edward Thomason, then Council Convener (leader), later conceded that "public relations could have been better handled."[36]

The local Labour Party had its concerns, as described by Jonathan Wills, Labour's candidate in both 1974 general elections. The party locally wanted to restrict the development of oil. Wills recounted a visit from a group of Labour MPs that included Dickson Mabon, who would become Minister of State for Energy in 1976. Wills had taken the group to Sullom Voe, while it was still a "calm backwater, beautiful to me and others for its birds and scenery" only to hear Mabon refer to the place as a "splendid site for a major petro-chemical complex."[37] The prospect of a petro-chemical complex in Shetland was anathema to most Shetlanders and the prospect of this was bound to provoke opposition. Wills himself was one of the islanders whose concerns focused on the potential environmental damage and found himself in disagreement with colleagues and friends which he explained was partly generational. Some older Shetlanders who had experienced harsh economic times viewed concern for the environment as relatively unimportant.[38] The threat to the environment led to the establishment of an environmental impact assessment produced by the Sullom Voe Environmental Advisory Group (SVEAG) set up in 1974 by the Council and oil industry. There were concerns that SVEAG was secretive and that its membership was skewed towards the interests of oil development but some concessions to these concerns were seen as necessary.[39]

Despite some local Shetland Tory opposition, a Scottish Office minister expressed the Conservative Government's support for the Bill and told the Commons that civil servants had offered the Council help. He acknowledged that what was proposed were "unusual powers, but they are being sought in order to deal with a very unusual situation in a very special part of Britain with peculiar local characteristics."[40] The change of government in February 1974 did not alter matters. A report to the Treasury from the new Secretary of State for Scotland outlined the thinking in March:

35 John Warden, "Land Developers Face Curbs in Shetland," *Glasgow Herald*, April 2, 1973, 1.
36 Thomason, *Island Challenge*, 71–72.
37 Wills, *A Place in the Sun*, 26.
38 Nicolson, *Shetland and Oil*, 81.
39 Wills, *A Place in the Sun*, 45.
40 George Younger, MP, *Hansard*, House of Commons, April 30, 1973, vol. 855, col. 893.

The Secretary of State considers that the Bill in its present form is desirable and necessary to deal with the situation arising in Shetland because of the discovery of oil in the Northern North Sea. The powers it gives to the County Council are necessary for the following reasons:

(a) The geographical nature of the coastline with a number of natural harbours makes close control and co-ordination of harbour development of great importance.
(b) The oil discoveries in the East Shetland Basin will have to be exploited by the construction of substantial oil storage and terminal works in Shetland within a limited timescale.
(c) These developments must be closely co-ordinated and carried out with minimum disturbance to the environment.
(d) The existing economy of Shetland is finely balanced and peculiarly delicate control of new development will be required to ensure its integration without economic damage.[41]

But this public statement did not reflect internal Whitehall concerns. In March 1974, the Scottish Office brought "a potentially awkward situation" to the attention of the Treasury. The Council in Shetland was proposing that oil companies make a substantial payment to the local authority "by way of a 'throughput charge' based on either the quantity or the value of oil passing."[42] Even with the new powers granted in the Zetland County Council Bill – at that stage still awaiting formal enactment – the Council would not have the power to require a payment. Instead, the Council had the power to "receive it if it is voluntarily paid as a gift by the companies." The Government had no way of preventing such gifts nor controlling how it could be spent, and this money would not affect entitlement to its central grant in paying for local services.[43] There were implications for central government:

a   the effect on the Government's own "take" in terms of royalty and tax;
b   the precedent it could set for other areas;
c   its effect on the political arguments about the hypothecation of oil revenues for Scotland.[44]

Central government had no powers to prevent oil companies paying the council, but "it might be possible to persuade the oil companies concerned to take a tougher line than they appeared to be likely to do at present" though this might

41 J.B. Fleming, *Report of the Secretary of State for Scotland on the Zetland County Council Bill*, Scottish Office, March 19, 1974, National Archives, T341/622.
42 Gavin McCrone, Letter to R.L. Workman, Treasury, with background paper, "North Sea Oil – Pipeline Terminals in Shetland," Scottish Office, March 25, 1974, National Archives, T341/622.
43 Ibid.
44 Ibid.

create "both political and administrative problems."[45] The Council would complain that Westminster was preventing the islands from getting proper recompense for disturbance caused by oil and this would, as the official noted, be supported by both the Scottish National Party and Liberal Party. It would also likely lead the Council to adopt a "non-co-operative attitude to planning applications from the oil companies" leading to complications and a drawn-out planning process with an impact on oil production.[46]

Cabinet ministers did not like the way the Council was operating. Ted Short, a senior Cabinet minister, agreed with Secretary of State for Scotland Willie Ross and the Paymaster General in objecting to the way the Council was operating. Short deplored the "way in which the County Council have gone about seeking such payments" but acknowledged the "political implications in Scotland of appearing to wield the big stick on behalf of wealthy oil companies and against a small and hardly prosperous county council," noting particularly the likely reaction of local MP Jo Grimond and the SNP. His view was that "our approach should be to try to get the political credit for helping to bring about a reasonable settlement; and thereby to demonstrate to the County Council that there are better ways of securing their objectives (to the extent that they are reasonable) than the very dubious one they have chosen."[47]

Concerns were also articulated in the second reading debate by a number of Labour MPs in Parliament reflecting a paternalist attitude. One referred to the "gentle, simple-minded people" who would be outwitted by "land-grabbing Mafia of Edinburgh and Texas."[48] Another questioned whether the Council had the expertise to become a harbour authority and whether the Government would support other authorities seeking similar powers.[49] This attitude may have worked to the islands' advantage in the tendency of oil companies and the UK Government to underestimate Shetland's leadership. The only MP to have been born in Shetland was Norman Lamont, who would become Chancellor of the Exchequer in 1990, and represented Kingston-upon-Thames in the Commons. Lamont viewed the arrival of oil and oil companies with "considerable trepidation" but he welcomed the Bill because it would enable the Council to "come to terms with considerable problems" that "will descend upon Shetland." He raised a concern frequently mentioned in discussions in Shetland: the prospect of an oil spill.[50]

A report on *Shetland's Oil Era* produced by Shetland Islands Council in 1978 reflected on the experience and noted the "stormy passage" of the legislation through Parliament.[51] Thirteen petitions were lodged against the Bill including

---

45 Ibid.
46 Ibid.
47 Ted Short, Letter to Willie Ross from Lord President of Council, April 26, 1974, National Archives, T341/622.
48 William Hamilton, MP, *Hansard*, House of Commons, March 30, 1973, vol. 853, col. 1760.
49 Tam Dalyell, MP, *Hansard*, House of Commons, March, 30, 1973, vol. 853, col. 866, 887.
50 Lamont, *Hansard*, April 30, 1973.
51 Shetland Islands Council, *Shetland's Oil Era*, vol. 1 (Lerwick: Research and Development of Shetland Islands Council, 1978), 15.

from Nordport Ltd, who argued that Sullom Voe would be adversely affected by the Council having control and that it was unprecedented for a Council to have such powers which exceeded those of any other councils. Nordport Ltd also objected that there was no right of appeal to any supervisory authority.[52] Total Oil Marine Ltd also objected and was the only oil company to have acquired land (at Scatsta Ness for a marine terminal). Total objected to the Council having a monopoly over construction works in a widely defined coastal area which might incorporate much of Shetland. Local residents, overlooking Sullom Voe, objected and suggested that greater benefits would accrue to the local community if development was in private hands with necessary resources to ensure development occurred. Shetland Fishermen's Association objected, as did Young's Seafoods Ltd plus a number of local individuals. Only one supporting petition was lodged. The Shetland Civic Society argued that the Council was best able to extract maximum community benefit with minimum disruption.

The objections were heard in Edinburgh beginning in June 1973 before a Select Committee consisting of two Labour and two Conservative MPs. Many of the objections made by local Shetlanders were addressed effectively by the Council with reassurances and minor amendments. Nordport Ltd proved the main objector. They argued that they were more competent than the Council, that the powers exceeded those of any other council, and that the compulsory purchase powers would be used in an unsatisfactory way. The Select Committee deliberated over 18 days and included a visit to Shetland. The MPs split along party lines with the two Labour MPs supporting compulsory purchase powers while the Conservatives opposed with the Conservative chair having a casting vote against. The Council challenged this and the Convener and senior official were allowed to address a meeting of Conservative MPs. By this stage, the discoveries of oil were such that it was clear that the impact on Shetland was set to be far greater than anticipated only a couple of years before. Compromises were found, notably in convincing Parliamentarians that the powers would be limited in their use. By the time the Select Committee in the Lords was considering the measure, there were few outstanding disputes. Nordport Ltd withdrew its objections. But it had been a long battle.

The Council suffered a setback at committee stage when the committee ruled against the Council's proposals for compulsory purchase. This led to a period of intense lobbying to have this decision reversed. The danger of development being held up due to this dispute proved advantageous to the Council. War in the Middle East, resulting in oil shortages, increased pressure to get oil ashore without delay. A consultant's report made it clear that the areas to be affected by development would be limited, helping to remove fears that the Council intended development throughout the islands with mass compulsory purchase of properties. By November 1973, the Bill was ready to return to the Commons and make its way through the House of Lords. The second reading was held in the Lords in January 1974, by which time the only objector was Nordport Ltd.[53]

52 John Warden, "Shetland Set for Battle with Oil Developers," *Glasgow Herald*, March 28, 1973, 1.
53 Shetland Islands Council, *Shetland's Oil Era*, vol. 1, 16.

But Parliament was dissolved on February 8th when an election was called by Prime Minister Heath. Heath had felt compelled to call an election in large measure due to the energy crisis and miners' strike. The election meant that the Bill would not be passed in time before dissolution. But unlike public bills, some categories of private bill can be carried forward into the next Parliament, avoiding having to start the whole process afresh with the resultant costs and delays. The carry-over motion was passed on the day Parliament was dissolved, allowing proceedings to be picked up where they were left off after the election. The Zetland County Council Act was finally given Royal Assent in April 1974. The legislation gave the Council considerable powers:

- as a harbour authority with jurisdiction to operate in Sullom Voe and other named ports;
- to issue licences to dredge and construct within three miles of coastal area;
- to invest in bodies corporate;
- to control development for conservation in the coastal area;
- to purchase land compulsorily;
- to construct, purchase or hire vessels to carry out these functions;
- to establish a reserve fund.

The last power would prove key in the continuing relations with the oil companies. Shetland's oil fund would provide the islands with a revenue source that would allow it to invest in local communities into the future.

Conclusion: Shetland's communities and the oil

Extractive industries will be required to engage with some authoritative body wherever they seek to exploit natural resources. Their first question asked by oil companies was likely to have been, who speaks for Shetland and its communities? The initial answer was confused. A variety of voices claimed to speak for Shetland. These included local communities, without necessarily having any official status, the local MP, various civic bodies, local government and central government. But alongside these were the myriad local interests, including the fishing and fish processing industries but also individuals and communities most likely to be directly affected by any development. The UK state also had an authoritative voice and one that the local council acknowledged but recognised would not necessarily act in Shetland's interests.

The challenge is that even in a small archipelago such as Shetland, there will be a range of divergent interests and views on a development that would have a transformative impact. Who then speaks for these communities? In liberal democracies, the answer is that these divergences are aggregated, differences resolved and decisions are made by elected representative bodies. But this can and did create tensions which were evident in debates and votes on the local council. Just as the UK Government took the view that this development had significant state-wide implications and thus it needed to be involved, so too did the local council seek to have involvement on behalf of the collective interest of the islands.

The main battle in this respect took place in the early years and focused on the role of the Council and the extent to which more local interests should be accommodated and how this would be achieved.

Leaving decisions to elected representatives, even when elections are held regularly, would be inadequate when faced with the need for continuous deliberation with local communities. The information asymmetries were stark: between the oil companies and government at all levels and between government and local communities. Shetland County Council was slow to appreciate the importance of deliberation but the experience of oil developments in the early 1970s would provide lessons. New formal community organisations were formed, debates were held at which various opinions and positions were debated. The key to the most successful community engagement appears to have been when there was transparency, deliberation, following a lengthy iterative process.

But the line dividing legitimate local community interests from individuals seeking a fast buck is unclear. Indeed, external interests were keen to take advantage of developments and to hide behind locals. This was evident in the case of Nordport Ltd, which sought to profit from a high profile development that attracted considerable external interest. Investigations and inputs from Members of Parliament representing constituencies well beyond Shetland played an important part in highlighting those seeking an easy profit. The *Scotsman* newspaper invested considerable staff time in covering oil developments and ensured that much light would be shed on developments that Shetland's local newspaper did not have the capacity to perform. The local paper played an important role in dissemination of information and as a forum for debate.

Time was a major factor, especially as the oil companies and UK Government were keen to extract the oil as quickly as possible. The Council's need to build capacity would take time and the process of gaining the legislative powers required was a slow one. The need to engage meaningfully with local communities involved the provision of information and many meetings. This could not be done quickly.

In the final analysis, the asymmetries were never, nor could ever have been, removed. But the Council demonstrated an ability to engage with the issues, identify its needs, and pursue these with external assistance in a determined fashion.

References

Blance, Thelma. "The Economy of Shetland, 1930–1952." M.A. dissertation., Aberdeen University, 1953.
Dalyell, Tam, MP. *Hansard*, House of Commons, March, 30, 1973, vol. 853, cols 866, 887.
Fenwick, J.M. "The Shetland Experience: A Local Authority Arms Itself for the Oil Invasion." *Scottish Government Yearbook 1978*: 33–50.
Fleming, J.B. *Report of the Secretary of State for Scotland on the Zetland County Council Bill*. Scottish Office, March 19, 1974. National Archives, T341/622.
Grimond, Jo, MP. *Hansard*, House of Commons, April 30, 1973, vol. 855, col. 863.
Grimond, Jo, MP. Speech moving second reading of Zetland County Council Bill. *Hansard*, House of Commons, April 30, 1973, vol. 855, col. 862.

Hamilton, William, MP. *Hansard*, House of Commons, March 30, 1973, vol. 853, col. 1760.
Harvie, Christopher. *Fool's Gold*. London: Hamish Hamilton, 1994.
Kilbrandon, Lord and The Nevis Institute. *The Shetland Report: A Constitutional Study Prepared for the Shetland Islands Council by The Nevis Institute under the Chairmanship of Lord Kilbrandon*. Edinburgh: Nevis Institute, 1978.
Lamont, Norman, MP. *Hansard*, House of Commons, April 30, 1973, vol. 855, col. 883.
McCrone, Gavin. Letter to R.L. Workman, Treasury with background paper, "North Sea Oil – Pipeline Terminals in Shetland." Scottish Office, March 25, 1974. National Archives T341/622.
McNicoll, I.H. and G. Walker. *The Shetland Economy 1976/77: Structure and Performance*. Unpublished report, Department of Business Studies, Edinburgh University, 1978.
Nicolson, James. *Shetland and Oil*. London: William Luscombe, 1975.
"Oil Notes from All Over." June 30, 1975. Edinburgh to London, Document number 1975 EDINBU00150. Department of State Telegrams, The National Archives and Records. Administration (NARA). Access to Archival Databases (AAD), Electronic Telegrams, 1975, Central Foreign Policy Files, created 7/1/1973–12/31/1979.
Report by County Clerk and General Manager on Visit to Pembrokeshire, September 17–18, 1973. Grimond Papers, National Library of Scotland, Dep. 363, Box 16.
Ross, William. "Landing of Offshore Oil Shetland." Note to Prime Minister from William Ross, Secretary of State for Scotland, April 11, 1974. National Archives. PREM 16/614.
Shetland Islands Council. *Shetland's Oil Era*, vol. 1. Lerwick: Research and Development of Shetland Islands Council, 1978.
Shetland Times. Editorial, October 11, 1972.
Short, Ted. Letter to Willie Ross from Lord President of Council, April 26, 1974. National Archives, T341/622.
Staerk, Gillian (ed.) *The Development of North Sea Oil and Gas*. London: Institute of Contemporary British History, 2002.
Stansbury, Michael. *Confidential Report on Land for Major Oil Development*. County Development Officer. April 6, 1972. Shetland Archives, CO7194/1-2.
Thomason, Edward. "Shetland in the Seventies: A Shetlander's View of Oil." In *Scandinavian Shetland: An Ongoing Tradition?*, edited by John R. Baldwin. Edinburgh: Scottish Society of Northern Studies, 1978.
Thomason, Edward. *Island Challenge*. Lerwick, Shetland: The Shetland Times Ltd, 1997.
UK. Private Legislation Procedure (Scotland) Act, 1936, c. 52.
Warden, John. "Land Developers Face Curbs in Shetland." *Glasgow Herald*, April 2, 1973, 1.
Warden, John. "Shetland Set for Battle with Oil Developers." *Glasgow Herald*, March 28, 1973, 1.
Wills, Jonathan. *A Place in the Sun: Shetland and Oil – Myths and Realities*. St Johns, Newfoundland: Institute of Economic and Social Research, 1991.
Younger, George, MP. *Hansard*, House of Commons, April 30, 1973, vol. 855, col. 893.
Zetland County Council Bill – Peculiarities of Shetland. Lerwick, May 28, 1973. Grimond papers, National Library of Scotland, Dep. 363, Box 16(2).

Part III
Participation improved

11 The relationship between host government contracts for oil and gas activities and public participation

Eduardo Guedes Pereira and Marianthi Pappa

Introduction

The extensive extraction of hydrocarbons during the past decades has caused a significant decrease in conventional reserves within easily accessible areas. Concerns about the "end of peak (or easy) oil"[1] have largely led states and energy companies to seek resources in marginal and/or frontier areas that were previously unexplored.[2] The rapid developments in technology and the use of advanced techniques[3] for the location of reserves have enabled the conduct of operations in

---

1 The term "peak oil" was introduced by King Hubbert in the 1957, in an attempt to determine when the US rate of production would reach its maximum level before it declines irreversibly. M. King Hubbert, *Nuclear Energy and the Fossil Fuels* (Houston TX: Shell Development Company, 1956), www.resilience.org/stories/2006-03-08/nuclear-energy-and-fossil-fuels. However, although Hubbert's prediction that the world's oil production would reach its peak during the 1990s has not come to pass, the discussion around peak oil remained. In 2009, the UK Energy Research Centre (UKERC) announced that "conventional oil production is likely to peak before 2030, with a significant risk of a peak before 2020." See, UKERC, "UKERC Report Finds 'Significant Risk' of Oil Production Peaking in Ten Years," October 8, 2009, www.ukerc.ac.uk/news/ukerc-report-finds-significant-risk-of-oil-production-peaking-in-ten-years.html
2 William Cummings, ExxonMobil, 2005, "All the easy oil and gas in the world has pretty much been found. Now comes the harder work in finding and producing oil from more challenging environments and work areas," cited in Ron Rhodes, *The Coming Oil Storm* (Eugene OR: Harvest House Publishers, 2010). Of course, this does not mean that exploration in easily accessible areas has ceased. The development of new technologies has enabled operations in mature provinces, like the North Sea, or exploration of unconventional resources, like shale, in relatively accessible locations.
3 The Offshore Robotics for Certification of Assets (ORCA) Hub seeks to develop robotics and artificial intelligence (AI) technologies for extreme and unpredictable environments. Recently, French oil major Total launched Argos (Autonomous Robot for Gas and Oil Sites) while Chevron is developing a similar technology. As stressed by Rebecca Allison, asset integrity solution centre manager at the Oil & Gas Technology Centre in Aberdeen, "the application for robotics in the [oil and gas] industry is almost limitless, and we have only just scratched the surface." See, "Rise of the Robot in Offshore Operations – Oil and Gas News," *Oil and Gas People*, January 15, 2008, https://www.oilandgaspeople.com/news/15886/rise-of-the-robot-in-offshore-operations/

deep and ultra-deep waters[4] and in areas with extreme climate or topographical conditions, like the Arctic.

The Arctic is estimated to host 13 per cent of the world's undiscovered oil and 30 per cent of the world's undiscovered natural gas.[5] Exploratory operations first began in Canada's Arctic region in 1960, with drilling following in Alaska, but the harsh polar conditions hindered further activities.[6] Lately, interest in the Arctic has resumed. A warming climate in the Arctic region has caused a significant ice melt in the area, making natural resources accessible and potentially creating new shipping routes for the surrounding countries. Also, unlike Antarctica, where there is an international, treaty-based moratorium on extractive industries until (at least) 2041, no international moratorium exists for petroleum operations in the Arctic.[7] The above factors have spurred increasing interest in the exploration of the Arctic's natural wealth. This is led by host states, as they typically hold sovereignty or sovereign rights over the oil and gas resources situated in their jurisdiction, even though their constitutions might refer to the common good, use or even ownership of resources by or for their own people/public.

The oil and gas upstream sector is fairly risky and costly. This is why most host nations delegate their powers to private investors (energy companies) who are willing to risk their capital in this endeavour. However, in order to do so, states need to issue regulations and grant permits (contracts).[8] These allow companies to

4 E.g. 3,000 metres from the water surface (as in the Cheyenne Gas Field in the Gulf of Mexico) while it is estimated that operations may soon be conducted to a depth of 12,000 metres. See, Tim Schröder, "Marine Resources – Opportunities and Risks," *World Ocean Review* 3 (2014): 17.

5 Donald L. Gautier, et al., "Assessment of Undiscovered Oil and Gas in the Arctic," *Science* 324, no. 5931 (2009): 1175–1179; Kenneth J. Bird, et al., "Circum-Arctic Resource Appraisal: Estimates of Undiscovered Oil and Gas North of the Arctic Circle," *US Geological Survey (USGS)*, 2008, https://doi.org/10.3133/fs20083049; Jacqulyn Coston, "What Lies Beneath: The CLCS and the Race to Lay Claim Over the Arctic Seabed," *Environmental and Energy Law and Policy Journal* 3, no. 1 (2008): 149–175, 152. However, these figures are not absolute. According to a US Geological Survey (USGA) conducted in 2008, the Arctic could contain about 22 per cent of the world's undiscovered oil and natural gas. Christopher Fettweis, "No Blood for Oil: Why Resource Wars are Obsolete," in *Energy Security Challenges for the 21st Century? A Reference Handbook*, eds Gal Luft and Anne Korin (Santa Barbara CA: Praeger Security International, 2009) 66.

6 Brian Beary, "Race for the Arctic: Who Owns the Region's Undiscovered Oil and Gas?" *CQ Global Researcher* 2, no. 8 (2008): 213, 230.

7 Protocol on Environmental Protection to the Antarctic Treaty, 1991, designates Antarctica as a "natural reserve, devoted to peace and science." States may introduce moratoria or prohibitions at national level. See, e.g., Dan Healing, "Canada, U.S. Announce Ban on Offshore Oil, Gas Licenses in Arctic," *The Star*, December 20, 2016, https://www.thestar.com/news/canada/2016/12/20/canada-us-announce-ban-on-offshore-oil-gas-licenses-in-arctic.html; and Harry Cockburn, "Norway Refuses to Drill for Billions of Barrels of Oil in Arctic, Leaving 'Whole Industry Surprised and Disappointed,'" *The Independent*, April 9, 2019, https://www.independent.co.uk/environment/norway-oil-drilling-arctic-ban-labor-party-unions-a8861171.html

8 Some states issue leases or concessions and others grant production sharing agreements or service contracts to their investors. However, for practical reasons, all permits are hereby referred to as "contracts" or "host government contracts."

conduct oil and gas exploration and production in the host country, and stipulate the conditions (legal, tax, environmental, etc.) under which operations will be performed. This practice is quite standardised all over the world, although different states tend to adopt different types of contracts with different provisions and conditions. However, what is less certain is how the public participates in negotiations and procedures before and after the awarding of host government contracts to oil and gas companies.

This chapter will analyse how certain Arctic states engage with public participation in the negotiation and implementation of host government contracts within the oil and gas industry. However, certain limitations must be set herein. First, the definition of public participation is fairly broad. For the purposes of this chapter, we will not refer to any specific region, location or community of the examined countries, nor address the rights of aboriginal people which are considered elsewhere in this volume.[9] Rather, we will provide an overview of public participation in general. Second, we will not analyse in detail the special conditions and challenges of operations in the Arctic.

Public participation in host state contracts in the Arctic

This section will analyse public participation in host state contracts in two Arctic countries, namely Norway and Canada. Both countries possess a developed petroleum regime and have expressed active interest in exploring the resources of the Arctic; they also have extensive legal provisions regarding public participation.

In this context, the chapter will analyse: the two countries' petroleum regimes; the impact of oil and gas contracts on society and local communities; and the role of the public in those contracts. Collectively, the above will determine whether public participation in the Arctic is effective or whether any changes should be effected in the examined regimes.

Host government contracts: types and features

Norway

To a large extent, the petroleum industry sustains Norway's economy. The country is among the world's largest oil and gas exporters.[10] In Norway, hydrocarbons belong to the State, and their utilisation is managed and controlled by the government with a view to promoting public interest and benefiting the Norwegian society as a whole.

The exploration and exploitation of hydrocarbons in Norway is governed by a series of laws and regulations. The Petroleum Act no. 72 of 1996 is the core of this regime, together with the supplementary Petroleum Regulation no. 653 of

---

9 See, Wilson; Johnstone; Buhmann; and Bankes, this volume.
10 Daniel Workman, "Crude Oil Exports by Country," World's Top Exports, October 7, 2019, www.worldstopexports.com/worlds-top-oil-exports-country/

1997.[11] They stipulate the legal status of hydrocarbons in Norway's Continental Shelf, the conditions for petroleum exploration and cessation of petroleum activities, as well as issues of health and safety, and environmental protection. Further rules are found in various regulations and EU Directives.[12]

As of 1965, all petroleum activities in Norway are offshore.[13] The Petroleum Act provides that the Norwegian State has the proprietary right to subsea petroleum deposits and the exclusive right to resource management.[14] In practice the State grants exploratory rights to oil and gas companies pursuant to a production licence.[15] The licence is the legal instrument which allows its holder to search for hydrocarbons in the Norwegian Continental Shelf and obtain ownership of resources upon extraction. Nevertheless, a non-exclusive exploration licence can be granted for the conduct of certain exploration activities, such as seismic surveys.[16]

The cycle of petroleum operations goes as follows: upon parliamentary approval, the government announces the new areas of the continental shelf where activities are planned to be conducted to the extent it obtained a positive outcome of the relevant impact assessment. That is known as the opening process.[17] Companies submit their applications through a bidding round and the successful ones receive a licence.[18] The first stage of petroleum operations is exploration.[19] During that time, hydrocarbons are searched for, located, and proved. If a commercial discovery is made, the stage of production follows after the approval of a development plan.[20] A production licence typically lasts for an initial period of up to ten years but can be extended for up to 30 or 50 years.[21] When operations are completed, the area is relinquished and installations may be removed with the process of decommissioning.[22]

11 Norway, Act no. 72 of November 29, 1996 relating to petroleum activities, last amended by Norway, Act no. 65, of June 19, 2015 (Petroleum Act 1996); Norway, Regulations to Act relating to petroleum activities, no. 653 of June 27, 1997 (Petroleum Regulations 1997).
12 E.g., Petroleum Regulations 1997. Although not a member of the European Union, Norway is part of the single market and applies European rules (e.g., directives regarding environmental protection).
13 Attempts at onshore exploration were made in the past but without result due to geological reasons. Eventually, the Norwegian continental shelf was opened to exploration in 1965 and four years later revealed large, commercial discoveries of offshore hydrocarbons. See, Norway, Ministry of Petroleum and Energy, "Norway's History in 5 Minutes," October 9, 2013, https://www.regjeringen.no/en/topics/energy/oil-and-gas/norways-oil-history-in-5-minutes/id440538/
14 Petroleum Act 1996, chapter 1–1.
15 Ibid., chapter 3–3.
16 Ibid., chapter 2–1.
17 Ibid., chapter 2–1. See also: https://www.npd.no/en/facts/news/general-news/2012/Opening-process-for-the-Barents-Sea–Impact-assessment-submitted-for-consultation/, accessed 17 April 2019.
18 See Petroleum Regulations 1997.
19 Petroleum Act 1996, chapter 2.
20 Ibid., chapter 4.
21 Ibid., chapters 3–9.
22 Ibid., chapter 5.

Canada

Canada is also one of the world's largest producers of oil and gas.[23] But unlike Norway, Canada's resources are located both onshore and offshore and include conventional (crude oil, natural gas) and unconventional tight formations (oil sands, shale oil).[24] Canada possesses a developed petroleum regime, combining the concessionary and the lease system. But since Canada is a federal state, its petroleum regime is subject to federal, territorial, and provincial bodies and laws.[25] The most important laws for the exploration of the Canadian Arctic in Nunavut and offshore are the Canada Petroleum Resources Act[26] and the Canada Oil and Gas Operations Act,[27] whereas Yukon and Northwest Territories have their own legislation.[28]

In Canada, ownership of natural resources is shared among: the Crown, the province, individuals, and aboriginal groups.[29] The Crown owns the vast majority of oil and gas located in federal or provincial areas.[30] However, in contrast to other jurisdictions, Canada also recognises private ownership of

---

23 U.S. Energy Information Administration – EIA – Independent Statistics and Analysis, "What Countries Are the Top Producers and Consumers of Oil?" April 22, 2019, https://www.eia.gov/tools/faqs/faq.php?id=709&t=6; Indexmundi, "Country Comparison > Natural gas – exports > TOP 10," January 1, 2018, https://www.indexmundi.com/g/r.aspx?t=10&v=138&l=en

24 The two main areas of production in Canada are the Western Canada Sedimentary Basin and the Eastern Canada Offshore Basins. See, National Energy Board, "Canada Energy Regulator," August 30, 2019. https://www.neb-one.gc.ca/index-eng.html

25 Federal regulatory bodies include: the National Energy Board, the Canadian Environmental Assessment Agency, the Department of Fisheries and Oceans. Each territory and province has its own bodies (e.g., the Alberta Department of Energy). The Arctic part of Canada hosts both onshore and offshore natural resources. The onshore ones are regulated by territorial governments, whereas the offshore are regulated federally by the National Energy Board.

26 Canada, Petroleum Resources Act, RSC 1985, c. 36 (2nd Supp.) (stipulating Crown ownership of natural resources).

27 Canada, Oil and Gas Operations Act, RSC 1985, c. O-7 (establishing the regulatory role of the Crown with regards to exploration and development of oil and gas). Other relevant federal laws include: The Constitution Act, 1982, Schedule B to the Canada Act 1982 (UK), 1982, c. 11; National Energy Board Act, RSC 1985, c. N-7; the Energy Safety and Security Act, SC 2015, c. 4; and the Investment Canada Act. RSC 1985, c. 28 (1st Supp.). Provincial laws include: Alberta Petroleum and Natural Gas Tenure Regulation, Alberta, Regulation 263/1997; and the Oil and Gas Conservation Act, RSA 2000, c. O-6.

28 Government of Yukon, "Legislation," accessed October 11, 2019, www.gov.yk.ca/legislation/legislation/page_o.html; Government of the Northwest Territories, "Oil & Gas," Tourism and Investment Industry, accessed October 11, 2019, https://www.iti.gov.nt.ca/en/oil-gas

29 Lewis Manning, Bernadita Tamura-O'Connor, and Lawson Lundell, "Oil and Gas Regulation in Canada: Overview," *Practical Law*, August 1, 2019, https://uk.practicallaw.thomsonreuters.com/3-633-1728?transitionType=Default&contextData=(sc.Default)&firstPage=true&comp=pluk&bhcp=1

30 The federal or provincial governments hold the land in the name of the Queen.

land and its resources.[31] Depending on the area in question, exploratory rights are granted either with a freehold lease or with a Crown licence and relevant payment of fees (rental or royalties).[32] In addition, land compensation agreements are equally important for onshore projects due to surface owners' rights, private ownership and/or aboriginal rights.[33]

The Crown retains ownership of resources and transfers only exploratory and production rights to oil and gas companies by virtue of exploration and production licences.[34] The licences are granted by a public bidding process. The exploration licence confers the right to search for, drill, and test for resources, whereas the production licence allows its holder to develop any commercial discoveries. The duration of a licence is typically nine years for exploration and 25 years for production.[35] Once operations are completed, all installations must be safely decommissioned.[36]

Public involvement in host government contracts

To what extent and in what ways is the public involved in host government contracts for the exploration of oil and gas in the Arctic? Given the number of Arctic states and their different regulatory systems, should the same answer be expected for two different countries, like Norway and Canada? A comparative analysis of these two case studies will provide some initial, but hopefully useful, information about the Arctic region.

Norway

Norway's petroleum regime is highly discretionary. The State announces the licensing rounds; considers applications; awards permits; decides on the formation of licensees' groups; and approves all stages of operations. Resource management is executed by the Norwegian Government in accordance with the provisions of Petroleum Act,[37] and decisions are made by the governmental authorities or by Storting (the Norwegian Parliament).[38] But since the law provides that resource management must promote Norwegian society, the public is involved across all stages of operations.

---

31 Constitution Act 1982, section 35. See also, Canada, Indian Act, RSC 1985, c. I-5. For example, in Alberta, 10 per cent of the oil and gas in situ is privately owned.
32 As this chapter is concerned with host state contracts, only Crown licences will be discussed.
33 See Bankes, this volume.
34 Parts III and IV of Canada Petroleum Resources Act.
35 Petroleum Resources Act 1985, sections 26(2) and 41(1).
36 See Canada, Oil and Gas Drilling and Production Regulations, SOR/2009-315.
37 See Petroleum Act 1996, section 1-2 (English translation): "resource management is executed by the King in accordance with the provisions of this Act and decisions made by the Storting (Parliament)."
38 Ibid., chapter 1-2. In practice, only the most important decisions are brought before the Parliament; otherwise they are taken by the executive or its subordinate Ministry of Petroleum and Energy.

Government contracts and public participation 251

As part of the opening process, the Ministry of Energy must perform an impact assessment to evaluate all possible impacts of operations on Norway's economy, society, and natural environment.[39] A three-month period is announced for public consultation, ensuring that the general public expresses its views or concerns.[40]

Similar, before the awarding of new production licences, the government opens a six-week period for public consultation.[41] All background documents and scientific reports are made available for public comments. Based on the outcome, the Ministry may announce additional assessment on certain aspects. These will be also submitted for consultation for two weeks.[42]

Before approval of the development plan, the licensee must prepare an impact assessment. This will also be submitted to public consultation for six weeks.[43] Likewise, the licensee must prepare an impact assessment for its plan for installation and operation of facilities not covered by the development plan (e.g., pipelines), as well as for its disposal plan.[44] These are also subject to public consultation.

The above might primarily suggest that Norway offers a significant level of public involvement in its host government contracts. That could be based on the extent of people's participation and the number of stages of petroleum operations which require public consultation. Yet, the same might not be argued about the actual effectiveness of public involvement. Although the current system of public consultation might be suitable for operations in previously explored areas, shallow waters, or areas with low environmental risks, it may not be adequate for operations in the Arctic parts of Norway. The sensitive environment and biodiversity of the Arctic and the presence of local populations whose survival and livelihood depend on the area might require a more effective public participation than mere consultation. For example, it may require the taking into consideration submissions from the public or even the possibility of a "veto" in certain circumstances.[45]

The issue was raised recently with regards to licences in the Barents Sea. The Barents Sea reportedly hosts 65 per cent of the undiscovered hydrocarbons of the Norwegian Continental Shelf.[46] Exploration in those waters began in 1980.[47] So far, 130 wildcat and appraisal wells have been drilled, while recently nine

---

39 Petroleum Act 1996, chapter 3–1; Petroleum Regulations 1997, chapter 2a.
40 Petroleum Regulations 1997, Section 6.
41 Petroleum Regulations 1997, section 6c.
42 Ibid.
43 Petroleum Regulations 1997, section 22.
44 Ibid., chapters 5 and 6.
45 See Wilson; and Johnstone, this volume.
46 Troy Bouffard, "Managing the Barents Sea: Comparing Norwegian & Russian Offshore Oil-Spill Prevention Policies," *Arctic Yearbook* (2017): 280–311.
47 Stig-Morten Knutsen, Jan Harald Augustson, and Pal Haremo, "Exploring the Norwegian Part of the Barents Sea: Norsk Hydro's Lessons from Nearly 20 Years of Experience," *Norwegian Petroleum Society Special Publications* 9 (2000): 99–112; R. M. Larsen, T. Fjæran, and O. Skarpnes, "Hydrocarbon Potential of the Norwegian Barents Sea Based on Recent Well Results," *Norwegian Petroleum Society Special Publications* 2 (1993): 321–333.

production licences were offered.[48] Still, petroleum operations in this area are subject to heated debate and public concern. Environmental groups (Greenpeace Nordic and Natur og Ungdom) protested against those activities, arguing that the Norwegian government violated section 112 of the Norwegian Constitution which guarantees the right to a safe and healthy environment, and also contravenes the 2015 Paris Agreement on Climate Change.[49] More specifically, the activists argued that the Arctic licences of 2016 were granted without sufficient impact assessments or adequate justification.

The environmental groups sued the government but the district court of Oslo dismissed the case in early 2018.[50] The court acknowledged the constitutional right to a healthy environment but found that the government did not violate the relevant article (112) of the Norwegian Constitution because it had fulfilled all necessary duties before announcing the licensing round for the Barents Sea.[51] In addition, it was held that the Norwegian Government cannot be held responsible for carbon dioxide emissions caused by hydrocarbons which the state exports to other countries.[52] The plaintiffs appealed on the basis that "[t]he District Court erred in interpreting Article 112 [of the Norwegian Constitution] in such a way that it limits the duty of the Norwegian government to guarantee the right to a healthy environment."[53] In particular, they argued that the court interpreted

48 Espen Erlingsen, "Barents Sea: Norway's New Oil Province," *Rystad Energy*, August 31, 2016, https://www.rystadenergy.com/newsevents/news/press-releases/barents-sea; "Licensing Position and Recent Rounds," Norwegian Petroleum, accessed October 13, 2019, https://www.norskpetroleum.no/en/exploration/licensing-position-for-the-norwegian-continental-shelf/

49 Norway. Constitution of the Kingdom of Norway, May 17, 1814, as amended in 2018, section 112; Paris Agreement, 2015. See also, "Environmentalists Appeal Ruling over Norway's Arctic Oil Licences," *News24*, February 6, 2018, https://www.news24.com/Green/News/environmentalists-appeal-ruling-over-norways-arctic-oil-licences-20180205; and Greenpeace, "The Climate Lawsuit against the Norwegian government, savethearctic.org accessed October 11, 2019, https://www.savethearctic.org/en/peoplevsarcticoil/background-documents

50 "The People versus Arctic Oil Litigation," *Environmental Justice Atlas*, March 15, 2018, https://ejatlas.org/conflict/the-people-versus-arctic-oil; "Greenpeace Norway v. Government of Norway," Grantham Research Institute on Climate Change and the Environment, accessed October 13, 2019, www.lse.ac.uk/GranthamInstitute/litigation/greenpeace-norway-v-government-of-norway

51 In particular, it was stressed that the *Storting* (the Norwegian parliament), had broadly agreed to open the Barents Sea Southeast to licensing and had considered proposals to halt that licensing or review whether it was inappropriate in light of the goals of the Paris Agreement on climate change. Hence, the government's duty to take measures had been fulfilled. However, the same Norwegian parliament recently withdrew support for exploration activities off the Lofoten Islands in the Arctic. See, Aris Folley, "Norway Refuses to Drill for Billions of Barrels of Oil in Arctic Region," *The Hill*, April 9, 2019, https://thehill.com/policy/energy-environment/438043-norway-refuses-to-drill-for-billions-of-barrels-of-oil-in-arctic

52 See, "The People versus Arctic Oil Litigation," and "Greenpeace Norway v. Government of Norway."

53 "Greenpeace Norway v. Government of Norway."

article 112 too restrictively in deciding that Norway is only responsible for the greenhouse gas emissions released within its territory. The appellate court will determine the final outcome of the case. Irrespective of the court's judgment, the case indicates that operations in the Arctic raise public concern and are likely to keep doing so in the future.[54]

In 2005, the Parliamentary Standing Committee of Justice (*Justiskomiteen*), which is responsible for judicial issues, declared that the interests of Sami (who possess historical fishing rights in the Barents Sea) are not sufficiently protected under the current laws of Norway.[55] The Committee proposed that the government should carry out an independent study on the matter. Although the issue did not specifically arise in the context of Norway's petroleum operations in the Arctic, any future policy changes for the promotion of Sami interests in the Barents Sea should also include participation of locals in the awarding of oil and gas contracts.

The above demonstrates that, although public involvement is required in Norway's petroleum system, tensions may arise over petroleum projects in the Arctic parts of the country. The law provides only for public consultation at various stages of operations, excluding other forms of public involvement, like advisory groups or committees. Also, participation is only indirect, via the route of environmental or social assessments, excluding the direct influence of decisions by the public under a veto right. Hence, even when the government receives public comments, it is not obliged to comply with them. Together, these factors raise serious concerns as to whether people in the Arctic actually have a voice and whether central authorities take local and wider public opinion into account. It remains to be seen whether the Norwegian Government will adapt its policies to respond to these issues.

Canada

Although Canada's licences are granted by the Crown, some degree of public involvement is also mandated. An analysis of the Canadian system brings to light some similarities and also some important differences from Norway. These concern both the means and the extent of public participation.

As in Norway, public participation in Canada is performed indirectly, via consultation during the preparation of environmental or social reports by the competent bodies. Depending on the area of operations (federal, provincial) and the nature of activities, an Environmental Impact Assessment (EIA) may need to be prepared.[56] When an EIA is required, the authority responsible for its preparation

---

54 See also Cockburn, "Norway Refuses to Drill for Billions of Barrels of Oil in Arctic" (on the withdrawal of support by Norway's opposition Labour party for explorative drilling off the Lofoten islands in the Arctic).
55 Øyvind Ravna and Kristoffer Svendsen, "Securing the Coastal Sami Culture and Livelihood," in *Governance of Arctic Offshore Oil and Gas*, eds Cecile Pelaudeix and Ellen Margrethe Basse (Abingdon: Routledge, 2017), 187.
56 See, e.g., Canada, Canadian Environmental Assessment Act, 2012, SC 2012, c. 19; and Alberta, Environmental Protection and Enhancement Act, RSA 2000, c. E-12, Part 17; Canada, the Inuvialuit Final Agreement, Bill C-49, June 21, 1984.

must ensure that the public is provided with the opportunity to participate in the process.[57] Upon completion, the report is submitted to the Minister of Environment for final decisions on the project.[58]

However, although public consultation is required for specific projects and areas, there is no general requirement for an EIA (and consequently for public participation) to be performed before the call for bids and the issuance of oil and gas licences under Canada's Petroleum Resources Act. Hence, in contrast to Norway, public participation in Canada applies only to designated projects and after the award thereof.[59] This raises serious concerns about the efficacy of public participation in the country. As criticised by Ecojustice Canada, "[t]his gap places Canada out of step with international best practices that every other Comparator Jurisdiction [Norway, Greenland and the USA] has adopted."[60] Other organisations have called on the Canadian government to ban all new offshore drilling in the Arctic and reject any deep-water drilling plans made without prior consultation with the local population.[61] Serious questions have also previously arisen as to when the Crown discharges its duty to consult with the public. In the recent cases of *Chippewas of the Thames*[62] and *Clyde River*,[63] the Supreme Court of Canada reached different conclusions on what constitutes an adequate

---

57 Canadian Environmental Assessment Act, 2012, section 24.
58 Ibid., section 25.
59 Ibid., sections 13 et seq.
60 Ecojustice Canada submission, April 11, 2016, cited in Rowland J. Harrison, "Review of the Canada Petroleum Resources Act Submitted by the Minister's Special Representative" (Government of Canada, May 30, 2016), https://www.rcaanc-cirnac.gc.ca/eng/1468946906852/1538587949255
61 See, "Protecting Life in the Arctic – U.S.," The Pew Charitable Trusts, accessed October 11, 2019, https://www.pewtrusts.org/en/projects/protecting-life-in-the-arctic
62 *Chippewas of the Thames First Nation v. Enbridge Pipelines Inc*, 2017 SCC 41 (Canada) (in which the National Energy Board (NEB) issued notice to Indigenous groups, including the Chippewas of the Thames First Nation (Chippewas), informing them of the project, the NEB's role, and the NEB's upcoming hearing process. The Chippewas were granted funding to participate in the process, and they filed evidence and delivered oral arguments delineating their concerns that the project would increase the risk of pipeline ruptures and spills, which could adversely impact their use of the land. The NEB approved the project, and was satisfied that potentially affected Indigenous groups had received adequate information and had the opportunity to share their views. The Chippewas appealed but the Court found that the NEB's duty to consult was sufficiently met).
63 *Clyde River (Hamlet). Petroleum Geo-Services Inc*. [2017] 1 SCR 1069, 2017 SCC 40 (Canada) (in which the proponents applied to the NEB to conduct offshore seismic testing for oil and gas in Nunavut. The proposed testing could negatively affect the treaty rights of the Inuit of Clyde River, who opposed the seismic testing, alleging that the duty to consult had not been fulfilled in relation to it. The NEB granted the requested authorisation. It concluded that the proponents made sufficient efforts to consult with Aboriginal groups and that Aboriginal groups had an adequate opportunity to participate in the NEB's process. Clyde River applied for judicial review of the NEB's decision. The Federal Court of Appeal found that while the duty to consult had been triggered, the Crown was entitled to rely on the NEB to undertake such consultation, and the Crown's duty to consult had been satisfied in this case by the NEB's process. However, the Court of Appeal quashed the NEB's authorisation).

consultation.[64] Hence, although it seems that governments bear a duty to consult with the public in oil and gas contracts, there are no fixed criteria to meet this requirement, nor a duty to implement any received public comments.[65]

Hence, although public participation is recognised in Canada, its effectiveness is questionable. The public can be involved in petroleum projects only indirectly, namely when an EIA must be prepared and when operations are planned in certain areas, but not in general and certainly not before the start of the licensing process. Also, even when public consultation takes place, its output is not binding upon public authorities.

Inefficacies in current Arctic regimes

The analysis of host government contracts of Norway and Canada within the oil and gas sector demonstrates two main points. First, the Arctic states' policy on public involvement in upstream activities appears to be severely fragmented.[66] It seems that there is not a unified and coordinated strategy; rather each country is more likely to follow its own path. This creates a great divergence among legal systems and hinders a balanced consideration of public interests across all regions of the Arctic. Second, even countries with long experience in petroleum exploration and a well-developed petroleum regime, like Norway and Canada, might fail to involve the public effectively in their host government contracts in the Arctic. This concern is even greater for other Arctic countries with more limited petroleum experience.

Of course, it can be argued that domestic laws are not the only means for the promotion of public interest in the Arctic. The consideration of the public is provided in international law instruments too, such as the Aarhus Convention[67] and the United Nations Declaration on the Rights of Indigenous Peoples (UNDRIP).[68] The

---

64 See also Bankes, this volume.
65 See, *Gitxaala Nation v. Canada*, 2016 FCA 187 (Canada); and Cecile Pelaudeix, "Governance of Offshore Hydrocarbon Activities in the Arctic and Energy Policies: A Comparative Approach between Norway, Canada and Greenland/Denmark," in *Governance of Arctic Offshore Oil and Gas*, eds Cécile Pelaudeix and Ellen Margrethe Basse (Abingdon: Routledge, 2017), 114. See also, David V. Wright, "Tsleil-Waututh Nation v. Canada: A Case of Easier Said than Done," ablawg.ca, September 11, 2018, https://ablawg.ca/2018/09/11/tsleil-waututh-nation-v-canada-a-case-of-easier-said-than-done
66 See Timo Koivurova and Kamrul Hossain, "Offshore Hydrocarbon: Current Policy Context in the Marine Arctic," *Arctic Transform*, September 4, 2008, https://www.ecologic.eu/sites/files/publication/2015/offshore_hydrocarbon_background_paper.pdf (on the issue of fragmentation in the general governance of offshore operations in the Arctic). See also, Cécile Pelaudeix, "Governance of Arctic Offshore Oil and Gas Activities: Multilevel Governance – Legal Pluralism at Stake," *Arctic Yearbook*, 2015, https://arcticyearbook.com/arctic-yearbook/2015 (arguing that there is no consistent policy or practice on public participation amongst the examined Arctic states).
67 Convention on Access to Information, Public Participation in Decision-Making and Access to Justice in Environmental Matters 1998 [Aarhus Convention].
68 UN General Assembly, Declaration on the Rights of Indigenous Peoples, UNGA Res. 61/295, September 13, 2007 (UNDRIP).

former guarantees public access to environmental information, participation through the process of consultation, and access to justice in environmental issues. The latter provides a universal framework of minimum standards for the rights of indigenous people, and provides that the state must obtain the free, prior, and informed consent of indigenous people before adopting and implementing legislative and administrative measures that may affect them. However, of the two instruments mentioned, only the former is a binding treaty – the latter instead is in the form of a UN General Assembly Declaration.[69] In the Arctic, the Nordic states have all adopted the Aarhus Convention, though Denmark has a territorial exemption for Greenland. Russia, Canada and the US are not parties. Meanwhile, they have all endorsed UNDRIP but with a high degree of caution regarding its legal status, and in Canada's case with significant reservations when it comes to the implementation of free, prior, and informed consent (FPIC).[70] A state that is not party to the Aarhus Convention would only be obliged to consult with the public if this duty was part of customary law. The International Court of Justice has refused to pronounce on this but the Inter-American Court of Human Rights has been more forthright, recognising a duty to consult at least in respect of indigenous and tribal communities.[71] This could support the view that the duty to consult indigenous peoples is part of customary law (or a general principle), though not necessarily a qualification for FPIC under UNDRIP. Still, the position of Arctic states regarding public consultation is fragmented at the level of both domestic and international law.

69 See also Wilson; and Buhmann, this volume. See also, Stephen M. Schwebel, "The Effect of Resolutions of the U.N. General Assembly on Customary International Law," *Proceedings of the ASIL Annual Meeting* 73 (1979): 301–309, https://doi.org/10.1017/s0272503700064934; and Marko Divac Öberg, "The Legal Effects of Resolutions of the UN Security Council and General Assembly in the Jurisprudence of the ICJ," *European Journal of International Law* 16, no. 5 (January 2005): 879–906, https://doi.org/10.1093/ejil/chi151 (for a more general discussion on UN instruments).
70 However, the Canadian government has not adopted the philosophy of Article 32 which refers to free, prior and informed consent (FPIC). See also, Canada, Bill C-262 (an Act to ensure that the laws of Canada are in harmony with the United Nations Declaration on the Rights of Indigenous Peoples). May 30, 2018, www.parl.ca/DocumentViewer/en/42-1/bill/C-262/third-reading (which at the time of writing is in the Senate for third reading but has not yet passed into law).
71 See, *Case concerning Pulp Mills on the River Uruguay (Argentina v. Uruguay)* 2010, International Court of Justice, *ICJ Reports* 2010: 14; and *Sarayaku, Kichwa Indigenous People of v. Ecuador (Merits and Reparations)* 2012, Inter-American Court of Human Rights, Petition 12465. See also, *Centre for Minority Rights Development (Kenya) and Minority Rights Group International on Behalf of Endorois Welfare Council v. Kenya* 2009, African Commission on Human and Peoples Rights, Communication 276/2003, AHRLR 75 (in which the African Commission followed the *Sarayaku* judgment, indicating that this may be a global standard). See also, Rachael Lorna Johnstone, *Offshore Oil and Gas Development in the Arctic under International Law: Risk and Responsibility* (Leiden: Brill, 2015), 88–89, 94–97 and 167.

Without a satisfactory threshold of public participation in at least one Arctic state, it is difficult for other Arctic countries to develop effective policies. Perhaps, then, they should turn to and learn from other jurisdictions.

Critical challenges for a meaningful public participation

The main challenge concerning public participation is its intended objective and outcome before you can assess its results. Should this public participation involve a meaningful consultation or a mere formality? Unfortunately, public consultation might be seen as a "compliance tool box" to be prepared and performed in order to proceed with the project.

For example, a public consultation might occur prior to the opening of a new area or bidding round such as in Brazil.[72] But it should also occur later on during the environmental and social impact assessments, as these should be performed prior to conduct of the relevant activities of the project, such as in the UK.[73] So arguably it would be good practice to allow public participation in different parts of the project. However, it might not be a meaningful process, as the local communities or even wider public might not be well informed about the positive and negative aspects of the project before making an informed decision.

Furthermore, in some cases, public participation might not require any feedback but rather a simple procedure to inform the public on what is going on. Questions might arise as to where the public might get access to information and who prepared this information, in order to understand if all different stakeholders could present their case or not. At least Norway and Canada have a strong presence of NGOs, a well informed population with high standards of academic education, and freedom of press, which might not exist in other countries (especially in developing nations).

Therefore, the public consultation is more likely to exist at some point before and/or during the execution of an oil and gas project. However, the definition of "public" might vary and the main challenge for the public perspective, regardless of its definition, is that people's concerns or views might be a mere formality without any real power or weight, unlike a right of veto. In other words, a number of host nations might welcome public participation in abstract terms but not actually *require* any public involvement in the negotiation of petroleum contracts. Moreover, even if the people are involved (as in Norway), the host government could ultimately ignore or reject their concerns and still move forward with the oil and gas development.

---

72 Ted Rhodes, "New Brazilian Oil & Gas Concession – Public Consultation – Energy and Natural Resources – Brazil," *Mondaq*, March 23, 2011, www.mondaq.com/brazil/x/126978/Oil_Gas_Electricity/New Brazilian_Oil_Gas_Concession_Public_Consultation
73 Ibid.

This is why public participation is often considered more generally as a part of the social licence to operate, which is commonly a good practice to achieve rather than a legal and compulsory obligation.

But any failure to obtain the social licence might present a real concern for oil and gas companies (especially those operating onshore), as local communities could provide serious challenges for these companies' operations by not supporting such development, as happened with Shell in Nigeria.[74]

In this sense, it is possible to argue that local communities and/or aboriginal people might have a stronger case for public participation due to their proximity to potential negative effects of an oil and gas development and/or due to historical rights, as both might be recognised under domestic legislation (e.g. in Australia[75] and Colombia[76]) and/or international legislation. However, a broader and more general public participation tends to be fairly limited and without a meaningful outcome.

In addition, a number of developing countries might prefer direct negotiations between the host government with the relevant investor. This might prevent a more transparent process and accountability on the part of the relevant host government. So other important tools to achieve an effective public participation might require the host country's legal system to allow free and open access to information as well as freedom of speech without fear of political persecution. If these basic elements are not present in the domestic jurisdiction, then it is much harder for the public to know what is going on, let alone to be actively involved.

Lessons to be learnt

The current laws of Norway and Canada provide for public involvement via certain avenues (public consultation in environmental reports and impact assessments) and in specific situations (certain projects, areas with indigenous people). However, we would argue that more could be done to make public involvement in host state contracts more effective. The lessons which can be drawn from the above analysis are summarised as follows.

First, information on oil and gas openings scheduled by the host government should be publicly available and accessible by convenient means (e.g., the internet, the gazette, the press) by large masses. This would secure transparency and increase the accountability of public authorities.

---

74 John Vidal, "Ogoni King: Shell Oil Is Killing My People," *Guardian*, December 3, 2016, https://www.theguardian.com/world/2016/dec/03/ogoni-king-shell-oil-is-killing-my-people

75 "Making Agreements on Aboriginal Land: Mining and Development," Central Land Council, accessed October 12, 2019, https://www.clc.org.au/index.php?/articles/info/mining-and-development

76 Guillaume Fontaine, et al., "The Politics of Accountability: Indigenous Participation in Colombian and Ecuadorian Oil and Gas Policies," *Colombia Internacional* 86 (2016): 17–50, https://doi.org/10.7440/colombiaint86.2016.01

Second, the right to information should be accompanied by the right of people to express their opinion without fear of retaliation. This is not the case in Norway or Canada, but it could be a real concern in certain parts of the world with no such established principle of freedom of speech.[77]

Third, the public should be involved in all stages of upstream operations – from the announcement of governmental decisions to award certain areas of exploration and the negotiation of host contracts with the potential investors, to the completion of projects and relinquishment of the explored area. This should not mean that decisions will be reached by the public, but rather that public opinion shall be requested and considered by the competent authorities in their decision-making.

Fourth, public consultation is one but not the only, nor necessarily the most effective method of public participation. Public participation can be secured in various other ways, such as via advisory groups or jury committees. The form of participation would rest on the country's legal system and institutions, as well as on the degree of collaboration which the government wishes to build with its people.

Fifth, the term "public" is much broader than indicated in the above laws, and consists of individuals of every age, occupation, educational and socio-economic status, as well as private groups, non-governmental organisations, and academic institutions. In addition, domestic and international laws might have different meanings and/or implications of public, local communities, and/or indigenous/aboriginal people. The latter might have further protections and rights compared to those of the general public, but it is outside the scope of this chapter to analyse such distinctions.

Finally, an important decision should be made by each host nation to determine if, when, and how members of the public should be able to exercise some sort of consent or even veto power with regards to oil and gas exploration and petroleum activities. Such an example occurred during the US midterm elections in 2018 when the voters in Colorado were asked to decide on certain oil and gas permissions allowing drilling closer to residential and other vulnerable areas and whether or not this buffer zone should be expanded.[78] In any case, consideration of this complex topic should not mean that individuals can halt all operations arbitrarily and potentially harm the operating company, but rather that a balance be drawn between the interests of host governments, the petroleum industry, the people associated with the area of operations, and the wider public interest. It is acknowledged that each of the above stakeholder groups possesses different interests and has divergent expectations of the applicable laws and policies. For instance, oil and gas companies perceive public participation as a means to inform potentially affected communities and as a requirement of their social licence to operate;

---

77 However, see also Johnstone and Hansen, this volume, on concerns about informal or social retaliation (bullying) for expressing unpopular views in close-knit communities.
78 Jacy Marmaduke, "Colorado Election: Proposition 112 Failed. What's next for Oil and Gas Setbacks?" *Fort Collins Coloradoan*, November 7, 2018, https://eu.coloradoan.com/story/news/politics/elections/2018/11/06/colorado-election-proposition-112-fails-oil-gas-setbacks/1893643002/

governments use it to create the trust and confidence of their citizens; whereas locals consider it as a way to influence the authorities' decisions.[79] A government's role is to consider those divergent (if not conflicting) interests carefully and weight them equitably.

Conclusion

Public participation is both an asset and a challenge. To the extent that it secures a meaningful engagement between governmental authorities, local communities, and the wider public, it is an element of an effective petroleum regime. It promotes transparency, and increases the legitimacy of political decisions. However, when public involvement is not substantial or does not actually influence political decision-making, serious problems may arise.

In order to be effective, public participation should not be restricted or indirect, but: *broad* (during all stages of operations, from the start of negotiations until completion of the project); *diverse* (providing for public consultation, advisory groups, jury committees, allowing for the exercise of a veto right or vote in certain circumstances); and *inclusive* (considering as many stakeholders from the public as possible, such as local residents, indigenous people, private groups, non-governmental organisations, educational units).

Norway provides more avenues for public participation in comparison to Canada. However, both Norway and Canada could improve their systems, as allowing public participation and conducting meaningful consultation are quite different concepts. Nevertheless, public involvement in both countries appears to be way more advanced than in states with limited or no public participation whatsoever (e.g., those countries that lack transparency and accountability mechanisms).

This chapter has only analysed the legal systems of two Arctic countries. It has identified certain strengths and serious weaknesses in the examined regimes, and made suggestions for making public involvement in host government contracts more effective. Further research is required for the remaining Arctic states, and steps should be taken in the entire Arctic region, as public needs should be equally important across all parts of the Arctic. Perhaps the optimal suggestion would be that Arctic countries align their strategies and accommodate public involvement across all stages of petroleum operations and in all areas of the Arctic. This should be done in consideration of the host governments' interests and industry's needs. More importantly, public opinion should be able to influence political decisions when the operations in question are expected to have an impact on people's lives. It is only then that public participation will serve its true purpose, which is to promote the principles of a democratic society (e.g., transparency, accountability, pluralism) and to contribute to the host government's management of oil and gas activities.

---

79 See, Anna-Sofie Hurup Olsen and Anne Merrild Hansen, "Perceptions of Public Participation in Impact Assessment: A Study of Offshore Oil Exploration in Greenland," *Impact Assessment and Project Appraisal* 32 (2014): 72, 75 (for an empirical study).

References

Alberta. Oil and Gas Conservation Act, RSA 2000, c. O-6.
Alberta Petroleum and Natural Gas Tenure Regulation, Alberta Regulation 263/1997.
Beary, Brian. "Race for the Arctic: Who Owns the Region's Undiscovered Oil and Gas?" *CQ Global Researcher* 2, no. 8 (2008): 213.
Bird, Kenneth J., Ronald R. Charpentier, Donald L. Gautier, David W. Houseknecht, Timothy R. Klett, Janet K. Pitman, Thomas E. Moore, Christopher J. Schenk, Marilyn E. Tennyson, and Craig R. Wandrey. "Circum-Arctic Resource Appraisal: Estimates of Undiscovered Oil and Gas North of the Arctic Circle." *US Geological Survey (USGS)*, 2008. https://doi.org/10.3133/fs20083049
Bouffard, Troy. "Managing the Barents Sea: Comparing Norwegian & Russian Offshore Oil-Spill Prevention Policies." *Arctic Yearbook* (2017): 280–311.
Canada. Bill C-262. An Act to ensure that the laws of Canada are in harmony with the United Nations Declaration on the Rights of Indigenous Peoples. May 30, 2018. www.parl.ca/DocumentViewer/en/42-1/bill/C-262/third-reading
Canada. Canadian Environmental Assessment Act, 2012, SC 2012, c. 19.
Canada. *Chippewas of the Thames First Nation v. Enbridge Pipelines* Inc, 2017 SCC 41.
Canada. *Clyde River (Hamlet) v. Petroleum Geo-Services Inc.* [2017] 1 SCR 1069, 2017 SCC 40.
Canada. Constitution Act, 1982, Schedule B to the Canada Act 1982 (UK), 1982, c. 11.
Canada. Energy Safety and Security Act, SC 2015, c. 4.
Canada. Indian Act, 1985, RSC 1985, c. I-5.
Canada. Investment Canada Act. RSC 1985, c. 28 (1st Supp.).
Canada. National Energy Board Act, 1985, RSC 1985, c. N-7.
Canada. Oil and Gas Drilling and Production Regulations, SOR/2009–315.
Canada. Oil and Gas Operations Act, 1985, RSC 1985, c. O-7.
Canada. The Inuvialuit Final Agreement, Bill C-49, June 21, 1984.
Cockburn, Harry. "Norway Refuses to Drill for Billions of Barrels of Oil in Arctic, Leaving 'Whole Industry Surprised and Disappointed.'" *The Independent*, April 9, 2019. https://www.independent.co.uk/environment/norway-oil-drilling-arctic-ban-labor-party-unions-a8861171.html
Convention on Access to Information, Public Participation in Decision-Making and Access to Justice in Environmental Matters 1998. Adopted June 25, 1998, entered into force October 30, 2001. United Nations Treaty Series 2161, 447 (Aarhus Convention).
Coston, Jacqulyn. "What Lies Beneath: The CLCS and the Race to Lay Claim over the Arctic Seabed." *Environmental and Energy Law and Policy Journal* 3, no. 1 (2008): 149–157.
"Environmentalists Appeal Ruling over Norway's Arctic Oil Licences." *News24*, February 6, 2018. https://www.news24.com/Green/News/environmentalists-appeal-ruling-over-norways-arctic-oil-licences-20180205
Erlingsen, Espen. "Barents Sea: Norway's New Oil Province." Rystad Energy, August 31, 2016. https://www.rystadenergy.com/newsevents/news/press-releases/barents-sea
Fettweis, Cristopher. "No *Blood* for Oil: Why Resource Wars Are Obsolete." In *Energy Security Challenges for the 21st Century? A Reference Handbook*, edited by Gal Luft and Anne Korin, 66–77. Santa Barbara CA: Praeger Security International, 2009.
Folley, Aris. "Norway Refuses to Drill for Billions of Barrels of Oil in Arctic Region." *The Hill*, April 9, 2019. https://thehill.com/policy/energy-environment/438043-norway-refuses-to-drill-for-billion-of-barrels-of-oil-in-arctic

Fontaine, Guillaume, Esther Sánchez, Marco Córdova, and Susan Velasco. "The Politics of Accountability: Indigenous Participation in Colombian and Ecuadorian Oil and Gas Policies." *Colombia Internacional* 86 (2016): 17–50. https://doi.org/10.7440/colombiaint86.2016.01

Gautier, Donald, Kenneth Bird, Ronald Charpentier, Arthur Grantz, David Houseknecht, Timothy Klett, Thomas Moore, Janet Pitman, Christopher Schenk, John Schuenemeyer, Kai Sørensen, Marilyn Tennyson, Zenon Valin, and Craig Wandrey. "Assessment of Undiscovered Oil and Gas in the Arctic." *Science* 324, no. 5931 (2009): 1175–1179.

Canada. *Gitxaala Nation v. Canada*, 2016 FCA 187.

Government of the Northwest Territories. "Oil & Gas." *Tourism and Investment Industry*. Accessed October 11, 2019. https://www.iti.gov.nt.ca/en/oil-gas

Government of Yukon. "Legislation." Accessed October 11, 2019. www.gov.yk.ca/legislation/legislation/page_o.html

"Greenpeace Norway v. Government of Norway." Grantham Research Institute on Climate Change and the Environment. Accessed October 13, 2019. www.lse.ac.uk/GranthamInstitute/litigation/greenpeace-norway-v-government-of-norway

Harrison, Rowland J. *Review of the Canada Petroleum Resources Act Submitted by the Minister's Special Representative*. Government of Canada, May 30, 2016. https://www.rcaanc-cirnac.gc.ca/eng/1468946906852/1538587949255

Healing, Dan. "Canada, U.S. Announce Ban on Offshore Oil, Gas Licenses in Arctic." *The Star*, December 20, 2016. https://www.thestar.com/news/canada/2016/12/20/canada-us-announce-ban-on-offshore-oil-gas-licenses-in-arctic.html

Hubbert, M. King. *Nuclear Energy and the Fossil Fuels, Shell Development Company, Exploration and Production*. Houston TX: Shell Development Company, 1956. www.resilience.org/stories/2006-03-08/nuclear-energy-and-fossil-fuels

Indexmundi. "Country Comparison > Natural Gas – Exports > TOP 10," January 1, 2018. https://www.indexmundi.com/g/r.aspx?t=10&v=138&l=en

International Centre for Minority Rights Development (Kenya) and Minority Rights Group International on Behalf of Endorois Welfare Council v. Kenya, 2009. African Commission on Human and Peoples Rights, Communication 276/2003, AHRLR 75.

Johnstone, Rachael Lorna. *Offshore Oil and Gas Development in the Arctic under International Law: Risk and Responsibility*. Leiden: Brill, 2015.

Knutsen, Stig-Morten, Jan Harald Augustson, and Pal Haremo. "Exploring the Norwegian Part of the Barents Sea: Norsk Hydro's Lessons from Nearly 20 Years of Experience." *Norwegian Petroleum Society Special Publications* 9 (2000): 99–112.

Koivurova, Timo, and Kamrul Hossain. "Offshore Hydrocarbon: Current Policy Context in the Marine Arctic." *Arctic Transform*, September 4, 2008. https://www.ecologic.eu/sites/files/publication/2015/offshore_hydrocarbon_background_paper.pdf

Larsen, R.M., T. Fjæran, and O. Skarpnes. "Hydrocarbon Potential of the Norwegian Barents Sea Based on Recent Well Results." *Norwegian Petroleum Society Special Publications* 2 (1993): 321–333.

"Licensing Position and Recent Rounds." Norwegian Petroleum. Accessed October 13, 2019. https://www.norskpetroleum.no/en/exploration/licensing-position-for-the-norwegian-continental-shelf/

"Making Agreements on Aboriginal Land: Mining and Development." Central Land Council. Accessed October 12, 2019. https://www.clc.org.au/index.php?/articles/info/mining-and-development

Manning, Lewis, Bernadita Tamura-O'Connor, and Lawson Lundell. "Oil and Gas Regulation in Canada: Overview." *Practical Law*, August 1, 2019. https://uk.practicallaw.

thomsonreuters.com/3-633-1728?transitionType=Default&contextData=(sc.Default)&firstPage=true&comp=pluk&bhcp=1.

Marmaduke, Jacy. "Colorado Election: Proposition 112 Failed. What's next for Oil and Gas Setbacks?" *Fort Collins Coloradoan*, November 7, 2018. https://eu.coloradoan.com/story/news/politics/elections/2018/11/06/colorado-election-proposition-112-fails-oil-gas-setbacks/1893643002/

National Energy Board. "Canada Energy Regulator." August 30, 2019. https://www.neb-one.gc.ca/index-eng.html

Norway. Act no. 65, of June 19, 2015.

Norway. Act no. 72 of November 29, 1996, relating to petroleum activities.

Norway. Constitution of the Kingdom of Norway, May 17, 1814, as amended in 2018.

Norway, Ministry of Petroleum and Energy. "Norway's History in 5 Minutes." October 9, 2013. https://www.regjeringen.no/en/topics/energy/oil-and-gas/norways-oil-history-in-5-minutes/id440538/

Norway. Regulations no. 653 of June 27, 1997, Act relating to petroleum activities.

Öberg, Marko Divac. "The Legal Effects of Resolutions of the UN Security Council and General Assembly in the Jurisprudence of the ICJ." *European Journal of International Law* 16, no. 5 (2005): 879–906. https://doi.org/10.1093/ejil/chi151

Olsen, Anna-Sofie Hurup and Anne Merrild Hansen. "Perceptions of Public Participation in Impact Assessment: A Study of Offshore Oil Exploration in Greenland." *Impact Assessment and Project Appraisal* 32 (2014): 72–80.

Paris Agreement, 2015. United Nations Treaty Series, C.N.63.2016.TREATIES-XXVII.7.d, February 16, 2016.

Pelaudeix, Cécile. "Governance of Arctic Offshore Oil and Gas Activities: Multilevel Governance – Legal Pluralism at Stake." *Arctic Yearbook* (2015). https://arcticyearbook.com/arctic-yearbook/2015.

Pelaudeix, Cécile. "Governance of Offshore Hydrocarbon Activities in the Arctic and Energy Policies: A Comparative Approach between Norway, Canada and Greenland/Denmark." In *Governance of Arctic Offshore Oil and Gas*, edited by Cécile Pelaudeix and Ellen Margrethe Basse, 108–126. Abingdon: Routledge, 2017.

"Protecting Life in the Arctic – U.S." The Pew Charitable Trusts. Accessed October 11, 2019. https://www.pewtrusts.org/en/projects/protecting-life-in-the-arctic

"Protocol on Environmental Protection to the Antarctic Treaty 1991," *International Legal Materials* 30 (1991): 1455.

Pulp Mills on the River Uruguay, Case Concerning (Argentina v. Uruguay) 2010. International Court of Justice. *ICJ Reports 2010*: 14.

Ravna, Øyvind and Kristoffer Svendsen. "Securing the Coastal Sami Culture and Livelihood." In *Governance of Arctic Offshore Oil and Gas*, edited by Cécile Pelaudeix and Ellen Margrethe Basse, 186–202. Abingdon: Routledge, 2017.

Rhodes, Ron. *The Coming Oil Storm*. Eugene OR: Harvest House Publishers, 2010.

Rhodes, Ted. "New Brazilian Oil & Gas Concession – Public Consultation – Energy and Natural Resources – Brazil." *Mondaq*, March 23, 2011. www.mondaq.com/brazil/x/126978/Oil

"Rise of the Robot in Offshore Operations – Oil and Gas News." Oil and Gas People, January 15, 2008. https://www.oilandgaspeople.com/news/15886/rise-of-the-robot-in-offshore-operations/

Sarayaku, Kichwa Indigenous People of v. Ecuador (Merits and Reparations) 2012. Inter-American Court of Human Rights. Petition 12465.

Schröder, Tim. "Marine Resources: Opportunities and Risks." *World Ocean Review* 3 (2014).

Schwebel, Stephen M. "The Effect of Resolutions of the U.N. General Assembly on Customary International Law." *Proceedings of the ASIL Annual Meeting* 73 (1979): 301–309. https://doi.org/10.1017/s0272503700064934

"The Climate Lawsuit against the Norwegian Government: Greenpeace." Accessed October 11, 2019. https://www.savethearctic.org/en/peoplevsarcticoil/background-documents

"The People versus Arctic Oil Litigation." *Environmental Justice Atlas*, March 15, 2018. https://ejatlas.org/conflict/the-people-versus-arctic-oil

U.S. Energy Information Administration (EIA)–Independent Statistics and Analysis. "What Countries are the Top Producers and Consumers of Oil?" April 22, 2019. https://www.eia.gov/tools/faqs/faq.php?id=709&t=6

UKERC. "UKERC Report Finds 'Significant Risk' of Oil Production Peaking in Ten Years." October 8, 2009. www.ukerc.ac.uk/news/ukerc-report-finds-significant-risk-of-oil-production-peaking-in-ten-years.html

UN General Assembly. Declaration on the Rights of Indigenous Peoples, UNGA Res. 61/295. September 13, 2007 (UNDRIP).

Vidal, John. "Ogoni King: Shell Oil Is Killing My People." *The Guardian*, December 3, 2016. https://www.theguardian.com/world/2016/dec/03/ogoni-king-shell-oil-is-killing-my-people

Workman, Daniel. "Crude Oil Exports by Country." World's Top Exports, October 7, 2019. www.worldstopexports.com/worlds-top-oil-exports-country/

Wright, David V. "Tsleil-Waututh Nation v. Canada: A Case of Easier Said than Done." ablawg.ca, September 11, 2018. https://ablawg.ca/2018/09/11/tsleil-waututh-nation-v-canada-a-case-of-easier-said-than-done

12 Achieving excellence in public participation and consultation

Penny Norton

Introduction

As earlier chapters have demonstrated, effective public participation is fundamental to the process of change brought about by extractive industries. Not only should residents be involved, whether as a legal requirement or simply through courtesy, but a proposal benefits substantially from feedback from the community – from anecdotes and folklore to information about current uses of a proposed site. In this context, "public participation" is viewed as the long term process of engagement, not necessary linked to a specific extraction project but concerning community relations between an extractives company (or companies) and a community over many years; in contrast to "consultation," which typically refers to the process of gaining feedback on a specific proposal and as such forms part of a broader public participation programme. Both involve extensive research, multiple stakeholders, an appropriate (and therefore diverse) selection of dialogue methods and comprehensive evaluation. A strategic approach provides the framework to do this in a cohesive manner.

While each unique project requires a unique approach to public participation, a standardised approach to strategy can ensure that all relevant factors are taken into account and produce an appropriate public participation programme.

The chapter will exemplify best practice strategy and tactics for consultation, and new methods of engagement as used in the UK, Australia and Canada. Clearly the Arctic faces some very specific limitations, particularly in relation to digital connectivity. However, as the latter part of the chapter demonstrates, recent technological development is not exclusively dependent upon internet access, and as such presents immediate opportunities.

Communications theorist Grunig identified four models to demonstrate "excellence" in communication: press agentry, public information, two-way asymmetrical and two-way symmetrical. His epitome of excellent communication is the *two-way symmetric* model – an entirely symmetrical relationship:

that is based on research and that uses communication to manage conflict and improve understanding with strategic publics.[1]

This is the definition of "excellence" used in this chapter to demonstrate a high standard of public participation.

The requirement to consult

The Aaarhus Convention provides an overview of effective public participation through its three public rights, or "Pillars": access to information, public participation in decision-making, and access to justice.[2] Although not legally binding in all Arctic regions, it is an important benchmark by which public participation can be measured.[3]

Individual countries' legal requirements to consult on a planning proposal vary considerably. For example, as explained in Chapter 3, the granting of an exploration licence for onshore mining activities in Greenland does not require a social impact assessment; which contrasts sharply with the UK, where community engagement in relation to similar schemes must follow a stringent process.[4]

Despite the apparent dichotomy between the two however, there is a critical commonality: regardless of whether there exists a legal obligation to consult, there is not a legal obligation to uphold the majority views revealed in the consultation. Consultation is not a referendum. According to the UK's Consultation Institute, consultation is:

> The dynamic process of dialogue between individuals or groups, based upon a genuine exchange of views, with the objective of influencing decisions policies or programmes of action.[5]

---

1 James E. Grunig, *Excellence in PR and Communication Management* (Mahwah NJ: Lawrence Erlbaum, 1992), 11.
2 Convention on Access to Information, Public Participation in Decision-Making and Access to Justice in Environmental Matters 1998 (Aarhus Convention).
3 Of the Arctic states, Denmark (excluding Greenland and the Faroe Islands), Finland, Iceland, Norway and Sweden and parties.
4 In the UK, large-scale energy projects are defined as Nationally Significant Infrastructure Projects (NSIPs) in the Planning Act 2008, c. 29. Due to their complex nature, the UK the planning system allows for consultation on the principle of the development to occur at a national level, while the local consultation is centred on design, community benefits and mitigating negative impacts on the neighbourhood. The process of consultation is strictly controlled and comprises seven stages: preparing a statement of community consultation; pre-application; acceptance; pre-examination; examination; decision; and post-decision (at which legal challenges may occur). See, Penny Norton and Martin Hughes, *Public Consultation and Community Involvement in Planning* (Abingdon: Routledge, 2018), chapter 13 (for more detail).
5 "The Consultation Institute," The Consultation Institute, accessed October 17, 2019, www.consultationinstitute.org/

Recommendations for change following consultation take into account both technical and financial factors alongside stakeholder views – which, technically, may or may not be upheld by the decision-makers.

So neither consultation nor public participation results in a definitive decision, but the notion that public participation *can* benefit planning decisions is unequivocal. Effective public participation can create lasting positive relationships between a developer and a community, can produce local insight which significantly benefits any resulting development (specifically in tailoring it to the local community), and through dialogue, identifies appropriate community benefits.

A strategic approach

In consulting on a specific proposal, the logical sequence of a strategy, however wide-ranging the involvement activities, establishes clear aims and objectives, enabling the development team to share values, expectations and understanding with local residents and organisations. A strategy is also the best means of identifying relevant issues, which provide context and insight as the programme progresses. The resulting communications programme is therefore a continuous cycle of research, engagement and evaluation, which can complement wider community development initiatives such as education, employment and healthcare.

A common mistake, often despite better intentions, is for a consultation strategy to become a retrospective document: the team launches into a series of tactics (perhaps based on past practice, experience or recommendation), results are collated, and then in a need to create a meaningful report, a "strategy" is drafted to justify the approach. Worse still, and all too common, is to "predict and provide," "plan, announce and defend," or "plan, monitor, manage." (These approaches are explained and critiqued elsewhere.)[6] Each of these examples is a distinctly asymmetrical approach which makes scant use of local insight. Due to presumptions about a lack of a strategic approach companies should constantly aspire to disprove potential or actual allegations of "tokenism," "box-ticking" and "done deals" through maintaining and communicating a highly transparent, symmetrical approach to consultation.

Table 12.1 describes the basic facets of a communications strategy and the corresponding elements of a public consultation.

A strategic approach to consultation, therefore, requires a symmetrical flow of information between a potential developer and the local community and must prioritise continual engagement, allowing development proposals to evolve in line with feedback, and for the process to adapt where necessary. The strategic framework is not a "to do" list, but a cycle: situational analysis, issues analysis and stakeholder database benefit from ongoing development; regular monitoring influences the ongoing selection of dialogue methods, and regular evaluation reinvigorates the strategic direction, as shown in Figure 12.1.

6 Norton and Hughes, *Public Consultation and Community Involvement in Planning*, 194.

Table 12.1 A strategic approach to public consultation

Stages of the strategic process	Purpose	Methods
Research		
Situational analysis	Gain background information to inform the programme.	Consider the possible influence of a wide range of factors. External issues include policies and political sensitivites, attitudes towards the principle of development and the potential for consultation fatigue. Internal factors include resourcing, past experience, local links and the developer's existing reputation.
Issues analysis	Develop an understanding of the issues likely to influence feedback on the specific proposals, adding context to the consultation responses and enabling the consultation team to address any misapprehensions.	Utilise local information including meeting records, reports, local press coverage, blogs, websites and social media. Research any past proposals by extractive industries and view responses to consultations.
Political analysis	Understand the political forces which may influence the consultation.	Research community/political/religious and special interest groups, their leadership, membership, policies and influences. Research the political make-up of political organisations. Understand the timing of local democratic processes and read key documents such as the Maniitsoq plan discussed in Chapter 6.
Stakeholder analysis	Understand the local community and the personalities and groups which shape it.	Utilise any national statistics or local data. Employ local community liaison officers to identity both potentially interested groups and those classified as "hard to reach." Use stakeholder mapping to determine the communications needs and expectations of specific groups and individuals so that they may be targeted appropriately.
Scoping	Begin a process of constructive dialogue with key stakeholders.	Hold initial meetings with community leaders, led by a community liaison officer (fluent in the native language) to develop an understanding of the issues and discuss the intended approach. Identify those within the local community who might be engaged as a bridge to the development team.

(Continued)

Table 12.1 (Cont.)

Stages of the strategic process	Purpose	Methods
Strategy		
Aims and objectives	Develop clear goals to ensure consistency within the development team.	Jointly determine what consultation is intended to identify and achieve measurable objectives.
Messages	Ensure consistency in communication.	Create an internal document which clarifies the key messages to be communicated, taking into account the aims and objectives and also issues identified previously.
Questions	Identify the questions that will deliver the required feedback.	Draft questions taking into account which aspects of the proposal can be changed in response to local views, and the information required to implement change. Take account of how responses will be analysed and test questions.
Target audience	Identify precisely who will be targeted so that resources can be focussed appropriately and monitoring can identify any gaps.	Determine the geographical and demographic scope, create and maintain a database of key stakeholders.
Strategic overview	Clarify the agreed strategy.	Ensure that the development team and as appropriate, local democratic organisations, are in agreement about the extent of the consultation and the aspects of the proposals upon which local residents can input. Draft a consultation mandate which clarifies: • The organisation running the consultation • The target audience • The aims and objectives • The subject for discussion • The way in which results will be used.
Dialogue methods	Select consultation tactics.	Consider the wide range of methods available and use the knowledge gained previously to identify those most suitable.
Resource allocation	Ensure that the proposed programme is deliverable.	Cost the proposed programme, taking into account human and financial resources.

(Continued)

Table 12.1 (Cont.)

Stages of the strategic process	Purpose	Methods
Create necessary documentation	Ensure that consultees have the adequate and appropriate information available to them.	Create informative resources which allow for intelligent consideration. Inclusion of a consultation mandate will provide the necessary introduction to a consultation, but the documents should also provide broader contextual information, explain the proposals in detail, present the options available and provide a means for response.
Timetable	Plan for the work to be completed in the time available.	Taking into account seasonal restrictions, create a timetable which details the methodology, timing, roles and responsibilities. Ensure that adequate time is allocated for responses, analysis and publication of feedback.
Monitoring	Continually check that the programme is running as intended.	Ensure that the agreed aims and objectives are met and be prepared to make changes if necessary.
Analysis	Gain an understanding of sentiment from the consultation responses.	Use quantitative and qualitative analysis to inform the development team of the feedback.
Report	Demonstrate the impact of the consultation feedback on the decision taken.	Present (and/or summarise) the analysis and demonstrate how feedback has influenced decision-making. Ensure that all personal data is redacted to comply with data protection law.
Respond	Thank respondents and assure them that their responses have been constructive.	Use both direct (one-to-one) and general communication to direct consultees to the consultation report and inform them of the next steps in the development process.
Evaluation	Review success based on the original aims and objectives.	Assess the consultation to address any criticisms and benefit future consultations.

Research: situational, stakeholder and issues analysis

Ideally the early stage of strategy formation should assess the context of the consultation as broadly as possible to ensure that all factors are taken into account. Useful methods for situational analysis are the PEST (political, economic, social, and technological) and SWOT (strengths, weaknesses, opportunities, threats) methods.

Achieving excellence in public participation 271

Figure 12.1 The circular approach to strategy development

Stakeholder analysis is central to any consultation and the spectrum of stakeholders for a single extractive project – let alone ongoing engagement with a wider community – is considerable. Stakeholders include not only those likely to be impacted by the proposed change, but those instrumental in communicating with the communities affected. Without understanding the quantity, diversity and informal spheres of power and influence that exist in the community, engagement runs the risk of failing to reach sections of the community and is thus asymmetrical. Stakeholder mapping enables the development team to understand specific individuals' likely views (be they positive or negative) and to assess the relative interest and potential impact of key individuals and groups.[7] A thorough understanding of the community also informs later stages of strategy development, for example, ensuring that tactics are well suited to specific groups.

Having identified a broad range of factors impacting upon the consultation and those most affected, development teams should consider the specific issues likely to dominate the conversation. In communications theory, an issue is regarded as *an unsettled subject ready for debate or discussion*. Knowledge of issues enables the potential developer to better understand the broad context of local sentiment, in

---

7 See Rhion Jones, "Stakeholder Mapping: Why Getting a Good Understanding of the Relative Positions of Your Key Stakeholders Is a Good Route to Successful Consultations," The Consultation Institute, July 14, 2016, https://www.consultationinstitute. org/stakeholder-mapping-why-getting-a-good-understanding-of-the-relative-positions -of-your-key-stakeholders-is-a-good-route-to-successful-consultations (for further information).

addition to existing and potential concerns. At the start of the engagement process, it benefits all parties for the developer to create a Frequently Asked Questions document which sets out each of the issues likely to arise alongside an agreed response. An embodiment of the transparency that any potential developer should aspire to, the document must above all be honest and open. It should also be flexible, as issues will change during the course of the project and themes will emerge or develop as new topics are introduced.

Scoping

It is common for a consultation strategy to be compiled internally, using research gathered informally from a variety of sources. However, excellent consultation requires direct and early dialogue with local communities. Those countries which require a Social Impact Assessment or Environmental Impact Assessment will routinely carry out scoping (otherwise known as pre-consultation dialogue), as does the UK's Nationally Significant Infrastructure Project (NSIP) consultation process. Regrettably, too few other public participation programmes begin with scoping, despite the clear advantages.

Messaging and questions

Messages should communicate the reason for the consultation, the features of the proposal and its likely impact, and the way in which people may wish to take part (as detailed in the consultation mandate).

The questions to be asked will be defined in the consultation objectives and should be both general and specific, inviting both qualitative and quantitative responses. Asking the right questions is crucial. In many cases questioning must be tightly controlled to avoid discussion focussing on larger and potentially controversial issues. For example, a UK NSIP project should not seek general views on the proposed development as it is not within the remit of the consultation to address the *principle* of development. Instead the consultation will focus on very specific questions such as design options and discussions about community benefits. In such cases, the consultation mandate should clearly stipulate that it is not within the remit to consider *whether* the development is to go ahead, but *how*. In all circumstances, the limits of the consultation must be stated clearly to avoid confusion.

Should a consultation request demographic data? For site-specific development it is useful to understand where people live in relation to their views, particularly if there is a danger of activists outside the locality seeking to influence a consultation outcome. Information relating to age, gender and employment status can also benefit analysis, but rarely is it worth requesting demographic data if it significantly deters potential respondents. A tried and tested technique is to seek this information at the end of the process, rather than early on: impart information, encourage feedback, acknowledge the contribution, and only then request personal information. It is also advised to make the provision of personal information voluntary, while both explaining its benefits and reassuring respondents that the information will remain confidential.

While anonymous data can lack validity, an anonymous contribution is more valid than none. In anonymous responses, consultees are more likely to express their views without fear of repercussions, hierarchies and bias are reduced, and greater expression may be used. Conversely, a consultation report carries greater value if comments can be attributed and consultees are less prone to exaggeration and dishonesty. Online consultation demonstrates that anonymity can benefit a consultation in removing hierarchies. In a typical online consultation by *ConsultOnline* over half of those taking part chose a username which bore no resemblance to their name, yet names, addresses and postcodes were supplied confidentially for the registration process. The absence of this data would have been detrimental to the consultation, and while respondents were reassured that their personal details would not be made public, the development team had access to the demographic data necessary to create a comprehensive consultation report.

Dialogue methods to inform and engage

In selecting dialogue methods, developers are advised to take into account accessibility (do the tactics selected give all sections of the community an opportunity to comment?), anonymity (consider the benefits and drawbacks in relation to the consultation objectives), appeal, and achieving both innovative and more established methods. Dialogue methods should be selected for ease of response and analysis (considering the outputs required for a convincing report, achieving a balance of qualitative and quantitative responses). Timing is important: time given for responses should assume no prior knowledge, provide ample opportunity to digest information, and also take into account local restrictions such as daylight hours, and the timing of breeding, hunting or berry-picking seasons. Developers lacking specific experience of Arctic communities should seek local advice on tactics which have particular local appeal such as story-telling and other oral forms of communication. A comprehensive scoping exercise will identify such opportunities.

The strategic framework described earlier ensures that the most appropriate tactics are selected: intelligence concerning stakeholders, issues, identification of objectives, consideration of practical viability and the potential to deliver meaningful results, creates an informed approach.

Three categories of dialogue methods are recommended for an effective consultation: information tactics, quantitative tactics and qualitative tactics.

A means of communicating the information necessary to make an informed response (for example, documents, videos, maps, hotlines, information kiosks, invitations, leaflets, letters, newsletters, presentations, websites) is of particular importance in extractive projects which are scientifically complex and liable to create further confusion as a result of misinformation. Earlier chapters in this volume identified that all too often, information is provided too little, too late and without the reassuring subjectivity that can be provided through neutral third parties.[8] Furthermore, the propensity of activist groups to spread unbalanced or

---

8 See, Johnstone, this volume; and Johnstone and Hansen, this volume.

inaccurate information reinforces the need for a variety of tactics aimed at communicating clear and relevant information, often targeted at very specific local communities.

While imparting information is vital to symmetrical communication, it is also important to ensure that the number of information-only tactics is limited: a consultation which informs a community about proposed changes but gives no opportunity for feedback does little to enable the public to participate: it is in fact one-way, or asymmetrical, and has potential to generate anger and mistrust.

Qualitative techniques are those which bring about an opinion or observation (in words) rather than a statistical result (in numbers) and are growing in popularity, partly because of their ability to bring about greater insight than quantitative tactics, also because of the increasingly sophisticated means of analysing such methods.

Online, qualitative tactics include blogging, chat rooms, forums, emails, interactive displays, layering and adapting maps, discussion groups, tech tapestries, video soapboxes and virtual meetings. Offline, they include social initiatives such as consultation cafés and art/theatre workshops; those techniques based around dialogue and discussion (in-depth interviews, discussion forums, discussion groups, face-to-face interviews and focus groups); collaborative planning techniques such as charrettes, citizens' juries, planning workshops and policy conferences; the setting up of task forces and think tanks, and opportunities to find out more about the proposal which then result in dialogue – such as exhibitions, roadshows and pop-up events, site visits and seminars.

Feedback generated by qualitative tactics, however, is not necessarily representative of the wider target audience. For example, activities which involve a considerable time commitment are likely to attract those in the 65–75 age group; conversely, online consultation is more popular among younger people and those in areas of greater digital connectivity. And if using pre-existing groups rather than focus groups it is important to consider that organisations may have a strong interest in a subject or a pre-formed bias. A stakeholder group set up for the specific purpose of the consultation can address these factors, but it is invariably difficult to create a group which is genuinely representative of the broad population.

In contrast, quantitative tactics – those which produce numerical data – typically target a wide audience. They include polls, budget simulators, referenda, questionnaires and surveys. The value of quantitative data relies both on a scientifically significant sample size and on information being readily available to those participating. As dialogue is not a feature of quantitative methods, such tactics are most appropriate when the target audience has some prior knowledge of the proposals. Typically, therefore, these tactics tend to be used specifically in consultation, as opposed to ongoing public participation.

Evolving tactics: co-production

Consultation has traditionally begun with a public meeting. Increasingly, however, the standard public meeting – which epitomises many features of asymmetrical, one-way communication – is being replaced with co-production, which is otherwise known as participatory planning, community planning, community visioning or collaborative planning.

The New Economic Foundation has identified six principles for co-production: assets (recognising people as assets), capacity (building on people's capabilities), mutuality (developing two-way reciprocal relationships), networks (encouraging peer support networks), blurred roles (blurring boundaries between delivering and receiving services) and catalysts (facilitating, not "delivering to"). Such collaborative features contrast strongly with the invariably adversarial public meeting.[9]

The process of co-production varies, but typically involves pre-engagement research and dialogue; a community planning day in which groups of residents, assisted but not directed by professionals, create visions and solutions which they then feed back to the larger group; development of a master plan by professionals following local insight; followed by an exhibition at which the master plan is formally consulted upon. Citizens' juries and appreciative inquiries also use co-production successfully.

The benefits of this approach are substantial. Early engagement can create a sense of ownership among the community, build trust with the development team and result in positive sentiment towards change. However, co-production is only effective if a considerable amount of time is invested at an early stage, providing an opportunity for the community to be involved in developing a vision, and it therefore requires considerable faith and an enlightened attitude on the part of the development team.

Co-production is well suited to projects at an early stage where there is an opportunity for the community to be involved in developing a vision. Where the potential for the community to shape proposals is limited it is less suitable, though in the case of large scale energy schemes, it may be used in determining community benefits.

Future online communication

In countries such as the UK (which has 89 per cent digital saturation[10]), online communication is increasingly used in public participation because of its accessibility: its ability to reach people at all times, with immediacy, through a variety of means; its ability to overcome language restrictions, access "hard to reach" groups (particularly commuters, families with young children, the elderly and disabled), and to break down social hierarchies.[11] Features such as voice recognition, directional controllers, use of screen readers, ensuring that websites are compatible with speech

---

9 New Economics Foundation, accessed October 17, 2019, https://neweconomics.org/
10 "Internet Access – Households and Individuals, Great Britain: 2018," Office for National Statistics, August 7, 2018, https://www.ons.gov.uk/peoplepopulationandcommunity/householdcharacteristics/homeinternetandsocialmediausage/bulletins/internetaccesshouseholdsandindividuals/2018
11 See also Skjervedal, this volume.

recognition software and providing "translations" of complex technical documents can potentially address specific accessibility issues. As such, online communication has significant potential for a future, connected, Arctic. Furthermore, many new methods of communication involving technology can be used offline.

Technological change impacts on the amount of information in circulation, the speed with which it travels and the potential for a message to spread. Online, a "level playing field" reduces hierarchies: communication can be on a one-to-one, one-to-many and many-to-many basis and the "filter" of traditional media is removed. Sophisticated communications tactics can allow for the formation of ideas or concepts, a more iterative approach, more responsive dialogue and a greater flexibility. Furthermore, new methodology enables efficient and extensive analysis.

The American University Center for Social Media identified internet usage as falling into five categories: choice, conversation, curation, creation, collaboration.[12] In a planning context, these behaviours might be described as follows:

Choice: finding information on strategic planning, policies and planning applications though search engines, recommendations (on or off line), news feeds and niche sites.

Conversation: entering into debates on discussion forums, blogs and microblogs, taking discussions into new forums by sharing links and mobilising action.

Curation: selecting and drawing together information on blogs to form powerful arguments, carefully targeted to specific groups; posting and reposting views and suggestions and sharing links.

Creation: posting brand new multimedia content, including text, images, audio and video.

Collaboration: creating groups of support or opposition for the purposes of campaigning both online and offline.

Writing about changes in methodology in 2016, I identified that online consultation fell into three categories: via social media (primarily Facebook, Twitter and YouTube); using "off the shelf" consultation websites (Citizen Space, Bang the Table), and through bespoke consultation websites (either produced in-house or using an adaptable template website such as ConsultOnline, possibly with additional third-party plug-ins and widgets such as Sticky World embedded).[13] In just four years, the selection of dialogue methods available has proliferated to the extent that there are now infinite categories.

---

12 Jessica Clark and Pat Aufderheide, *Public Media 2.0: Dynamic Engaged Publics* (Washington DC: Center for Social Media, 2009), https://cmsimpact.org/resource/public-media-2-0-dynamic-engaged-publics/
13 Norton and Hughes, *Public Consultation and Community Involvement in Planning*, chapter 16.

Consultation websites are no longer single dialogue methods. ConsultOnline, for example, provides a range of tactics including polls, forums, infographics, videos, blogs, vlogs, blog posts and podcasts which offer immediate and very effective means of analysis.[14] Data collected both online and offline can be processed via the online platform, thus creating a consultation report instantaneously.

In addition to websites, consultation apps are now increasingly used in consultation.

Give-My-View, created by Built-ID, is a web-based platform which encourages collaboration and data-sharing. It connects development teams and local communities through a visually appealing and highly accessible website app and enables a development team to guide and educate the community as a project evolves. An interactive timeline manages expectations while a newsfeed enables the development team to counteract the spread of misinformation. Other features include polls, questionnaires, and "quick facts" which provide information in relation to specific questions. Geofencing (the use of GPS technology to create a virtual geographic boundary) provides the ability to restrict online interaction to a specific geographical areas. To encourage use among younger audiences and simultaneously benefit relationships between the developer and the community, the app provides the opportunity to earn points in return for engaging and sharing. Points translate into money for a selection of local charities. Community members are able to browse "influenced decisions" from previous phases, which assists in building trust between the developer and the community.

The principles of gaming are increasingly incorporated into public participation. A consultation carried out by the University of Dundee's Centre for Environmental Change and Human Resilience successfully attracted young people to planning through use of the popular game, Minecraft.[15] A youth camp was held at the University, where secondary school pupils worked together to develop hypothetical visions for the Dundee waterfront through interactive sessions using Minecraft. Each participating school team was given an individual plot on a model of the Dundee waterfront and encouraged to develop a vision. At the end of the day, a winning team was presented with a Future Planner Award. A central aim of the Youth Camp was to encourage young people to think differently about their communities and to help them understand their potential to influence change. Minecraft's classroom edition enables pupils to work as a team and engage in a co-production of knowledge in the design of shared spaces.[16]

CHLOE (Conceptual Hexagonal Land Use Overlay Engine) is an online mapping and reporting tool developed by David Lock Associates to enhance engagement and improve information capture during community and stakeholder workshops. In small groups, participants are encouraged to create conceptual

---

14 "Welcome to ConsultOnline," ConsultOnline, accessed October 17, 2019, www.consultonlinewebsites.com
15 Working with Geddes Institute for Urban Research.
16 "Minecraft: Education Edition," Minecraft, accessed October 17, 2019, https://education.minecraft.net/

masterplans for potential growth locations by populating an empty grid, tile-by-tile, with a selection of land uses. An aerial photo overlaid with local constraints helps to inform the group's discussion on where development can and cannot be placed. As development tiles are added to the grid, CHLOE feeds back live alerts to guide the group through the design process, allowing them to make informed decisions. Adjustable parameters, including residential densities, are combined with open space standards and demographic data (specific to each local authority) to highlight the impact that housing has on associated land use composition. Different scenarios, based on changes to the parameters, can be tested, recorded and compared. CHLOE has proved extremely successful in enabling stakeholders to discuss and consider development that is appropriate, proportionate and represents the existing community's needs.

A tool which uses similar technologies is VU.CITY, the first complete fully interactive 3D digital model of several international cities.[17] Through VU.CITY, consultees can visualise proposed developments within the existing context of the area. VU.CITY can overlay the model with transport data, sightlines, wind modelling, pollution and sunlight paths. Dropping down to street level further helps consultees understand the proposed new developments in context. VU.CITY also incorporates information in relation to protected views and both existing and consented developments.

The logical extension of 3D modelling is augmented reality projection of proposed schemes onto actual landscapes. Along with a vision of how a new scheme could fit with existing infrastructure, augmented reality could enable the user to access additional information data-tagged onto the projected image.

Public participation which utilises modern technology is evolving rapidly, and over the next decade we expect to see increasing use of large format touchtables and touchscreens which use geospatial data, weblinks and videos to provide additional information. Walk-through 3D models and virtual reality theatres will enable a shared experience of a digital representation in a planning workshop.[18] Online "story maps" which link text and images to a map have the potential to provide information about a proposal either though a desktop app or as part of a walking tour, supported by information on constraints and current land uses and proposals for development. Increasingly photorealistic, high-resolution representation of proposals will have the ability to depict alternative scenarios almost equivalent to reality.

Although it does much to benefit consultation, online consultation is not a panacea: this new selection of tactics presents a new set of risks. The fast dissemination of information online, although beneficial in many circumstances, can also be a disadvantage. In cyberspace, information can fragment quickly and become used by pressure groups to reinforce opposition. The extractive sector in the Arctic has been targeted by headline-grabbing activists and protestors from

17 VU.CITY is the product of leading PropTech agency Wagstaffs, and GIA Surveyors, specialists in rights of light and daylight and sunlight.
18 David Miller, et al., *Use of Digital and 3D Visualisation Technology in Planning for New Development*, Report of the James Hutton Institute for Scottish Government (Livingston: Scottish Government, 2016), https://www.gov.scot/publications/use-of-digital-3d-visualisation-technology-research-report/

around the world who can rapidly spread news of their latest protests as well as misinformation regarding the extractive sector globally. The internet should be consistently monitored and procedures put in place to respond to concerns and misinformation.

Furthermore, online consultation, particularly social media, can be seen as superficial and lacking in the emotional power and empathy that face-to-face communication can bring. Online profiles can mask identities and if measures are not put in place, it can become impossible to monitor the geographical origin of comments. Standardised response mechanisms which give online consultations a bad reputation should be avoided in most circumstances. And despite the increase in online communication, a digital divide still exists, particularly affecting rural, indigenous and older groups.

Certainly online consultation should not be used a means to reduce costs or labour. As with any tactic, the decision to use online consultation should relate directly to the consultation's overall objectives, including the need to produce meaningful analysis.

As the capabilities of the internet, along with digital connectivity, grows, the opportunities for involvement within each of these categories will undoubtedly increase. Individuals' power to use the internet as a means of protest will increase and therefore prospective developers must adapt and respond to this changing communications landscape.

Developments in monitoring, analysis and evaluation

Monitoring, analysis and evaluation are important elements of strategic consultation.

Monitoring, the process of overseeing engagement and interacting as appropriate, occurs throughout.

Analysis is the collection of data generated by the consultation – percentages from polls, comments from emails, reports from workshops – and the process of making sense of it. It is both simpler and more effective if the analysis of each tactic is planned in advance. A so-called consultation tactic which does not produce data in a form that can be analysed is asymmetrical, counter-productive and risks destroying trust. It goes without saying that electronic communication has enabled a more scientific approach to analysing both quantitative and qualitative data, and with the move towards participatory planning, consultation responses are becoming increasingly qualitative.

Evaluation is the process by which a consultation is reviewed. Its dual purpose is to demonstrate that an effective consultation has been carried out, and to benefit future consultations. The former gives credibility to the results and can also make sense of any inconsistencies. Although it takes place at the end of the process, evaluation should be considered at the inception. Objectives, when drafted, should be assessed on their evaluation potential. Ideally, evaluation is formative rather than summative: making sense of the consultation throughout and amending it as necessary. There is also an argument for evaluation to be carried out externally to allow for objectivity; although the counter-argument is that the process of evaluation is a useful learning experience for the team at the heart of the project.

Addressing common challenges

Opposing factors and risks are common to public participation: the very notion that developers bring change to established local communities; the wide-ranging views which exist within a community; the sentiments of those wary of engagement and exponents of it. Significant time and financial resources are expended with no guarantee that the investment will be realised, and the focus on inviting comment on a potentially contentious issue can appear counter-productive to its eventual delivery.

However, an understanding of the potential challenges from the outset (and using issues analysis to further enlighten the process of understanding) can assist in mitigating risk.

In reality, potential problems fall into just a handful of categories, to which there are solutions. Two problems are common to the development team itself: resistance to public participation and a lack of dedicated resources. The first can be addressed by using workshops and training to gain buy-in from internal audiences, and the second by taking into account limitations at the outset and planning accordingly. In the Arctic, travel poses particular challenges in terms of costs and staff time, and the use of technology is limited where a reliable internet connection is required.

Within the community, a common problem is a lack of understanding. This can be mitigated through provision of adequate information at the start of the process, in an appropriate voice and level of detail for the target audience; simplifying complex information and utilising professional communications skills as necessary. It goes without saying that those running a local consultation must be fluent in the native language. When inviting responses, it is beneficial to present information alongside questions to encourage understanding immediately prior to the questions being asked. Political interference is common whether in relation to national or local politics or in a powerful individual seeking influence others. Research and pre-consultation dialogue can develop an understanding of the community pressures and hierarchies, and steps taken to mitigate undue influence. Initial research can be used to determine the most appropriate dialogue methods for each sub-group. Lack of engagement is a common problem, especially when a community is suffering from "consultation fatigue." To encourage engagement, a broad audience should be targeted, with the messages tailored to specific demographics and cultural sub-groups, particularly those "hard to reach" groups.[19] New, creative and enticing methods can be used to increase engagement and time

---

19 Previously the elderly, disabled, black and minority ethnic, and women were singled out as requiring additional outreach support. Today, older age groups and women may be among those most likely to respond to a consultation but issues still remain: whereas the 65–75 age group is very likely to contribute to a consultation, the very elderly remain unrepresented; and whereas women are now much more likely to engage in consultations independently of their husbands than 50 years ago, parents of young children are hard to reach due to time pressures and the practical difficulties of attending evening events. Recent entrants to the list of hard to reach are those who work, particularly commuters. In Arctic communities specifically, those who do not have good English so find it hard to understand the official documentation and recent immigrants can be particularly difficult to engage in public participation.

invested in both promoting the varied engagement tactics and the purpose (and potential impact) of public participation. Monitoring can be used to identify those successfully and, as necessary, the strategy and tactics adapted to focus on the "missing" demographic.

Developers are inevitably concerned when a consultation returns a negative set of results, though this generally inevitable given that a community faced with change is likely to respond only if it resists change – it is notoriously difficult to gain feedback from those who tacitly accept change. This will be taken into account and balanced with other factors when a decision is taken. Research can be used to identify potential negativity and address issues at the first opportunity. Development teams should bear in mind that criticism is frequently constructive, and so negative responses should be interrogated to gain useful information and identify the true cause of concern. Further dialogue and the use of facts can counter misinformation. Negative responses which are a result of pressure groups or activists can be identified as such and, where appropriate, such feedback viewed as separate from the results of the target community. To counter the impact of such groups, it may be possible to use local "ambassadors" to provide a bridge between the developer and the community. Developers are also advised to work closely with the media from the early stages of the project with the aim of securing balanced coverage.

It is immediately apparent when considering challenges to public participation that a majority of problems likely to arise are in the domain of the development team: issues relating to access, clarity, communication, creativity, failure to respond, inadequate promotion of information, resistance to engagement, a lack of resources and time, are common issues with communications plans generally and can each be addressed prior to the consultation commencing.

Advice on how to address the external issues is provided in greater depth in my earlier book.[20] In considering the challenges, it was immediately clear that most problems can be resolved by following the strategic process: situational and issues analysis and pre-consultation dialogue enables the development team to identify many of the potential problems that may occur, understand and manage expectations, and determine the most appropriate tactics to use; stakeholder analysis will identify the range of local audiences to be involved, from political and community leaders to those regarded as "hard to reach," and develop an understanding of how best to involve them; the aims and objectives, as communicated through the consultation mandate, help address any criticisms of the consultation in terms of its breath, reach and use of the results; consistent messaging in the form of a Frequently Asked Questions document will ensure that the whole development team is able to address difficult questions, and agreement with the local authority over the strategic overview will provide the basis for a good relationship between the development team and local planning authority. Resource allocation will prevent issues such as capacity to respond, and monitoring will help identify and

---

20 Norton and Hughes, *Public Consultation and Community Involvement in Planning*, chapter 18.

respond to any problems as they occur. Finally, monitoring, analysis and evaluation all play an important role in explaining the reasons for consultation results.

Maintaining good ongoing relationships with a local community

Much of this chapter has focused on the public participation implemented before an exploration or exploitation licence application is submitted. With pre-planning consultation complete and planning consent won, a significant amount of public participation has been accomplished. But as the project moves into the construction phase, community engagement too enters a new phase.

Inclusive and engaging consultation creates a foundation for the next stage of public participation. But rather than a continuation of the work to date, community engagement post-planning has new aims and objectives, new stakeholders and new challenges. A proactive approach towards community relations is required to ensure a constructive relationship between all parties.

The process of construction is rarely popular, and where negative sentiment already exists within a local community, a developer has an uphill struggle to deliver a project while maintaining a good reputation. And once work begins, that relationship can be further strained due to frequent movements by construction vehicles, the noise of pile driving, road closures, parking cessations, occasional cuts to power supplies and numerous other, often unpredictable, consequences of construction.

A good relationship with the local community enables the development team to minimise disruption and pre-empt future problems: regular dialogue with residents can identify problems before they occur.

As with consultation, a community relations strategy should begin with local dialogue. Meetings with those most affected and stakeholder groups representing the wider area will enable the developer to understand both fears and expectations and put in place channels of communication for the future. While previous research is a useful starting point, the developer must be cognisant that interested parties may change at this stage, especially with the addition of new users and occupiers.

Good community relations is both proactive and reactive and is not limited to mitigating the impact of construction. The community relations strategy for a medium or large scheme might also include outreach activities, perhaps involving education, the environment, art and employment initiatives. This proactive approach is a positive means of reaching a local audience and involving them in the project through relevant and appealing tactics.

The appointment of a community liaison officer is an excellent starting point, as this ensures a single point of contact for local residents and a co-ordinated and consistent approach. In some cases, this may be served by a Construction Impacts Group or development forum. Newsletters, emails, a community relations website and social media, telephone helplines, and exhibitions in local community centres have been found to be useful in imparting information. Face-to-face and small community group meetings enable the development team to speak directly with those affected and respond to concerns. Community liaison panels are a more formal means by which the construction project can understand residents' concerns, but are smaller and more manageable than public meetings. A simple means of sharing news about the development is to provide plastic windows in hoardings, enabling local residents to view progress on site. This can also be provided through the use of a webcam or time-lapse photography, hosted on a website or social media page. Other ideas used to encourage local residents to engage with the development team include the creation of community reporters (local people given the opportunity to interview the development team and report back to the community in the form of a newspaper or blog) and a regular drop-in cafe to encourage direct communication between the construction team and community. Contact with the local media can be a useful means of providing updates to the wider community and also establish a positive relationship with the local media, which can be useful in the case of complaints. The development team also has the opportunity to involve the community in events, such as "topping out" a significant building or opening a community facility.

When the last construction vehicle has left the site, what is the developer's responsibility to the new development? The Impact Benefit Agreement negotiated between the developers, local and central government and possibly other local organisations will set legally binding requirements or targets for local employment and training as well as contributions to local projects. While this provides an opportunity for the developer to work constructively with the local community, that good intention can misfire if problems arise elsewhere, or if the needs of certain sections of the community area not met, hence the ongoing need for research and dialogue.

Conclusion

The enduring answer to achieving excellence in public participation is a strategic and symmetrical approach: appropriate early dialogue, stakeholder research, situational analysis, a clear strategy communicated via a consultation mandate and an appropriate selection of two-way dialogue methods has the greatest chance of success.

While this chapter has recommended a best practice approach to public participation, I do not presuppose that such advice will result in an ideal public participation programme: no public participation programme will conform to an ideal, because issues will always arise which challenge the best laid plans. However, in implementing a strategy with appropriate aims and objectives, the realisation of these aims is more likely to be achieved. With this in mind, the chapter concludes with a table outlining ten principles which determine good public participation (Table 12.2).

Table 12.2 Ten principles of good public participation

Accessibility	Provides access to all stakeholder groups, taking into account cultural, physical, intellectual and technological limitations.
Accountability	Assumes responsibility for the impact of the development team's approach and interpretation of the results.
Engaging	Uses appropriate and creative dialogue methods to involve and inspire.
Informative	Provides adequate, unbiased information to enable good decision-making, ensures that complex information is explained clearly, and considers adapting consultation materials for different audiences.
Management of expectations	Uses scoping, research and monitoring to understand attitudes and expectations and responds accordingly.
Responsive	Responds to all communication quickly and positively; allows development proposals and the process to evolve in line with feedback; ensures that all consultees receive feedback.
Strategic	Follows the strategic approach to ensure that the consultation is well researched, based on firm objectives, and designed to produce meaningful analysis and evaluation. The strategy is well understood within the development team and communicated to wider audiences in the form of a consultation mandate.
Transparent	From setting realistic objectives, communicating the purpose of the consultation, drawing up agendas for discussion and imparting information; to analysing results and providing feedback, openness is paramount. The report provides a clear audit trail of analysis and recommendations so that the impact of the dialogue upon subsequent decisions is identified, and where feedback which has not been used to inform the final decision, demonstrates the rationale for doing so.
Timely	Allows ample time to develop the early stages of the strategy, to engage fully and provide adequate time for responses.
Two-way	Aims to achieve a symmetrical flow of information between the development team and the local community.

References

Clark, Jessica and Pat Aufderheide. *Public Media 2.0: Dynamic Engaged Publics.* Washington DC: Center for Social Media, 2009. https://cmsimpact.org/resource/public-media-2-0-dynamic-engaged-publics/

Convention on Access to Information, Public Participation in Decision-Making and Access to Justice in Environmental Matters 1998. Adopted June 25, 1998, entered into force October 30, 2001. United Nations Treaty Series 2161, 447 (Aarhus Convention).

Grunig, James E. *Excellence in PR and Communication Management*. Mahwah NJ: Lawrence Erlbaum, 1992.

"Internet Access – Households and Individuals, Great Britain: 2018." Office for National Statistics, August 7, 2018. https://www.ons.gov.uk/peoplepopulationandcommunity/householdcharacteristics/homeinternetandsocialmediausage/bulletins/internetaccesshouseholdsandindividuals/2018

Jones, Rhion. "Stakeholder Mapping: Why Getting a Good Understanding of the Relative Positions of Your Key Stakeholders Is a Good Route to Successful Consultations." The Consultation Institute, July 14, 2016. https://www.consultationinstitute.org/stakeholder-mapping-why-getting-a-good-understanding-of-the-relative-positions-of-your-key-stakeholders-is-a-good-route-to-successful-consultations

Miller, David, Jane Morrice, Margaret McKeen, Gillian Donaldson Selby, Chen Wang, and Jose Munoz-Rojas. *Use of Digital and 3D Visualisation Technology in Planning for New Development*. Report of the James Hutton Institute for Scottish Government. Livingston: Scottish Government, 2016. https://www.gov.scot/publications/use-of-digital-3d-visualisation-technology-research-report/

"Minecraft: Education Edition." Minecraft. Accessed October 17, 2019. https://education.minecraft.net/

New Economics Foundation. Accessed October 17, 2019. https://neweconomics.org/

Norton, Penny and Martin Hughes. *Public Consultation and Community Involvement in Planning*. Abingdon: Routledge, 2018.

"The Consultation Institute." The Consultation Institute. Accessed October 17, 2019. www.consultationinstitute.org/

UK. Planning Act 2007, c. 29.

"Welcome to ConsultOnline." ConsultOnline. Accessed October 17, 2019. www.consultonlinewebsites.com

13 Arctic voices

Strategies for community engagement

Anne Merrild Hansen and Rachael Lorna Johnstone

Our presentation and account of the international standards and the examples provided of extractive projects implemented with indigenous and local participation in the Arctic is inspired by the increasing recognition of the political, territorial and cultural sovereignty of indigenous peoples globally. Rights to land and natural resources are a critical element of this sovereignty. Participation in decision-making processes around extractive projects is hence a central element in ensuring that international standards and conventions are met by governments, while business standards for responsible conduct are met by investors and enterprises. It seems, however, that expectations related to the present implementation of free, prior and informed consent (FPIC) through participation processes, for example in impact assessment processes, are rather higher than their modest implementation in practice.

In the contemporary Arctic, where social adaptation and transformation are taking place as a response to ongoing environmental, cultural, economic and political changes, we have pointed to extractive industries as a potential major driver of change in Arctic communities. Both alone and together with other ongoing processes of change, these may cause adverse impacts on Arctic communities and peoples. We have demonstrated the impacts of extractive projects already at very early stages of development prior to production, and we found that future impacts cannot always be foreseen, while criticism and conflict in relation to developments have been found in areas of heavy development even after periods of general acceptance and support from locals.

Participation in decision-making processes is to a large extent expected to ensure that development takes place in a manner that is in line with local and indigenous people's wishes and aspirations for the future, while also supporting the possibility of realising these aspirations. Public participation should follow international standards applicable in Arctic states as well as the domestic legal requirements in all the Arctic countries.

Throughout the chapters of this book, we have identified a range of both positive and negative experiences related to public participation processes. In the first part of the book regarding the general frameworks for public participation in the Arctic and the current international standards and their application, Wilson, Buhmann, and Johnstone describe international standards for meaningful public participation processes, often beyond the present legislative requirements and practices. In the second part of the book, the six case studies on participation in practice explain and explore extractive projects, their impacts and participation strategies at different development stages. These include two on early mining and oil exploration in Greenland; studies of well-established hydrocarbon activities in the Komi Republic; inclusion of indigenous peoples in decision-making in Arctic Canada; a historic study of the early years of oil exploration offshore close to the Shetland Islands; and the accelerated petroleum development over the past decade on the North Slope of Alaska. The studies presented identify amongst other things a lack of transparency related to the length and content of the decision-making processes, and a need for better communication strategies taking into account informal pathways of knowledge and opinion-sharing. Across the chapters, there is agreement that participation processes need to be context-dependent and designed to be relevant and culturally appropriate for the particular communities affected in each unique case. They also show that conflict can arise when frustrations accumulate. The third part of the book explores the potential to improve public participation and community engagement. Pereira and Pappa make some recommendations for improvements within the Norwegian and Canadian systems, whereas Norton reflects on the goals and expectations of participation from different perspectives and how to realise those objectives. The conclusions are very much in line with what was found in the case studies regarding the need for context-dependent procedures and exploration of alternative ways of citizen engagement. They also show that people in impacted communities do not always agree on support or opposition to projects and have varying perceptions of desired futures. This in turn creates difficulties in securing FPIC, as it is not always easy to determine when and how consent is reached. Part III highlights that no single set of guidelines can ensure ideal public participation programmes as no public participation programme will conform to an ideal. As Norton explained: "issues will always arise which challenge the best laid plans."

In this final chapter, we sum up some of the key findings arising across the three parts and reflect on how in future improved public participation can contribute to mitigating profound and undesired impacts of extractive projects on the living conditions of peoples across the region.

Protecting and respecting human rights and the rights of indigenous peoples require practices that meet international standards

Our first key finding is that, according to international standards and principles, indigenous peoples have the right not only to influence but to determine priorities and strategies, and to participate in the formulation of development plans and programmes, before the award of any licences to extractive companies and ongoing throughout the industrial process. This is however, not always reflected in national legislation or in the actions of governments or of companies. Even while modern land claim agreements in Canada actually contain operative provisions emphasising the importance of indigenous participation in decision-making concerning the use of land water and resources, Bankes' review of the litigation demonstrates that the government has not always been willing to live up to its responsibilities under these agreements. It is not sufficient for companies to refer only to the regulations most pertinent to their projects; they must have a profound understanding of the international and constitutional rights of indigenous peoples as the background against which any regulations will be interpreted (or, more realistically, they need to hire lawyers who are experts in indigenous rights). Wilson explains that a greater understanding is needed of the range of international standards and instruments, the key principles inherent in them, and how they are implemented in practice in order to ensure that projects only go ahead with support of indigenous and other local communities and with full respect for their rights. Wilson's contribution, alongside those of Johnstone and Buhmann, makes significant contributions to increasing that understanding. Johnstone considers the intricacies and complications of FPIC in the Greenland context. She concludes that even if there is still some dispute about the applicability of indigenous rights in Greenland and of FPIC in particular as a matter of international law, it is still a useful framework for improving the understanding of an acceptance of large-scale developments. Buhmann argues in Chapter 4 that even if the legislation does not fulfil international standards there could be other motivating factors for companies to go beyond the domestic law and aim higher. For example, institutions charged with assessing responsible business conduct can issue recommendations to companies that can help companies understand what is expected of them. Buhmann recognises that practice among the OECD National Contact Points (NCPs) varies, but reminds us that the Norwegian and Swedish NCPs have proposed that companies ensure their policies and practices uphold ILO C169,[1] even when this is not required by domestic law. Buhmann suggests that companies defer also to the UN Declaration on the Rights of Indigenous Peoples (UNDRIP).[2] Loginova and Wilson's case study of oil development in Russia's Komi Republic in Chapter 7 likewise demonstrates the importance for companies of following international good practice standards even if this means going beyond the domestic law. Their case study suggests that sticking strictly to the letter of the law can be a high-risk strategy for companies. Similarly, Bankes' close study of participation requirements under Canadian indigenous land claims settlements and case-law shows that meeting the minimum standards laid down in regulations is no bar to lengthy and costly litigation and even overturning of licensing decisions based on constitutional protections. Although the Canadian courts have yet to require FPIC, the Canadian government has endorsed UNDRIP, including the principle of FPIC. Constitutional law in Canada is always evolving and the courts are not afraid to "fill the gaps." It would be a hasty project manager who pressed on with a project without even *seeking* the consent of an indigenous people on whose territory the activity would be carried out. Pereira and Pappa call for development of international standards as they

1 Indigenous and Tribal Peoples Convention 1989, ILO Convention 169, 1989.
2 UN General Assembly, Declaration on the Rights of Indigenous Peoples, UNGA Res 61/295, September 13, 2007.

suggest that the right to information should be accompanied by the freedom to express one's opinion without fear of retaliation. While constitutional and international human rights law guarantee such a right throughout the Arctic and this right is largely upheld in seven of the Arctic states *vis à vis* the state, the Greenland case study uncovered a fear of bullying or social exclusion by other citizens were people to express an unpopular view, and this may be an issue in other small or close-knit communities. Johnstone and Hansen recommend the maintenance of safe channels of communication in Greenland, whereas Norton explores the selection of dialogue methods and the advantages and disadvantages of anonymous submissions more generally in Chapter 12.

What a meaningful process entails depends on who the "public" or "community" is

Securing the rights of citizens in communities potentially affected by extractive projects requires one first to define who is a member of the community and how they will be reached. Pereira and Pappa underline the need to define the term "public" in relation to each project, and strategies for including them in consultation processes. The public is very seldom a homogeneous group. A community is typically constituted by different groups of age, gender, income group, occupation, education, culture, socio-economic status and more. Furthermore, a community will often include private groups, non-governmental organisations, and academic institutions. Skjervedal touches upon this in Chapter 5 when she observes that it is mostly middle-aged men who have participated in many of the public meetings held in Greenland, and that youth is not being reached in the dialogue about how extractive industries will impact on their futures. She emphasises further that recognising who the public are may call for a broadening of the range of participation formats and providing opportunities for inclusion of a broader representative voice among the local communities, through tailoring the participation format(s) to the specific project, local context, and target group. Norton examines "stakeholder analysis" to identify different interest groups and relations within and between them as a necessary step before selecting the most suitable means of reaching them. Mitchell's historic study of the Shetland oil negotiations also demonstrates that in certain cases, individual characters can make a big difference, for example, skilled negotiators who can take the time to inform themselves about the practicalities, the economics and the politics of proposed developments.

Public expectations – what different people and organisations expect from participation and hence their understanding of the purpose of the engagement – also affect people's views as to whether their involvement will be meaningful or not and in turn their evaluation of whether it is worth the effort. Skjervedal found that disagreement on the purpose of public participation between different stakeholders causes frustration and creates a situation where no-one considers consultation processes a success. Pereira and Pappa also find that there are different perceptions of the purpose of consultation and participation. They exemplify this by highlighting that oil companies perceive public participation as a means to inform potentially affected communities and as a condition of their social licence to operate; governments use it to create trust and confidence with their citizens; whereas locals consider it as a way to influence the authorities' decisions. Norton's contribution brings in a business perspective to show the advantages of quality participation strategies for developers and investors and counter-suspicions (justified or not) that participation requirements are merely "box-ticking" exercises for projects that have already been agreed.

Meaningful consultation with affected stakeholders is a core element in the process of adequately identifying and managing risks to individuals and groups, as Buhmann explains in Chapter 4. There are many guidance documents available, for instance related to public participation in impact assessment processes. The general agreement is that excellence in public participation requires sensitivity to the local context. What is meaningful will differ from case to case, depending on the individual project's context. This includes the ethnic mix of local communities, levels of resource dependency, and the nature of cultural practices and decision-making structures.

International standards and guidance recommend that project proponents and communities agree processes, procedures and values in advance of engagement, consultation and consent processes, as Wilson explains in Chapter 2. Wilson suggests that so-called "community protocols" – charters of rules and responsibilities, in which communities set out their rights and their position regarding any proposed development on their territories – can be an effective way for communities to establish and articulate their expectations and demands in advance of engaging with external developers. Skjervedal expands on these considerations, observing in Chapter 5 that for ordinary citizens, issues that relate to their everyday lives are much higher on the agenda and much more relatable than extractive ventures that may take a decade or more to come to fruition, if they ever come to fruition at all. Thus, effective participation processes must be framed in a manner that takes as its point of departure what people find important in their everyday lives and the visions they hold for their children and their grandchildren (and this will vary between different groups of citizens).

Alternative forms of participation could increase diversity of participation

Another finding that stands out from the chapters in this book is the critique of the most common methods employed during participation processes and their limitations. In Chapter 5 Skjervedal calls for a reassessment of the current format and practices of public participation in Greenland, and concludes that there is a need for new approaches to ensure active and meaningful engagement, as a-prerequisite for sustainable development. Johnstone suggests that people be given the opportunity to meet with or hear from people from other communities where exploration and/or production of minerals or hydrocarbons have taken place during the participation phases to inform and develop their views and understanding of the potential impacts and benefits of industrial development. She also argues that companies and authorities ought to consider how to accept and consider confidential information and to facilitate anonymous submission of views. Norton explains that good practice requires that the public is provided adequate, unbiased information. She also explores the need to adapt consultation materials for different audiences. This also relates to a call for accessible information, as presented below.

In addition, the traditional public meeting needs to be rethought. Johnstone recommends that companies and authorities consider holding smaller, targeted meetings, both to ensure a safe space and to encourage people to speak up without meetings being dominated by the usual suspects. Johnstone and Hansen also find in Greenland that the timing of meetings is an issue. Pereira and Pappa suggest creation of advisory groups or jury committees. Skjervedal explores the use of social media as a forum for dialogue during participation processes in Greenland today. She found that it is important to adapt participation approaches and methods to the specific target group, to assure that marginalised future stakeholders are interested in being involved. Norton also considers electronic fora for discussion, including social media. However, poor and expensive communications services in remote Arctic communities mean that online participation must be carefully designed. Glossy, high-graphic websites that work in cities and that take for granted cheap, 24-hour connectivity, are entirely unsuitable for communities relying on satellite internet connections.

Besides the format of knowledge transmission, Johnstone also considers the need to cross epistemologies to ensure fully-informed decision-making. It is necessary to consider and integrate indigenous knowledge and local knowledge, including when it is presented in formats with which the developers are unfamiliar, such as story-telling and other traditional forms of communication. To ensure that the parties understand each other, indigenous experts should be engaged in the process. Further emphasising the importance of sensitivity to various knowledge systems as a platform for dialogue and mutual understanding, Johnstone and Hansen find in the case study from Greenland that informal pathways of knowledge and opinion-sharing are often used, and suggest that citizens be reached on platforms they use already, as also emphasised by Skjervedal's Facebook study. Johnstone and Hansen also suggest that participation processes should be based on long-term strategies for consultation. This involves not necessarily pivoting on a single project and bringing in a wide range of participants. Also, allowing citizens time to consider alternative opportunities for development is important; and it is also important for them to be able to seek out improvements to promote a strong community network with a good level of public trust already in place, should an extractive company come into town. The community protocols highlighted by Wilson could be a relevant tool in this regard.

Sufficient time and accessible information are essential for public acceptance of consultation processes

Various contributions identify time as a major factor influencing performance in relation to participation processes. There is a need to engage meaningfully with local communities, including the provision of adequate time to disseminate and receive information, and meetings held at the right place and at the right time. Reviewing the Shetland case, Mitchell states that: "This could not be done quickly." Norton further stresses the need for ample time during the early stages of participation, both to engage fully and to provide adequate time for responses. Yet in some cases, the public consultation period is only eight weeks.

The case studies also find that information needs to be more accessible so that citizens have the opportunity to become fully acquainted with the materials and prepare for consultations. Loginova and Wilson observe that local people frequently want to understand the technical side of projects but find it difficult to find clear information on potentially damaging environmental impacts, and this leads to anxiety and frustration. Johnstone and Hansen note that information should not be internet-dependent, especially in regions where internet access is slow and expensive, and that it must be provided in all relevant languages as many indigenous groups continue to speak their own languages or dialects and not all members will be confident in reading technical materials in their second or third language. Johnstone and Hansen further call for a transparent timeline and process, so that everyone involved has a realistic idea of when decisions can be expected. Mitchell's case-study indicates that the keys to a successful community engagement include transparency and deliberation, following a lengthy iterative process.

In Loginova and Wilson's case study from Russia's Komi Republic, the consistent failure of companies to provide information prior to certain oil industry activities taking place, such as seismic testing and exploration activities, or after incidents such as oil spills into local rivers, led to mounting frustration among local communities. Despite many local citizens being broadly in favour of the petroleum industry as a generator of local employment and income, the lack of information was interpreted as a lack of respect. This resulted in the breakdown of trust and ultimately led to lengthy local protests against the industry – protests that could have been avoided or reduced through better communication from the outset.

Power relations and justice are important in the process

Justice in the participation process includes defining who "the public" is, as described above, and determining who should be targeted and how. From a justice perspective, there are circumstances in which key issues arise as to whether to target and prioritise some groups for more participation, and whether sometimes the views of certain individuals or groups are more important than others. Not everyone will be equally affected by resource developments and the views of those facing the most significant impacts should be particularly sought out. Furthermore, international law – for example, in ILO C169 and UNDRIP – promises rights to indigenous peoples that other local communities do not enjoy.

Johnstone and Hansen explain that Greenlanders mostly shared the view that those closest to a project should have more influence on decision-making. Although all opinions should be considered, there was a general consensus that those of people most directly affected and who bear the greatest risk, as opposed to international campaign groups who might be campaigning on points of higher principle, should have greater weight. Hansen and Ipalook find that in Nuiqsut on the North Slope of Alaska, there was support for greater attention to the views of those with longer connections to the land and family histories in the area, in preference to those of relative newcomers who may have come to the region only after the oil development started.

How then should governments and companies identify and weigh the views of different (purported) stakeholders? Is it a matter of one person, one vote? Should certain groups be preferred, based on location, indigeneity or other considerations? The location from where a submission is made can be taken into account by decision-makers even when submissions are semi-anonymous or anonymised, as Norton explains. How should a "group" view be ascertained? FPIC is a community view – the consensus of an indigenous people, not a majority, winner-takes-all decision – but how is the community view determined? Indigenous views can be delivered by indigenous leaders in the area, identified by the people's internal governance system; but there must always be space for a member of an indigenous group to express his or her contrary view as an individual. Bankes' examples from Canadian jurisprudence show us that indigenous (communities') views can be identified – and the case law that he discusses also provides examples of where efforts to ascertain that view are inadequate.

Besides the power relations amongst citizens are the power relations between the public, the government and companies. Loginova and Wilson address the unequal distribution of power by showing what can happen if local government and oil companies develop close relations without proper consideration of the implications of a lack of engagement with local citizens. The residents of northern Komi Republic found themselves in a situation where they felt out of control of the resource development process, yet forced to endure repeated oil spills and other livelihood impacts from the industry. The experiences documented in the study, however, illustrate that rural people can institute a form of local politics oriented to achieving relational justice. The northern Komi people mobilised internal and outsider networks and communities, social media and international scrutiny, to challenge injustices they perceived in relation to the opportunity to express their voice about development on the land they depend on for their livelihoods. By opening up debates to wider issues of sustainability and justice, they succeeded in drawing considerable attention to their cause, owing to the impact of their protests against "business-as-usual."

In Alaska, Inuit residing on the North Slope shared thoughts about how to empower the local communities in the negotiations with companies and governments in relation to oil development. When they felt that mitigation measures implemented in relation to such activities were not effectively protecting the interests of the locals, they organised across communities in a Whaling Commission, which they stated gave them a stronger voice during negotiations with governments and companies. The Whaling Commission is today considered a central participant in many debates around oil and gas development, and reminds the other stakeholders of the importance of subsistence hunting and sharing for the locals' physical and mental wellbeing.

Participation and dialogue are essential throughout the life of a project

Citizens are primarily involved and participate in a particular period in the life cycle of an extractive project, namely in relation to impact assessment processes carried out by companies to prepare for an application for a production licence. We recognise that it is important to involve people in deciding on whether or not a project should move forward from exploration to production. However, the findings presented in this book echo what many previous studies have also pointed out – that it is equally important to involve people early, prior to, and during decision-making regarding licensing, and preferably by governments before companies even begin exploration in an area. This right is written into international standards and guidelines for government and industry, as Wilson highlights in Chapter 2. Wilson points to the need to develop a nuanced understanding of what level of decision-making and at what stage in a project life-cycle affected communities have the right to influence or even determine the outcomes of decision-making. Norton likewise explains the benefits to developers from maintaining early communication and examines the concept of "co-production."

Johnstone and Hansen find that early information is not only a right, but also something the citizens in Greenland call for in practice. They want to learn about the mineral potential of the mountains amongst which they live and hunt before prospectors show up. We further develop the discussion by asking different sectors to examine the role they might play to prepare the public to participate effectively in extractive decision-making.

Johnstone explains in Chapter 3 that citizens in Greenland asked for actors such as authorities, research institutions, educational institutions and the media, to take initiatives to inform and engage the public about extractive projects before or during early exploration. Mitchell also discusses in Chapter 11 the role that the Scottish national newspaper, the *Scotsman* and local paper, the *Shetland Times*, played by consciously contributing to the "education" of the public by running a series of articles about the industry, to prepare people to develop a nuanced and informed opinion about the projects being implemented in their area. Wilson observes that well-organised communities can develop community protocols that set out communities' rights to land and resources and general position regarding proposed developments. The "co-production" strategies that Norton discusses can also result in general principles for cooperative development.

In addition to the need for early engagement and dialogue, we further emphasise that it is important to follow up and communicate with communities throughout the life of projects, including the decommissioning stages, especially if projects are revised or new permits are granted in an area. Unanticipated or cumulative impacts might be adverse and lead to an intensity of activities that was not foreseen and may not be supported by citizens who had earlier expressed support during the planning phase and who, in principle, favour industrial development in broad terms. We highlight therefore the need to continue the dialogue and to ensure that citizens have a chance of making their voices heard during production. Wilson and Buhmann highlight the various mechanisms established by international standards bodies, investors and companies to ensure access to remedies and the resolution of public grievances as they arise. Johnstone and Wilson also highlight the importance of seeing FPIC not as a one-off process. Citizen participation should be continuous, through, for example, ongoing stakeholders' groups. In this context, the "prior" of FPIC is misleading: it is not only "prior" but "prior and ongoing" consent that is required for legitimacy.

There is also a knowledge gap when it comes to our understanding of the way peoples' opinions regarding development in their area change over time. Citizens' expectations and aspirations may change, not only as they become accustomed to the industry and rely on income from that industry, but also if and when they experience undesirable and adverse consequences associated with projects. Hansen and Ipalook suggest that arenas for dialogue be set up or a system created whereby people can express their opinions and receive responses from the authorities and companies, including, but not only, through social media or other media, in order to be able to mitigate and manage potential or emerging conflicts before they escalate. They suggest that proactive efforts by companies and authorities to engage more consistently and meaningfully with local communities throughout a project's lifecycle and during production can serve to avoid or minimise local frustrations. Loginova and Wilson find that conflict can arise as a response to accumulated frustration built up throughout the lifecycle of a project or due to activities intensifying in a given area. They point to a lack of a legal imperative in Russia for companies in the northern Komi Republic to consult meaningfully with communities prior to a whole range of industrial activities throughout the lifetime of an extractive project. The accumulated frustrations in the Komi case resulted in local protests which affected project operations. The Komi case study underscores the importance of adequate and timely community consultation and the need for companies to go over and above legal requirements as a risk-mitigation measure, especially if the domestic law is insufficient to protect people's rights or not adequately enforced.

There is not always local consensus on future aspirations and not always disagreement between locals and industry

Another take-away from the preceding contributions is that there seems to be a need for a more nuanced understanding of communities and a clear definition of "consent," since communities are not homogeneous (as also described in relation to the discussion above on defining the public). Citizens in each community have different values, priorities and preferences regarding development, and this represents one of the key associated challenges which complicates endeavours to establish FPIC. It raises the questions of whose consent is required and how it is expressed, and of who should grant consent on behalf of a community. Mitchell addressed this issue in Chapter 11 and demonstrated that even in a close-knit archipelagic community such as the Shetland Isles there was a range of different interests and views on a development that would have a transformative impact.

While consent is supposed to be granted through elected representatives, that presupposes some form of internal discussion, negotiation and compromise.

Additional challenges might arise where community leaders take on responsibility for representing community views. Even if there is a general sense of agreement and consent in a community to begin with, this does not always mean that they will continue to be supportive throughout the lifetime of a project. In the case studies in Alaska and in Russia, many respondents who expressed strong opposition to the way that the industry was being developed in their regions did not necessarily oppose the oil industry per se. This finding is echoed by Pereira and Pappa, who state that there is not always disagreement between local and industry development and suggest that host nations should determine if, when, and how members of the public should be able to exercise some sort of consent or even veto powers with regard to extractive projects. Seen in the light of the findings of Hansen and Ipalook, one could add that there needs to be consideration of the circumstances in which a community might revoke consent, should a project be radically altered or have unanticipated negative impacts.

Final words

People in the Arctic have goals for their own futures and those of their families and communities. Resource development decisions and decision-making processes can make it easier or harder to realise those goals. Extractive projects can cause social disruption but also create opportunities for economic gain and development, which in turn can support sustainable communities and the preservation of traditions. It is hence extremely important to plan and manage extractive projects in a wise manner that ensures that developments benefit local communities and facilitate their abilities to pave a path towards and reach their desired futures. To do that, it is necessary to understand their views on impacts, both positive and negative, and their hopes and fears regarding resource activities and community development.

Most of the researchers involved in the creation of this book live or work in the Arctic. We recognise that the Arctic is not a single place but is a wide and diverse region that is in a constant state of change. It is a region that is experiencing increasing global attention. It is also a place that has had thriving communities and economies for centuries in some areas, for millennia in others. Decisions to exploit natural resources are based on global market demand and supply. General policies to promote or restrict mining or hydrocarbon projects are led by governments in capital cities south of the Arctic Circle. Leakage of the benefits of development out of the region is endemic. Campaigns to "save the Arctic" from industrialisation are trumpeted by millions of people who have never set foot there.

With this book, we explain the importance of bringing Arctic voices to the fore in decision-making about extractive industries, by not only including local voices in Arctic extractive decision-making but also paying particular attention to them. We provide examples of how to do so more effectively, and it is our hope that the strategies explored in this collection will inform governments and companies of their legal and ethical responsibilities and enhance the capacity of members of civil society to participate in the decisions that affect first and foremost themselves, their children and their communities.

Whatever happens, decisions on whether, where and how to conduct extractive projects in the Arctic will continue to shape the futures and the fate of the people of this region.

References

ILO Convention 169 (1989). "Indigenous and Tribal Peoples Convention. Adopted 27 June 1989, entered into force 5 September 1991." *International Legal Materials* 28, 1382.

UN General Assembly. Declaration on the Rights of Indigenous Peoples. UNGA Res 61/295. September 13, 2007 (UNDRIP).

Index

Note: Information in figures and tables is indicated by page numbers in italics and bold.

Aarhus Convention *see* Convention on Access to Information, Public Participation in Decision-Making and Access to Justice in Environmental Matters
accountability, in public participation **284**
Agenda 21 20, 29, 87, 106
Agreement Respecting a New Relationship Between the Cree Nation and Government of Quebec 210n63
Alaska 185–197, **192**, 293
Alaska Natives Claims Settlement Act 187–188, 190
Alaska Permanent Fund 188
Anaya, James 56–57
Avannaata 133, **134**, 142

Beckman v. Little Salmon Carmacks First Nation 214, 214n80
Brundtland Report *see Our Common Future* (World Commission on Environment and Development)

Callaghan, Jim 227
Canada 200–222, 249–250, 253–255
capacity building 231–233
CBD *see* Convention on Biological Diversity (CBD)
CEACR *see* Committee of Experts on the Application of Conventions and Recommendations (CEACR)
CERD *see* Convention on the Elimination of All Forms of Discrimination (CERD)
Chippewas of the Thames First Nation v. Enbridge Pipelines Inc 254–255, 254n62
CHLOE *see* Conceptual Hexagonal Land Use Overlay Engine (CHLOE)

"citizen councils" 144, 152
Clark, Ian 232
Clyde River (Hamlet) v. Petroleum Geo-Services Inc 217–219, 254–255, 254n63
colonialism 50
Committee of Experts on the Application of Conventions and Recommendations (CEACR) 30–31
Committee on the Elimination of Racial Discrimination 64
community engagement: legal and voluntary aspects of 163–167
community relationships 282–283
Conceptual Hexagonal Land Use Overlay Engine (CHLOE) 277–278
Convention on the Elimination of All Forms of Racial Discrimination (CERD) 63–65
consent: requirements for 156–157; *see also* free, prior and informed consent (FPIC)
Constable Point *see* Nerlerit Inaat
consultation: accessibility of information in 291–292; analysis in 279; common challenges in 280–282; community relationships and 282–283; co-production and 274–275; defined 266; dialogue methods in 273–274; duty of 212–222, 266–267; elderly individuals in 280n19; evaluation in 279; fatigue 280–281; messaging in 272–273; online communication and 275–279; strategic approach in 267, **268–270**
consultation meeting, public 104–105
continuous environmental impact assessment 71

Index

contracts *see* host government contracts
Convention on Access to Information, Public Participation in Decision- Making and Access to Justice in Environmental Matters (Aarhus Convention) 1, 20, 28–29, 88, 255, 266
Convention on Biological Diversity (CBD) 20, 38, 163
Convention on Environmental Impact Assessment in a Transboundary Context (Espoo Convention) 20
co-production 274–275
corporate responsibility 22–23; to respect 79–80
corporate social responsibility (CSR) 78, 159
cultural preservation 194–195
culture: integration of, in extractive planning 147–150, **148**

De Beers v. Mackenzie Valley Environmental Impact Review Board 207, 207n49
decolonisation 52–53
Denmark 16
due diligence: indigenous rights and 15; risk-based 84–94
duty to consult and accommodate 212–222

Earth Summit *see* UN Conference on Environment and Development (UNCED)
Egede, Hans 50–51
EIA *see* environmental impact assessment (EIA)
elderly individuals, in consultation 280n19
environmental impact assessment (EIA) 163, 164, 253–254; continuous 71; land claims agreements and 207–212
Espoo Convention *see* Convention on Environmental Impact Assessment in a Transboundary Context
expectation management, in public participation **284**

Facebook 107–109
First Nation of Nacho Nyak Dun v. Yukon 202–203, 206
foreign workers 139
Forest Stewardship Council (FSC) 27, 166
FPIC *see* free, prior and informed consent (FPIC)

free, prior and informed consent (FPIC) 2–3, 11, 13; application of 157; in Greenland 47–72; human rights treaties and 63–66; indigenous rights and 13–14, 31–32, 35; treaty law and 61–63
FSC *see* Forest Stewardship Council (FSC)
future, citizens' ideas of 143–144

GCM Resources case 92–93
Give-My-View 277
government: indigenous rights responsibilities of 28–32
Greenland 1, 16, 47–72, 89n48, 101–120, 125–152, 288
"green transitions" 12
Grimond, Jo 231, 235

Holm, Gustav 51–52
host government contracts: participation and 245–260; public involvement in 250–255; types of 247–250
human rights 287–289; business and 79–83; *see also* Convention on the Elimination of All Forms of Racial Discrimination (CERD), International Covenant on Civil and Political Rights (ICCPR), International Covenant on Economic, Social and Cultural Rights (ICESCR); Indigenous and Tribal Peoples Convention (ILO C169); UN Declaration on the Rights of Indigenous Peoples (UNDRIP)
hunting management 144–145

IBA *see* impact and benefit agreement (IBA)
ICCPR *see* International Covenant on Civil and Political Rights (ICCPR)
Iceland 2
ICESCR *see* International Covenant on Economic, Social and Cultural Rights (ICESCR)
ICMM *see* International Council on Mining and Metals (ICMM)
ICP *see* informed consultation and participation (ICP)
IFC *see* International Finance Corporation (IFC)
ILO C169 *see* Indigenous and Tribal Peoples Convention (ILO C169)
Ilulissat **134**
impact and benefit agreement (IBA) 202, 202n16

300 *Index*

impact assessments (IA) 207–222
Indigenous and Tribal Peoples Convention (ILO C169) 9, 13, 16, 25, 29–32, 48, 54–55, 83, 163
indigenous peoples 1–3; qualification as 24–28; in Russian law 158, 170
indigenous rights: background in 12–17; business responsibilities with 32–36; and Committee of Experts on the Application of Conventions and Recommendations (CEACR) 30–31; context to 12–17; due diligence and 15; and free, prior and informed consent 13–14, 31–32, 35; government responsibilities with 28–32; in Greenland 56–58; "green transitions" and 12; ILO C169 and 9, 13, 16, 25, 29–32, 48; and International Covenant on Civil and Political Rights (ICCPR) 18; and International Covenant on Economic, Social and Cultural Rights (ICESCR) 18; justice access and 36–38; and Organization for Economic Co-operation and Development (OECD) Guidelines for Multinational Enterprises 21, 32–33, 35–36; remedy access and 36–38; standards and principles with 18–24; and UN Declaration on the Rights of Indigenous Peoples 13–14, 19; voluntary standards and 21–22
inefficiencies 255–257
informed consultation and participation (ICP) 25–26, 34
Innarsuit **134**
International Council on Mining and Metals (ICMM) 23
International Covenant on Civil and Political Rights (ICCPR) 18, 49, 62–63, 89
International Covenant on Economic, Social and Cultural Rights (ICESCR) 18, 62–63, 83, 163
International Finance Corporation (IFC) 17, 33–34, 34n95, 38
issues analysis **268**, 270–272
Isukasia iron ore project 69–70
Ittoqqortoormiit **134**, 138–139, 141, 144

justice, relational: oil development and 167–177; power imbalances and 162–163; relational injustice and 170–172

Ka'a'Gee Tu First Nation v. Canada (Attorney General) 219–220

Ka's'Gee Tu First Nation v. Canada (Minister of Indian Affairs) 208
Kiev Protocol *see* Protocol on Strategic Environmental Assessment to the Convention on Environmental Impact Assessment in a Transboundary Context
Komi people 24, 156–179, *161*
Kvanefjeld *see* Kuannersuit
Kuannersuit 57–58, 68, 72, 128, 137–138, **148**; *see also* Narsaq
Kujalleq 136
Kullorsuaq **134**

Labrador Inuit Land Claims Agreement (LILCA) 214–215
London Mining *see* Isukasia iron ore project

Mackenzie Valley Resources Management Act (MVRMA) 201–202, 201n14, 208, 211
Maniitsoq **134**, 138–139, 141, 144, **148**, 152
Manson, John 232
Moriusaq 133, **134**
MVRMA *see* Mackenzie Valley Resources Management Act (MVRMA)

Narsaq **134**, 136–138, 144, 147, **148**
Narsarsuaq **134**
National Contact Points (NCPs) 38, 80, 90n48, 92–94; *see also* Organization for Economic Co-operation and Development (OECD) Guidelines for Multinational Enterprises
Nerlerit Inaat **134**, 139
NGOs *see* non-governmental organizations (NGOs)
non-governmental organizations (NGOs) 174
North American Tungsten Corp Ltd v. Mackenzie Valley Land and Water Board 211
Norway 247–248, 250–253
Nuiqsut 189–196, **192**
Nunatsiavut Government v. AG Canada 214–216
Nunatsiavut Government v. Newfoundland and Labrador 202n18
Nunavut Tunngavik Inc v. Canada (Attorney General) 205n35
Nutaarmiut **134**
Nuttall, Mark 69

Nuuk **135**, 136, 151
Nuussuaq **134**

Olsvig, Sara 59
opportunity perception 137–140, **148**
Organization for Economic Co-operation and Development (OECD) Guidelines for Multinational Enterprises 21, 32–33, 35–36, 79–80, 84, 89–92; *see also* National Contact Points (NCPs)
Our Common Future (World Commission on Environment and Development) 106

Paix des Braves 210n63
participation, public: achieving excellence in 265–284, **268–270**, **271**, **285**; alternative forms of 290–291; as aspect of risk-based due diligence 87–92; benefits of 103–104; challenges for meaningful 257–258; defined 265; difficulty of, in Greenland 104–105; diversity of 290–291; enhanced 200–222; expectations and 289–290; host government contracts and 245–260; justice and 292–293; over life of project 294–295; power relations and 292–293; principles of **284**; rights of 195–196; *see also* consultation
"peak oil" 245, 245n1
Peary, Robert Edwin 52
Peasants Declaration 49
photo-elicitation 109
political analysis **268**
power imbalances: relational justice and 162–163
power relations 172–177, 292–293
Protocol on Strategic Environmental Assessment to the Convention on Environmental Impact Assessment in a Transboundary Context 20, 28–29
public consultation meeting 104–105

Qaanaaq **134**
Qaqortoq **134**, 136–137, 147
Qikiqtani Inuit Association (QIA) 209
Qikiqtani Inuit Association v. Canada (Attorney General) 208–209
Qullissat 138

regional land use planning commissions (RLUPC) 203
relational justice: oil development and 167–177; power imbalances and 162–163; relational injustices and 170–172
Rio Declaration 20, 87–89, 106
Rio Summit *see* UN Conference on Environment and Development (UNCED)
risk-based due diligence 84–94
risk perception 137–140, **148**
RLUPC *see* regional land use planning commissions (RLUPC)
Russia 156–179, *161*

sacrifice zones 149–150
Saramaka case 50, 60
Savissivik **134**
scoping **268**, 272
Sermersooq 72, 133, 136, 142
Shetland 225–241
SIA *see* social impact assessment (SIA)
situational analysis **268**, 270–272
social impact assessment (SIA) 131
social media 107–109
sovereignty claims 1
stakeholder analysis **268**, 270–272
stakeholder engagement: risk-based due diligence and 86
Statkraft case 93
Strateco Resources Inc v. Québec (Attorney General) 210
sustainable development 20, 87, 125, 186, 191, 290

Tasiilaq **134**, 135, 144
Tauli-Corpuz, Victoria 63
transparency, in public participation **284**

UDHR *see* Universal Declaration of Human Rights (UDHR)
UK Private Legislation Procedure (Scotland) Act 234n30
Umbrella Final Agreement 200–201
UN Conference on Environment and Development (UNCED) 20
UN Declaration on the Rights of Indigenous Peoples (UNDRIP) 2–3, 13–14, 19, 19n36, 25, 29, 37, 47–49, 55, 62, 64, 163, 255–256, 288
UN Guiding Principles on Business and Human Rights (UNGPs) 14, 16–17, 21, 23, 33, 78–79, 82–83, 89
United Kingdom 225–241
United States 185–197, **192**
Universal Declaration of Human Rights (UDHR) 18, 82, 89, 89n45

UN Protect, Respect and Remedy Framework 78–79, 82–83
Upernavik **134**

Vienna Declaration 88–89
voluntary standards 21–22
VU.CITY 278

Weeramantry, Judge 71
White River First Nation v. Yukon 220–222
Wills, Jonathan 236
World Commission on Environment and Development 106

Yellowknives Dene First Nation v. Minister of Aboriginal Affairs and Northern Development 219n110

youth: challenges for engagement of 106–107; culture as priority of 111–114; education as priority of 110; and Greenlandic independence 114–117; identity as priority of 111–114; lack of engagement of 101–105; potential for engagement of 106–107; priorities and concerns as perceived by 110–114; quality of life as priority of 110–111; social media as engagement tool for 107–109; social relations as priority of 110; visual methods as tools for engagement of 107–109; wellbeing as priority of 110–111; work as priority of 110
Yukon Environmental and Socio-Economic Assessment Act (YESAA) 210–211, 220–221